Housing and Mortgage Markets in Historical Perspective

**A National Bureau
of Economic Research
Conference Report**

Housing and Mortgage Markets in Historical Perspective

Edited by **Eugene N. White, Kenneth Snowden, and Price Fishback**

The University of Chicago Press

Chicago and London

EUGENE N. WHITE is Distinguished Professor of Economics at Rutgers University and a research associate of the National Bureau of Economic Research. KENNETH SNOWDEN is professor of economics at the University of North Carolina at Greensboro and a research associate of the National Bureau of Economic Research. PRICE FISHBACK is the Thomas R. Brown Professor of Economics at the University of Arizona and a research associate of the National Bureau of Economic Research.

The University of Chicago Press, Chicago 60637
The University of Chicago Press, Ltd., London
© 2014 by the National Bureau of Economic Research
All rights reserved. Published 2014.
Printed in the United States of America

23 22 21 20 19 18 17 16 15 14   1 2 3 4 5
ISBN-13: 978-0-226-07384-2 (cloth)
ISBN-13: 978-0-226-09328-4 (e-book)
DOI: 10.7208/chicago/9780226093284.001.0001

Library of Congress Cataloging-in-Publication Data

Housing and mortgage markets in historical perspective / edited by
    Eugene N. White, Kenneth Snowden, and Price Fishback.
        pages cm. — (National Bureau of Economic Research conference report)
    "Early versions of many of the papers in this volume were presented at a Universities-Research Conference on Housing and Mortgage Markets in Historical Perspective held in Cambridge, Massachusetts, on September 23 and 24 in 2011"—ECIP data.
    Includes bibliographical references and index.
    ISBN 978-0-226-07384-2 (cloth : alk. paper) — ISBN 978-0-226-09328-4 (e-book)
    1. Residential real estate—United States—History. 2. Housing—Prices—United States—History. 3. Mortgage loans—United States—History. 4. Housing policy—United States—History. I. White, Eugene Nelson, 1952– editor of compilation. II. Snowden, Kenneth A., editor of compilation. III. Fishback, Price Van Meter, editor of compilation. IV. Series: National Bureau of Economic Research conference report.
    HD7293.Z9H6775 2014
    333.33′80973—dc23

                                                                                    2013040456

Relation of the Directors to the
Work and Publications of the
National Bureau of Economic Research

1. The object of the NBER is to ascertain and present to the economics profession, and to the public more generally, important economic facts and their interpretation in a scientific manner without policy recommendations. The Board of Directors is charged with the responsibility of ensuring that the work of the NBER is carried on in strict conformity with this object.

2. The President shall establish an internal review process to ensure that book manuscripts proposed for publication DO NOT contain policy recommendations. This shall apply both to the proceedings of conferences and to manuscripts by a single author or by one or more co-authors but shall not apply to authors of comments at NBER conferences who are not NBER affiliates.

3. No book manuscript reporting research shall be published by the NBER until the President has sent to each member of the Board a notice that a manuscript is recommended for publication and that in the President's opinion it is suitable for publication in accordance with the above principles of the NBER. Such notification will include a table of contents and an abstract or summary of the manuscript's content, a list of contributors if applicable, and a response form for use by Directors who desire a copy of the manuscript for review. Each manuscript shall contain a summary drawing attention to the nature and treatment of the problem studied and the main conclusions reached.

4. No volume shall be published until forty-five days have elapsed from the above notification of intention to publish it. During this period a copy shall be sent to any Director requesting it, and if any Director objects to publication on the grounds that the manuscript contains policy recommendations, the objection will be presented to the author(s) or editor(s). In case of dispute, all members of the Board shall be notified, and the President shall appoint an ad hoc committee of the Board to decide the matter; thirty days additional shall be granted for this purpose.

5. The President shall present annually to the Board a report describing the internal manuscript review process, any objections made by Directors before publication or by anyone after publication, any disputes about such matters, and how they were handled.

6. Publications of the NBER issued for informational purposes concerning the work of the Bureau, or issued to inform the public of the activities at the Bureau, including but not limited to the NBER Digest and Reporter, shall be consistent with the object stated in paragraph 1. They shall contain a specific disclaimer noting that they have not passed through the review procedures required in this resolution. The Executive Committee of the Board is charged with the review of all such publications from time to time.

7. NBER working papers and manuscripts distributed on the Bureau's web site are not deemed to be publications for the purpose of this resolution, but they shall be consistent with the object stated in paragraph 1. Working papers shall contain a specific disclaimer noting that they have not passed through the review procedures required in this resolution. The NBER's web site shall contain a similar disclaimer. The President shall establish an internal review process to ensure that the working papers and the web site do not contain policy recommendations, and shall report annually to the Board on this process and any concerns raised in connection with it.

8. Unless otherwise determined by the Board or exempted by the terms of paragraphs 6 and 7, a copy of this resolution shall be printed in each NBER publication as described in paragraph 2 above.

Contents

Acknowledgments

We would like to acknowledge our debts to a number of people who contributed to the development and publication of this book. Early versions of many of the chapters in this volume were presented at a Universities-Research Conference on Housing and Mortgage Markets in Historical Perspective held in Cambridge, Massachusetts, on September 23–24, 2011. The National Bureau of Economic Research sponsored and provided the funding for the conference. We owe special thanks to Jim Poterba and Claudia Goldin for their enthusiasm and encouragement as we developed the idea for the conference. They insisted that we should publish this volume and have been very generous in their support.

The discussants of the papers at the conference were Gary Richardson, Susan Wachter, Shawn Kantor, Ed Glaeser, Jim Kau, Andra Ghent, Kris Mitchener, and David Wheelock. Their presented and written comments offered valuable insights that helped to greatly improve the revisions of the papers and our editorial suggestions. In addition, there were a number of other scholars at the conference who contributed to the conversations about the papers. We also thank the anonymous reviewers of the book proposal who provided valuable guidance for organizing the book, as well as useful comments to the authors.

We are most thankful for the help of the NBER's conference staff—Carl Beck, Rob Shannon, Lita Kimble, and Brett Maranjian—who organized a seamless conference. Most importantly and notably among the other NBER staff, we thank Helena Fitz-Patrick for her many patient hours of editing and formatting the manuscript. We would also like to thank our editor at the University of Chicago Press, Joe Jackson, for ably squiring us through the publication process.

Introduction

Kenneth Snowden, Eugene N. White, and Price Fishback

The central role of housing in the "Great Recession" of 2007 raises a series of questions that need to be addressed in historical perspective. Were the underlying causes of housing crises similar in earlier episodes? Has the propagation and transmission of housing and mortgage crises changed over time? Have previous policy interventions mitigated or increased the damage from crises? Have earlier regulatory responses to crises improved the long-run performance and stability of housing and mortgage markets? This volume begins to offer answers to these questions by treating past housing and mortgage crises as multifaceted, complex episodes that represented watersheds in the long-run development of these markets, their institutional structure, and the broader economy.

Economic historians are not alone in taking broad views of the origins and impacts of severe disruptions in housing and mortgage markets. At the beginning of the recent crisis, for example, Martin Feldstein (2007) laid out a concise, but prescient, description of three forces that were by then buffeting the economy: a sharp decline in housing prices and home production, disruptions in the arrangements used to finance mortgage credit, and spillovers from both to consumer spending. Feldstein pointed out at the time that each development taken alone was substantial enough to trigger an economic downturn, and that the confluence of the three was likely to

Kenneth Snowden is professor of economics at the University of North Carolina at Greensboro and a research associate of the National Bureau of Economic Research. Eugene N. White is Distinguished Professor of Economics at Rutgers University and a research associate of the National Bureau of Economic Research. Price Fishback is the Thomas R. Brown Professor of Economics at the University of Arizona and a research associate of the National Bureau of Economic Research.

For acknowledgments, sources of research support, and disclosure of the authors' material financial relationships, if any, please see http://www.nber.org/chapters/c12792.ack.

cause a particularly serious recession. His framework has continued to be useful for understanding the course of the crisis since 2007 and the policy choices and trade-offs that we faced during that time. In this volume Alexander Field, Steven Gjerstad and Vernon Smith, and Eugene White employ similar broad frameworks to examine the interactions between the interwar business cycle and the housing and mortgage crisis of the 1930s. Like Feldstein, these chapters integrate into their analyses decreases in housing prices, disruptions in credit markets, and household consumption behavior and monetary policy before and during the crisis. The goal of all three chapters is to identify common and dissimilar elements through which housing markets influenced the economy during the Great Depression and our own Great Recession.

John Campbell (2012) provided additional insights into the recent crisis, drawing on the scholarship that has boomed since 2007. This new research indicates that the US mortgage system generated significant inefficiencies during the crisis, resulting from the negative externalities associated with foreclosures, the instability of the financial system, and the high mortgage lending costs that were borne by unsophisticated borrowers. Against this backdrop, Campbell promotes the Danish system as a promising model of reform because its structural elements mitigate weaknesses within the US system that he argues are responsible for the inefficiencies.[1]

The historical analysis in this volume offers additional insights from the United States and other counties for a deeper understanding of the weaknesses in the current US mortgage system. Michael Brocker and Christopher Hanes and Price Fishback and Trevor Kollmann, for example, provide the first detailed and systematic examinations of the decreases in housing prices and home construction that occurred during the early 1930s. Their work represents an important first step in determining whether the housing market was as fragile eight decades ago, and susceptible to spillovers from foreclosures, as the current system. Campbell cites recent research that identifies the risk-sharing incentives, which are built into mortgage contracts and are designed to encourage homeownership, as an important source of fragility in the current US market. The chapters here by Daniel Fetter and Matthew Chambers, Carlos Garriga, and Don Schlagenhauf provide measures of how the introduction of federally insured and guaranteed mortgages contributed to the rapid rise in homeownership in the United States between 1940 and 1960.

In his overview, Campbell also discusses how our understanding of the sources of instability in the mortgage and financial markets influenced the

---

1. The Danish system relies heavily on fixed-rate, long-term mortgages but, unlike the United States, imposes restrictions on prepayment and recourse on borrowers. Mortgages are funded, in addition, with callable covered mortgage bonds.

course of events beginning in 2007. Jonathan Rose offers a similar but very detailed exercise for the 1930s focusing on the severe disruption arising from the collapse of the New Jersey building and loan (B&L) industry. His analysis is important because at that time B&Ls were the most important source of institutional residential mortgage credit in New Jersey and the United States as a whole. The weaknesses Campbell points to as specific to the pre-2007 American system lead him to view the Danish covered bond system as more stable and less prone to disruption. Yet, securitization has a long history of failure and success in Europe. The studies by Rik Frehen, K. Geert Rouwenhorst, and William Goetzmann and Kirsten Wandschneider of eighteenth- and nineteenth-century Dutch and German markets provide important historical background for evaluating these claims by examining the structure, performance, and failure of earlier innovations in securitization.

The historical analysis in this volume, therefore, speaks to a broad range of issues that are central to our understanding of the current US mortgage system's problems and many of the proposed reforms. However, the current explosion of research is actually a second wave of work on housing markets and institutions. A large amount of research on housing was begun in the wake of the 1930s housing crisis and provided the statistics and stylized facts that helped to shape both the post-Depression institutions and markets and the views of economists and policymakers. To set the stage for this volume, Kenneth Snowden gives a brief account of the development of the housing and mortgage markets in the United States during the first half of the twentieth century and a historiography of the extraordinary burst of scholarship that was conducted under the auspices of the National Bureau of Economic Research (NBER) between 1935 and 1960. It is particularly important that we acknowledge this body of NBER scholarship early in the volume because it provides the foundation for most historical research.

The rest of this volume is divided into four sections of related chapters. In the first section, "Housing and the Interwar Business Cycle," three chapters examine the sources, magnitude, and impact of the real estate boom and bust of the 1920s and 1930s with an eye toward comparing that experience to events from 2001 to 2011. In the section "A Closer Look at the Interwar Housing Crisis," the second group of chapters refines our understanding of the boom and bust in housing production, the changes in home prices, and the failures of the building and loan associations during the 1930s. The focus shifts away from the interwar period in the final two sections of the book. Part of the European experience is examined in the section, "Securitization in Earlier Times" where two chapters provide perspective for the ongoing debate concerning alternative systems of funding mortgage credit, while the chapters in the section "Postwar Housing Policies" address the role that public policy played in promoting homeownership between 1940 and 1960.

Housing and the Interwar Business Cycles

Alexander Field examines how the housing crisis of the interwar period compares to events in the early twenty-first century. He shows that the decrease in residential building that began in 1926 was more severe and protracted than the one that began in 2007. On the basis of this observation, he argues that the collapse in home construction, once transmitted to consumption spending through the multiplier, likely contributed more to the decrease in aggregate output in the early 1930s than the existing scholarship recognizes. Field notes that this impact was reinforced by the unplanned character of residential construction during the 1920s building boom that left significant legal and financial barriers to recovery in the 1930s.

Although the decline in housing production was greater during the 1930s crisis, Field argues that the financial shocks associated with it had smaller impacts than those felt between 2007 and 2011. Home price movements are central to his analysis. Nominal home prices fell modestly between the 1926 peak and 1929, and more rapidly over the next four years. These decreases were much smaller in magnitude than those that occurred during and after 2007. In addition, the relatively sharper decline in nominal prices between 1929 and 1933 was accompanied by similar decreases in the general price level so that real home prices fell only modestly between 1926 and 1929 and then actually increased slightly over the next four years. Field also observes that the stability in real housing prices during the interwar crisis was connected to relatively low leverage among home owners—fewer households owned homes in 1930 than 2007, fewer financed their homes with mortgages, and those that did were subject to more conservative underwriting requirements.

Field acknowledges that the fall in housing prices had negative impacts on the balance sheets of households and lenders in the early 1930s, but concludes that their influence on output and employment was not as strong as after 2007. According to Field, this explains why New Deal regulation focused heavily on reforming the securities markets and the commercial banking system—these, and not residential mortgages, were considered to be the important source of financial distress that helped to start and prolong the Depression.

Steven Gjerstad and Vernon Smith see things differently. They argue that the role of housing was "remarkably similar" during the financial crises of the interwar period and 1997 to 2011, although the parallels in the origins and transmission of the two crises have been largely neglected in the literature. One reason for the neglect is that Friedman and Schwartz's authoritative emphasis on monetary collapse as the source of the Great Depression leaves little room for the possibility that expansionary monetary policy by itself could not have eliminated or reversed the impacts of a "debt-fueled real estate bubble." To make the case that such a bubble occurred during the interwar period, Gjerstad and Smith assemble a broad range of evidence for the 1920s and 1930s that includes housing production, household spending, total output, mortgage indebtedness, housing prices, housing sales, rents, unemployment, and foreclosures. Using this information, they argue that the interwar crisis was transmitted to the broader economy through five channels that were also at work between 2000 and 2011.

The first is the direct impact of reduced residential construction. Gjerstad and Smith, like Field, find that the decrease in homebuilding was relatively larger in the late 1920s and early 1930s than after 2007. They also point out that the share of construction spending in aggregate output was higher in the earlier period, which made its impact on total output even larger. A second channel that Field also mentions was the deterioration in the balance sheet of households as home values fell in the face of fixed nominal debt burdens. Gjerstad and Smith argue that this influence was more powerful and important and show evidence that the fall in nominal house prices was substantial in several markets relative to fixed mortgage debt burdens. Moreover, the deterioration in household balance sheets was closely connected to three other channels of influence. Deteriorating balance sheets led households to cut back spending, especially on durables, leading businesses to reduce production and their demand for inventories and fixed investments. In turn, this created a feedback effect on households' employment and incomes that created further uncertainty and distress. As distress turned into mortgage delinquency and foreclosure, the balance sheet of banks and mortgage lending specialists also deteriorated and the supply of credit to housing and other forms of investment was curtailed. According to Gjerstad and Smith, this fifth and last channel completed the powerful transmission mechanism that operated after the real estate booms of both the 1920s and the early twenty-first century.

Eugene White also sees similar forces at work during the "Great American Real Estate Boom and Bust of the 1920s" and the events leading up to the crisis of 2007. He argues that bubble-like behavior was evident during both episodes and supports that characterization for the earlier period by examining patterns in homebuilding, home prices, and foreclosure rates. His primary objective, however, is to better understand why the banking system was not threatened by the real estate bust in the late 1920s, in contrast to the early twenty-first century. To this end, White enumerates twelve factors that have frequently been identified as important forces behind the recent real estate bubble. His project is then to assess which of these were also operating in the 1920s.

Not surprisingly, given the role of banks in the recent crisis, six of White's factors relate to monetary policy and bank regulation. To assess the potential role of easy money during the 1920s White uses interwar data to examine how a Taylor rule would have influenced the economy and finds that the short-term time rate fell below its predicted Taylor rule level for two years in the mid-1920s when the building boom was at its height. He identifies and estimates the impact of the 1920s version of the "Greenspan put," which he argues was driven by the Fed's commitment to reduce the uncertainty associated with seasonality in interest rates. White finds that these two forces contributed to the production of about 200,000 additional housing units that represented a large share of the starts that he classifies as overproduction relative to the number of units needed to catch up for low wartime production. However, he notes that total homebuilding in the 1920s was so great (in excess of 1 million units) that there would have been a large boom in construction during the 1920s even had monetary policy been more restrictive. White's analysis of bank regulation focuses on elements that influenced the willingness and ability to engage in risky real estate lending. He argues that the double liability rule faced by bank shareholders and the restrictions on mortgage lending meant that both national and state-chartered banks were well capitalized relative to the modest risks that they carried on real estate loans.

White argues that although there were some common factors that affected the banks during the building booms of the 1920s and the early twenty-first century—including easy money, a "Greenspan put," and the development of new securitization products—the banking system was not undermined by the real estate boom of the mid-1920s. The important difference between the two episodes is that banks were induced in the modern period to participate in risky real estate finance by a set of policies that were missing in the 1920s—deposit insurance, the "Too Big to Fail" doctrine, and federal subsidization of risky mortgage lending and securitization.

A Closer Look at the Interwar Housing Crisis

Michael Brocker and Christopher Hanes begin their examination of the 1920s real estate boom by noting that it was national in scope even though some popular accounts give the misleading impression that it was confined to Florida. To investigate the broad geographic character of the episode in their chapter, Brocker and Hanes examine differences in the timing and volume of homebuilding activity across many of the nation's largest cities during the 1920s. Their analysis is designed to assess whether high levels of construction during the boom were associated with higher rates of foreclosure, larger declines in home values, and greater reductions in home ownership after 1930. Brocker and Hanes argue that finding a pattern like this provides evidence that the 1920s boom actually contributed to the depth and severity of the Depression and was not, primarily, simply one more consequence of it. They employ an empirical cross-city approach that has been exploited in examinations of postwar building booms and real estate bubbles.

To conduct the historical analysis, Brocker and Hanes use city-level data drawn from the annual Bureau of Labor Statistics (BLS) surveys of building permits that lie beneath its annual housing start series; home ownership and housing values from the 1920, 1930, and 1940 censuses; and foreclosure data from Federal Home Loan Bank Board and the *Financial Survey of Urban Housing* (1937). In combining these, the authors touch many of the primary sources that lie behind earlier NBER work, but use them in a new way and for a different purpose. In their analysis, contemporaneous and future home values, home ownership rates, and the numbers of households and foreclosures are regressed on the number of new units that were permitted to be built for residential use. Brocker and Hanes measure the number of permitted units within multiyear windows in order to capture cross-city variation in building activity for the early, middle, and end of the 1920s. They also use separate measures for single- and multifamily housing permits to investigate the impact of variations in the composition, as well as the timing, of residential building activity.

Brocker and Hanes argue that their results are consistent with a "bubbles" interpretation of the 1920s building boom. More specifically, they conclude that the Depression of 1929 hit just after many local urban real estate markets had seen increases in the number of housing units, in home values, in home ownership and in mortgage indebtedness that had been driven by bubble-like expectations. As a result, housing markets were already in disequilibrium in the late 1920s, and were fragile in ways that made the subsequent depression even worse.

Price Fishback and Trevor Kollmann provide new measures of the changes in home values over the course of the interwar boom and bust. We have seen earlier that changes in home values, home prices, and housing wealth represent important evidence regarding the fragility of the interwar housing markets and its role in transmitting or amplifying macroeconomic shocks. Fishback and Kollmann make clear that there are important flaws in all of the available evidence for the period on home prices and values, and that care must be taken when using and interpreting these series. They focus most attention on a price series reported in the 1956 NBER monograph by Grebler, Blank, and Winnick (GBW) that Robert Shiller (2006) used to extend the widely cited Case-Shiller/S&P repeat sales home price index back to 1890.[2] The original GBW series was constructed from data reported in the *Financial Survey of Urban Housing* for twenty-two cities. During the mid-1930s home owners in each of these cities were asked to retrospectively report the value of their homes in 1934, 1933, 1930, and in the year they had acquired the home. From these data GBW constructed a housing price index for the period 1890 to 1934, which Shiller linked to a five-city index of advertised housing prices for the period 1934 to 1953 in order to derive a continuous annual series extending from 1890 to the present.

Fishback and Kollmann provide an alternative to the GBW-Shiller index

---

2. The potential problems in linking these two different series are discussed in chapter 4 of this volume.

by combining additional data drawn from the *Financial Survey of Housing* with information on housing values and rents drawn from the 1920, 1930, and 1940 censuses and information on the value of building permits reported annually for the period by the BLS. The authors construct a variety of multicity indexes of home values from these sources for the years 1920, 1930, 1933, 1934, and 1940. The exercise reveals that all nominal measures of home values, including GBW-Shiller, show declines in home values of between 20 and 30 percent between the late 1920s and 1934. Outside this interval, however, the indexes tell different stories. Only the GBW-Shiller index, for example, shows a mild decrease in home values during the 1920s—all the other indexes show a stronger upward trend in values for the same period. The GBW-Shiller index is also unique in showing that housing prices had almost recovered to 1930 levels by 1940. All of Fishback and Kollmann's alternatives show housing values remaining well below 1930 levels a decade later. Fishback and Kollmann conclude that GBW-Shiller index understates the increase in housing prices during the 1920s and overstates their recovery during the 1930s.

To compare changes in housing prices during the early twenty-first century and the 1920s and 1930s, Fishback and Kollmann construct comparable modern housing value indices using reports on home values in the 2000 and 2010 census and the American Community Surveys. The housing value indexes rose more rapidly between 2000 and 2006 to 2007 than in the 1920s boom, while nominal housing prices fell rapidly during both the post-2006 bust and the bust from 1930 to 1933. However, the rapid deflation from 1929 to 1933 meant that inflation-adjusted housing prices rose to a new peak in 1933, in contrast to the sharp drop in inflation-adjusted housing prices between 2007 and 2010. After 1933, the Fishback and Kollmann estimates adjusted for inflation fall sharply.

Drawing on a new and highly detailed data set, Jonathan Rose ends the section about the interwar housing crisis with an analysis of the resolution of the severe problems faced by building and loan associations in Newark, New Jersey, during the 1930s. Rose is one of the first to illuminate the specific institutional channels through which financial shocks associated with the housing crisis were transmitted to the larger economy. He provides a detailed analysis of the lending operations and performance of the major mortgage lending groups during the interwar period. Building and loan associations represented the largest institutional source of residential mortgage credit in 1930 and were the only lending group at that time active in all regions of the country and in cities of all sizes. As residential mortgage lending specialists, moreover, B&Ls were more adversely affected by the housing crisis than other mortgage lenders. So even though Rose focuses his analysis on B&Ls that were active in Newark, New Jersey, he is providing insight into an industry that would have played a major role in transmitting financial shocks from the housing crisis.

Rose explains that B&Ls are particularly interesting because they did not operate under contractual requirements that forced them to speed up resolution if they became troubled. In 1930 B&Ls were member-owned corporations that could indefinitely delay paying out equity and dividends to their members. As a result, thousands of B&Ls in the United States became "frozen" when their mortgage portfolios generated losses and foreclosed real estate became a major asset on their balance sheets. It took years for many of these organizations to liquidate their assets and resolve their liabilities to owners.

Most importantly, Rose shows that an endogenous, market-based resolution mechanism emerged during the 1930s to facilitate the resolution of B&Ls that were contractually frozen. This mechanism took the form of secondary markets in B&L shares that opened up in dozens of major urban markets throughout the nation. Rose also explains how these secondary markets facilitated two elements of the resolution process. First, by selling their shares at discounts in this market, B&L members could liquidate their investments in the association, although at deep discounts. Second, investors who purchased these shares could then use them to buy the foreclosed real estate held by the B&L at similar deep discounts. The secondary market in B&L shares during the 1930s represents an unusual and intriguing example of financial innovation under market distress.

Securitization in Earlier Times

Starting in 1970, securitization transformed the US mortgage market as portfolio lenders who funded and held whole loans were displaced by marketable securities that were issued against the collateral of underlying mortgage loan pools. These securities came to dominate all segments of the market, including subprime loans. Since the crisis of 2007, there has been a virtual shutdown of the securitization in the US mortgage market, raising policy concerns about its viability moving forward. When the distinctively American form of securitization was developed in the 1970s, there was little attention given to earlier successful forms of securitization that had been implemented in the United States, and especially in European markets, for more than two centuries. The two chapters in this section provide new evidence on alternative forms of securitization that may help inform current debates on how to reform the US system.

Rik Frehen, K. Geert Rouwenhorst, and Will Goetzmann (FRG) investigate two forms of mortgage-backed securities that were issued in Dutch securities markets in the 1790s to finance property development in western New York state and Washington, DC. The emergence of these "negotiaties" were part of a larger process of experimentation and innovation in eighteenth-century Dutch capital markets. FRG explain that these negotiaties were similarly structured to plantation loans that had been issued, starting in the 1750s, to finance Dutch sugar plantations in South America and the Caribbean. These were fixed-income securities that collateralized not only revenue from sugar production, but also all of the plantation owner's property, including slaves. Plantation loans were themselves variations on earlier asset-based securities in the Dutch market that were secured only by the revenue generated by trade in commodities. The negotiaties examined in this chapter represent an innovation because the Holland Land Company and the consortium in Washington, DC issued bonds that were securitized only by mortgages on land and the income from future development of that land—the collateral for these asset-based securities did not include any revenue from commodity trade.

FRG find it puzzling, for example, that these securities did not offer investors any part of the returns associated with income from future land development; the payoff, instead, was restricted to fixed interest. They argue that this feature of the security was curious because earlier Dutch capital markets had used equity contracts to fund projects of similar durations that involved similar levels of risk. In this light, the fixed yield offered to investors was also curiously modest—only 5 percent on the securities of the Holland Land Company. Despite this feature, both issues of that company's negotiaties were fully subscribed when issued in 1793. By 1804 cash flows from property sales turned out to be insufficient to support both the company's investment activities and its interest expense. Under these pressures, the company's debt obligations to investors were reduced in exchange for their participation on the returns from land sales. FRG conclude that this transaction reflected the complexity and sophistication of capital markets at the time and the need to replace the mortgage-backed, fixed-income negotiatie with some form of equity.

This historical episode points to the conditions under which fixed-income, mortgage-backed securities may not be a viable financing vehicle. This became even more apparent when another negotiatie failed to be fully subscribed, after being issued in 1794 to finance land development in Washington, DC. FRG conclude that the two experiments "pushed the debt-based financial infrastructure of the Netherlands to the limit," because these real estate ventures would have been more efficiently funded with equity-like instruments rather than asset-backed, fixed-income securities.

Kirsten Wandschneider tells a very different story about eighteenth-century mortgage securitization. Her focus is on Prussia and on a mortgage-backed security that met with great success for more than a century after being introduced in 1770. The history of the Pfandbriefe that were issued by the Prussian Landschaften is particularly important because this security was ultimately transformed into the covered mortgage bond that became a major source of real estate finance in European markets and is currently being considered as a replacement for US-style securitization in the wake of our mortgage crisis.

Wandschneider explains that the Landschaften were publicly sponsored, cooperative credit associations that had some unusual and important institutional features. The original institutions were established in five provinces and noble landowners within each province were required to join. Membership meant that a landowner was eligible to apply for a mortgage from the organization, and the mortgage was then used as collateral for the Landschaft's bonds. Even if members had not borrowed, they were still jointly liable for the outstanding bonds and participated in appraising and approving all mortgage applications and monitoring indebted fellow members. Wandschneider shows how these, and other institutional features of the Landschaften, mitigated the effects of adverse selection and moral hazards that are inherent in mortgage lending. The success of these organizations is documented by the fact that their bonds sold at some of the lowest yields in the German market until well into the twentieth century. The performance of the bonds was particularly impressive since the Landschaften expanded their operations in the 1800s to accommodate smaller landowners and offer mortgages with longer maturities and amortization.

Postwar Housing Policies

The nonfarm home ownership rate in the United States increased from 37 to 46 percent between 1890 and 1930, and fell back to 41 percent during the Depression and the housing crisis of the 1930s. After this half century of modest change, nonfarm home ownership increased by nearly 20 percentage points between 1940 and 1960 and has stayed above 60 percent ever since. During the early twenty-first century, in fact, home ownership rates in the United States approached 70 percent and public policies that support home ownership have been implicated as important source fragility in the crisis that began in 2007. As we debate modifying these policies, we will be well served by understanding the market forces and policies that broadened home ownership in the United States during the mid-twentieth century. The two chapters in this section are devoted to this theme.

Dan Fetter examines the facts behind this rise in home ownership between 1940 and 1960 and identifies important questions that remain unanswered about the sources and impacts of the change. He analyzes previously underutilized data from the 1940s to show that much of the increase was a wartime, rather than a postwar, phenomenon. By 1945, in fact, the home ownership rate had recovered enough to exceed its 1930 level. Fetter also identifies several potential explanations that could account for this poorly appreciated but important phenomenon, including rising incomes and savings, the growing importance of tax incentives for home ownership, and unusual conditions in wartime housing markets. Fetter also stresses the importance of studying home ownership at the individual level, which helps to illuminate striking changes in individuals' paths to home ownership between the 1920s and the postwar era. During the earlier decade, the dominant path was for an individual to first live with relatives, then to rent, and finally to move to an owned home. After the war, as both the period of living with relatives and that of renting were sharply reduced, rental rates rose at the youngest ages while ownership displaced both renting and living with relatives at slightly older ages. He argues that we need to explore the forces that drove this change, as well as its impact on age-specific rates of home ownership and the rental-owned mix of residential construction and the housing stock.

Fetter provides an extended survey of factors that have been shown or hypothesized to have driven the broad upward movement in home ownership between 1940 and 1960. The existing literature provides compelling evidence that changes in demographic composition, income, tax incentives, and access to affordable mortgage finance all played major roles in the upsurge in home ownership, and that suburbanization and old-age assistance were also supportive. Fetter emphasizes that the discussion must move beyond investigation of the individual sources of the increase and move to assessing the interactions between the factors responsible for the increase in home ownership.

Matthew Chambers, Carlos Garriga, and Don Schlagenhauf (CGS) take up the challenge and close our volume by asking, "Did Housing Policies Cause the Postwar Boom in Home Ownership?" They explore the issue within a dynamic, general equilibrium model of tenure choice that incorporates many of the forces that Fetter enumerates—age, income, taxes, and mortgage credit. In their model, a household that is renting chooses between continuing to rent or buying a home; a home owner, on the other hand, must choose whether to stay put, to trade up to a bigger house, or to rent. Households use mortgages to finance the purchase of homes, and these contracts are structured to allow for different down payment requirements, amortization structures, terms to maturity, and interest rates. By modeling mortgages in this way CGS provide a flexible theoretical structure within which to assess the net impact on home ownership of two housing policies: improvements in mortgage terms and the tax deductions for mortgage interest payments.

To identify how actual changes in the terms of residential mortgages changed over the period, CGS rely on the results of surveys of mortgage lenders that were conducted in the late 1940s under the NBER's Urban Real Estate Program. Generally, these indicate that post–World War II mortgages had lower interest rates, longer maturities, higher loan-to-value ratios, and more amortization than mortgages in the 1920s and 1930s. Most of these changes, of course, were due to the incentives created by the Veterans Administration guarantees and Federal Housing Administration (FHA) insurance programs for home mortgage loans. Increasing marginal income tax rates at all levels helped to increase the benefits associated with mortgage interest deductibility. In their simulations, they assess how much of the change in home ownership during the postwar period was due to these two policies. The effects turn out to be substantial; the lengthening of mortgage maturity from twenty to thirty years by itself explains one-quarter of the rise in home ownership, while the change income tax deductibility contributes about half that amount.

Conclusion

The central role played by housing in the Great Recession of 2007 leads us to pose the question: "What was different this time?" This volume is designed to bring historical perspective to the answers to this question. Until the recent crisis, this area of economic history received little attention in the past half century after the burst of scholarship into residential housing and finance sponsored by the NBER before 1960. It is fitting, therefore, that the NBER once again takes the lead by sponsoring a project to show how historical analysis provides a unique perspective on contemporary housing and mortgage markets. The reforms engineered in the aftermath of the 1930s were a direct response to the immediate perceived problems of the housing and mortgage markets. Generally, they were designed and implemented without a broader investigation of potential alternative institutions and in part, because of this lack of perspective, these New Deal innovations set the stage for the crisis of 2007. By offering a broader historical and international appreciation of housing and mortgage markets, this volume provides new information that should help to inform future policy debates.

References

Campbell, John Y. 2012. "Mortgage Market Design." NBER Working Paper no. 18339, Cambridge, MA.
Feldstein, Martin. 2007. "Housing, Credit Markets and the Business Cycle." NBER Working Paper no. 13471, Cambridge, MA.

1

A Historiography of Early NBER Housing and Mortgage Research

Kenneth Snowden

As the United States grew rapidly and urbanized between 1870 and 1930, nonfarm residential construction and home mortgage debt became increasingly important to the nation's capital formation, financial structure, and short-run aggregate performance. However, both activities remained highly localized, institutionally diverse, and unevenly regulated during this period. As a result, residential construction and mortgage credit were poorly measured and largely unexamined before 1930. This all changed during the Great Depression when the federal government responded to the worst housing and mortgage crisis in the nation's history with a five-year burst of regulatory initiatives. Some of these were temporary, emergency interventions, while others permanently transformed the nation's homebuilding and residential mortgage lending sectors. These interventions created a more institutionally mature and integrated national housing market, and provided new sources of data and opportunities for research.

The National Bureau of Economic Research (NBER) played a central role in the academic discussion of residential construction and mortgage finance that blossomed over the next quarter century.[1] Between 1935 and

Kenneth Snowden is professor of economics at the University of North Carolina at Greensboro and a research associate of the National Bureau of Economic Research.

I acknowledge the insights of participants of a Universities-Research Conference on Housing and Mortgage Markets in Historical Perspective held in Cambridge, Massachusetts, September 23–24, 2011. The National Bureau of Economic Research sponsored and provided the funding for the conference. I also acknowledge the improvements that resulted from comments and suggestions by Price Fishback, Jean Rosales, Eugene White, and anonymous reviewers. Financial support has been provided by National Science Foundation Grant SES-1061927. For acknowledgments, sources of research support, and disclosure of the author's material financial relationships, if any, please see http://www.nber.org/chapters/c13003.ack.

1. The work of Richard Ely's Institute for Research in Land Economics and Public Utilities needs to be acknowledged because it was, according to Marc Weiss (1989, 115), "[t]he orga-

1960, the NBER sponsored six distinct research programs that produced thirteen major monographs examining the performance and transformation of the housing and mortgage markets. The appendix to this chapter provides a complete enumeration of these contributions. When viewed collectively, these works provide a broad and deep analysis of residential construction and financing before World War I, through the boom and bust of the interwar years, and during a remarkable post–World War II expansion. To set the stage for the discussion of these early NBER research initiatives, we begin with a brief account of the development of the housing and mortgage markets between 1920 and 1950.

1.1   Setting the Stage: Housing and Home Mortgages, 1920–1950

The earliest formal investigation of the US housing market was conducted by the Calder Committee, created by US Senate Resolution 350 that was passed on April 17, 1920.[2] The committee was asked to make legislative recommendations to respond to the acute excess demand for housing that had developed by the end of World War I. The committee's first observation in its final report was that private enterprise, rather than public intervention, should be relied on to alleviate the imbalance.[3] At the time, this recommendation was more than a generic endorsement of free markets. It was, instead, a response to groups of architects, labor organizations, and even the military services who, at the time, advocated for the continuation, and even the expansion, of wartime federal housing programs that had originally been established for defense workers (Wood 1931, 76, 8). Moreover, by this time, several European countries had established public housing programs to address their own postwar housing problems. The Calder Committee examined the foreign programs and gave particularly harsh assessments of

nization most responsible for studying the economics aspects of housing policy during the 1920s." Weiss documents the contributions of Ely and associates of his institute through the late 1930s, including publication of *The Journal of Land & Public Utility Economics* and important monographs on all elements of urban property development, participation in Hoover's 1931 conference on homeownership (see following), close connections to the National Association of Real Estate Boards and the American Savings and Loan Institute, and influence during the 1930s on the development of the Federal Home Administration. Ely was a strong advocate of increasing homeownership throughout the period, and one of his institute's first research projects was the *Report on Mortgages* (1923), which was written for the Bureau of the Census from data on homeownership and encumbrance that it collected in the 1920 population census.

2. The resolution instructed the committee to inquire into and report on "(a) The existing situation in relation to the general construction of houses, manufacturing establishments, and buildings, and the effect thereof upon other industries and the public welfare and; (b) such measures as it may deem necessary to stimulate and encourage such construction work, to encourage popular investment rather than spending, to foster private initiative in building, and to insure cooperation between labor and persons or corporations engaged in transportation, banking, or other businesses necessary to the development of such construction" (*Congressional Record*, vol. 59, pt. 6, p. 5765).

3. The Calder Committee's report was presented as Senate Report 829 dated March 2, 1921.

the British and French initiatives.[4] In the end, the federal wartime housing programs were soon discontinued.

Although skeptical of direct federal intervention in the housing market, the Calder Committee recognized the inadequacies in the nation's housing stock and recommended the implementation of a set of public programs and policies for the purpose of assisting, rather than replacing, private market initiatives and local governments. The first was to compile and maintain a comprehensive statistical record of national building activity. In response, the Bureau of Labor Statistics (BLS) took over a small program from the US Geological Service to collect annual building permit series from local governments. Beginning in 1921, the BLS used these data to compile an annual report of planned nonfarm construction activity in 257 principal cities. The Calder Committee also endorsed federal sponsorship of a national clearinghouse for information about residential zoning regulation and building standards that varied widely across local markets. The Division of Building and Housing in the Department of Commerce was charged with compiling this information and, in 1926, began to publish *Zoning Progress in the United States* to inform local governments and their constituents about new and best practices within the urban planning community (Hubbard and Kimball 1929, 162–63).

The Calder Committee identified the residential mortgage market as a third area where federal policy could make a positive contribution. It recommended a relaxation of strict prohibitions on urban mortgage lending by nationally chartered commercial banks—and policies that did so were gradually adopted during the 1920s. The committee also gave its support for proposals to establish a new Federal Home Loan Bank (FHLB) system that could provide liquidity and oversight for residential mortgage lenders in much the same way as the recently created Federal Reserve and Federal Farm Loan Bank systems were doing for commercial banks and farm mortgage lenders. The proposal was championed by, and designed to assist, building and loan associations, which at the time were the nation's leading institutional residential mortgage lenders and the only ones that specialized in home mortgages. The proposal foundered when other mortgage lenders— mutual savings banks, life insurance companies, and state banks—strongly opposed the new system. These latter groups prevailed, and the federal government continued to play a small role during the 1920s in a residential mortgage market that remained fragmented in structure and subject to a patchwork of state regulation.

The Calder Committee's confidence in the productive capacity of the private housing sector was borne out as the nation's postwar housing demands were soon satisfied by a historic building boom. After averaging just over 300,000 nonfarm housing starts between 1905 and 1916, produc-

---

4. See pp. 13–16 in S. Rep. 829 (1921).

tion reached a peak of more than 700,000 units in 1925 and averaged more than 600,000 units per year between 1921 and 1928. Ultimately, 8 million new housing units were added to an initial stock of 24 million during the 1920s, as the nonfarm homeownership rate surged from 41 to 46 percent. Because the BLS began to record housing starts as the committee had recommended, we know that the jump in building occurred in all regions of the country, in both single- and multifamily markets, and especially in the new suburban ring areas of metropolitan areas (Kimbrough and Snowden 2007). Additionally, the discussion of housing regulation and building standards intensified during this period as groups such as the National Housing Association, the Better Homes movement, and the National Association of Real Estate Boards promoted new policies and approaches as the physical layout of US cities were being transformed by increased density and suburbanization (see Veiller 1929).[5]

The home mortgage market of the 1920s grew even more rapidly than the nonfarm housing stock, with nonfarm residential debt tripling (from $9 to $30 billion) in less than a decade as the ratio of debt to residential wealth doubled to nearly 30 percent (Snowden 2010). The credit was supplied by a diverse set of lenders. Life insurance companies and mutual savings banks expanded their mortgage portfolios rapidly, while building and loans (B&Ls) grew both in number and size and spread geographically. At the same time, two new innovations—private mortgage insurance and two early forms of mortgage securitization—served noninstitutional investors, who remained the largest single source of residential mortgage credit.[6] Lenders of second mortgages also appeared in great numbers during the lending boom to provide borrowers with the opportunity to purchase homes with smaller down payments than the 40 to 50 percent generally required by first mortgage lenders. Besides requiring low loan-to-value ratios, these first mortgage contracts also differed from the familiar long-term, amortized modern mortgage loan by being short in term and structured as balloon or sinking-fund loans. Despite the rapid growth and innovation, by the end of the 1920s, the American home mortgage market remained highly localized, regionally fragmented, and institutionally immature relative to modern standards.[7]

One sign of the federal government's "hands off" attitude toward the home mortgage market during the 1920s, and a development that continues to this day to impair our understanding of the mortgage lending boom of the

---

5. Despite these efforts, Field (1992) argues that the uncontrolled pattern of development during the 1920s created physical and legal impediments to recovery in homebuilding throughout the 1930s.

6. Participation certificates were issued by private mortgage guaranty companies and single-property real estate bonds by bond houses (see Goetzmann 2009; Snowden 2010).

7. National banks were allowed to hold urban mortgages in 1916, but only with maturities of one year until 1927. The size of their mortgage portfolios was also limited to one-half of time deposits (Behrens 1952, 17–21). Morton (1956, 21) and Gray and Terborgh (1929, 14) document regional disparity in mortgage rates in the 1920s.

1920s, was the Census Bureau's decision to remove the question regarding home mortgages from the 1930 population census form, even though it had regularly been asked since 1890. As a result, we do not know with any precision the role that mortgage credit played during one of the greatest home-building booms in US history. The federal indifference ended quickly, however, when the 1920s housing expansion turned into a severe and protracted foreclosure crisis in 1930. The change was signaled by President Hoover's decision to organize a national housing conference in the summer of 1931. The purpose of this conference was to provide a comprehensive examination of the state of the nation's housing and mortgage markets (Gries and Ford 1932a, 2).

Hoover enlisted more than five hundred housing professionals, experts, and practitioners—organized into twenty-five different subcommittees—to collect and assess information on topics as diverse as planning and zoning, house design and construction, slums and large-scale housing, and home improvement and repair. These reports were transformed into an eleven-volume conference report that provides a remarkable, detailed, and comprehensive snapshot of the state of US homebuilding and finance in 1930. However, by the time the participants convened as a group in December 1931, the discussion focused on the economic crisis and a mortgage credit system that was identified as "the greatest hindrance" to progress toward the national goal of increasing homeownership (Gries and Ford 1932b, 9).

Conference participants identified several problems in home mortgage lending: high interest rates that varied substantially across the country, contracts that were short in term and renewable only with additional costs, and the widespread use of second liens. To address the rising number of foreclosures, the conference endorsed Hoover's plan to revive the Calder Committee's recommendation for a federal home loan discount bank. Just as in the early 1920s, banks and life insurance companies opposed the creation of such a system because it was structured to serve the building and loan industry.[8] The proposal succeeded this time, and the Congress passed the Federal Home Loan Bank Act on July 22, 1932. Its advocates argued that the new system was established "not only to relieve the present financial strain . . . but [to] have permanent value . . . as a means of promoting home ownership in the future."[9]

The Federal Home Loan Bank system began operation in the spring of 1932, but, as its critics had warned, it was designed for, and used only by, building and loan associations. While the FHLB system was successful in gradually transforming B&Ls into the modern savings and loan industry,

8. Bodfish and Theobald (1938, 288–90) describe in their account of the bill's legislative history that officials of the United States Building & Loan League actually helped draft the legislation.
9. This language appeared in the first of two resolutions approved by the participants of the President's Conference on Home Building and Home Ownership. See p. 21 in Gries and Ford (1932b).

it proved to be incapable of stemming the general mortgage crisis of the early 1930s. Against this backdrop, Roosevelt promoted several initiatives between 1933 and 1935 that immediately addressed the mortgage crisis and permanently changed the market's institutional structure. The first was the Home Owners' Loan Corporation (HOLC), which was proposed in the spring of 1933 "[t]o provide emergency relief with respect to home mortgage indebtedness, to refinance home mortgages, [and] to extend relief to owners of homes . . . who are unable to amortize their debt elsewhere."[10] The HOLC was a publicly owned entity that purchased one million defaulted home mortgage loans from private lenders between 1933 and 1936 and refinanced them on a long-term, low interest basis. Along with the HOLC, Congress created a new system of federal savings and loan (S&L) charters, and even more support for the new S&L industry came when the Federal Savings and Loan Insurance Corporation was created in 1935. The other major New Deal initiative was the Housing Act of 1934, which created the Federal Housing Administration (FHA) and its program to insure long-term, low down payment, amortized mortgages. The volume of FHA lending was disappointingly small at first, but grew robustly after the Federal National Mortgage Association (the FNMA or "Fannie Mae") was created in 1938 to support a secondary market for these insured loans.

Five years of New Deal legislation forged a new framework through which housing was built and financed in the United States for the next three decades. Savings and loan associations served local mortgage markets and small-scale builders; commercial banks and mortgage companies used FHA and VA loans to finance large-tract builders and multifamily projects; and life insurance companies and mutual savings banks dominated the interregional residential mortgage market through networks of dedicated mortgage companies. Within this structure, institutional portfolio lenders came to dominate the residential mortgage market as never before or since; regulatory boundaries limited competition among lender groups; financial innovation was deemphasized; and loan origination, servicing, and credit risk management were integrated within single or small networks of institutions. A historic surge in both homebuilding and homeownership was financed through this new structure during the post–World War II era, and the research programs of the NBER documented both its institutional structure and its accomplishments.

1.2 The Early NBER Housing Programs

The National Bureau of Economic Research was a decade old when the Great Depression presented the young organization with both opportunities and challenges. Survival was foremost among the latter—a significant loss

---

10. Language taken from H.R. 5240, the Home Owners' Loan Act.

of external support in 1932 forced the NBER to suspend several research programs and to contemplate dissolution.[11] Even after the severe fiscal challenges were resolved in 1933, the NBER still had inadequate resources to maintain its research agenda into general features of economic life—including the measurement of national income, wholesale prices, and industrial production—while responding to the opportunities that arose during and because of the economic crisis. The trade-off became even more complicated when "a Federal administration proclaiming a philosophy of 'rugged individualism' [was] succeeded by an administration seeking to secure a 'New Deal' by governmental action."[12] The NBER maintained its traditional detachment concerning specific policy proposals, but recognized "the need for a more effective science of economics" to support "a policy of public control over many economic activities in the hope of increasing common welfare."

The diversion of attention to New Deal policy was so demanding that Wesley Mitchell declared in 1935 that the NBER's "chief embarrassment" was a lack of progress on its long-term research projects.[13] By then, one-half of the NBER's permanent research staff were on loan at least part-time to federal agencies—Leo Wolman as chairman of the Labor Advisory Board of the National Recovery Administration, Simon Kuznets with the Department of Commerce to form national income estimates, and Mitchell himself as a member of the National Resources Board. Although these activities delayed progress on important elements of the bureau's agenda, Mitchell noted that they also "brought fresh information, wider contacts and often keen insights into economic problems." These all turned out to be important advantages as the NBER turned its attention to residential housing.

1.2.1 The Program on Real Estate Financing and Economic Stability: 1935–1941

While the 1930 census did not ask households about their mortgage indebtedness, it continued to collect information about the value of their owned homes and the amounts of rent paid by tenants. These data provided valuable information about the total value of the occupied housing stock in 1930. One limitation, however, was that the census still defined a dwelling unit as the domicile of a census family.[14] Within this survey structure, no information was collected concerning the physical structure or characteristics of the buildings in which units were located. Consequently, we have no information on how much of the nation's housing stock in 1930 was in

---

11. "Report of the Director of Research of the NBER for the Year 1933 (1934)," pp. 5–6.
12. "Report of the Director of Research (1933)," p. 26.
13. Material in this paragraph drawn from pp. 5–6 of the "Report of the Director of Research of the NBER for the Year 1934–1935 (1935)."
14. The census does provide counts of the number of "dwellings" in 1930 and before with all residential structures, single- as well as multifamily, counted as one dwelling.

single-family versus multifamily structures, how much was substandard in quality, or even its age. In fact, the census did not even collect or report data on the number of dwelling units that were vacant at the end of one of the largest building booms in US history.

To provide at least some information on the housing stock and temporary employment for white-collar workers, the New Deal's Civil Works Administration conducted detailed Real Property Surveys in 1934 for sixty-four cities that varied in size, location, age, and rate of growth.[15] The survey instrument and procedures were developed under the Bureau of Domestic and Foreign Commerce and were designed to capture information about the type and age of structure, heating, and plumbing facilities, and the value, rent, and mortgage status for both occupied and vacant units. This first wave of real property inventories was so well received that similar surveys were conducted in an additional 140 cities in 1934, 1935, and 1936. Nearly all of these questions were included in the first census of housing in 1940; so, from 1934 on, we have much more detailed information about the composition and quality of the US housing stock in major urban areas.

The available information about the financial condition of housing markets and homeowners was increased markedly when the Department of Commerce decided to follow up its Real Property Survey with an extensive Financial Survey of Urban Housing for samples of households in sixty-one of the original sixty-four inventoried cities (Wickens 1937). This survey asked homeowners and tenants additional questions regarding the value of their homes and the debt owed on them in 1930, 1933, and 1934; rent and income in 1929, 1932, and 1933; and the sources and terms of the mortgage debt. The Financial Survey was conducted by mail and captured an average of 12 percent of tenant families and 15 percent of homeowners across the sixty-one cities.

The Social Science Research Council (SSRC) took immediate note of the Financial Survey as an opportunity to investigate the structure and stability of the channels through which capital formation was being financed in the United States. The SSRC found the survey particularly important because "real estate finance had been commonly under-stressed in the discussions of banking and credit phases of stabilization problems," even though construction was the largest component of aggregate capital formation (Wickens 1941, vii). For this reason, the SSRC and NBER joint committee on banking and credit decided in 1934 to sponsor an examination of "Real Estate Financing and Economic Stability."

The project got underway in 1935 when David L. Wickens, the government economist who had supervised the collection of data for both the Real Property Surveys and the Financial Survey of Urban Housing, was

---

15. Stapp (1938, ix–xii). CWA was within the New Deal's Federal Emergency Relief Administration.

appointed chief investigator and an NBER research associate. The first output from the project was a series of national estimates of "Non-Farm Residential Construction, 1920–1936" by Wickens and Ray Foster.[16] To construct the estimates, Wickens and Foster used the building permit activity of the 257 cities, which the BLS had been reporting since 1921, to construct separate estimates of building permits and housing starts for nonreporting urban localities and the entire nonfarm rural sector. Wickens did so by fitting relationships between population growth rates and permit activity in reporting areas and then using these to predict building activity in nonreporting areas on the basis of their own population trends. These estimates were then combined with adjusted permit data from the reporting areas to construct national estimates of authorized dwelling units and starts.[17]

The project was designed to provide for the first time a comprehensive picture of the nonfarm housing stock. To do so, Wickens relied heavily on the primary data collected in the Financial Survey of Urban Housing, information on rents and values from the 1930 census, and the BLS permit data. The result was *Residential Real Estate* (NBER 1941) which, according to the foreword, "remove[s] real estate and mortgage financing from the list of economic and financial factors about which we know the least" (vii–viii). Much of the monograph describes data and explains the methods used to compile and draw estimates from them. The essential resource for historical research within the volume, however, is nearly 100 tables that provide detailed measures of housing values, rents, mortgage indebtedness, and family income across cities, states, and regions.

1.2.2   The Urban Real Estate Finance Project: 1945–1955

In 1937, the NBER's Exploratory Committee on Financial Research surveyed existing research in the field and suggested directions for further study. Its conclusion about the urban real estate market will sound familiar to modern readers:

> The financing of real estate constitutes one of the most basic and essential financial activities in our economy. It is widely felt, however, that the real estate mortgage was subjected to more abuse and over-extension during the expansion of the twenties than any other credit instrument. During the [D]epression the real estate mortgage market was probably more completely frozen than any other domestic financial market. Stimulated by recent legislative changes designed to remedy the most conspicuous abuses in this type of financing, banks and other financial institutions are again expanding their mortgage loans. The recent crisis made material

16. Foster and Wickens's work appeared as NBER Bulletin 65, September 1937.
17. The BLS adopted Wickens's estimates for 1920–1936 as its official housing start series and then employed similar techniques to construct estimates for the 1937–1944 period. In 1942, BLS used the results of the 1940 census of housing to revise Wickens's estimates for 1930–1936 and its own estimates for 1937–1939. See notes to table Dc510-530 in Carter et al (2006).

available for a broad analysis of our experience with mortgage financing and for a formulation of fundamental credit standards designed to maintain sound conditions in the mortgage market. Immediate analysis of this material would be of incalculable value to our national economy as a whole as well as to the specific institutions that specialize in mortgage financing.[18]

Despite the apparent urgency, the exploratory committee decided to delay an additional urban mortgage project until Wickens completed his analysis of real estate financing and stability. The wait turned out to be far longer than expected when the United States entered World War II. Once the war ended, the NBER outlined a second and more elaborate research program into the urban mortgage market. Beginning in 1945, a team of seven researchers worked on the "Urban Real Estate Finance Project" for nearly a decade to produce a set of NBER monographs that examined the development and performance of the US mortgage market over the period 1920 to 1950.[19] The project had three components.

The first part was designed to document the legal, contractual, and institutional foundations of the nonfarm residential mortgage market and the changes that occurred between 1920 and 1950, including the growing influence of government within the market. The two monographs commissioned for this work were written by individuals who had actually helped shape the transformation that they described. Ernest Fisher was a prolific real estate scholar in the 1920s and had participated in Hoover's 1931 housing conference.[20] During the 1930s, he became active in the National Association of Real Estate Boards and served as director of research for the Federal Housing Administration, later becoming the first director of the Institute for Urban Land Use and Housing Studies at Columbia University. Miles Colean began his career as an architect in Chicago but moved to Washington in the early 1930s to help draft the legislation that created the Federal Housing Administration, and then served as its first technical director.[21] In subsequent years, Colean was a long-term consultant to both the Mortgage Bankers Association and the federal government; in the latter capacity, he was credited with coining the term "urban renewal" in the late 1950s.

18. NBER (1937, NBER Bulletin 64, p. 9).
19. The Urban Real Estate Project was a joint project of the Institute for Urban Land Use and Housing Studies of Columbia University and the staff and research associates of the National Bureau of Economic Research.
20. Fisher was professor of real estate management at the University of Michigan in the 1920s and moved to Columbia in 1945, where he was appointed as first director of the Institute for Urban Land Use and Housing Studies in 1948.
21. Colean's early career was in architecture (he helped design the Palmer House in Chicago), but after becoming involved in government policy, he briefly served as director of the Twentieth Century Fund, became associated with the Institute for Urban Land Use and Housing, and worked extensively as a consultant with the Mortgage Bankers Association.

The two monographs reflect the depth of their authors' experience and knowledge. Fisher's *Urban Real Estate Markets: Characteristics and Financing* (1951) surveys the legal background and development of institutional structures governing real estate transactions, homeownership, rental arrangements, and mortgage finance. His chapter on "Instruments of Real Estate Finance," for example, provides the most complete treatment available of the wide range of contracts used in the mortgage market over the first half of the twentieth century. Colean displays the same instincts in his *Impact of Government on Real Estate Finance in the United States* (1950), which neither apologizes for nor defends policies he helped to create. His general approach is to detail how government policy had influenced the size and composition of the investment flows that financed real estate development. For example, he argued that the FHA program created a structure through which federal regulation would reshape housing policy that had previously been local in character—including zoning regulations, building regulation, and town planning. Colean emphasized that residential mortgage lending policies implemented in response to crises were likely to generate unintended long-run effects.

The second part of the Urban Real Estate Finance Project focused on the four largest groups of institutional urban lenders between 1920 and 1950. Studies on life insurance companies, commercial banks, and the Home Owners' Loan Corporation were published as monographs between 1950 and 1952, while the draft manuscript for the fourth, savings and loan associations, was never published.[22] A key component of each of these studies was a detailed survey based on the mortgage records of a sample of institutions drawn from each lending group. These surveys yielded samples of 8,000 individual loans for life insurance companies and commercial banks, 6,000 for savings and loan associations, and more than 3,000 mortgages for the HOLC. All of these loans were made between 1920 and 1950 and, together, they provide a detailed view of changes in the structure and terms written into mortgage contracts over this period. Information and documentation for all of these samples, as well as the loan data itself, remain available on the NBER website, in digitized form for the HOLC and on microfilm for the other three lender groups.

Beyond the similarities in research designs, all four investigations detail the specific lending and contractual structures used by the lenders and the specific role each played in the nonfarm mortgage market. Raymond Saulnier's *Urban Mortgage Lending by Life Insurance Companies*, for example, establishes that the lending activities of most of the large insurance

---

22. The NBER project did not investigate the fifth important institutional lender because John Lintner, *Mutual Savings Banks in the Savings and Mortgage Markets* (1948) had just appeared.

companies were national in scope and became increasingly focused during the period on residential, as opposed to commercial, mortgage lending. The majority of the companies used correspondents to originate and service loans rather than their own internal branch networks. By 1946, more than one-half of the insurance companies' home mortgages were federally insured or guaranteed. As a result, their loan contracts were written for longer terms, carried higher loan-to-value ratios, and required full amortization—a radical change from the terms of pre-1930 loan contracts.

Carl Behrens was a member of the Federal Deposit Insurance Corporation's research staff when he was enlisted by the NBER to research and write *Commercial Bank Activities in Urban Mortgage Financing*. Changes in regulation between 1913 and 1930 set the stage by permitting nationally chartered commercial banks to become more active in nonfarm, and especially residential, mortgage lending. After joining in the mortgage boom, commercial banks curtailed their residential lending until the second half of the 1930s, when they returned to the market by providing federally insured and guaranteed mortgages to an even greater extent than insurance companies. These generalizations refer only to the mortgage loans that banks held in their portfolios, not, as Behrens cautions, to bank lending that was used to finance short-term construction loans or the activities of independent mortgage originators and correspondents. Both proved to be critical components of the home financing system in the 1950s as shown in a later NBER study by Saul Klaman (1961).

Edward Edwards completed a draft of *Urban Real Estate Financing by Savings & Loan Associations* in 1950, but a final version of the monograph was never approved for publication by the NBER. His task was particularly difficult because B&Ls were more affected by the 1930s mortgage crisis than any other lending group. By 1929, some twelve thousand building and loan associations were operating in the home mortgage market but, over the next decade, one-third of these institutions failed while most of the remainder were transformed into new savings and loan associations. Edwards's draft describes little of this transition, but his quantitative evidence identifies three important trends associated with it. First, by 1948, S&Ls had almost regained the position of being the largest single source of institutional home mortgage credit that B&Ls had maintained throughout the 1920s. Second, Edwards shows that the transition from B&Ls to S&Ls involved a change in the mortgage contracts used within the industry from the traditional B&L sinking fund contract to the modern, fully amortized loan. Finally, the transition in contracts occurred primarily in the conventional mortgage market because S&Ls were less involved in FHA lending than all the other lending groups during the postwar era.

The loan surveys conducted within the Urban Real Estate Finance Project provided new and granular detail about the practices, lending costs, and returns of the leading urban mortgage lenders during a period of significant market turmoil and institutional change.[23] The data indicated that life insurance companies, commercial banks, and S&Ls all experienced average rates of foreclosure between 15 and 20 percent on mortgage loans made during the last half of the 1920s. They also establish a clearer view of the diversity that existed in the structure of mortgage loan contracts before 1930, the liberalization of mortgage lending terms between 1935 and 1950, and the differential impact that the introduction of government mortgage loan insurance and guarantee programs had on the major lending groups. It is important, at the same time, to acknowledge that the NBER loan surveys were subject to substantial response and survivorship biases, so all of these patterns need to be interpreted with care. These problems with the sampling methodology might explain why the data for commercial banks, life insurance companies, and savings and loan associations remain unused by other researchers more than sixty years after they were collected.

The same cannot be said for the sample of loans that Lowell Harriss collected for *The History and Policies of the Home Owners' Loan Corporation*. The HOLC was an unusual mortgage lender in a couple of important respects. To begin with, it was created as an emergency federally financed corporation in 1933 and, over the next three years, it became the nation's largest holder of residential mortgage debt after it had purchased and refinanced more than one million home loans. Second, after finally liquidating its mortgage portfolio in 1951, the HOLC was dissolved as originally intended. The agency's business was restricted to purchasing and refinancing only existing home loans that were in default and facing foreclosure. Borrowers like these were plentiful in the mid-1930s, and, by 1936, the HOLC held loans on one out of every ten of the nation's owner-occupied homes. Harriss had access to the HOLC's staff and documents just before it dissolved, so his study provides unusual detail about the costs and profitability of its operation, the procedures it used to appraise property values, and how it set loan terms and serviced its loan portfolio. Because the HOLC was the key New Deal intervention designed to ameliorate the home mortgage crisis of the 1930s, its performance and effectiveness has been of great interest since 2007. Harriss's monograph has proved to be invaluable to both policymakers and academics in these discussions, and his sample of more than three thousand HOLC loans from the New York region has recently been used by Jonathan

---

23. Saulnier enlisted twenty-four of the largest life insurance companies, a group that held nearly two-thirds of the industry's urban mortgage loans, to report detailed information from origination to retirement for a 1 percent sample of the mortgage loans that they had made each year between 1920 and 1946. In addition, he secured information from dozens more concerning their costs and returns on urban mortgage lending. Behrens's bank survey was distributed to just under 500 commercial banks, of which 116 reported detailed information about loans made between 1920 and 1947 and several dozen more about their activities in 1947. Edwards received retrospective loan data from 92 of 500 surveyed savings and loans and contemporaneous information (for 1947) from more than 100 others.

Rose to show that the HOLC brought substantial benefits to lenders as well as to delinquent borrowers.[24]

The third component of the NBER's Urban Real Estate Finance Project was designed to integrate the examinations of the principal mortgage lenders provided by Saulnier, Behrens, Edwards, and Harriss with the institutional environment described by Fisher and Colean.[25] This task was undertaken by J. E. Morton, who provided the project's seventh and last monograph *Urban Mortgage Lending: Comparative Markets and Experience.* The volume by Morton offers a wide-ranging picture of the nonfarm mortgage market during a period in which outstanding home mortgage debt grew rapidly in size relative to both residential wealth and other types of debt. In it, he documents how the home mortgage market was transformed between 1920 and 1950 as residential mortgage finance became dominated by a differentiated set of institutional portfolio lenders that were each shaped by federal regulation, policies, and subsidies. By focusing on the activities and experience of these principal lending agencies, the NBER's Urban Real Estate Finance Project contributed significantly not only to our understanding of the development of the supply side of the mortgage market between 1920 and 1950, but also the forces that affected mortgage investment experience before, during, and after the worst mortgage crisis in the nation's history.

1.2.3   Capital Formation in Residential Real Estate: Trends and Prospects, 1950–1954

Contemporaneously with the Urban Real Estate Finance Project, the NBER sponsored a project that focused more narrowly on residential housing and its mortgage market. *Capital Formation in Residential Real Estate: Trends and Prospects* was part of Simon Kuznets's larger project on "Capital Requirements in the American Economy." Kuznets structured the project as a series of independent studies of capital formation and financing in agriculture, manufacturing, regulated industries, and government, as well as residential housing. Each was published as a separate monograph by the NBER and then integrated by Kuznets in his own analysis of *Capital in the American Economy: Its Formation and Financing* (1961). Leo Grebler was chosen to lead the effort on residential capital. Grebler was a German émigré who worked between 1939 and 1946 for the Federal Home Loan Bank system and as chief of the FHA's housing finance division before becoming a research professor with the Institute for Urban Land Use and Housing Studies at Columbia University, which cosponsored his NBER study.[26]

---

24. See Rose (2011), Fishback et al. (2011), and Courtemanche and Snowden (2011). Fishback, Rose, and Snowden (2013) provide additional background about the HOLC and a unified view of recent research about it.

25. Morton (1956) also makes extensive use of Lintner's study of mutual savings banks to complete the institutional picture.

26. In later years, Grebler served with the President's Council of Economic Advisors and as a consultant with the Commission on Money and Credit, the President's Task Force on Low

Kuznets envisioned that each component of the capital formation project would analyze available data for the 1870 to 1950 period rather than collect new evidence. However, no systematic or reliable statistics were available for the period before 1920 for either residential construction or mortgage finance. Grebler's coauthor David M. Blank attacked the former problem by extending back to 1889 the estimates of housing starts that Foster and Wickens had constructed for the post-1920 period. This work was accomplished using building permit data for the pre-1920 era that had been collected during the 1930s by the Works Progress Admininstration (WPA) but never used. Like Wickens and Foster, Blank relied on relationships between population and building permits to derive his estimates, but his approach was considerably more sophisticated. Blank reports his estimates and a complete description of his methodology in *The Volume of Residential Construction, 1889–1950* (1954). The BLS adopted Blank's annual estimates for 1889 to 1919 as its official housing starts series for that period.

There was also a need for comprehensive historical estimates of the size and structure of the nonfarm residential mortgage market. Grebler, Blank, and Winnick assembled these estimates beginning in 1896 by combining several sources, including data that appeared in Raymond W. Goldsmith's NBER volume, *A Study of Saving in the United States, Volume I* (1955), and estimates of institutional residential mortgage holdings that the FHLB had assembled for the period beginning in 1925. Using this information, Grebler, Blank, and Winnick estimated the total amount and institutional distribution of residential mortgage debt each year beginning in 1896, with a disaggregation of the totals into debt on one-to-four family and multi-family dwellings beginning in 1925. The derivation and reliability of the annual series are laid out meticulously in two lengthy appendices, and these estimates continue to provide the best and most comprehensive view of the size and structure of the American mortgage market before 1950.

Grebler, Blank, and Winnick did much more than fill obvious gaps in the statistical record. Their monograph provides a broader and more detailed analysis than earlier NBER contributions into the forces that shaped the performance and development of housing and home mortgage markets between 1890 and 1950. The scholarship brought to this task was exhaustive, well documented, and a major contribution in its own right. Two-fifths of the monograph is taken up by seventeen appendices that report and document information not only about housing starts and mortgage holdings, but also conversions and demolitions of housing units, depreciation, housing prices and costs, household formation, and mortgage lending terms. As we shall see in this volume, some of these ancillary estimates and discussions have ended up playing a much larger role in subsequent literature than Grebler, Blank, and Winnick could have envisioned in the mid-1950s.

Income Housing, the Board of Governors of the Federal Reserve System, and the United Nations. In 1958, he moved to UCLA and its Real Estate Research Program.

Grebler, Blank, and Winnick also differed from the previous NBER authors by focusing on longer, six-decade trends in the residential housing and mortgage markets. They establish, for example, that additions to the housing stock over this period in the United States were closely connected to population growth and influenced by the declining size and changing composition of nonfarm households. As a result, they link a declining aggregate importance of residential construction between 1890 and 1950 to the deceleration in population growth over the same period. This trend was reinforced, according to the authors, by a surprising decrease in the average size and real investment made in individual housing units over the same period.[27] While the importance of residential construction activity diminished in this relative sense, households showed a marked increase in their willingness to purchase homes on credit. This behavior, in turn, drove the spectacular growth and rapid development of the home mortgage market between 1890 and 1950 that was driven in large part after 1930 by federal programs, regulation, and subsidies.

1.2.4   Postwar Residential Mortgage Market: 1955–1961

In 1955, the NBER established a program to examine the three major components of the postwar capital market: the markets for government securities, corporate securities and loans, and nonfarm mortgage loans. Saul Klaman, an economist on leave from the Federal Reserve Board of Governors, was chosen to conduct the examination of the residential mortgage market.[28] As Raymond Goldsmith points out in his introduction to *The Postwar Residential Mortgage Market* (1961), the home mortgage market after World War II was central to the performance of the entire capital market because it grew faster than all other components between 1946 and 1955. In addition, the home mortgage market experienced a fundamental structural change during the period as institutional lenders became increasingly dominant and federal credit programs reshaped the channels through which mortgage finance flowed.

Klaman's monograph focuses primarily on institutional lenders and the supply side of the market, so it can be read as an extension of the earlier Urban Real Estate Finance Project. The time period examined by Klaman is much shorter than those examined in previous NBER studies, and he responded by offering a more detailed and technical analysis of the topic. Klaman shows that the institutional transformation of the nonfarm, residential mortgage market in the postwar decade produced a larger discontinuity than had previously been understood. At the center of the transition was the influence of the federal credit programs that gave institutional lenders

27. Margaret Reid (1958) offers a detailed critique of this particular result. See Grebler, Blank, and Winnick (1959) for a rejoinder.
28. Klaman later served as chief economist and president of the National Association of Mutual Savings Banks.

greater liquidity and access to an active secondary market in mortgage loans. With this new foundation in place, Klaman demonstrates that the single-family residential market expanded much faster than all other components of the urban mortgage market after the war, and that the four big institutional lenders—savings and loans, life insurance companies, commercial banks, and mutual savings banks—achieved dominance within this segment of the market. Klaman documents marked differences across these lending groups in their reliance on the FHA program, the methods they used to acquire mortgage loans, the extent of participation in interregional lending, and how they balanced lending activity across the single-family, multifamily, and commercial property markets. Klaman also describes and explains how innovation reshaped the methods these institutions used to facilitate connections between construction, interim, and permanent mortgage financing.

To lay a foundation for this analysis, Klaman constructed new estimates of the volume of residential mortgage debt that were first reported in his *Volume of Debt in the Postwar Decade* (1958). Klaman's goal in constructing these estimates was to improve on previous studies that examined net flows of mortgage credit measured with changes in the volume of outstanding debt between two dates. Klaman believed that measures of the gross flows of mortgage debt—which accounted for the total volumes of originations, secondary market transactions, and retirements for each period—could provide a much clearer picture of how mortgage credit actually flowed between investors and borrowers. Klaman was able to construct tentative estimates of gross flows for S&Ls, insurance companies, and savings banks, but not for commercial banks. By doing so, he established for the first time a statistical record of the complex interinstitutional networks that emerged during the postwar decade to facilitate greater scale and geographic reach in lending activities.

Klaman's second noteworthy contribution in *The Postwar Rise of Mortgage Companies* (1959) was to document the institutional developments during the postwar period that facilitated these mortgage flows. During the 1920s, mortgage companies had expanded their mortgage loan origination and servicing activities by writing private mortgage loan insurance and issuing mortgage-backed securities. These techniques disappeared when nearly all of the urban mortgage companies failed during the 1930s. Klaman establishes that a new breed of mortgage companies emerged in the post–World War II decade to originate and service mortgage loans as correspondents for life insurance companies and mutual savings banks. Federally insured and guaranteed loans dominated the flow of funds through these networks, while innovations such as forward and standby commitments were developed to smooth the transitions between interim and permanent financing. Klaman's scholarship in *The Postwar Residential Mortgage Market* is first rate in all dimensions, and the monograph remains the definitive account of the postwar development of the US residential mortgage market.

1.2.5   Extensions of Earlier NBER Projects: 1958–1964

Between 1958 and 1964, two final projects extended earlier NBER research contributions into the nonfarm housing market. The first was a comprehensive examination of federal credit programs that served agriculture, business, and, most importantly here, the FHA-insured and the VA-guaranteed home loan programs. Raymond Saulnier, Harold Halcrow, and Neil Jacoby began this work in 1951. It then took six years to assemble data on the volume and lending experience within each category of the programs and to analyze their economic impacts.[29] In *Federal Lending and Loan Insurance* (1958), they show that federal housing credit programs had reduced the costs of mortgage credit to borrowers, decreased regional differences in mortgage loan rates, increased the ratio of debt to equity, lengthened the final maturities of loans, and promoted the principle of periodic amortization. More surprisingly, they also conclude that the introduction of the programs had not appreciably increased the economy-wide use of mortgage credit or significantly influenced the institutional structure of the mortgage market.

The last NBER housing project of this early era extended annual estimates of aggregate residential construction back to 1840. Interest in this subject arose in the early 1950s when Kuznets identified fifteen- to twenty-year "long swings" in economic growth, demographics, and construction that appeared to be closely connected to historical "building cycles" that had been widely examined in the 1930s. Abramovitz provides an extensive survey of this literature in his NBER volume, *Evidences of Long Swings in Aggregate Construction since the Civil War* (1964). More specifically relevant to residential housing, however, is Manuel Gottlieb's *Estimates of Residential Building, United States, 1840–1939* (1964).

Gottlieb's estimates were designed to provide an alternative to the Blank/BLS estimates before 1915 and to extend that series back an additional fifty years in order to capture additional evidence of Kuznets's long swings. To do so, Gottlieb introduced a new approach and new data. Rather than relying on building permits, Gottlieb assembled his housing production series from housing stock and vintage data that were collected in the 1940 census of housing and from an almost complete 1890 inventory of housing in Ohio. His method involved first estimating decadal totals of new housing and then distributing these totals across housing age categories by using weighted averages of the annual building indexes constructed by several earlier authors. His monograph contains a detailed description of the methodology used along with comparisons with competing estimates. Gottlieb's argument that his urban housing production series represented an improvement on the BLS official housing start series convinced Nathan

---

29. Saulnier, Halcrow, and Jacoby produce a particularly detailed examination of the business loan program of the Reconstruction Finance Corporation.

Balke and Robert J. Gordon (1989) to use it as a central part of their analysis of long-run changes in the US business cycle.

1.3 Conclusion

Between 1935 and 1960, the National Bureau of Economic Research sponsored a series of programs that documented the structure, performance, and institutional development of the markets for nonfarm housing and residential mortgages going back to the nineteenth century. This volume attests not only to the value of these early NBER efforts, but also to the enduring quality of that work. Seven of the ten contributions within this volume cite NBER monographs from this era, and in most of them these sources are relied upon heavily. There can be no better evidence that historical research provides unique and important insights than its capacity to instruct even after being completed and in ways that could not have been anticipated when the work was being done. The contributors to this volume hope that their own work will stand up equally well to this test of time.

Appendix

National Bureau of Economic Research Programs, Monographs, and Papers on Housing Markets, 1935–1964

Below we list the resources discussed in this chapter. All except those indicated with an asterisk are available at http://data.nber.org/booksbyyear/.

1935–1941: The Program on Real Estate Financing and Economic Stability

> Ray Foster and David L. Wickens. 1937. *Non-Farm Residential Construction, 1920–1936.* NBER Bulletin 45.
> David L. Wickens. 1941. *Residential Real Estate: Its Economic Position as Shown by Values, Rents, Family Incomes, Financing, and Construction, Together with Estimates for All Real Estate.*

1945–1955: The Urban Real Estate Finance Project

> Raymond J. Saulnier. 1950. *Urban Mortgage Lending by Life Insurance Companies.*
> Miles L. Colean. 1950. *The Impact of Government on Real Estate Finance in the US.*
> Ernest M. Fisher. 1951. *Urban Real Estate Markets: Characteristics and Financing.*
> C. Lowell Harriss. 1951. *History and Policies of the Home Owners' Loan Corporation.*
> Carl F. Behrens. 1952. *Commercial Bank Activities in Urban Mortgage Financing.*
> J. E. Morton. 1956. *Urban Mortgage Lending: Comparative Markets and Experience.*

Edward E. Edwards. 1950. "Urban Real Estate Financing by Savings and Loan Associations" (unpublished draft).*

Mortgage Loan Experience Cards (data on 27,000 mortgage loans from Lender Surveys: Data and Documentation) available at http://data.nber.org/nberhistory/.

1950–1954: Capital Formation in Residential Real Estate: Trends and Prospects

Leo Grebler. 1953. *The Role of Federal Credit Aids in Residential Construction.*
David M. Blank. 1954. *The Volume of Residential Construction, 1889–1950.*
Leo Grebler, David M. Blank, and Louis Winnick. 1956. *Capital Formation in Residential Real Estate: Trends and Prospects.*

1955–1961: Postwar Residential Mortgage Market

Saul B. Klaman. 1958. *The Volume of Mortgage Debt in the Postwar Decade.*
Saul B. Klaman. 1959. *The Postwar Rise of Mortgage Companies.*
Saul B. Klaman. 1961. *The Postwar Residential Mortgage Market.*

1957–1964: Other Housing Monographs

Raymond J. Saulnier, Harold G. Halcrow, and Neil H. Jacoby. 1957. *Federal Lending: Its Growth and Impact.*
Raymond J. Saulnier, Harold G. Halcrow, and Neil H. Jacoby. 1958. *Federal Lending and Loan Insurance.*
Moses Abramovitz. 1964. *Evidences of Long Swings in Aggregate Construction Since the Civil War.*
Manuel Gottlieb. 1964. *Estimates of Residential Building, United States, 1840–1939.*

References

Abramovitz, Moses. 1964. "Evidences of Long Swings in Aggregate Construction since the Civil War." NBER Occasional Paper 90. New York: National Bureau of Economic Research.

Balke, Nathan S., and Robert J. Gordon. 1989. "The Estimation of Prewar Gross National Product: Methodology and New Evidence." *Journal of Political Economy* 97 (1): 38–91.

Behrens, Carl F. 1952. *Commercial Bank Activities in Urban Mortgage Financing.* New York: National Bureau of Economic Research.

Blank, David M. 1954. *The Volume of Residential Construction, 1889–1950.* NBER Technical Paper 9. New York: National Bureau of Economic Research.

Bodfish, H. Morton, and A. D. Theobald. 1938. *Savings and Loan Principles.* New York: Prentice Hall.

Carter, Susan B., Scott S. Gartner, Michael R. Haines, Alan L. Olmstead, Richard Sutch, and Gavin Wright, eds. 2006. *Historical Statistics of the United States: Earliest Times to the Present.* Millennial edition. Cambridge: Cambridge University Press.

Colean, Miles. 1950. *The Impact of Government on Real Estate Finance in the US.* Princeton, NJ: Princeton University Press.

Courtemanche, Charles, and Kenneth Snowden. 2011. "Repairing a Mortgage Crisis: HOLC Lending and Its Impact on Local Housing Markets." *Journal of Economic History* 71 (2): 307–37.

Edwards, Edward E. 1950. *Urban Real Estate Financing by Savings and Loan Associations*. Unpublished manuscript of the Financial Research Program of the National Bureau of Economic Research.

Field, Alexander. 1992. "Uncontrolled Land Development and the Duration of the Depression in the United States." *Journal of Economic History* 52 (4): 785–805.

Fishback, Price, Shawn Kantor, Alfonso Flores-Lagunes, William Horrace, and Jaret Treber. 2011. "The Influence of the Home Owners' Loan Corporation on Housing Markets During the 1930s." *Review of Financial Studies* 24: 1782–813.

Fishback, Price, Jonathan Rose, and Kenneth Snowden. 2013. *Well Worth Saving: How FDR Safeguarded Homeownership during the 1930s*. Chicago: University of Chicago Press.

Fisher, Ernest M. 1951. *Urban Real Estate Markets: Characteristics and Financing*. New York: National Bureau of Economic Research.

Foster, Ray, and David L. Wickens. 1937. *Non-Farm Residential Construction, 1920–1936*. NBER Bulletin 45. New York: National Bureau of Economic Research.

Goldsmith, Raymond W. 1955. *A Study of Saving in the United States*, Volume 1. Princeton, NJ: Princeton University Press.

Gottlieb, Manuel. 1964. *Estimates of Residential Building in the United States, 1840–1939*, NBER Technical Paper 17. New York: National Bureau of Economic Research.

Gray, John H., and George Terborgh. 1929. *First Mortgages in Urban Real Estate Finance*. Washington, DC: The Brookings Institution.

Grebler, Leo. 1953. *The Role of Federal Credit Aids in Residential Construction*. NBER Occasional Paper 39. New York: National Bureau of Economic Research.

Grebler, Leo, D. Blank, and L. Winnick. 1956. *Capital Formation in Residential Real Estate*. Princeton, NJ: Princeton University Press.

———. 1959. "Once More: Capital Formation in Residential Real Estate." *Journal of Political Economy* 67 (6): 612–19.

Gries, John, and James Ford. 1932a. *Home Finance and Taxation*. President's Conference on Home Building and Home Ownership (Volume II). Washington, DC.

———. 1932b. *Housing Objectives and Programs; Reports*. President's Conference on Home Building and Home Ownership (Volume XI). Washington, DC.

Harriss, C. Lowell. 1951. *History and Policies of the Home Owners' Loan Corporation*. New York: National Bureau of Economic Research.

Hubbard, Theodora Kimball, and Henry Vincent Kimball. 1929. *Our Cities Today and Tomorrow*. Cambridge, MA: Harvard University Press.

Kimbrough, Gray, and Kenneth Snowden. 2007. "The Spatial Character of Housing Depression in the 1930s." Working Paper, University of North Carolina at Greensboro, August.

Klaman, Saul. 1958. *The Volume of Mortgage Debt in the Postwar Decade*. NBER Technical Paper 13. New York: National Bureau of Economic Research.

———. 1959. *The Postwar Rise of Mortgage Companies*. NBER Occasional Paper 60. New York: National Bureau of Economic Research.

———. 1961. *The Postwar Residential Mortgage Market*. Princeton, NJ: Princeton University Press.

Kuznets, Simon. 1961. *Capital in the American Economy: Its Formation and Financing*. Princeton, NJ: Princeton University Press.

Lintner, John. 1948. *Mutual Savings Banks in the Savings and Mortgage Markets*. Boston: Harvard University.

Morton, J. E. 1956. *Urban Mortgage Lending: Comparative Markets and Experience.* Princeton, NJ: Princeton University Press.

National Bureau of Economic Research (NBER). Various years. Annual Report of the Director of Research. http://data.nber.org/nberhistory/.

———. 1937. *A Program of Financial Research.* NBER Bulletin 64. New York: NBER. http://data.nber.org/nberhistory/.

Reid, Margaret G. 1958. "Capital Formation in Residential Real Estate." *Journal of Political Economy* 66(2): 131–53.

Rose, Jonathan. 2011. "The Incredible HOLC? Mortgage Modification during the Great Depression." *Journal of Money, Credit and Banking* 43 (6): 1073–1107.

Saulnier, Raymond J. 1950. *Urban Mortgage Lending by Life Insurance Companies.* Princeton, NJ: Princeton University Press.

Saulnier, Raymond J., Harold G. Halcrow, and Neil H. Jacoby. 1957. *Federal Lending: Its Growth and Impact.* Princeton, NJ: Princeton University Press.

———. 1958. *Federal Lending and Loan Insurance.* Princeton, NJ: Princeton University Press.

Snowden, Kenneth. 2010. "The Anatomy of a Residential Mortgage Crisis: A Look Back to the 1930s." NBER Working Paper no. 16244, Cambridge, MA.

Stapp, Peyton. 1938. *Urban Housing: A Summary of Real Property Inventories Conducted as Work Projects, 1934–1936.* Washington, DC: Government Printing Office.

Veiller, Lawrence. 1929. "The Housing Problem in the United States." *The Town Planning Review* 13 (4): 228–56.

Weiss, Marc A. 1989. "Richard T. Ely and the Contribution of Economics Research to National Housing Policy, 1920–1940." *Urban Studies* 26:115–26.

Wickens, David. 1937. *Financial Survey of Urban Housing.* Washington, DC: Government Printing Office.

———. 1941. *Residential Real Estate: Its Economic Position As Shown by Values, Rents, Family Incomes, Financing and Construction, Together with Estimates for All Real Estate.* New York: National Bureau of Economic Research.

Wood, Edith. 1931. *Recent Trends in American Housing.* New York: Macmillan Company.

I

Housing and the Interwar Business Cycles

2

The Interwar Housing Cycle in the Light of 2001–2012
A Comparative Historical Perspective

Alexander J. Field

The financial crisis of 2008 to 2009 and the Great Recession it precipitated forced a rethinking among macroeconomists about the origin, prevention, and potential mitigation of such events. One of the conclusions emerging from a considered examination of the run-up to and the fallout from the events is the limitation of framing the policy issues solely in terms of whether Chairman Bernanke and the Federal Reserve System, as well as President Obama and the Congress, did the right thing when the crisis hit. Most observers believe that the response to the immediate crisis was correct in the sense that they believe that the appropriate remedy, once the seizing up of credit markets began, was indeed large scale fiscal and monetary stimulus.

As the Fed reduced short-term rates close to the zero lower bound, it almost tripled the size of its balance sheet, and this ongoing monetary accommodation was augmented by the Treasury's Troubled Asset Relief Program (TARP, October 2008) and, beginning in February of 2009, the fiscal stimulus associated with the American Recovery and Reinvestment

Alexander J. Field is the Michel and Mary Orradre Professor of Economics at Santa Clara University.

I am grateful for comments from Michael Bordo, Jean-Jacques Dethier, Price Fishback, Fred Foldvary, Mason Gaffney, Steven Gjerstad, Leslie Hannah, Eric Hilt, Natacha Postel-Vinay, Gary Richardson, Ken Snowden, Bill Sundstrom, Richard Sylla, Eugene White, Larry White, Gavin Wright, and other participants at the NBER Universities-Research Conference on Housing and Mortgage Markets in Historical Perspective, Cambridge, Massachusetts, September 23–24, 2011; at the presentations at Columbia University and New York University, October 6–7, 2011; at the London School of Economics, October 12, 2011; at Santa Clara University, November 9, 2011; and at the Business History Conference, Philadelphia, Pennsylvania, March 30, 2012. For acknowledgments, sources of research support, and disclosure of the author's material financial relationships, if any, please see http://www.nber.org/chapters/c12793.ack.

Act (ARRA).[1] The Republican takeover of the House of Representatives in the November 2010 midterm elections ended prospects for additional fiscal stimulus, at least from the expenditure side, but the Fed's expansionary monetary stance continued as it sustained its expanded balance sheet, purchasing, through its programs of quantitative easing, longer term securities as some of the troubled assets acquired at the height of the crisis matured.

Analysis of the appropriate response to the crisis drew inspiration from the experience of the country during the Great Depression. Two of the key policymakers, Christina Romer and Ben Bernanke, were both serious students of the Great Depression. Bernanke is famous for saying, at a 2002 conference honoring Milton Friedman on his 90th birthday, "Regarding the Great Depression, you're right, we did it. We're very sorry . . . we won't do it again" (Bernanke 2002). Or to put it slightly more accurately, we won't *not* do it again, since Friedman and Schwartz's (1963) brief against the Fed was not their action, but their inaction in the face of bank failures and the consequent shrinkage in the country's money supply.

But this approach to thinking about the lessons of either the Great Recession or the Great Depression, by focusing only on the policy response once the crisis emerged full blown, may dissuade us from examining the process whereby balance sheets become increasingly levered and increasingly risky over time—in other words, the process, which may extend over several years or even decades, whereby an economy can become increasingly financially fragile (Minsky 1964, 1975, 1986). Ignoring this aspect of the run-up to the most recent episode makes it difficult to understand why or how the collapse of an asset price bubble in housing, and the consequent reduction of spending in an overbuilt sector could have threatened such catastrophic consequences for the United States and the world economy. To be sure, residential construction is an important component of gross private domestic investment, but it still contributes a small portion of overall planned spending. Even allowing for a generous multiplier, it is hard to see on the face of it how this relatively small tail could have had the potential to bring down a much larger economic dog.

The answer, which I think is appreciated more now than before 2008, is the significance of balance sheets, and in particular the ways in which high leverage in both the financial and household sectors can generate tight interconnections and the potential for domino effects (systemic impacts) as well as, in the context of house price declines, significant wealth and liquidity effects. To focus only on Fed action or inaction once the crisis hit draws attention away from the multiple acts of legislative and regulatory commission and omission that allowed financial fragility to grow in the first place. It is much clearer now that balance sheets, debt, and leverage can make a big

---

1. Most of the effects of the ARRA on employment and output were experienced in 2010 and 2011. See Congressional Budget Office (2013, 3, table 1).

difference in how an economy responds to an asset price, and/or spending shock. The financial fragility of an economy can spell the difference between whether the system shrugs off a shock or potentially goes into a tailspin.

If the history of the Great Depression enriched our understanding of and influenced the policy response to the Great Recession, reverse intellectual influences are also probable—and desirable. In particular, postmortems on policy issues associated with the Great Recession should cause us to reconsider the shared beliefs among many (aside from real business cycle proponents) that the Great Depression was indeed principally caused by the absence of adequate Federal Reserve response. The thesis that massive monetary accommodation in the early 1930s could almost entirely have eliminated the output cost of the Great Depression needs to be reexamined. Balance sheet considerations were likely implicated in the slow recovery then as well as now, and might have resulted in persistent output losses, even in the presence of a different monetary policy. In the Great Recession, the Fed drove short rates close to the zero lower bound, and also engaged, in sustaining a balance sheet that increased almost by a factor of three, in buying large amounts of longer term Treasury securities. It is not clear how much more monetary accommodation could have been applied. And yet, in its April 27, 2011, release, the Fed forecast unemployment in 2013, a full five years after the worst months of the crisis, to still be in the 6.8 to 7.2 percent range (central tendency), with some within the Fed projecting an unemployment rate of 8.4 percent (Federal Reserve Board 2011a).

The Fed's forecast was overly optimistic. The actual unemployment rate in June 2013 was 7.6 percent, and more than half the unemployed had been out of work for fifteen weeks or longer. It will likely be years before the economy reaches a prerecession forecast of the trajectory of potential output (this is written in 2013) and the cumulative output loss associated with the Great Recession may ultimately exceed one and a half years of gross domestic product (GDP) at 2007 rates.[2]

If massive monetary accommodation will not be able to avoid a very large output loss over the years 2008 to 2017 and beyond we must reconsider whether, in fact, as conventional wisdom seems to hold, massive monetary accommodation in 1929 to 1933 would have avoided most of the output loss associated with those worst years of the Depression. The more recent monetary accommodation made a difference and without it the cumulative output loss would likely have been larger. Similarly, more Fed accommoda-

---

2. After the start of the recession the Congressional Budget Office revised downward its projections of potential GDP, in part because of anticipations of the deleterious effects on labor productivity growth of long-term unemployment. This will reduce a calculation of cumulative output loss if we define the recession and slow recovery as ending at the point where actual output again reaches potential. Such an estimate of cumulative output loss will be too small, since the permanently reduced trajectory of potential is also a consequence of the recession and slow recovery and the financial fragility and crisis that precipitated it. See Field (2013) for calculations.

tion in the early 1930s would probably have meant a less severe Depression. The question on the table, however, is whether that was all that would have been needed to avoid a significant cumulative output loss.

Carmen Reinhardt and Kenneth Rogoff (2009) provide historical evidence that recessions associated with financial crises require significantly longer for recovery than those that do not.[3] And financial crises involving institutions that are not just illiquid but effectively insolvent (because of a prior history of poor and/or risky lending, augmented in some cases by fraud) pose a much more serious policy challenge. Richard Koo's (2009) analysis of Japan and the International Monetary Fund's 2012 survey emphasize that highly leveraged balance sheets in the financial, nonfinancial, and/or household sectors can make a big difference both in the resilience of an economy when faced with an asset price or spending shock, and on the effectiveness of monetary policy in avoiding a large output loss.[4]

But if balance sheet issues hindered recovery in the 1930s, we also need to ask whether housing was implicated in the same ways and to the same degree as has been true in the Great Recession. In 2007–2012, bad real estate lending clearly impaired financial sector balance sheets more than did poorly performing stock market–related loans. Was this true as well in the 1920s? In other words, compared to more recent experience, and other categories of lending, how much did residential mortgage lending in the 1920s contribute to weakening bank balance sheets, making them vulnerable in the 1930s to runs, insolvency, and failure? Secondly, at the level of household balance sheets, was bad residential mortgage debt linked in some direct way to the anomalous drop in consumer durables spending that marked the initial stages of the economic downturn in 1929 and 1930 (Temin 1976)? Or did this have more to do with the loss of stock market wealth (Mishkin 1978) or increased burden of consumer loans (Olney 1999), or an effect running from increased postcrash stock market volatility (Romer 1990)?

In this chapter I tread a narrow line, arguing on the one hand that we cannot understand the onset, depth, and duration of the Great Depression

3. Reinhardt and Rogoff (2010) have been criticized for aspects of that paper suggesting that ratios of government debt to GDP above 90 percent represented a break point associated with much lower growth rates. In *This Time Is Different* (2009), they had cast a considerably broader net, with as much emphasis on private as on public debt. One of the central messages of *This Time Is Different* was that recoveries from recessions associated with financial crises tended to be slower; neither the 2010 paper nor criticism of it undermined or confirmed that generalization. Based on US data, Bordo and Haubrich (2011) did express doubt, although much depended on the criteria used to define a financial crisis. And they granted three important exceptions consistent with the Reinhardt and Rogoff claim: the Great Depression, the recession of the early 1990s, and the recovery after the Great Recession.

4. Chapter 3 of the IMF's 2012 *World Economic Outlook* offers an overview of international and to some extent historical evidence that housing slumps associated with prior run-ups in household debt tend to be more severe and require more time for recovery. Koo (2009) emphasizes how high degrees of leverage contributed to years of slow economic growth in Japan, although the emphasis in the Japanese case is on corporate and bank as opposed to household balance sheets.

without giving as much attention to balance sheet issues as we are now devoting in the analysis of more recent events. At the same time I will maintain that the residential housing cycle, and lending associated with it, played a smaller role in the interwar business cycle compared to what has been true in the first cycle of the twenty-first century. To argue that housing was at the epicenter of the downturn in 1929 to 1931, as it was in 2007 to 2009, and as Gjerstad and Smith (see chapter 3, this volume) maintain, would require significant changes in what have become established narratives of the origin of the downturn in the interwar period. That does not mean the claim is wrong, but rather that it needs to be carefully considered.

There are many similarities between the Great Depression and Great Recession, not least of which is that each was preceded by asset price bubbles (boom and bust) in both equities and real estate. But there were also important differences. The timelines are roughly inverted.[5] In the 1920s a residential real estate boom peaked in 1926, although it was followed by a boom in apartment building and one in central business district construction that extended into the early 1930s. The stock market boom was particularly strong in 1928 and 1929, and the crash in equity values is often taken as symbolic of the start of the Great Depression. Although the causal link has been questioned—scholars have pointed to the fact that industrial production began to decline in the summer of 1929, or claimed that stock ownership was concentrated among a small portion of the population,[6] or that the market recovered considerably in the first four months of 1930, or that big declines in output and employment did not begin until months after the crash—the October 1929 drop and subsequent downward trajectory retain a central place in narratives of origin.[7]

In the Great Recession, the sequence was roughly reversed. The boom in equities, particularly tech-based securities, began to collapse in 2000. This was followed, however, by a major boom in the prices and construction of residential housing, which peaked in early 2006. A commercial construction boom followed, as had been the case in the 1920s.[8]

5. Another difference is that net inflows of foreign capital, an important factor in the early twenty-first century, were entirely absent in the 1920s, when the United States, running current account surpluses, was a net capital exporter.
6. Romer (1990) suggests that less than 2 percent of American households held stock at the time of the crash, citing Galbraith (1955, 78). But the empirical basis for this assertion is problematic. Galbraith cited a 1934 Senate investigation, in which 29 exchanges reported 1,548,707 customer accounts. Assuming no more than one account per household, and with approximately 30 million occupied housing units in the country in 1930, this is closer to 5 percent than 2 percent. I am indebted to Gavin Wright for drawing my attention to the open question of how extensive stock ownership was at this time.
7. See, for example, Mishkin (1978), who emphasized wealth and liquidity effects; Romer (1990), who argued that post-1929 stock market volatility adversely affected consumer durables purchases; or Eichengreen and Mitchener (2004, 190), who reference stock market effects on balance sheets throughout the economy.
8. The S&P 500 index temporarily exceeded its 2000 peak in 2007, although it remained, in inflation adjusted terms, about 18 percent below it. In November of 2011 it was, in real terms,

But whereas the real economy appears to have largely shrugged off the end of the residential real estate bubble in 1926, that does not appear to have been the case with the stock market crash of 1929 and the slow, sickening slide to a trough in 1932, marked as it was by some of the largest one-day percentage increases in stock prices. And whereas the real economy largely shrugged off the collapse of the tech stock bubble in 2000 and 2001, that does not appear to have been the case with the real estate collapse that began in early 2006 and continued through the first quarter of 2012. This asymmetrical real economy response to asset price deflation is associated with almost diametrically opposed opportunities for leveraged asset acquisition in housing and equities during the run-ups to the two crises.[9]

During the 1920s, mortgages commonly required 50 percent down payments, were generally nonamortized, and were for relatively short periods (five years or less). In the case of federally chartered commercial banks, these limits were legally mandated. Other lenders exercised restraint for some of the same reasons national banks had been restricted in their ability to lend on housing: real estate had an historical record as a very risky asset. As the result of innovations in the 1920s by building and loans, then responsible for more than half of institutional lending on residential housing, it did become possible in some instances for borrowers to obtain a second mortgage and thereby, through this mechanism, increase leverage (Snowden 2010). But not all building and loans were enthusiastic about the practice—the larger ones opposed it—and the overall norm remained short mortgages with modest loan-to-value ratios.

In stocks, however, the situation was almost exactly the reverse. Particularly in the early and middle twenties, one could buy stocks for as little as 10 percent down, with the remainder borrowed. The stock purchaser typically received margin from his broker, who in turn financed this by securing a brokers' loan from a bank or, in the late 1920s, directly from a corporation or private individual. If the stock price declined such that borrower's equity fell below an agreed upon minimum (which might be above 0), the borrower added margin or the lender sold out the position.[10]

---

still close to 40 percent below its year 2000 high point. The NASDAQ index, which peaked at 5,408 in March of 2000, remained in inflation-adjusted terms, almost 60 percent below its peak. By May of 2013 the S&P 500 had risen substantially, but still stood in real terms below its 2000 peak.

9. The asset-side wealth effects of the dot.com and real estate busts were of similar magnitude; the decline in stock values actually somewhat larger. Between December 1999 and September 2002 approximately $10 trillion of stock market value disappeared (Gjerstad and Smith 2009). By the end of 2011, the housing crash had erased about $7 trillion dollars of house value (the comparison between these losses does not factor in the mild inflation that characterized the early twenty-first century). Although the asset-side loss from stock market decline was somewhat larger than that associated with the housing bust, the real economy damage from the latter was worse, suggesting that a focus on the liability side of balance sheets is the key to understanding why this was so.

10. White (1990) argues that credit was not "pushed" on borrowers, but rather "pulled" by speculative fever in the stock market. His evidence is that when, under pressure from the Fed,

In 1934, following the worst years of the Great Depression, the Securities and Exchange Act gave the Federal Reserve authority to set margin requirements on stocks. Since 1975 these have been fixed, for new purchases by individuals, at 50 percent. When the tech bubble collapsed, many investors did see their balance sheets shrink. Nevertheless, because the acquisition of stocks had, to a lesser degree than in the 1920s, been financed with borrowed money, the collapse of the price bubble had lower potential to transmit distress to other entities (financial institutions) that, indirectly or directly, held equities on the left-hand (asset) side of their balance sheets.[11] The end of the tech boom also meant some retardation in the acquisition of information technology (IT) equipment which, through multiplier effects, influenced consumption spending and the retardation of GDP growth. From a comparative perspective, however, the 2001 recession saw few financial failures and was of mild severity and duration. Only in the quarterly data (2001:1) do we see a slight (one quarter) decline in real GDP (see US Department of Commerce 2013, NIPA table 1.1.6).

---

member banks in 1928 and 1929 cut back on brokers' loans, this lacuna was, in the presence of very strong demand, quickly filled by private investors, corporations, and foreign banks. Rates on brokers' loans rose during 1928 and 1929, along with the general level of interest rates, as the Fed allowed increases in the face of a rise in the transactions demand for cash associated with the upsurge in stock trading (Field 1984). The Fed rationalized these rate increases, along with member bank restrictions on brokers' loans, as part of a program that would help control speculation in the stock market. Rappoport and White (1994) summarize evidence that margins rose from 10 to 25 percent in the early to mid-1920s to 40 to 50 percent in 1928 and especially 1929. A brokers' loan was in principle collateralized, but creditors still bore risk because of the possibility, if prices went into free fall, that a lender might not be able to sell quickly enough to secure his initial investment. Higher margins provided additional protection against this risk. Rappoport and White also show that the premium on brokers' time loans rose relative to Treasury rates, also consistent with the likelihood that lenders had increasing concerns about a possible crash. Nevertheless, through whatever channels, and at whatever price, credit supported the run-up in stock purchases and prices, as evidenced by the close correlation between outstanding brokers' loans and security prices (White 1990, figure 4, 75).

11. Mishkin (1978) argued that the stock market decline between 1929 and 1932 affected household demand through both wealth and liquidity effects. Romer (1990) questioned the empirical significance of the wealth effect. Typical econometric estimates are that a dollar decline in household wealth will reduce consumption by four or five cents. The liquidity mechanism predicts that if financial liabilities rise, or if the illiquid portion of assets rises, then demand for new durables and house ownership may decline. The composition of the household balance sheet, therefore, has the potential to influence the amount and composition of consumption. Leveraged acquisition by households of stocks, as opposed to real estate or consumer durables, was less likely to generate liquidity effects because of the nature of margin loan contracts. If prices fell, the borrower could add margin to retain the position, but in cases of rapid price decline, the more likely outcome was that the lender simply sold out the position, removing the stock from the asset side of the balance sheet but at the same time extinguishing the associated liability. Banks in the aggregate did have considerable exposure. On December 31, 1929, loans on securities comprised 39 percent of all member bank loans, more than triple the amount of real estate loans, and loans on securities remained substantially above real estate loans throughout the worst years of the Depression (Board of Governors of the Federal Reserve Board 1943, *Banking and Monetary Statistics*, table 19, 76). But loans on securities were heavily concentrated in the large money center banks, which in general did not fail, suggesting that for the thousands of banks that did, bad real estate loans may have played a more important role than is suggested by the aggregate data.

In contrast, the collapse of the real estate bubble[12] starting in 2006 set in motion rows of falling dominoes that threatened to bring the United States and the world economy to its knees.

These observations suggest that the pre-2008 complacency among economists and policymakers about how real estate acquisition was financed was not justified. We should have been more concerned. Leverage mattered. This is a matter of continuing and more general concern. In spite of the passage of the Dodd-Frank bill in July of 2010, there has to date (May 2013) been little movement to alter the incentives that even bigger and more interconnected financial institutions have to make risky bets with borrowed money.[13]

As we try to parse the lessons from the most recent cycle, there is much to be learned by going back and reexamining the history of housing during the interwar period. In particular, it would be helpful to understand better why the end of the residential real estate boom in 1926 appears to have had such a limited adverse effect on the real economy, as compared to what happened in the early twenty-first century (on this question, see White, chapter 4, this volume). At the same time, we need to understand why private sector construction remained so depressed for such a long time during the 1930s. More than two decades ago I argued that this was principally due to the physical and legal detritus of premature subdivision in the 1920s (Field 1992), and that in the postwar period, housing booms have created fewer obstacles to recovery from this source, due to the development of zoning and land use regulation. That is likely to be true as well for the most recent boom, since land use regulation, unlike that applicable to financial institutions, was less affected by the deregulatory enthusiasms of the 1980s and 1990s (see also Field [2011], chapters 10 and 11).[14] More than six years after it peaked in

12. By a bubble I mean an increase in asset prices unrelated to improvements in fundamentals. It is always easier to see and say this after the fact, but even before the crash it was apparent to a critical observer that the unprecedented increase in the ratio of house prices to median household income in the early twenty-first century could not continue indefinitely.

13. The failure in November 2011 of Jon Corzine's firm, MF-Global, was a reminder that a newer and more effective regulatory regime, one less subject to exploitation of loopholes and political manipulation, remained a work in progress. Corzine had placed highly leveraged bets (using leverage ratios of more than 30 to 1—higher than investment banks, somewhat chastened, were then risking) that troubled European sovereign debt would recover. Because of the very slim equity cushion, it did not take much of a continued slide in the prices of these bonds to push the firm into bankruptcy. Corzine also took advantage of weakening restrictions on what trading firms could do with supposedly segregated customers' accounts (see Burrough, Cohan, and McLean 2012), and had personally intervened to help fight back efforts by the Commodity Futures Trading Commission to tighten these. See http://blogs.wsj.com/deals/2011/10/31/mf-global-bankruptcy-the-biggest-losers/.

14. The implications of the failure of construction spending to revive are significant. Throughout the 1920s, gross investment in equipment, residential structures, and nonresidential structures were each of similar magnitude. In 1937, both construction categories remained substantially short of equipment investment. I calculate that had these three categories retained their rough equality with the rates exhibited by equipment investment, and assuming a multiplier of 1.78, GDP in 1937 would have been $102.2 billion rather than the actual $91.9 billion. I estimate potential output in that year at $110.9 billion (all magnitudes in 1937 dollars). According

2006:1, expenditures on residential construction began to recover in 2012, although in 2013:1, a full seven years after the peak, these expenditures proceeded at less than half peak levels in nominal and real terms.[15]

On the other hand, leverage, debt overhang, and foreclosure played a major role in amplifying the impact of the housing bust in 2006 to 2012, posing obstacles to full economic recovery (Financial Crisis Inquiry Commission 2011). An open question historically is how much the debt overhang of the residential housing boom of the 1920s, as compared to the direct legacy of premature subdivision, contributed to slow recovery during the 1930s. Looking at the two booms using a comparative approach can give us some perspective on this.

What happened in the early twenty-first century was quite different in a number of respects from what happened in the interwar period. The epicenter of the problems causing the initial downturn in 2007 was clearly housing, which most argue was not the case in the Depression.[16] And whereas Irving Fisher's debt deflation mechanism affected mortgaged housing between 1929 and 1933, the problems in the sector in the recent episode were caused only marginally by increasing debt burdens due to deflation. Although Bernanke and other policymakers feared more severe deflation, in part as a result of their actions, the annual rate of change of the consumer price index (CPI) for all urban consumers was negative only in 2009, declining at .37 percent per year, as compared with 3.8 percent growth in 2008, and returned to positive territory (1.6 percent per year) in 2010 (US Department of Labor 2011). This is to be compared with the 8 percent per year deflation that characterized 1929 to 1933.[17]

Bad mortgage debt contributed directly to failures of building and loans, the provider of the majority of institutionally financed mortgages during the 1920s, and this bears some relationship to the ways in which housing travails ended up threatening system-wide damage to the economy by jeopardizing the solvency of financial institutions in the 2007 to 2011 period. But the argument (Gjerstad and Smith, chapter 3, this volume) that balance sheet issues associated with housing were central both to the initial downturn in the Great Depression and to the slow recovery must overcome the long lag of several years between when the residential housing boom ended (1926) and the beginning of the downturn in the real economy in 1929. It must also overcome the relatively small share of institutional lending on residential

---

to these calculations, more than half the output gap remaining in 1937 can be accounted for by the failure of construction to revive. The contribution of the residential housing shortfall considered alone is about a third. For details, see Field (2011, 271).

15. US Department of Commerce 2013, NIPA table 1.1.5, accessed May 30, 2013.

16. For a contrasting view see Gjerstad and Smith, chapter 3, this volume.

17. Home owners in the most recent episode faced increasing real debt burdens, but this was more typically due to their use of innovative financial products such as negative amortization loans with low teaser rates that subsequently reset.

housing contributed by commercial banks: a fifth or less prior to 1937 (Morton 1956, table C-2, 170).

We have abundant historical evidence that commercial bank failures can pose a systemic threat to an economy. It is less clear that this would have been so with building and loans. Such institutions did not issue demand deposits, and so their failure could not reduce the money supply. Moreover, unlike commercial banks, they did not typically borrow from or lend to other financial institutions, and thus contributed little to the interconnections among financial sector balance sheets that can facilitate contagion.

On the other hand, there is little doubt that bad real estate lending contributed to the vulnerability and failure of specific commercial banks, particularly state-chartered banks, which faced fewer constraints on their lending in this area than did their nationally chartered counterparts. Natacha Postel-Vinay (2011) has found, based on longitudinal analysis of balance sheet data for Chicago-area state banks, that real estate lending in the 1920s influenced which banks were vulnerable to failure in the early 1930s. In particular, as did Elmus Wicker (1980), she disputes the view that bank runs were simply liquidity events inspired by irrational fear, crises that could have been averted by temporary intervention from the Fed. She suggests instead that most failed banks were insolvent, and that they were so in particular because of bad real estate lending. In other words she tells a story—admittedly one based on the Chicago data alone—that bears analogues to 2001 to 2010, and is in this sense supportive of what Gjerstad and Smith are trying to advance.

Indeed, it does sometimes appear that wherever and whenever one digs into the failure of a commercial bank during the Depression, the words "bad real estate lending" are likely to follow. This is true for the famous case of the Bank of United States (see Lucia 1985; O'Brien 1992; Trescott 1992), although stock market loans, in particular loans to affiliates and others to support holding the bank's own stock, were also implicated in its failure.[18] Bad real estate loans were also prominent in the collapse of the Bain group of banks in Chicago in June 1931, which spread to the Forman banks (Guglielmo 2011, 35). A third case in point is the failure of the Tennessee-based banking empire of Caldwell and Company, which figures prominently in the Gjerstad and Smith narrative. Wicker (1980) attributed the failure of Caldwell and 120 other banks to poor loans and investments made in the 1920s (1980, 572).

Still, categories such as "real estate lending," or "urban mortgages" include loans not only on residential housing, but also on commercial and industrial property; the focus here is mainly on the comparative contribution of the residential housing cycle to recession/depression. Caldwell's problems, for example, appear to have been largely in commercial real estate and

18. Temin (1976, 92) also attributed the failure of the Bank of United States to bad loans, particularly real estate loans.

municipal investment complementary to it rather than strictly residential lending (Tennessee Encyclopedia 2011).

Wicker saw his interpretation as supporting Friedman and Schwartz (1963) in what was then an ongoing debate with Temin (1976). But Wicker's analysis is really quite inconsistent with the narrative Friedman and Schwartz advanced. Friedman and Schwartz downplayed the extent to which failing banks were insolvent as a result of a prior history of risky or poorly selected loans and investments, emphasizing instead that the banking panics were almost entirely liquidity events. This is particularly evident in their characterization of the failure of the Bank of United States, which they considered a solvent bank, attributing the fact that it was not rescued in part to anti-Semitism. Friedman and Schwartz mention, although they do not pursue further, the possibility that "the great surge in bank failures that characterized the first banking crisis after October 1930 may . . . have resulted from poor loans and investments made in the twenties" (Temin 1976, 85; Friedman and Schwartz 1963, 355).

As does Wicker, Guglielmo (2011) links vunerability in the 1930s to poor lending in the 1920s, attributing a weakening of Illinois state bank portfolios to the drying up of opportunities to make short-term commercial loans—as many corporations shifted from debt to equity financing. To make up for lost business, he suggests, banks shifted into loans backed by real estate or stock. Although such loans may have been viewed as safe at the time they were made, they turned out, ex post, to be quite risky. Unlike commercial loans, neither category was discountable at the Fed. In the case of real estate, the relatively low loan-to-value ratios of 1920s loans did not end up protecting bank collateral as effectively as may have appeared to have been the case when they were originated, largely due to the perhaps unexpectedly high cost of foreclosure. Similarly, loans on stock (e.g., brokers' loans), although championed in the 1920s as almost as liquid as cash, turned out not always to be so when the free fall of equity prices made it impossible to sell out fast enough to recover collateral.

Therefore, there is considerable evidence linking bad lending in the 1920s, including bad real estate lending, to financial institution vulnerability in the 1930s, suggesting that failures, which were already high in the 1920s and rose much further in the 1930s, were not pure liquidity events but often involved institutions driven to insolvency by a prior history of risky lending (Calomiris and Mason 1997, 2003). This suggests strong parallels with the early twenty-first century, and would again seem to provide support for the Gjerstad and Smith position. While acknowledging the importance of this dynamic in understanding the interwar cycle, I will nevertheless continue to make the case that the residential housing cycle in the 1920s was not the epicenter of the Great Depression in the way it so clearly has been for the Great Recession. To the degree that real estate lending was implicated in bank failures in the 1920s, and it was considerable, the loans tended to be farm mortgages, rather than loans on residential real estate per se (Alston, Grove, and Wheelock 1994).

It is indeed tempting to conclude that the 1920s were like the early twenty-first century, and that the foundations for the Depression were established in housing in the 1920s. To some degree this was no doubt true. As I have previously argued, premature subdivision in the 1920s posed legal and infra-structural impediments to the revival of house construction in the 1930s (Field 1992). But the financial groundwork differed in important ways. In the earlier period a smaller fraction of houses was mortgaged, and loan-to-value ratios were lower—in other words the sector was much less levered. Bad real estate loans adversely affected building and loan societies (fore-runners of savings and loans), but their failures had little systemic impact. In spite of the role that poor real estate (and in general poor and in some cases fraudulent) lending played in notable bank failures in the 1930s, the fact remains that commercial bank holdings of institutional mortgages on one-to-four family houses never rose above 20 percent of the total until 1937 (Morton 1956, table C-2).

Because of a history of wild real estate booms and busts prior to the Civil War, the National Banking Act (1864) tightly restricted the loans national banks could make on land or housing. Although these prohibitions were weakened in the face of competition from state chartered institutions, total lending on mortgages by federally chartered commercial banks remained very low until the second decade of the twentieth century. On June 4, 1913, real estate loans accounted for just .7 percent of national bank assets (Behrens 1952, 16).

Loosening began with the Federal Reserve Act (1913), which for the first time allowed loans on farmland with loan-to-value not to exceed 50 percent and a period of time not to exceed five years, provided such loans in the aggregate did not exceed 25 percent of bank capital and surplus or a third of time deposits. The 1916 legislation went somewhat further, freeing national banks to lend on nonfarm real estate for a period of time not to exceed one year, again with a maximum 50 percent loan-to-value. The one-year restriction was serious: prior to the McFadden Act, many commercial bank mortgage loans were effectively demand loans after the first year. The McFadden Act (1927) increased the allowable term on nonfarm mortgages to five years with the total amount of such loans not to exceed 50 percent of time deposits. In most cases commercial banks could not lend across state lines, and indeed were restricted to lending on real estate within 100 miles of the bank's principal place of business.

State-chartered banks did not face the same restrictions in the 1920s, perhaps one reason their failure rates were so much higher in the 1930s. Still, even with more liberal real estate lending on the part of state banks, total commercial bank lending as a fraction of institutional lending on one-to-four family houses did not rise above 20 percent until 1937. The rise at that point was partly the result of an amendment to the Federal Reserve Act in 1935 that allowed national banks to make ten-year loans, with up to 60 percent loan-to-value, if the loan was sufficiently amortized to reduce principal by at least 40 percent within ten years. This was part of a coordinated program of mortgage liberalization advanced during the New Deal, reflected in the establishment of the Federal Housing Authority in 1934 and the Federal National Mortgage Association in 1938. These legislative and policy initiatives led ultimately to the thirty-year, fully amortized fixed rate instrument that became common after the Second World War.

Finally, although mortgage-backed securities appeared in the 1920s, their development was much less advanced than became the case in the early twenty-first century (White 2009, figure 4.14). During the 1920s they were largely limited to pools of mortgages on apartments or other commercial properties, as opposed to first mortgages on owner-occupied houses. (Goetzmann and Newman 2010). Robert J. Gordon has noted that more skyscrapers higher than 250 feet tall were built in New York between 1922 and 1931 than in any ten-year period before or since. Securitization and other innovations played a significant role in financing this capital formation, and the balance sheet consequences, in terms of the duration of the interwar cycle, remain to be investigated. But this dynamic is distinct from what we normally understand as the residential housing cycle, and is not the central focus of this chapter.

Turning now from financial sector to household sector balance sheets, we can consider other channels through which asset price deflation might have contributed to the propagation of the Great Depression. In the presence of a central bank with an asymmetric commitment to price stability, and thus in the presence of deflation, even the moderate (relative to the early twenty-first century) expansion of debt in housing that took place during the 1920s could have contributed, through the debt deflation mechanism, to declines in demand, particularly for durables and houses themselves. Frederick Mishkin's breakdown of the household balance sheet during the Depression shows mortgage liabilities increasing in real terms from $29.6 billion in 1929 to $33.6 billion in 1930, to $36.9 billion in 1931, and to $40.5 billion in 1932. He shows security loans jumping in real terms from $16.4 billion in 1929 to $21.6 billion in 1930, before falling off to $17.4 billion in 1931 and $12.4 billion in 1932. Consumer credit liabilities (for automobiles, for example) increased from $10.1 billion in 1929 to $12 billion in 1930, to $12.3 billion in 1931, and then fell to $11.3 billion in 1932 (Mishkin 1978, 921; all figures in 1958 dollars). These numbers suggest that the biggest negative shock coming from the liabilities side of the household balance sheet between 1929 and 1930 was the increase in the real value of security loans: $5.2 billion. The increase in the real value of real estate liabilities, $4 billion, was about a fourth less. The stock of real estate debt, however, was larger than securities and consumer credit debt combined, and persisted at high, and in the case of real estate lending rising levels (in real terms) much longer, in part perhaps because of less adequate resolution mechanisms.

Mishkin's data suggest that the liability-side wealth effects on consumption emanating from stock acquisition in the 1920s were stronger than those from real estate debt in producing the initial shocks that led to the downturn in the economy between 1929 and 1930. However, there are unresolved issues about the data underlying his analysis of equities. Mishkin's table A-1 gives as the source for the stock market loan data column (4) of table L-25 in Goldsmith (1955, vol. 1, 410). That table shows that nominal commercial bank loans for purchasing or acquiring securities fell from $8.278 billion in 1929 to $7.251 billion in 1930 (these are listed in the table as end-of-year values).[19] That is what one would have expected to have happened if, in the presence of rapid price declines, lenders sold out the positions of their leveraged borrowers, thus extinguishing the loans. The only circumstance in which we might have expected nominal loans to have increased is if, in the face of collapsing stock values, many borrowers met their margin calls and even acquired new stock on margin in the expectation that price declines represented a buying opportunity. This is possible, especially given that most of the largest one-day price increases in the market during the twentieth century took place between 1929 and 1932. But it seems much less likely than the first scenario, which would be consistent with the numbers in Goldsmith.

The problem with reconciling these numbers with Mishkin (1978) is that there is too little deflation between 1929 and 1930 to turn these nominal decreases into real increases, let alone real increases of the magnitude reported in his table 2. The stock market crash may have adversely affected spending in such areas as consumer durables because of a reduction in stock market values or because of the influence of volatility on perceived uncertainty, as emphasized by Romer. It appears questionable, however, at the household level, whether the balance sheet effects of declining stock values on the asset side was reinforced by a rising real value of stock market loans on the liabilities side. Between 1929 and 1933 the wealth effects of declines in the values of equities were considerably more serious than were those associated with declines in the value of real estate. On the asset side of the household sector balance sheet, corporate stocks in 1929 were worth more than real estate ($128.8 billion vs. $109.7 billion), a situation dramatically reversed by 1933 ($50.9 billion vs. $81.7 billion) (data are nominal and are from Woolf and Marley 1989, table 15.A.1, 817). Stocks fell in value more than real estate, and much more than consumer prices, and so the asset-side wealth effect was quite large. Woolf and Marley give a 1929 value of

19. Board of Governors of the Federal Reserve Board 1943, *Banking and Monetary Statistics* (table 19, 76) shows end-of-year member bank loans on securities falling from $10.148 billion in 1929 to $9.439 billion in 1930, although the average level of brokers' loans was higher in 1930 than in 1929. Even a generous allowance for deflation cannot generate the increase in real value of loans on securities reported by Mishkin.

total equities held of $235.4 billion. That included unincorporated business equity, trust fund equity, insurance and pension equity, as well as corporate stock ($128.8 billion). The Dow Jones index fell 89 percent in nominal terms and 60 percent in real terms between its peak in August of 1929 and trough in July of 1932, although it recovered somewhat in 1933. Using the data from Woolf and Marley, limiting ourselves to corporate stock and assuming 30 percent goods and service price deflation between 1929 and 1933, we have stock values dropping 60 percent in nominal terms and 44 percent in real terms over this four-year period for a loss in wealth of $57 billion in 1929 dollars. Using the Goldsmith numbers from table L-25, we have stock market borrowing dropping from $8.278 billion to $3.078 billion (nominal). Again, assuming 30 percent deflation, we have stock market liabilities declining 63 percent nominal and 47 percent real, for a decline of $4.4 billion in 1929 dollars. Combining the effects of declines of both stock market assets and liabilities between 1929 and 1933, we have a negative net wealth effect of $52.6 billion ($57 billion drop on the asset side, counterbalanced by a $4.4 billion decline on the liabilities side).

In real estate, the locus of the balance sheet effects differed, and overall impact on net worth was much smaller. If we accept Shiller's numbers (see following) the price of houses fell, but only along with the general deflation, so real values were largely unaffected, and therefore the asset-side wealth effects in the aggregate were on average small. On the liabilities side, a much smaller fraction of the housing stock was mortgaged, and loan-to-value ratios were much lower than was true in the early twenty-first century. Woolf and Marley (1989, table 15.A) show nominal housing values dropping from $109.7 billion to $81.7 billion between 1929 and 1933, a decline of 25 percent. Shiller has nominal prices dropping 30 percent over those years. If we make allowance for a modest increase in the number of structures over that four-year period, these estimates are roughly consistent with each other.

On the other hand, the interactions of real estate debt and deflation clearly became important in 1931 and 1932, and the negative wealth effect on the liability side was nonnegligible. Woolf and Marley (1989) have nominal mortgage debt falling from $16.6 billion in 1929 to $13.3 billion in 1933. Again assuming an approximately 30 percent decline in goods and services prices over the four-year period, this means real mortgage debt rose from $16.9 billion in 1929 to $19 billion in 1933, a 14 percent increase, a total of $2.1 billion in 1929 prices. Since we are assuming essentially no effect in inflation-adjusted terms on the asset side of the balance sheet, this is the total deflationary impact from real estate. Even if Woolf and Marley are off by a factor of two or three, and the rise in real estate liabilities is closer to what Mishkin reports, it is clear that the stock market effects on household balance sheets in the first four years of the Depression were much larger than those emanating from real estate—probably an order of magnitude larger.

To summarize, from the stock market, we have for the household sector very large negative wealth effects from the assets side, only modestly counteracted by the reduction in liabilities from the closing out of margined positions. In the case of real estate, we have little if any effect on the asset side from change in real housing values, along with a negative wealth effect of an increase in mortgage liabilities through the debt deflation mechanism. The relatively modest impact on household balance sheets from the real estate sector over the worst years of the Great Depression, in comparison with the impact of stock market decline, contrasts sharply with the respective impacts from these two asset classes during the 2006 to 2012 period. In the latter period, as I will show, not only were the housing price declines, both nominal and real, comparatively larger, but so too was the impact of the rising nominal and real value of mortgage liabilities.

Note that, with respect to real estate, debt deflation had conflicting effects on lending institutions' balance sheets. To the degree that households managed to remain current on their nominally fixed mortgage payments, deflation benefited lenders, because the real value of debt repayment went up. Indeed, bond interest was the one category of income to capital that increased in real terms between 1929 and 1933 (Field 2011, 269). Similarly, declines in short rates should, ceteris paribus, have increased the value of the higher interest longer term mortgages. But to the degree that deflation drove borrowers to default, lenders were harmed. When real estate borrowers defaulted, of course, this may have been attributable to loss of income as the consequence of unemployment, to rises in the real burden of payments due to the debt deflation mechanism, or because the loan was of poor quality in the first place—and likely would not have continued to perform even in the absence of deflation or increases in the unemployment rate.

The most recent housing cycle has been marked by a sharp decline in both the nominal and real value of housing. In contrast, although housing prices dropped in the early 1930s, they did so only in line with the general deflation. Unlike the early twenty-first century, however, goods and service price deflation raised the real burden of nominally fixed mortgage payments, which did contribute to foreclosure.

The wave of foreclosures in the early twenty-first century, on the other hand, required neither deflation nor falling income to precipitate it. Falling (indeed, no longer rising) nominal house prices combined with high loan-to-value and "innovative" financing instruments such as negative amortization loans with teaser initial rates were enough to get many home owners into very serious trouble. Because average loan-to-value ratios were so much lower as were nominal price declines, the phenomenon of underwater homes (loan balances greater than house values), still endemic today (2013), was less common during the Depression (but see also Guglielmo 2011, 13, who asserts the contrary, although without evidence). In the nation as a whole more than one in four home owners with a mortgage remained underwater in the first quarter of 2013.[20]

It was much more the case, particularly after 1929, that people got into trouble not because housing prices had fallen per se, but because income had fallen as the result of other causes, combined with the effects of deflation in raising the burden of mortgage payments fixed in nominal terms. In a number of respects, therefore, the precipitators of foreclosure differed in the two cycles.

2.1 Shiller's Series

As part of the research for his book *Irrational Exuberance* (2006), Robert Shiller assembled a series on real and nominal house prices going back to 1890. His source for nominal house prices for 1890 to 1933 is Grebler, Blank, and Winnick (1956), whose data were based on a survey of home owners in twenty-two cities who were asked to report the value of their house in 1934 and what they originally paid for it and when. Since the index created from these reports tracks prices for the same housing units at different times, it is not subject to the compositional bias that can bedevil comparisons of median house prices over time (see Shiller 2006, 234).

Shiller's data for 1934 to 1941 are based on advertised home prices in newspapers in five cities: Chicago, Los Angeles, New Orleans, New York, and Washington, DC. His students collected about thirty house prices for each city for each year, except that the Washington data are based on a median price series from Fisher (1951). Data for those years may therefore be partially affected by the upward bias characteristic of median sales price data, which can in part reflect improvements in house quality. Given the relatively low level of house construction during the 1930s, however, the bias is probably small. Shiller uses the Consumer Price Index to deflate nominal house values both pre- and post-1934 to get a series on real house prices, which appear in his book as part of figure 2.1.

For most readers of the second edition of *Irrational Exuberance* (the first dealt only with the stock market boom), the principal takeaway from the longtime series on real housing prices was the strikingly dramatic run-up in real estate prices between 2000 and 2006. In percentage terms the increase in the real price of a house (approximately 60 percent between 2000:1 and 2006:1) was larger during this period than during any comparable period going back to 1890. The increase in house prices following the Second World War (measuring from 1944 to 1953) came close in percentage terms, but it took place over a larger number of years and, in contrast with the run-up

20. http://www.zillow.com/visuals/negative-equity/#12/43.8065/-71.5023, accessed May 30, 2013.

over the 2000 to 2006 period, the new higher level of real house prices was sustained for half a century.

As Shiller updated his numbers, they revealed a staggering fall in the value of an asset that conventional wisdom held should and could never decline nationally. According to his quarterly data, nominal prices through 2012:1 declined 34 percent from their peak in 2006:2. The economy also experienced mild inflation over this period. Data on real housing values indicate that they declined 42 percent over the period 2006:1 through 2012:1; the index drops from 198.1 to 113.9. Widespread reports of price appreciation in 2013, particularly in certain markets, such as the San Francisco Bay Area, did reflect a real phenomenon, but the positive news was much amplified by the real estate industry. Shiller's real price index for houses had risen to 121.7 by the fourth quarter of 2012, a 7 percent increase from the trough, but a long way from 198.1.

In a 2005 interview with *New York Times* correspondent David Leonhardt, Shiller predicted house prices could fall 40 percent in inflation-adjusted terms (Leonhardt 2005). Because of the mechanics of simple percent calculations, the 60 percent increase followed by 42 percent decrease in real housing prices left the index in 2011:4 below where it had been in 1998:4, thirteen years earlier. By 2012:4 it had recovered to where it was in 1999. The price recovery to date (May 2013) has been, on a national level, quite modest. With one out of four home owners with a mortgage still underwater (see footnote 20) the magnitude and severity of this housing cycle should not be downplayed.

Investors are taught that they must be prepared to take substantial losses if they are to enjoy the upside potential of assets such as stocks. But it is not what individuals expected from housing, certainly in the postwar period. The expectation that houses would hold and possibly increase their value helped justify and reinforce institutional changes that allowed lower down payments (higher leverage) in house purchases starting in the 1930s. New norms and mechanisms of housing finance originating in the 1930s established an institutional regime that helped real house prices remain basically stable for fifty years, from the early 1950s through 2001. Boomlets marked the last part of the 1970s and, associated with the Savings and Loan Crisis, 1988 through 1990. But in both cases the price rises, modest compared to what were experienced in the early twenty-first century, quickly subsided.

Looking at Shiller's entire series since 1890, it is clear that the degree of real house price decline between 2006 and 2012 in the United States does have historical precedent. But if we study the series closely we discover something else that is quite remarkable: *no such decline took place during the interwar years*. It is true, according to Shiller's index data, that a house purchaser buying at the peak in 1907 and selling in the trough of 1921 would have experienced a 40 percent decline in real value, similar to that experienced since 2006. And a house purchaser buying at the peak in 1894 and selling at the trough in 1921 would have lost 47 percent of the value of the house in real terms.[21] These house price losses, however, would have been experienced over twenty-seven- and fifteen-year holding periods, not a five-year period. Moreover, these calculated losses are partly an artifact of the sharp post–World War I inflation, which home owners probably—and correctly—did not expect to last.

In contrast with evidence of large declines in the real price of housing in 2006 to 2012, what is striking for a student of the interwar period is the relative tameness of price movements during the 1920s and 1930s. There was indeed a real estate boom during the 1920s, one whose details have been seared into the consciousness of economic historians by the lurid descriptions of it contained in J. K. Galbraith's *The Great Crash* (1955). In terms of overall construction activity, there were, as noted, actually three consecutive booms, a boom in single-family residences that peaked in 1926, an apartment building boom that peaked a year later, and a central business district building boom that extended into the early 1930s (because of semicompleted projects such as the Empire State Building). And, looking at residential prices, there was appreciation and depreciation prior to and following the construction peak. But the magnitudes of these price swings, compared with 2001 to 2012, are mild.

Let's look first at nominal prices (figure 2.1).[22] We can see house prices increasing from 1919 through a peak in 1925, then declining to about the 1919 level in 1930 and then continuing to fall along with the general deflation in the economy before beginning to increase again in 1934.

The relative tameness of house price movements in the interwar period is even more apparent when we look at real price movements (figure 2.2). Comparing figure 2.2 with figure 2.1, one can see that the main effect of moving to a real index is to moderate the decline evident in the early 1930s. As for the 1920s, after 1922, the nominal and real indexes move very closely with each other, because the CPI was basically stable between 1922 and 1929.

Examining the real house price series one cannot help but be struck by the almost complete absence of a 2001 to 2012–style price bubble and collapse. There is actually a slight *upward* trend in real housing prices, comparing the 1930s with the 1920s, which might or might not be due to the change in the data source post-1934. Of course, even if the decline in real house prices between 1925 and 1932 was only 12.6 percent (as compared with a real decline of 42 percent between 2006 and the end of 2012), the nominal decline

21. Both 1893 and 1907 are peaks associated with financial panics that ended NBER business cycle expansions. Indeed, the ending of the 1907 crisis benefited from the intervention of J. P. Morgan (Friedman and Schwartz 1963, 160), and set in motion forces that would lead to the creation of the Federal Reserve System in 1913.

22. This series is described in Fishback and Kollmann's figure 6.1 (chap. 6) as "Shiller GBW hybrid." They normalize on 1930 whereas, following Shiller, I normalize on the year 2000. The other difference is that my *y* axis begins at the origin, which produces a less exaggerated impression of the degree of house price fluctuations during the interwar years.

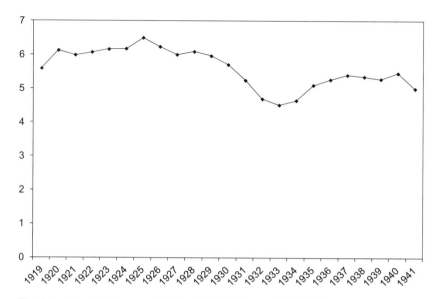

Fig. 2.1   Nominal house price index, United States, 1919–1941
Source: Shiller (2012), housing data, available at http://www.econ.yale.edu/~shiller/data.htm.
Note: 2,000 = 100.0.

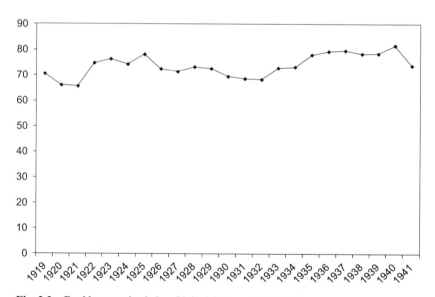

Fig. 2.2   Real house price index, United States, 1919–1941
Source: Shiller (2012), housing data, available at http://www.econ.yale.edu/~shiller/data.htm.

in the context of mortgages with fixed nominal interest payments had the potential to contribute to debt deflation and persisting problems with debt overhang and contagion in the 1930s. As noted in the earlier discussion of Mishkin, however, the lower fraction of houses mortgaged and lower loan-to-value ratios meant that the adverse effect on household balance sheets of deflation in the face of fixed nominal mortgage payments was modest.

As already mentioned, I argue that the difficulties construction had in recovering in the 1930s had more to do with the legacy of premature sub-division (see Field 1992) than with debt overhang from real estate. This view is strengthened by looking at the interwar housing cycle in the light of 2001 to 2012. Assuming house prices bottomed out in 2012:4, the 2006 to 2012 peak-to-trough decline in real housing prices of 42 percent was more than triple the 1925 to 1932 decline in percentage points. And, as I will show, housing was much more highly leveraged in the more recent episode, which enabled it to pose more of a systemic threat.

2.2   Critiques of Shiller's Series

A number of scholars, including contributors to this volume, have raised doubts about the reliability of Shiller's series for the 1920s and the years 1934 to 1940. Eugene White (2009, see also chapter 4, this volume) has argued that the data disguise the true magnitude of the house price boom and bust in the interwar period. White finds the series too volatile in the early years, which he attributes to the declining sample sizes as one goes back further in time, but he also suggests that the level of the series in the 1920s, and thus its interwar volatility, is biased downward because the series does not include the prices of houses bought at the peak and subsequently abandoned or foreclosed upon. Such houses, he argues, would not have shown up in Grebler, Blank, and Winnick's 1934 survey. He notes, however, that the size of the possible bias is "difficult to assess in the absence of sufficient additional national or regional data" (White 2009, 9; 2014, x). Price Fishback and Trevor Kollmann (chapter 6, this volume) note that GBW also produced a house price series adjusted for depreciation, and, reinforcing White's view, suggest that Shiller's use of the unadjusted series biases downward the price increases during the 1920s.

In their 2011 paper in the *Review of Financial Studies*, Fishback et al. reported data derived from the US census on the ratio of the value of owner-occupied housing in 1930 to the value of mortgaged owner-occupied housing in 1920 for 272 large cities in the United States (Fishback et al. 2011, 1784).[23] They found that the average ratio was 1.45, meaning that nominal

---

23. Fishback and Kollmann expand on this work, proceeding to develop an index of house prices of owner-occupied mortgaged homes. What we aspire to, however, is an index of quality-adjusted house prices, irrespective of whether they are owner occupied, and irrespective of whether they are mortgaged. Their calculated average owner occupied mortgaged (AVOOM) index is not necessarily a representative index of the price of the entire universe of prices, only those that are owner occupied and mortgaged.

prices in 1930 were 45 percent higher than they had been in 1920. In contrast, the Grebler, Blank, and Winnick (GBW) data show nominal house prices *lower* in 1930 by about 7 percent than in 1920. The Fishback and Koll-mann chapter in this volume (chapter 6) supersedes the comparisons made in the 2011 paper, although the data presented still suggest that the GBW data understate nominal price rises between 1920 and 1930, and overstate increases between 1934 and 1940.

Fishback et al. (2011) compared census data for all owner-occupied houses in 1930 with mortgaged occupied houses in 1920. It is difficult to know if this difference in the sample space between the 1920 and the 1930 census data they rely upon introduces a bias, and if so in which direction. Fishback and Kollmann's contribution to this volume achieves consistency in comparing 1920 and 1930 by concentrating on data on mortgaged owner-occupied units, at the expense of focusing on a somewhat narrower subset of the residential housing stock (the GBW data are for single-family, owner-occupied units, irrespective of mortgage status).

An issue of particular concern in making comparisons of median house prices is one upon which Shiller placed a great deal of emphasis. It has to do with changes in the composition of the housing stock and the necessity of comparing the prices of similar housing units through time. Houses are a heterogeneous asset category. If over time the average unit becomes larger or in other respects better (or the reverse), then comparisons of changes in median house prices may not accurately reflect what is happening with respect to quality-adjusted prices. Careful attempts to correct for changes in the composition and characteristics of housing inform the construction of the widely referenced indexes which in part bear his name. As the methodology section for the currently produced S&P/Case-Shiller indexes states,

> The indices measure changes in housing market prices given a constant level of quality. Changes in the types and sizes of houses or changes in the physical characteristics of houses are specifically excluded from the calculations to avoid incorrectly affecting the index value.

That is one reason Shiller found the data underlying the GBW series appealing: the survey asked people what their house was currently worth and what they paid for it and when. The index was constructed based on comparisons of value over time for the same housing units. The modern Case-Shiller indexes are based on repeat sales of similar houses. In other words, they rely on comparisons over time of prices of individual houses that have sold at least twice. The index is constructed by sampling recent real estate transactions and then searching prior transaction records to create matched sales pairs for individual houses. As the document describing the methodology states, "The main variable used for index calculation is the price change between two arms-length sales of the same single-family home" (Standard and Poor's 2009, 6). All repeat sales pairs are candidates for inclusion, but non-arms-length transactions, such as those between family members, are excluded, as are transactions in which the property type is changed; for example, when a property is converted to a condominium. Statistical techniques are used to reduce the weighting of outlier transactions that are not likely to truly be matched pairs because, for example, maintenance has been neglected or the house has been extensively remodeled, and to reduce the weight of transactions that are far separated in time.

The statistical underpinnings of the Shiller-GBW series for the years 1934 and earlier are, to be sure, sparser and noisier than those that underlie the modern Case-Shiller series. The raw materials were estimated values and remembered sales prices observed during 1934 rather than actual transactions data covering a number of years. GBW acknowledge the likelihood of purchase year "heaping" on years ending in 0 or 5. For each city, the price relatives to 1934 were calculated as the ratio of aggregated recalled purchase price to estimates of aggregated estimated 1934 values (the indexes might more closely have approximated the repeat sales methodology had they, for each year, averaged the price relatives for each individual housing unit). Despite its limitations, however, the GBW index is closer conceptually to the repeat sales (matched pairs) methodology than are some of the comparisons reported by Fishback et al. (2011) or Fishback and Kollmann (chapter 6, this volume).

GBW also produced a second "adjusted" series, which assumed that housing service flow and "real" value depreciated at a compound rate of 1 and 3/8 percent per year. Fishback and Kollmann note that GBW believed this series superior, and wonder why Shiller did not use it. GBW argued that houses deteriorated in value over time because of wear and tear and obsolescence. They acknowledged that structural additions and alterations worked in the opposite direction but cited evidence supporting their view that the former effect dominated (1956, appendixes C and E). There remains, however, a theoretical and empirical question as to whether the service flow from a well-maintained house truly declines through time. A well-maintained house, like a chair, may have a depreciation profile more akin to the proverbial one-horse shay.[24] Shiller may have been receptive to this view, and thus preferred the unadjusted series.

24. The reference is to a poem by Oliver Wendell Holmes Sr. The shay was so well constructed that it lasted 100 years before falling apart. The Case-Shiller methodology emphasizes the importance of controlling for changes over time in the size and physical characteristics of the average housing unit. The age of a unit might be considered a physical characteristic, but, again, the service flow from a well-maintained house, like a shay, may not necessarily decrease with age. The size and physical characteristics (electrification, for example) of the over seven million units constructed in the 1920s, in relation to what was in place in 1920, and the units that were withdrawn from service during that decade, are in my view issues of greater empirical significance than whether one uses the "adjusted" series constructed by GBW that factors in depreciation on the housing stock. None of the alternate series investigated by Fishback and Kollmann (chapter 6, this volume) changes the conclusion that house price movements, both nominal and real, were more moderate during the interwar period than has been true in 2001 to 2012.

Returning to the comparisons Fishback et al. make between the 1930 and 1920 census data, there are several reasons these might depart substantially from what would be yielded by matched pair reports of the same houses sold in 1920 and 1930. The most important is that the housing stock was different in 1930. Over the years 1920–1929 inclusive, over 7 million new private, permanent, nonfarm housing units were built (Grebler, Blank, and Winnick 1956, table B-1, 332). The 1930 census reported 23.2 million occupied nonfarm housing units. Since few of the units built in the 1920s would have been abandoned, unoccupied, or torn down in 1930, we can conclude that at least 30 percent of the units in 1930 simply were not there in 1920. Moreover, although few of the newly built units would have vanished, been torn down, or been unoccupied in 1930, some of the units whose prices had been reported in the 1920 census of mortgaged units were, by 1930, abandoned, torn down, or unoccupied, and they were likely to have been smaller units with less desirable physical characteristics.[25] The 1920 census reported about 17.6 million occupied housing units, and the 1930 census 23.2 million, an increase of 5.6 million. Since there were roughly 7 million units constructed, we can infer that about 1.4 million units fall into the category of present in 1920 but absent in 1930.

Because the 1930 enumeration included 7 million generally higher quality houses not present in 1920, and because it did not include approximately 1.4 million generally lower quality units that had been in the enumeration in 1920, the 1920 to 1930 comparisons reported by Fishback et al. and Fishback and Kollmann may give a misleading picture of quality-adjusted house price change between 1920 and 1930.

Fishback and Kollmann emphasize the outlier nature of the unadjusted GBW series, although other data are consistent with the picture it paints. Fisher (1951, 55, table 7), for example, looked at a sample of 3 percent of Home Owners' Loan Corporation (HOLC) mortgage loans in the states of New York, New Jersey, and Connecticut. The underlying data included appraisal values for those refinancing loans in 1933 and 1934 and purchase prices in 1925 and 1927. These are for the same houses, and thus the data approximate the repeat sales data that underlie the current Case-Shiller indexes, although the HOLC appraisals may have overstated the market value of the homes in 1933 and 1934 because of a rule limiting the loan-to-value ratio of the mortgage they could offer to 80 percent. Median prices in Fisher's sample decline 31 percent between 1925 and 1933 to 1934. Grebler, Blank, and Winnick report approximately the same percentage decline in their twenty-two city sample over these years. In the Fisher sample, homes purchased in 1926 and 1927 had a decline of 26.9 percent nominal to 1933 to

---

25. For example they may have been less likely to have had hot and cold running water, had an interior bathroom, or been wired for electricity.

1934. Using the Grebler, Blank, and Winnick series for a similar calculation yields a 25.2 percent decline.

Another regional series is the National Housing Agency's compilation of monthly price data for Washington, DC, from 1918 through 1948, which was based on asking prices for houses listed for sale in newspapers. The annual average for 1930 is 13.5 percent higher than for 1920 (see Carter et al. 2006, series Dc 828), compared with Fishback et al.'s 45 percent increase and Grebler, Blank, and Winnick's 7 percent decline. The Fisher numbers can be reconciled with the Grebler, Blank, and Winnick series, given the fact that the housing stock in 1930 was possibly of better quality and that these are not and do not approximate matched sales.

Fishback et al. (2011) also compare housing prices reported in the 1940 census with those reported in the 1930 census, and find them in nominal terms to be 48.6 percent lower; Shiller has them about 5 percent lower.[26] The issue of changes in the composition of the stock is less important in the 1930s than the 1920s, since many fewer units were constructed than had been true in the 1920s. The number of occupied nonfarm housing units increased just 19 percent during the 1930s (4.4 million), as opposed to the 30 percent jump during the 1920s. The number of housing starts in the years 1930 through 1939 inclusive was even less, totaling only 2.586 million (Grebler, Blank, and Winnick 1956, table B-1). This means, since the number of occupied units rose 4.4 million, that approximately 1.8 million units abandoned or unoccupied at the time of the 1930 census were now again in use. We can infer that these were lower quality units (after all, they had been abandoned during the boom time of the 1920s) and their reintroduction into the occupied housing stock may be one of the reasons the Fishback et al. data show a sharper drop in reported values between 1934 and 1940.

All of this discussion speaks to the significance of the matched sale methodology pioneered and championed by Case and Shiller in developing meaningful price indexes for a heterogeneous housing stock whose composition changes over time. Fishback et al. and Fishback and Kollmann have done yeoman work in digging up new data. But the alternatives they explore may not necessarily do a better job than the GBW series preferred by Shiller of reflecting changes in quality-adjusted house prices for the 1920 to 1934 period.[27]

---

26. Fishback and Kollmann (chapter 6, this volume) suggest somewhat smaller price declines after 1934, but still substantially larger than the Shiller numbers. As Shiller acknowledges, the five-city survey his students conducted for years after 1934 makes no claim to approximate a repeat sales methodology.

27. Fishback and Kollmann also augment the GBW series by adding data for thirty-one cities to the twenty-two originally used by GBW. But the expanded coverage does not change the picture much. Compare "GBW adjusted" in their figure 6.1 with "New GBW-Style Adjusted" in their figure 6.4. In both cases these series include the adjustment for depreciation, which Shiller eschewed.

Both nominal and real prices matter in thinking about the impact of housing price fluctuations on the real economy. In an institutional environment characterized by fixed nominal debt obligations, nominal prices matter, because their decline can decrease the value of an owner's equity. When both house prices and goods and service prices are declining (as was true between 1929 and 1933), the real burden of debt repayment can go up if mortgage payments are fixed in nominal terms. But not all home owners had a mortgage. Indeed, the majority did not. For those who did, loan-to-value ratios were smaller than they are today. If we are interested in possible wealth effects of consumption caused by declines in housing equity, real prices matter. If you own your house free and clear, or have a small mortgage on it, and it drops in value 30 percent, but so does the CPI, it should not have a great effect on your behavior.

All of the decline in real house prices in the interwar period had already taken place by 1929, with no apparent ill effects on the economy. Real housing prices were actually higher in 1933 than they had been in 1929. In order for the magnitude of the decline in real house prices in the interwar period to approach what has taken place since 2006, either the 1929 figure suggested by Shiller and Grebler, Blank, and Winnick would have to be 40 percent too low or the 1933 figure 40 percent too high, or there would have to be some combination of too low earlier and too high later yielding biases in the nominal data sufficient to disguise a 40 percent drop in the real price. We should accept that the real price decline in the most recent cycle has been substantially greater in magnitude—the collapse has been more severe—than what took place during the interwar years.

2.3   Construction

There are of course at least two dimensions to a housing boom—price and quantity—and so one might expect from the more modest price movements between 1919 and 1941 that the boom and collapse of construction was also more moderate in the interwar period than it was in the early twenty-first century. And one would be quite mistaken (see figures 2.3 and 2.4). From a construction standpoint the interwar boom was in fact the greatest in terms of the fluctuations of construction activity, both in absolute terms and as a proportion of GDP, that the US economy has ever experienced. In 1924, 1925, 1926, and 1927, residential housing construction comprised more than 5 percent of GDP (over 6 percent in 1925), a figure not exceeded until the most recent boom.[28] In the 2001 to 2005 boom, the share of residential

28. See Carter et al. (2006) series Dc256 for construction and Ca213 (Balke-Gordon) for the gross national product (GNP), which yields a residential construction share of 5.8 percent for 1924, 6.0 percent for 1925, 5.7 percent for 1926, and 5.3 percent for 1927. Kendrick's GNP estimates (series Ca188) are very similar. Both Balke-Gordon and Kendrick are intended conceptually to be comparable to the Bureau of Economic Analysis estimates published from

construction rose from 4.6 percent in 2000 to 6.2 percent in 2005 (the year that housing prices peaked nationally) before falling to 3.4 percent in 2008 and 2.5 percent in 2009. By 2011:1 it had declined further to 2.2 percent, in 2013:1 it had recovered only to 2.7 percent (US Department of Commerce 2013, NIPA table 1.1.5, accessed May 31, 2013).

In comparison, by 1929 the housing construction share of GDP had fallen to 3.9 percent and by 1933 to 1 percent of a greatly reduced GDP (US Department of Commerce 2013, NIPA table 1.15). So in terms of GDP shares, housing construction went from 6 percent to 1 percent of GDP between 1925 and 1933, and from 6.2 percent to 2.2 percent from 2005 to 2011. If we looked at residential construction as a fraction of potential rather than actual GDP, the contrasts between these two episodes would be even greater.

The drop is especially dramatic in the interwar period, as figure 2.3 indicates, if we look at the absolute decline in inflation-adjusted residential construction. The years 1926 to 1933 witnessed an 89 percent decline in real construction activity. In comparison, assuming that the housing construction cycle bottomed out in 2011, we see a peak-to-trough decline of 57 percent in real construction activity between 2006 and 2011(see figure 2.4).[29] From the standpoint of construction activity, the 1920s boom and bust was proportionately larger. Yet the price movements associated with that housing cycle were more modest.

The absence of big real house price movements in the interwar period means that the mechanisms whereby housing contributed to recession/depression were different in the two cycles. In the 1930s, the collapse of construction spending and its weak recovery contributed to a slow revival in private sector aggregate demand primarily through standard multiplier mechanisms. Since the collapse of the building boom was associated with modest movements in the real price of housing, and the impact of the debt deflation mechanism was softened by the smaller fraction of houses mortgaged and lower loan-to-value ratios, the impact of the housing bust on household balance sheets was also more modest. In comparison with the wealth and liquidity effects on consumption of collapsing stock prices, the influence of the end of the housing boom on consumption expenditures through this mechanism was weaker, at least initially.

Between 2006 and 2011, in contrast, the collapse of the housing boom was associated with an approximately $7 trillion hit to household balance sheets (in comparison, the flow of US GDP in 2011 was about $15 trillion per year). This decline in home equity was the result of a pincer movement: nominal mortgage debt continued to increase through 2007 and then

---

1929 onward. Using Kuznets's variant 1 for the denominator (series Ca184) puts residential construction's share at 6.2 percent for 1924, 6.4 percent for 1925, 6.1 percent for 1926, and 5.7 percent for 1927.

29.US Department of Commerce 2013, NIPA table 1.1.3, accessed May 30, 2013.

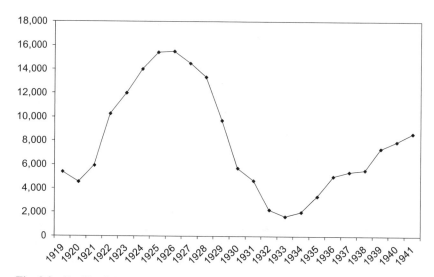

Fig. 2.3   Residential construction, United States, 1919–1941
Source: Carter et al. (2006, series Dc262).
Note: Millions of 1957–1959 dollars.

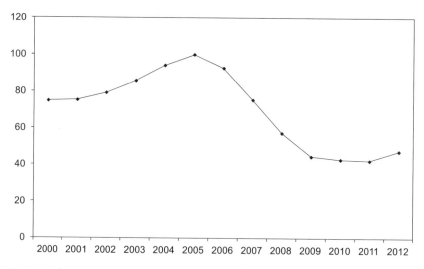

Fig. 2.4   Index of real residential construction, United States, 2000–2012
Source: http://www.bea.gov, NIPA table 1.1.3, accessed May 30, 2013.

declined only modestly, while nominal house prices fell sharply (see figure 2.6). The consequence was a big reduction in household real estate wealth. Given the uneven distribution of mortgage debt this pushed millions of home owners underwater, in the sense that they owed more than their homes were worth. The 2006 to 2008 American Community Survey showed that of approximately 75.4 million owner-occupied US housing units, 51.4 million had a mortgage (US Bureau of the Census 2011, series B25087). Of these, more than one in four remained underwater in the first quarter of 2013. Even though there were tens, indeed hundreds of thousands of foreclosures during the Depression, the phenomenon during the most recent episode has been more widespread and more severe in its consequences, particularly if we try and restrict our attention to residential housing, as opposed to the farm foreclosure problem. During the Depression the problem was not typically that people owed more on the house than it was worth.[30] The problem was simply that they could not make the mortgage payments, in part because their nominal income had fallen, and in part because the drop in goods and service prices had increased the real burden of their mortgage payments.

Case, Quigley, and Shiller (2005) estimate that a 10 percent decline in household wealth has somewhere between a .4 and a 1.1 percent effect on consumption (although see Calomiris, Longhofer, and Miles 2009 for a more skeptical view of the size of this coefficient). Whatever the number we agree on, we are dealing here with a drop in owner's equity of more than 50 percent, from $13.1 trillion in 2005 to $6.3 trillion in 2010. Nothing comparable happened with respect to real estate wealth in the interwar period. In contrast, the contractionary effect of lower *construction* expenditures was relatively more significant during the interwar housing boom.

Why were the price movements and wealth effects so much more muted during the interwar period than in 2001 to 2012? The most compelling answer is simply that residential housing was less leveraged in the 1920s than it became in the early twenty-first century. Mortgage "innovations" such as option adjustable rate mortgages (ARMs), no documentation loans, and no money down loans magnified the upward price movements during the boom, as they did the downward movements in the bust. These institutional innovations helped upend an institutional equilibrium that, by and large, had kept real house prices relatively stable for half a century.

Another way to look at this question is to ask why housing leverage was so low in the 1920s when, as evidenced by the stock market, the financial system was clearly capable of financing highly leveraged asset acquisition. Why was it that mortgage lenders in the 1920s were so stingy with down payment and maturity terms? Again, common terms were 50 percent down, five-year mortgages with a balloon payment at the end. It is true that innovations pioneered by small building and loan societies enabled some borrowers to take a second mortgage and thus borrow a larger share of the house value (Snowden 2010). But these innovations were opposed by larger building and loan societies, and overall, especially in comparison with the early twenty-

---

30. Since loan-to-value ratios rarely exceeded 50 percent in the 1920s, and the average nominal price decline between 1929 and 1933 appears to have been about 30 percent, simple arithmetic tells us that the phenomenon of underwater houses, or negative equity, with the outstanding loan value exceeding the house value, must have been infrequent in comparison to what has been the case in the post-2005 period.

first century, the overall picture is one of conservatism (White [2009], 26 reaches a similar conclusion).

One might argue, and indeed it was argued in the 1930s that the typical loan contract from the 1920s was in fact risky to lenders (Morton 1956). It was the heavy and perhaps unanticipated costs of foreclosure that made it so (see Ghent 2010, 11). Given the experience with the foreclosure process that had by then manifested itself, one can perhaps understand the argument from an ex post standpoint. But if foreclosure had been costless, requiring a 50 percent down payment surely would have given considerable protection to the lender, who always, of course, had the option of rolling the balloon loan over. It is hard to see how, absent the large transactions costs associated with foreclosure, an 80 percent, thirty-year loan, even one fully amortized, was, on the face of it, *less* risky for the lender than a 50 percent, five- year, nonamortized loan.

There was in fact a large percentage increase in mortgage lending in the first half of the 1920s. But that increase was from a modest base, and considering loan-to-value ratios and other metrics, it is fair to say that lending on residential real estate, in comparison to what transpired in the early twenty-first century, remained conservative.[31]

This conservatism was in part because legislation governing lending by national banks mandated higher down payments. And even though state-chartered commercial banks and building and loans were not so constrained, the prior history of land and real estate speculation, in which lending standards had been at times lax, leading to sometimes extreme cycles of boom and bust in house prices prior to the 1920s, which lay behind the National Banking Act restrictions, acted as something of a deterrent on lending by institutions that were not constrained.

White (2009) has argued that conservatism in the 1920s was reinforced by the absence of a "too big to fail" expectation,[32] although it is not clear that the major players in the residential mortgage market (building and loans, mutual savings banks, insurance companies) could have had this expectation even had the government or Fed announced a willingness to rescue systemically important institutions. For a financial institution to be systemically important it must have liabilities serving as assets for other institutions, so that if it fails its creditor financial institutions are threatened as well, or like a commercial bank, have demand deposits as liabilities, so that collapse reduces the means of payment (money supply).

31. Whether the same can be said for loans on commercial and central business district structures remains an open question. See Postel-Vinay (2011) for evidence on the role bad real estate loans played in failures of Chicago-area state banks.

32. White also emphasizes the typical absence of deposit insurance (state schemes generally covered smaller banks in more rural or agricultural areas) as well as the imposition in some states of double liability on shareholders of failed banks, both of which, it can be argued, increased the incentives of depositors or shareholders to monitor the liability side of financial institutions of which they were creditors.

To be sure, by the last years of the 1920s, there was plenty of excess in real estate lending. Declines in lending standards (see Saulnier 1956), self-dealing, fraud, all of this was evident in absolute terms. *But not in comparison with what took place between 2001 and 2008.* Decades of experience of real estate cycles in the nineteenth and early twentieth centuries had persuaded lenders—and legislators—that real estate was a very risky asset, by no means certain or even expected to appreciate, and one for which lenders should take moderate and short-lived stakes, and ensure that borrowers had plenty of skin in the game.

An implication of this is that although the failure of housing construction to revive during the 1930s helps explain the duration of the Depression, balance sheet aspects of housing sector finance are today more important in obstructing recovery than was true in the Great Depression. As has been noted, there are several distinct mechanisms whereby housing can affect a downturn. A decline in construction can, amplified by multiplier effects, lead directly to a decline in equilibrium output, associated with drops in both consumption and gross private domestic investment. In the 1920s the decline in residential construction was, from an aggregate demand perspective, compensated for by the apartment building boom followed by central business district (CBD) construction, which extended into the 1930s. Strong exports helped as well. But when construction went south big time in the 1930s, this mechanism became very important in accounting for the prolonged downturn and the failure to recover.

A second depression-inducing, housing-related mechanism involves borrowers on real estate who cannot service their mortgages, become delinquent, and eventually face foreclosure. As they struggle to meet their mortgage obligations, nonhousing consumption is adversely impacted. Foreclosures were an important feature of the early 1930s (see Wheelock 2008), but they were not primarily produced by the cessation of increases and then actual declines in house prices, which was the main driver after 2006. Rather, during the early years of the 1930s, it was declines in income (among those unemployed, for example), that predisposed to foreclosure. Of course as deflation set in during the early 1930s, the real value of debt service obligations fixed in nominal terms did increase, aggravating the pressure on borrowers in difficult positions. Because of lower leverage, however, shorter average durations of mortgages, and a smaller fraction of the housing stock encumbered by loans, bad mortgage debt from housing did not play as significant a role in transmitting a financial shock to lending institutions as was the case in 2007 to 2009.

2.4   Foreclosures

There was indeed a serious foreclosure problem during the Great Depression, but it was more specifically a farm foreclosure problem. Two decades of farm prosperity came to an end at the conclusion of World War I, and farm incomes and land values declined steadily during the 1920s, a major factor in bank failures during that decade (Alston, Grove, and Wheelock 1994; Field 1992, 2001). The precipitous decline in agricultural commodity prices between 1929 and 1933 made a fragile situation worse, and attempts to foreclose led to actual or threatened violence and multiple state-level foreclosure moratoria.

Foreclosures on residential housing during the 1930s, although a very real and painful phenomenon, were, however, proportionately less common than has been true in the years since 2006. To show this, we begin with interwar data for nonfarm housing units, over three-fourths of the occupied housing units in 1930, for which the statistical information is less ambiguous. The number of foreclosures for nonfarm occupied housing units, 68,100 in 1926, rose to 134,900 by 1929, and peaked in 1933 at 252,400, before gradually subsiding to 58,559 by 1941 (Carter et al. 2006, series Dc1255). The 1930 census reported 23,235,982 occupied nonfarm housing units (Carter et al. 2006, series Dc697-698). Using the 1930 occupied housing number as a denominator, and the peak 1933 foreclosure number as numerator, we can conclude that 1.08 percent of the nonfarm occupied housing stock was foreclosed upon in the worst year of the Depression. This number is probably biased slightly upward because we have not attempted to correct for the possible growth in occupied housing units between 1930 and 1933.

In contrast, RealtyTrac (2011) reported that in 2010, 2,871,891 housing units in the United States experienced a foreclosure filing.[33] This represented 2.23 percent of all US housing units; the total of about 130 million in 2010 includes seasonal units as well as occupied all year units and those that were vacant. Note that the 1933 calculation has occupied units in the denominator. If that calculation were comparable to that made for 2010, the denominator would include vacant and seasonal units as well, and the foreclosure rate would be lower.

The fact that more than twice the proportion of all housing units were foreclosed upon in 2010 as compared with the proportion of nonfarm units foreclosed upon in 1933 is indicative of the higher fraction of the housing stock encumbered by a mortgage, the substantially higher degree of leverage, and the much greater decline in nominal and real housing prices that have marked the more recent cycle.

The data for the 1930s in the aforementioned calculations are, of course, for the nonfarm housing sector. Adding in data on farm-occupied housing units will increase our estimate of the rate for all occupied units. The 1930 census shows that there were about a third as many occupied farm housing units (6,668,881) as there were nonfarm units (there were 29,904,663 total units, so farm housing units were about a quarter of the total). The rate

---

33. The data on filings include notices of default, scheduled auctions, and real estate owned (REO) property.

of foreclosure on farm housing would have had to have been substantially higher than on nonfarm housing to yield a foreclosure rate on the entire occupied housing stock approaching that experienced in 2010. I calculate that 424,473 farm housing foreclosures—6.2 percent—or one of every sixteen farm housing units would have had to have been foreclosed upon in 1933 in order to make the overall foreclosure rate on residential housing equal to what it was in 2010.

The rate of foreclosure on farm housing is inextricably entangled with the rate of foreclosures on farms, and these are not exactly the same. They are, nevertheless, closely related, and we do have some data on the latter. Alston (1983, 886) reports that in 1933, the worst year of the Depression, over 200,000 farms were foreclosed—3.88 percent of all farm units. This is significantly below the 6.2 percent rate that would have been needed to equate the overall 1933 foreclosure rate to that experienced in 2010. Since a number of states passed laws instituting moratoria on farm foreclosures, it is possible that in their absence, we would have had foreclosure rates at that level.

Citing Federal Reserve Board data, Alston, Grove, and Wheelock (1994, 415) indicate that 42 percent of owner-occupied farms had a mortgage in 1930. Parker (2005, 57), reviewing early research by Galbraith, reports that half of all farm mortgages were in default by 1933. This suggests that approximately a fifth of owner-occupied farms were potentially vulnerable to foreclosure during the worst year of the Depression. In comparing foreclosure rates on residential housing in the early twenty-first century with those in the 1930s, a difficulty thus arises: how should we treat a foreclosure or potential foreclosure on a farm property that also includes a residential housing unit? Since roughly a quarter of all residential housing units were on farms the issue can be neither dismissed nor easily resolved.

Some conclusions can, however, be stated without qualification. If we restrict our attention to nonfarm residential housing units, or to *actual* foreclosures on all residential units (considering a foreclosure on a farm as equivalent to a foreclosure on a farm housing unit) the foreclosure rates in 2010 were unambiguously higher than those during the worst year of the Depression. These higher foreclosure rates were, moreover, generated in an environment in which the unemployment rate did not break 10 percent (as opposed to 25 percent in 1933), which gives us additional appreciation for how fragile the housing finance situation had become by 2006.

In the 1930s, and under the aegis of the Federal Housing Authority, institutional changes ushered in an era of higher leverage in housing than had prevailed in the 1920s. These changes were associated with a one-time permanent upward movement in real housing prices in the years immediately after the war. In part because of organizational and procedural controls on the quality of lending, however, this rise was sustained, leading to a half century of relative stability in real housing prices, from the early 1950s through 2001. Prior to the twenty-first century, this was disrupted at the

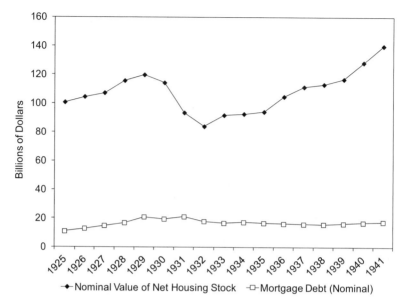

Fig. 2.5   Nominal housing value and mortgage debt, United States, 1925–1941

Sources: Nominal value of net housing stock, US Department of Commerce, Bureau of Economic Analysis (2011, fixed asset table 1.1, http://www.bea.gov, accessed June 6, 2011); nominal value of mortgage debt on residential structures, Carter et al. (2006, sum of series Dc916-922).

national level only by boomlets in the late 1970s and again during the savings and loan (S&L)–fueled 1988 to 1990 period, but each of these subsided relatively quickly.

Beginning in the 1980s under President Reagan, gathering steam under President Clinton in the 1990s, and continuing under President George W. Bush at the turn of the twenty-first century, financial deregulation and changes in the financial services industry destroyed the previous institutional equilibrium. Out of this witches' brew (much more than simply the low interest rates of the early twenty-first century, on which it is often blamed), emerged the housing boom and the near catastrophic financial meltdown that followed.

Figures 2.5 and 2.6 illustrate the very different degrees of housing leverage in the interwar cycle as compared with 2001 to 2012. Figure 2.5 shows the nominal value of the net housing stock along with the nominal value of residential mortgage debt from 1926 through 1941. The debt-to-asset ratio never rose above 25 percent during these years (see figure 2.7), starting at 10.9 percent in 1925, ending at 12.5 percent in 1941, and peaking in 1932 at 22.6 percent under the influence of temporarily declining nominal house prices, and a relatively stable nominal debt burden. It is certainly true that

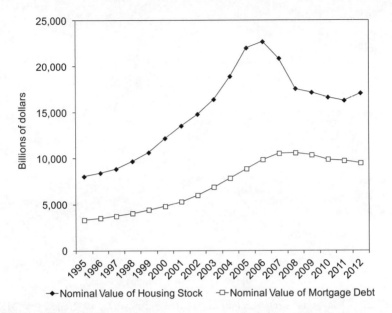

Fig. 2.6   Nominal value of housing stock and mortgage debt, United States, 1995–2012

Sources: US Department of Commerce, Bureau of Economic Analysis (2011, fixed asset table 1.1, http://www.bea.gov); Carter et al. (2006, series Dc916-922); http://www.federalreserve .gov, Flow of Funds accounts, table B-100, lines 4 and 33, accessed May 30, 2012.

in 1932 home owners were stressed. But the degree of leverage is dwarfed by what transpired in the first decade of the twenty-first century. The debt-to-asset ratio averaged roughly 40 percent during the run up to the housing price explosion, and then jumped to over 60 percent starting in 2006 in the face of rapidly declining house prices and a nominal debt burden that continued to increase through 2007 and then fell off only slightly. It remained at that level through 2011.

The comparative trends in housing debt-to-asset ratios, comparing 1925 to 1941 with 1996 to 2012, are illustrated in figure 2.7.

2.5   Conclusion

Using a comparative historical approach, this chapter has identified several important differences in the housing sector's characteristics and contributions to macroeconomic instability in the interwar period as compared with 2001 to 2012. First, in terms of fluctuations in residential construction activity, and whether measured in absolute terms or as a share of GDP, the interwar housing cycle was more severe than 2001 to 2012. But it was *less*

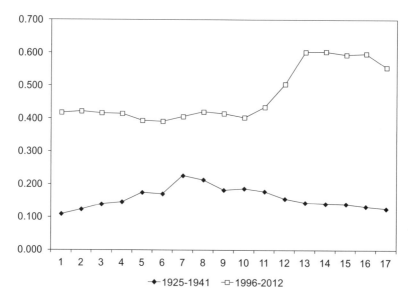

Fig. 2.7   Debt-to-asset ratios in housing, United States, 1925–1941 and 1996–2012

Sources: US Department of Commerce, Bureau of Economic Analysis (2011, fixed asset table 1.1, http://www.bea.gov); Carter et al. (2006, series Dc916-922); http://www.federalreserve. gov, Flow of Funds accounts, table B-100, lines 4 and 33.

severe in terms of fluctuations in the real price of housing and their impact on household and banking institution balance sheets. Finally, housing was much less levered in the 1920s than was true in the run up to the most recent crisis.

The chapter argues that the second and third of these differences are related. During the 1920s, a prior historical experience of housing booms and busts had disciplined lenders to treat housing as a very risky asset, and made them at least initially unwilling to lend liberally on it, with the standard for "liberalism" being what transpired between 2001 and 2008. Although these inhibitions, which had been reinforced by legislation and government regulation, weakened as the decade of the 1920s proceeded, the overall outcome was still a housing sector that was much less leveraged than in 2001 to 2012. In contrast, between 2001 and 2006 institutional restraints on lending that had for the most part obtained for half a century broke down under the banner of deregulation, innovative ways to finance housing, and shoddy and sometimes fraudulent work by mortgage appraisers, originators, securitizers, and ratings agencies.

The channels through which a housing bust affected the rest of the economy were different across these two periods. The impact of the collapse in construction spending in the 1930s was felt particularly strongly through its effect on real gross private domestic investment, and, through multiplier mechanisms, indirectly on consumption. In the housing bust of the early twenty-first century, this mechanism was weaker. On the other hand, the relative stability of housing values in the interwar period meant that the effect of the end of the boom on household consumption through a direct wealth effect was weaker, certainly in comparison to the effect of the collapse of stock prices.

In contrast, in 2001 to 2012, with an almost $7 trillion drop in house values, this effect was stronger. And because of the much higher degree of leverage in 2001 to 2012, the problems of debt overhang and underwater home owners were more severe than was true in the interwar period. Moreover, because of the interconnections between high leverage in households and highly leveraged and interconnected financial institutions, the ability of a prior real estate lending boom to pose a systemic threat to United States and world financial institutions was higher in the first decade of the twenty-first century than was true in the interwar period. The mechanisms and interconnections that allowed this to happen in the early twenty-first century are documented in the final report of the Financial Crisis Inquiry Commission (2011).

Compared to what happened in the 1920s, postwar subdivisions were more efficiently designed for an automobile age, and, because of the integration of the subdivider/developer function there was much less of a postboom problem of subdivisions with a few houses built here and there. Subdivisions in the postwar period tended to be opened in sections, with a new one not opening until the previous one had been built out. This was not true in the 1920s. As bad as things may have been after the savings and loan bubble or the most recent upswing, they were worse in this respect during the interwar period. That is, the physical legacy of premature and partially completed subdivisions in the 1920s posed a greater hindrance to the recovery of construction in the 1930s than has been true in postwar cycles. True, some overbuilt subdivisions from 2001 to 2010 left vacant and allowed to deteriorate, may ultimately have to be bulldozed; this was true as well after the S&L insolvencies. But the physical legacies of postwar housing booms, including the most recent one, pose less of an obstacle to long-term recovery than was true during the interwar period.

On the other hand, the financial legacies pose a *more* serious threat to economy-wide recovery today than was true during the Depression. That is because housing was much less leveraged in the 1920s than was true in the early twenty-first century. In the more recent episode, more houses had mortgages, loan-to-value ratios were much higher on average, and securitization has meant that there were many more avenues for contagion from household to financial institution balance sheets.

When New Deal reformers set their minds to mitigating the likelihood of a recurrence of the Great Depression, they addressed housing, but placed much more emphasis on the travails of the stock market. They insisted on separating commercial and investment banking.[34] During the 1920s housing boom, commercial banking had been involved to only a limited degree in housing finance, and although investment banking activities did include placements of some mortgage-backed securities, these tended to be for the purposes of financing commercial and other nonresidential structures (Goetzmann and Newman 2010). The insistence on separating commercial from investment banking (Glass-Steagall) was motivated by what were perceived as improper or imprudent commercial bank lending on stocks, not real estate. The Securities Act of 1933 and the Securities and Exchange Act of 1934 mandated new transparency in security issues and corporate reporting in the hopes of mitigating the magnitude and impacts of subsequent booms and busts in the market for equities.

New Deal legislation, including acts establishing the Home Owners' Loan Corporation (1933), the Federal Housing Administration (1934), and the Federal National Mortgage Association (1938) did address issues in the housing sector. While these organizations aimed at alleviating Depression era problems, their mandates do not suggest that housing and its financing per se was perceived as a locus of the origins of the economic downturn. The HOLC engaged in remedial intervention, and indeed stopped making new loans after 1935. The FHA pioneered in establishing the viability of the thirty-year, fixed-term, fully amortized mortgage, and promulgating better designs for residential subdivisions, and the Federal National Mortgage Association, chartered in 1938, established a secondary market for home mortgages. These changes helped usher in a half century of relative stability in real house prices.

But these changes in the institutional mechanisms of residential finance were not primarily oriented toward mitigating a systemic risk that lending on real estate was perceived as having generated during the 1920s. Remedial efforts to mitigate such risk concentrated much more on the stock market, focusing on the purchase, sale, and financing of equities, with the twin objectives of increasing transparency and limiting leverage. Unlike real estate, which declined in nominal terms by 30 percent but in real terms hardly at all, the 89 percent nominal (60 percent real) decline in the Dow Jones index reflected a drop in the value of the highly levered stock market that had more severe consequences.[35] Indeed, while the Securities and Exchange Act of

34. Investment banking profits, among other sources, derive from commissions earned marketing new bond and stock issues to retail customers, advice provided to potential merger candidates, and income from trading on the bank's own account (proprietary trading). There is abundant evidence that proprietary trading by depository institutions was implicated in the 2008 financial crisis, and some evidence that its frequency, and the share of profits from this source, increased prior to the crisis (see "Obama to Propose Limits on Risks Taken by Banks," by Jackie Calmes and Louis Uchitelle, *New York Times*, January 20, 2010; Financial Crisis Inquiry Commission 2011). The "Volker rule" was intended to prohibit proprietary trading by commercial banks.

35. As Eichengreen and Mitchener observed, "the Great Crash bequeathed a legacy of problems for banks, corporations and households, which had assumed heavy debt loads and packed their portfolios full of now poorly performing assets" (2004, 190).

1934 was tightening margin requirements on stock purchases, amendments to the Federal Reserve Act in 1935 loosened margin requirements in terms of the ability of federally chartered national banks to lend on real estate. And while those amendments relaxed constraints on lending by banks on real estate, perhaps the most famous legislation of the New Deal era, the Glass-Steagall Act (1933–1999), drastically restricted the ability of commercial banks or their affiliates to take positions in equities. This emphasis on the market for stocks rather than real estate as ground zero for the unfolding Great Depression stands in sharp contrast to the diagnoses of the locus of the onset of the 2008 and 2009 financial crisis and ensuing economic recession and slow recovery. The differential legislative attention during the New Deal is consistent with the narrative developed in this chapter.

There is broad consensus that the 2007 to 2012 financial crisis and aftermath originated in US housing markets, precipitated by imprudent real estate loans, enabled by lax regulation and associated behavior by ratings agencies, and facilitated by innovations in mortgage products and derivatives, particularly credit default swaps and tranched mortgage-backed securities. There is as well much evidence that, for both the interwar period and the early twenty-first century, the quantity and quality of credit extended during the boom created obstacles to recovery that prolonged depression/recession.

But history never repeats itself exactly. Although no doubt contributory, bad residential housing lending in the interwar period did not play as central a role in blocking recovery as it does today. The legacies of the explosion of mortgage debt between 2001 and 2007 and the 42 percent drop in real house prices between 2006 and 2012 included impaired household balance sheets, effectively insolvent financial institutions, and extensive, lengthy, and drawn out foreclosure processes. These legacies exercised a persistent retardative effect on the macroeconomy, the result of which will be a cumulative output loss substantially exceeding that associated with the 1982 recession, which had heretofore been the worst since the Great Depression.

References

Alston, Lee J. 1983. "Farm Foreclosures in the United States during the Interwar Period." *Journal of Economic History* 43 (December): 885–903.

Alston, Lee J., Wayne A. Grove, and David Wheelock. 1994. "Why do Banks Fail? Evidence from the 1920s." *Explorations in Economic History* 31:409–31.

Behrens, Carl Frederick. 1952. *Commercial Bank Activities in Urban Mortgage Financing*. New York: National Bureau of Economic Research.

Bernanke, Ben. 2002. Speech given at birthday party for Milton Friedman. http://www.federalreserve.gov/BOARDDOCS/SPEECHES/2002/20021108/default.htm.

Board of Governors of the Federal Reserve Board. 1943. *Banking and Monetary*

Statistics, 1914–1941. Washington, DC: Board of Governors of the Federal Reserve System.

Board of Governors of the Federal Reserve Board. 2011a. April 27 release. http://www.federalreserve.gov/newsevents/press/monetary/fomcprojtabl20110427.pdf

Board of Governors of the Federal Reserve Board. 2011b. "Flow of Funds Accounts." http://www.federalreserve.gov.

Bordo, Michael D., and Joseph G. Haubrich. 2011. "Deep Recessions, Fast Recoveries, and Financial Crises: Evidence from the American Record." Working Paper, Federal Reserve Bank of Cleveland.

Burrough, Bryan, William D. Cohan, and Bethany McLean. 2012. "Jon Corzine's Riskiest Business." *Vanity Fair*, February, 94–153.

Calomiris, Charles W., and Joseph R. Mason. 1997. "Contagion and Bank Failures during the Great Depression: The June 1932 Chicago Banking Panic." *American Economic Review* 87 (December): 863–83.

———. 2003. "Fundamentals, Panics, and Bank Distress During the Depression." *American Economic Review* 93:1615–47.

Calomiris, Charles, Stanley Longhofer, and William Miles. 2009. "The (Mythical?) Housing Wealth Effect." NBER Working Paper no. w15075, Cambridge, MA.

Carter, Susan B., Scott S. Gartner, Michael R. Haines, Alan L. Olmstead, Richard Sutch, and Gavin Wright, eds. 2006. *Historical Statistics of the United States: Earliest Times to the Present.* Millennial edition. Cambridge: Cambridge University Press.

Case, Karl E., John Quigley, and Robert Shiller. 2005. "Comparing Wealth Effects: The Stock Market vs. the Housing Market." *Advances in Macroeconomics* 5. http://www.bepress.com/bejm.

Congressional Budget Office. 2013. "Estimated Impact of the American Recovery and Reinvestment Act on Employment and Economic Output from October 2012 Through December 2012." Accessed May 29, 2013. http://www.cbo.gov/sites/default/files/cbofiles/attachments/43945-ARRA.pdf.

Eichengreen, Barry, and Kris J. Mitchener. 2004. "The Great Depression as a Credit Boom Gone Wrong." *Research in Economic History* 22:183–237.

Field, Alexander J. 1984. "Asset Exchanges and the Transactions Demand for Money, 1919–1929." *American Economic Review* 74 (March): 43–59.

———. 1992. "Uncontrolled Land Development and the Duration of the Depression in the United States." *Journal of Economic History* 52 (December): 785–805.

———. 2001. "Bankruptcy, Debt, and the Macroeconomy." *Research in Economic History* 20:99–133.

———. 2011. *A Great Leap Forward: 1930s Depression and U.S. Economic Growth.* New Haven, CT: Yale University Press.

———. 2013. "The Savings and Loan Insolvencies in the Shadow of 2007–2017." Paper prepared for the World Cliometrics Conference, Honolulu, Hawaii.

Financial Crisis Inquiry Commission. 2011. *Final Report of the National Commission on the Causes of the Financial and Economic Crisis in the United States.* Washington, DC: Government Printing Office.

Fishback, Price V., Alfonso Flores-Lagunes, William C. Horrace, Shawn Kantor, and Jaret Treber. 2011. "The Influence of the Home Owners' Loan Corporation on Housing Markets during the 1930s." *Review of Financial Studies* 24:1782–813.

Fisher, Ernest M. 1951. *Urban Real Estate Markets: Characteristics and Financing.* New York: National Bureau of Economic Research.

Fisher, Irving. 1933. "The Debt-Deflation Theory of Great Depressions." *Econometrica* 1:337–57.

Friedman, Milton, and Anna J. Schwartz. 1963. *A Monetary History of the United States, 1867–1960*. Princeton, NJ: Princeton University Press.

Galbraith, John Kenneth. 1955. *The Great Crash 1929*. Boston: Houghton Mifflin.

Ghent, Andra C. 2010. "Residential Mortgage Renegotiation during the Great Depression." Working Paper, Baruch College, CUNY.

Gjerstad, Steven, and Vernon L. Smith. 2009. "From Bubble to Depression." *Wall Street Journal*, April 9. http://online.wsj.com/article/SB123897612802791281 .html.

———. 2014. *Rethinking Housing Bubbles: The Role of Households and Bank Balance Sheets in Modeling Economic Cycles*. New York: Cambridge University Press.

Goetzmann, William N., and Frank Newman. 2010. "Securitization in the 1920's." NBER Working Paper no. 15650, Cambridge, MA.

Goldsmith, Raymond. 1955. *A Study of Saving in the United States*. (3 volumes). Princeton, NJ: Princeton University Press.

Grebler, Leo, David M. Blank, and Louis Winnick. 1956. *Capital Formation in Residential Real Estate: Trends and Prospects*. Princeton, NJ: Princeton University Press.

Guglielmo, Mark. 2011. "Illinois Bank Failures during the Great Depression." Working paper, University of Chicago.

International Monetary Fund. 2012. "Dealing with Household Debt." In *World Economic Outlook 2012*, chapter 3. http://www.imf.org/external/pubs/ft/weo/2012 /01/index.htm.

Koo, Richard. 2009. *The Holy Grail of Macroeconomics, Revised Edition: Lessons from Japan's Great Recession*. New York: Norton.

Leonhardt, David. 2005. "Be Warned: Mr. Bubble's Worried Again." *New York Times*, August 21. http://www.nytimes.com/2005/08/21/business/yourmoney/21real .html?pagewanted=1.

Lucia, Joseph L. 1985. "The Failure of the Bank of United States: A Reappraisal." *Explorations in Economic History* 22:402–16.

Minsky, Hyman. 1964. "Longer Waves in Financial Relations; Financial Factors in the More Severe Depressions." *American Economic Review* 54 (May): 324–35.

———. 1975. *John Maynard Keynes*. New York: Columbia University Press.

———. 1986. *Stabilizing an Unstable Economy*. New Haven, CT: Yale University Press.

Mishkin, Frederic S. 1978. "The Household Balance Sheet and the Great Depression." *Journal of Economic History* 38 (December): 918–37.

Morton, J. E. 1956. *Urban Mortgage Lending: Comparative Markets and Experience*. Princeton, NJ: Princeton University Press.

O'Brien, Anthony Patrick. 1992. "The Failure of the Bank of United States: A Defense of Joseph Lucia." *Journal of Money, Credit, and Banking* 24 (August): 374–84.

Olney, Martha L. 1999. "Avoiding Default: The Role of Credit in the Consumption Collapse of 1930." *Quarterly Journal of Economics* 114 (February): 319–35.

Parker, Richard. 2005. *John Kenneth Galbraith: His Life, His Politics, His Economics*. New York: Farrar, Straus and Giroux.

Postel-Vinay, Natacha. 2011. "From a 'Normal Recession' to the "Great Depression. Finding the Turning Point in Chicago Bank Portfolios." London School of Economics Working Paper #151/11, March.

Rappoport, Peter, and Eugene N. White. 1994. "Was the Crash of 1929 Expected?" *American Economic Review* 84 (March): 271–81.

RealtyTrak. 2011. "Record 29 Million US Properties Receive Foreclosure Filings in 2010." http://www.realtytrac.com/content/press-releases/record-29-million-us-properties-receive-foreclosure-filings-in-2010-despite-30-month-low-in-december-6309 .

Reinhart, Carmen, and Kenneth Rogoff. 2009. *This Time is Different: Eight Centuries of Financial Folly*. Princeton, NJ: Princeton University Press.

Reinhart, Carmen M., and Kenneth Rogoff. 2010. "Growth in a Time of Debt." *American Economic Review* 100:573–8.

Romer, Christina D. 1990. "The Great Crash and the Onset of the Great Depression." *Quarterly Journal of Economics* 105:597–624.

Saulnier, Raymond J. 1956. *Urban Mortgage Lending*. Princeton, NJ: Princeton University Press.

Shiller, Robert. 2006. *Irrational Exuberance*, 2nd ed. New York: Crown Publishers.

Shiller, Robert. 2012. Housing Data. http://www.econ.yale.edu/~shiller/data.htm.

Snowden, Kenneth. 2010. "The Anatomy of a Residential Mortgage Crisis: A Look Back to the 1930s." NBER Working Paper no. 16244, Cambridge, MA.

Standard and Poor's. 2009. "S&P/Case-Shiller Home Price Index Methodology." http://www.standardandpoors.com/.

Temin, Peter. 1976. *Did Monetary Forces Cause the Great Depression?* New York: Norton.

Tennessee Encyclopdia. 2011. s.v. "Caldwell and Company." Accessed October 31, 2011. http://tennesseeencyclopedia.net/entry.php?rec=171.

Trescott, Paul B. 1992. "The Failure of the Bank of United States: A Rejoinder to Anthony Patrick O'Brien." *Journal of Money, Credit, and Banking* 24 (August): 385–89.

US Department of Commerce, Bureau of Economic Analysis. 2011. Fixed Asset Tables. http://www.bea.gov.

US Department of Commerce. 2013. National Income and Product Accounts (NIPA). http://www.bea.gov.

US Department of Labor. 2011. Consumer Price Index—All Urban Consumers. http://www.bls.gov.

Wheelock, David. 2008. "The Federal Response to Home Mortgage Distress: Lessons from the Great Depression." *Federal Reserve Bank of St. Louis Review* 90 (3, part 1) (May/June): 133–48.

White, Eugene N. 1990. "The Stock Market Boom and the Crash of 1929 Revisited." *Journal of Economic Perspectives* 4 (Spring): 67–83.

———. 2009. "Lessons from the Great American Real Estate Boom and Bust of the 1920s." NBER Working Paper no. 15573, Cambridge, MA.

Wicker, Elmus. 1980. "A Reconsideration of the Causes of the Banking Panic of 1930." *Journal of Economic History* 40 (September): 571–83.

Woolf, Edward N., and Marcia Marley. 1989. "Long Term Trends in U.S. Wealth Inequality: Methodological Issues and Results," In *The Measurement of Saving, Investment, and Wealth, Studies in Income and Wealth*, vol. 52, edited by Robert E. Lipsey and Helen Stone Tice, 765–844. Chicago: University of Chicago Press.

3

Consumption and Investment Booms in the 1920s and Their Collapse in 1930

Steven Gjerstad and Vernon L. Smith

> As explanations of the so-called business cycle, or cycles, when these are really serious, I doubt the adequacy of over-production, . . . over-confidence, over-investment, over-saving, over-spending, and the discrepancy between saving and investment. I venture the opinion . . . that in the great booms and depressions each of the above named factors played a subordinate role as compared with two dominant factors, namely over-indebtedness to start with and deflation following soon after.
>
> Over-investment and over-speculation are often important; but they would have far less serious results were they not conducted with borrowed money.
>
> The same is true as to over-confidence. I fancy that over-confidence seldom does any great harm except when . . . it beguiles its victims into debt.
>
> —Irving Fisher (1933, 340–41)

3.1 Interpretations of the Great Depression

Similarities between the financial crisis in September 2008 and the collapse of the financial system during the Depression have been widely noted. Yet the comparability of the origins and transmission of the crises have been neglected. The recent downturn, which originated with a pronounced housing boom and collapse, led to severe household balance sheet problems that were transmitted to lenders and mortgage security investors. Damage to household balance sheets weakened household demand—especially for housing and durable goods—which adversely affected employment, production, and nonresidential fixed investment. This pattern, however, is not

Steven Gjerstad is the Presidential Fellow Professor at the Economics Science Institute at Chapman University. Vernon L. Smith is professor of economics and law and holds the George L. Argyros Endowed Chair in Finance and Economics at Chapman University. He is a Nobel Laureate in Economics.

For acknowledgments, sources of research support, and disclosure of the authors' material financial relationships, if any, please see http://www.nber.org/chapters/c12794.ack.

recognized in the dominant view as a possible cause of the Depression. Contrary to prevailing views of the origins of the Great Depression, we argue in this chapter that changes in levels of mortgage finance, residential construction, and the broader economy preceding and during the initial phases of the Great Depression shared many features with the recent Great Recession. Based on data collected in Wickens (1937) we estimate that by the end of the Great Depression, losses on mortgage loans exceeded estimates of losses in the Great Recession, either as a percentage of loans outstanding or as a percentage of aggregate output.

3.1.1   Friedman and Schwartz versus Real Business Cycle Interpretations

The interpretation of the Depression that Friedman and Schwartz articulated in *A Monetary History of the United States* is probably the most influential. Friedman and Schwartz (1963, 300) argued that during the Depression the "monetary collapse was not the inescapable consequence of other forces, but rather a largely independent factor which exerted a powerful influence on the course of events." They further argued that "different and feasible actions by the monetary authorities could have prevented the decline in the stock of money—indeed, could have produced almost any desired increase in the money stock" (301). But they also admit that while "monetary expansion . . . would have reduced the contraction's severity . . . the contraction might still have been relatively severe." Much effort has been expended in efforts to understand the monetary contraction that took center stage in 1931. In this chapter we focus on the background for the stresses that emerged in the financial system. Before the serious deterioration of the banking system developed at the end of 1930, the United States had already experienced a deep downturn in output. In the aftermath of a debt-fueled residential real estate bubble, expansionary monetary policy could not entirely eliminate the effects of the resulting household balance sheet problems, financial sector losses, and the collapse in mortgage lending. Misallocation of resources and investment losses could not be reversed by central bank provision of liquidity in an environment in which a significant portion of households and their lenders faced insolvency.

In contrast to the monetary policy explanation of Friedman and Schwartz, the real business cycle (RBC) literature initiated by Kydland and Prescott (1982) contends that economic downturns have their origin in serially correlated negative productivity shocks that reduce aggregate output. Although this view has been influential, in its current form it is implausible. It would be difficult to argue that the decline in US automobile and light truck production from 10.47 million units in 2007 to only 5.56 million units in 2009 resulted from a shock to productivity. If a productivity shock drove the decline of this magnitude, then the relative scarcity of automobiles should have resulted in an increase in automobile prices, but in fact, the Consumer Price Index component for new cars and light trucks fell 0.5 percent from

2007 to 2009.[1] Construction of new single-family and multifamily residences fell 78.7 percent between Q1 2006 and Q1 2011, during a period when the Case-Shiller National Home Price Index fell 35.5 percent. If the contraction of output in these two sectors resulted from a shock to productivity that disrupted supply, that should have led to rising prices. The pattern of decline seems much more consistent with a demand shock initiated by a shock to household credit.

3.1.2   Economic and Banking Conditions in 1930

The rapid accumulation of mortgage debt, the housing bubble and collapse, and its impact on the financial and real sectors up to the time of the financial crisis in September 2008 share many similarities to events between the end of the 1920 to 1921 recession and the collapse of the banking system that began in late 1930. The fact that the recent financial crisis and recession did not lead to an economic calamity equal to the Great Depression is strong evidence that an aggressive monetary policy response can mitigate the consequences of a financial crisis. On the other hand, the depth and duration of the recent recession and the slow recovery suggest that expansionary monetary policy cannot entirely compensate for the contraction caused by a residential real estate bubble and collapse; it also suggests that there may have been more to the Depression than "a largely independent" monetary collapse, as Friedman and Schwartz argued.

A very serious downturn had already occurred before the first banking crisis. By the end of 1930, GNP had fallen 9.5 percent from its peak in 1929. As Wicker (1996) has noted, the number of bank suspensions and the level of deposits in suspended banks were only slightly higher between January and October 1930 than they had been throughout the 1920s. The wave of bank suspensions in November 1930 was concentrated primarily in the St. Louis Federal Reserve District; in December 60 percent of the deposits of suspended banks were in three banks, two in New York and one in Philadelphia.

Receivers' reports from the liquidation of failed national banks compiled by the Comptroller of the Currency provide strong evidence that the large majority of suspended banks both before and during the Depression were insolvent. After November 1930 the frequency of insolvent banks entering receivership escalated. The contention by Friedman and Schwartz that the banking system was facing only liquidity problems and not solvency problems is difficult to reconcile with the record of liquidated national banks.[2]

---

1. Automobile production figures are taken from http://oica.net/category/production -statistics/. The CPI new car and light truck component series is CUSR0000SS4501A from the Bureau of Labor Statistics.

2. In an article titled "Bernanke is Fighting the Last War," Carney (2008) interviewed Anna Schwartz. As the title suggests, her position was that circumstances in 2007 and 2008 were quite different from those in 1930 and afterward. "'If the borrowers hadn't withdrawn cash, they [the

The extent of insolvency versus illiquidity during the Depression is placed in context by first examining it during the boom years. The 103 national bank receiverships that were completed in the twelve months ending October 31, 1929 paid only 49.2 cents on each dollar of unsecured liabilities, even after stock assessments were collected that amounted to 9.8 percent of unsecured liabilities. Only 21 of these 103 liquidations resulted in repayment of over 75 percent of unsecured liabilities.[3] Given that asset values had not yet suffered when these liquidations were completed, the results should have been better if there was only a liquidity problem. Insolvency persisted at a similar level in 1930, and became far more prevalent in 1931. For all national banks that entered receivership in the year ending October 31, 1929, 66.1 percent of $41.8 million in unsecured liabilities were paid during liquidation. In 1930, 61.1 percent of $47.0 million in unsecured liabilities were paid. In 1931, the percentage of unsecured claims paid increased to 72.2 percent, but the level of unsecured claims surged to $294.2 million.[4] The percentage of failed banks that were deeply insolvent did not change appreciably from 1925 to 1933, but the number of banks that entered liquidation—and the deposits and other liabilities involved—escalated sharply in the reporting period beginning on November 1, 1930. Although we do not have data on the condition of state banks, they were much more encumbered with illiquid assets, especially real estate, so it is unlikely that their record with respect to solvency was better than that of the failed national banks. The hypothesis that the banking system collapsed due to a contagion of fear and widespread runs on solvent banks seems suspect, so an examination of the sources of banks' losses is warranted. Losses on residential real estate lending were one important category of losses.

3.1.3   Mortgage Leverage and a Housing Collapse Amplify Distress in a Downturn

The same pattern of contraction evident in the 2008 crisis—starting with declining expenditures on residential construction followed first by declining house prices and then by declining nonresidential fixed investment—was clearly present before the effects of monetary contraction appeared late in 1930 and accelerated in 1931. In fact, the 40.4 percent decline in residential construction from 1925 to 1929 was the largest decline from housing peak

---

banks] would have been in good shape. But the Fed just sat by and did nothing, so bank after bank failed. And that only motivated depositors to withdraw funds from banks that were not in distress. . . . [T]hat's not what's going on in the market now,' Ms. Schwartz says."

3. These data on the results of liquidations that were completed in 1929 are drawn from table 43 in Comptroller of the Currency (1929).

4. These data on the results of liquidations by the year the bank entered receivership are compiled in table 83 in Comptroller of the Currency (1941) for all liquidations closed by October 31, 1941. We have added to these figures by collecting the results of other liquidations that were completed and reported in later years.

to economic cycle peak in any economic downturn between the 1920 to 1921 recession and the 2001 recession.[5]

The typical recession begins with a downturn in expenditures on residential construction, and this directly affects employment and consumption, but if home prices do not decline substantially the problems are not further compounded by households' losses on their real estate assets, with corresponding negative impacts on bank equity.[6] In both the 2007 to 2009 Great Recession and the Great Depression, large house price declines against fixed mortgage debt reduced household wealth, and damaged the balance sheets of financial sector firms. This in turn amplified the usual downturns in consumer durables expenditures and nonresidential fixed investments.

One consequence of the focus on monetary policy mistakes has been a clearer understanding of the importance of an aggressive central bank response to a developing crisis. But another consequence of the focus on monetary factors was a lack of attention to and concern about the housing bubble and the precarious buildup of household debt that accompanied the bubble. If the Federal Reserve had paid more attention to the risk accumulating in the housing and mortgage markets, that might have obviated the need for the aggressive policy measures that it subsequently pursued.

In this chapter we demonstrate that the real estate boom in the 1920s began to unwind three years before the general contraction began: households' consumption of durable goods, firms' investments in inventories, equipment, and structures, the stock market, and output all continued to climb for three years after the contraction in residential real estate began, and the broader economic collapse coincided with the collapse of credit to households that had supported residential real estate purchases and consumer durable goods consumption.[7] These events all preceded the first banking crisis in late 1930 as well as the missed opportunities by the Federal Reserve to try to counteract the declining money supply.

3.1.4   Household Balance Sheet Stress and the Consumption Decline in 1930

Prior to subsequent problems with monetary policy, a serious contraction was already underway in 1930 before the escalation of bank failures in late 1930 and in 1931. Temin (1976) claimed that the consumption decline

---

5. The only larger decline in residential construction between housing peak and economic cycle peak during the past ninety-four years in the United States was the 43.9 percent collapse between Q1 2006 and Q4 2007.

6. For a comparison of the somewhat typical 1973 to 1975 recessions and the 1980 and 1981 to 1982 recessions with the atypical 2007 to 2009 recession see Gjerstad and Smith (2012). Buchanan, Gjerstad, and Smith (2012) compares the 1980 and 1981 to 1982 recessions with the 2007 to 2009 recession.

7. Figure 3.2 in section 3.3 shows that mortgage lending collapsed well before the money supply declined, and before the first large failures of financial firms occurred in November and December 1930, or the serious decline in the money supply began in early 1931.

in 1930 was much sharper relative to the declines in household income and wealth than it was during the other two interwar recessions in 1920 to 1921 and 1937 to 1938.[8] Friedman and Schwartz argue that a series of monetary policy failures—starting with the failure to provide liquidity during the first banking crisis in November and December 1930—turned a normal cyclical downturn into an inexorable economic collapse. Temin's observation that the decline in consumption in 1930 was unusually large is consistent with the hypothesis that household balance sheets were stressed before the monetary collapse in 1931. Particularly unusual, in comparison with other downturns in the last century, was the decrease in nondurable consumption. (See figure 3.1.) This decline, suggesting unusual household belt tightening, preceded the monetary collapse described by Friedman and Schwartz, which leaves open the possibility that both consumption decline and an inadequate monetary response are consistent with the broad course of events. White (1984) has argued that the first banking crisis was indistinguishable from the banking troubles that had plagued rural areas throughout the 1920s. White notes that "Friedman and Schwartz argue that the surge of failures was prompted by a loss of confidence in the banking system, while Temin believes that the failures and depression grew out of a downturn in the real sector" (119) and concludes that "depictions of events by Temin and by Friedman and Schwartz are not really in conflict. The weakening of assets and the lack of easy credit put the squeeze on all banks, and many weak ones were doomed" (137).

Although we cannot unambiguously identify the cause of the collapse in consumption, the buildup of household debt almost surely played a significant role. The period prior to the Depression contrasts sharply with the period leading up to the 1920 to 1921 recession. Before the 1920 to 1921 recession, the price level—including housing prices—rose sharply. The Consumer Price Index (CPI) and nominal GDP doubled from December 1915 to June 1920. Consequently, even as households took out new mortgage loans, real household mortgage debt fell over 20 percent between 1915 and 1920. During the deep 1920 to 1921 recession and again in the shallow 1923 to 1934 recession, while fixed investments and inventories fell, real household expenditures on nondurable goods and services, on durable goods, and on new residential structures all increased. As we show in our discussion of the Depression, all major components of households' expenditures declined sharply early in the Great Depression. Even though there

---

8. Note that declines in total wealth alone do not measure the impact on households of a decline in home values against fixed mortgage debt. During the Great Recession, mean household wealth fell 14.7 percent between 2007 and 2010, but median household wealth fell 38.8 percent. (These figures are calculated from the 2007 and 2010 Survey of Consumer Finance from the Federal Reserve.) For many households, home equity is a major store of wealth, and a collapse of housing prices can affect the wealth of a large fraction of households to an even greater extent than it decreases national wealth.

were sharp monetary contractions in both the 1920 to 1921 recession and in the Great Depression, the persistence of the monetary contraction in the Depression was most likely catalyzed by the stressed balance sheet conditions among households.

3.2   Changes in Output by Sector

During the 1920s residential and commercial construction, manufacturing, and consumer durable goods production all expanded rapidly, but mortgage and consumer credit were the factors that expanded most sharply. The expansion had two distinct phases—a strong expansion from 1921 to 1925 supported by a rapid expansion of residential construction and consumer durable goods expenditures followed by a moderate expansion from 1925 to 1929 that continued in spite of declines in residential construction that began in 1927. These two phases indicate the important role that residential construction played over the entire decade from 1921 to 1930, so it is worthwhile to decompose the growth and decline in the economy during that period into its major components. We examine changes in GNP and four of its major components: consumption of nondurable goods and services (C), investment in new residential structures (H), expenditures on durable goods (D), and fixed investment less investment in new residential structures (I).[9]

Table 3.1 shows annual growth rates of GNP and several of its primary components between 1921 and 1933. Looking at the growth rates of these components from 1925 to 1929, nothing looks surprising moving down the table from GNP to the sum of residential fixed investment and nonresidential fixed investment ($H + I$). Toward the end of the expansion, $H + I$ flattened out for a long period, from 1925 to 1929. But nonresidential fixed investment grew by 5.3 percent per year during those four years. It was residential construction that was collapsing. Given its size relative to the economy, that should not be a serious problem. But it plays an outsized role in the household balance sheet because it became increasingly leveraged during the decade, and the price collapse during the Depression seriously reduced household wealth and solvency.

Changes in output by sector in the Great Depression are uncharacteristic of recessions primarily in their magnitudes, but also by the fact that there

---

9. For brevity we refer to personal consumption of services and nondurable goods as "consumption" (C), households' durable goods expenditures as "durables" (D), expenditure on new single-family and multifamily housing units as "housing" (H), and nonresidential fixed investment as "investment" (I). Expenditure on new single-family and multifamily housing units is from Grebler, Blank, and Winnick (1956, table B-3); consumption and durable goods expenditures are from Swanson and Williamson (1972, table A1); investment is from Swanson and Williamson (1972, table A2, Column 3), minus expenditure on new housing units from Grebler, Blank, and Winnick (1956, table B-3); and GNP is from Swanson and Williamson (1972, table 1). All series are converted from nominal to real figures by dividing by GNP deflators from Balke and Gordon (1989, table 10); the Balke-Gordon GNP deflators are HSUS series Ca215.

Table 3.1	Annual growth rates of GNP and components, 1921–1933		
	1921–1925 (%)	1925–1929 (%)	1929–1933 (%)
GNP	6.1	3.7	−7.8
C	3.4	4.7	−4.6
D	12.9	2.7	−15.6
D + H	17.7	−1.7	−19.8
H + I	17.6	0.6	−27.6
H	29.4	−10.9	−40.1

was a large decrease in consumer spending on nondurable goods and services. With the single exception of the 2001 recession, consumer durables, residential construction, and investment all declined in every postwar recession, but their percentage declines have never matched the declines during the Depression.[10] During the Great Depression, durable goods expenditures declined 49.2 percent, investment declined 68.6 percent, and housing declined 92.5 percent. In the average of eleven postwar recessions from 1948 to 2007, the corresponding declines were 11.4 percent (durables), 11.8 percent (investment), and 32.5 percent (housing).[11]

In the Depression, real GNP declined 27.7 percent and every major component of output declined: even nondurable consumption fell by 17.3 percent—a figure dramatically larger than the decline in consumption of nondurable goods and services in any downturn since the depression.[12] Figure 3.1 shows the movement of GNP and several of its major components between 1922 and 1937. Each data point in a series measures the difference between the value of the series in that year and its value at the peak of the economic cycle in 1929. For example, residential construction was 30.3 percent higher in 1923 than it was in 1929; it was 46.4 percent lower in 1930 than it was in 1929. In figure 3.1 housing peaked in 1925 at a level 58.7 percent higher than its 1929 level. Other major components of GNP—and GNP itself—all continued to rise until 1929. Every major component of GNP fell in 1930, but none fell as much as housing. By 1933, housing was only 12.5 percent of its 1929 level and a paltry 7.5 percent of its peak level in 1925.

10. In the 2001 recession, nonresidential fixed investment was the only sector that declined. *This* has only happened once before in the past ninety-four years, in the 1923 to 1924 recession, when a downturn in consumption was averted by large infusions of mortgage credit, just as in 2001. See figure 3.2 in section 3.3 for a depiction of the highly unusual growth of net mortgage credit in 1923 and 1924.

11. These figures on the average size of sectorial changes in postwar recessions are drawn from table 1 in Gjerstad and Smith (2012).

12. Real expenditures on nondurable goods and services have fallen in only three postwar recessions (1980, 1981–1982 and 2007–2009), and the only year-over-year decline in households' consumption of nondurable goods and services between 1934 and 2012 was the 1.4 percent decline in 2009.

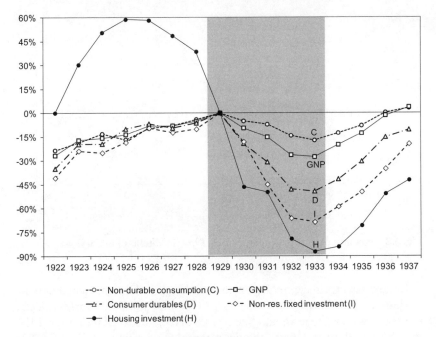

--○-- Non-durable consumption (C)   -□- GNP
-△- Consumer durables (D)   -◇- Non-res. fixed investment (I)
-●- Housing investment (H)

Fig. 3.1   Percentage changes to GNP and its major components relative to 1929 levels

3.3   Residential Mortgage Debt Boom and Increasing Leverage

Grebler, Blank, and Winnick (1956, table L-6) report residential mortgage debt outstanding from 1896 to 1952. Mortgage debt increased fairly steadily from 1896 to 1922. The rapid decline in foreign lending after World War I combined with the pent-up demand for housing led to a surge in residential mortgage finance starting in 1919. From 1919 to 1929, nominal residential mortgage debt rose from $7,998 million to $29,440 million, an increase of 268 percent. Mortgage debt outstanding grew rapidly from 1923 to 1928 and then slowed in 1929 and 1930. From 1931 to 1937, total mortgage lending outstanding fell in every year. Figure 3.2 shows the net growth of mortgage funds outstanding from 1905 to 1939.

The nominal declines in mortgage debt outstanding between 1931 and 1937 were remarkable in view of the historical record of mortgage lending in the United States. Residential mortgage debt increased every year from 1897 to 1952 except the period from 1931 to 1937 and during the war years 1942 to 1944. Combining the Grebler, Blank, and Winnick annual data from 1896 to 1952 with the Federal Reserve Flow of Funds quarterly data from 1952 on, mortgage loans outstanding increased in every reporting period from 1945 until Q1 2008. It then declined for twenty-one consecutive quarters, from Q2 2008 through Q2 2013 before rising in Q3 2013.

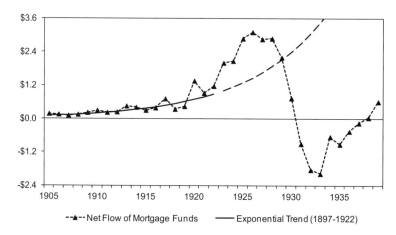

Fig. 3.2   Net flow of mortgage funds, 1905–1939 (in billions of dollars)

Residential mortgage credit growth over this period was much higher than during any other period over the past 110 years. Nominal mortgage debt increased at an average annual rate of 13.9 percent between the end of 1919 and the end of 1929. During the same period the consumer price index fell 11.4 percent, so the net effect was a rapid growth of household mortgage debt. This rapid buildup of mortgage debt enabled increased residential construction.

Mortgage bonds financed large construction projects to a greater extent than at any previous time, with results that ultimately proved very costly to investors. Losses on Chicago residential apartment building bonds began before 1929. More than 10 percent of apartment building bonds were in default by the end of 1929 and 35 percent of them were in default at the end of 1930. Almost every indicator in the residential real estate market turned down before the stock market bubble began in 1928. Sales, prices, the net flow of mortgage funds, and residential construction all peaked in 1925 or 1926, but the net flow of mortgage funds continued at an elevated level in 1927 and 1928 while house prices, housing sales, and new residential construction were all falling. From this we can conclude that household leverage—the fraction of home sales paid for with mortgages—was rising in 1927 and 1928.

In 1934 the Department of Commerce conducted a Financial Survey of Urban Housing in fifty-two cities. The survey included a broad range of questions about household and housing finance. Wickens (1937) tabulated the results of these surveys in up to eighty tables per city for twenty-two of the fifty-two cities in the original survey. Table 29, which was tabulated for each of the twenty-two cities, provides the total number of respondents who acquired their home in each year from 1901 to 1933, and the amount of the original purchase price that was financed by a mortgage, grouped into percentage ranges. The three highest ranges were 70 percent to 84 percent, 85 percent to 99 percent and 100 percent. There is widespread belief that mortgages were limited to 50 percent of the purchase price in the 1920s—for example, see chapter 1 in this volume—yet the results of the survey indicate very high levels of mortgage leverage.

Aggregated across the 27,795 respondents who originally purchased their homes between 1920 and 1929, 23.4 percent of all home buyers (whether they had a mortgage or purchased entirely with equity) had mortgages at the time of purchase that were 85 percent of the purchase price or higher. The time trend was also consistent with increasing leverage: the percentage of new purchases made with 85 percent borrowed money or more increased every year from 1920 (when it was 16.3 percent) until 1926 (when it reached 26.4 percent).

If we set the threshold lower, 42.7 percent of homeowner occupants in the survey had borrowed 70 percent or more of their purchase price. The survey also reports the number of homeowners who did not take out a mortgage when they purchased their homes. If we consider only those homeowners who took out a mortgage at the time of purchase, 55.8 percent of those borrowed 70 percent or more of their purchase price. Most measures of the nominal decline in housing prices are close to 30 percent for the period from 1930 to 1933, so by this measure about half of mortgaged properties could have been at risk of being "underwater" (that is, with a mortgage greater than the value of the home).

Research on the housing market in Franklin County, Ohio, complements the evidence we have reported from aggregate data and from the Financial Survey of Urban Housing. The Bureau of Business Research (1943), a study conducted at Ohio State University, examined deed and mortgage recordings from 1917 through 1937. The study reports tax assessment values of properties with new mortgages by year and type of structure. We use these data to determine the loan-to-value ratio for years from 1921 to 1930, which we report in table 3.2.[13]

As with the data from the Financial Survey of Urban Housing, the deed and mortgage survey data show a gradual increase in loan-to-value ratios, and the average mortgage debt is well above the 50 percent commonly believed to be the norm in the 1920s. Table 3.2 shows that, averaged across all mortgages recorded in 1928 in Franklin County, Ohio, debt amounted to

13. The data on number of residential mortgages are from table 21 in Bureau of Business Research (1943). Data on the ratio of mortgage to assessed value and average assessed value are calculated from data in table 24 for appraised value of mortgaged residential structures and from table 27 on the amount of residential mortgages. We have restricted attention from 1921 to 1930 because the same data source also includes assessed values on properties acquired under sheriff's deeds and on the sale prices for those properties, and those prices and assessed values are close. For 1921 through 1930, the average ratio of sales price to assessed value was 1.018. These ratios are calculated from data in table 87 and table 96.

Table 3.2   Mortgage leverage in Franklin County, Ohio, 1921–1930

Year	Number of mortgages	Mortgage to assessed value (%)	Average assessed value ($)	Index of assessed values
1921	8,599	61.6	3,998	0.76
1922	12,097	62.1	4,352	0.83
1923	14,303	62.1	4,906	0.94
1924	13,526	57.6	5,227	1.00
1925	16,896	64.2	4,885	0.93
1926	18,195	67.8	4,798	0.92
1927	15,735	68.8	4,890	0.94
1928	14,120	69.1	4,968	0.95
1929	9,997	65.4	4,936	0.94
1930	8,400	66.6	4,806	0.92

69.1 percent of assessed value.[14] Data on properties with junior liens in the Bureau of Business Research (1943) volume indicate that the loan-to-value ratio was far worse for homes with junior liens. Table 69 in that volume indicates the number of properties with junior liens, the assessed value of the properties, the principle amount of the junior lien, and the amount of the senior lien. For properties that had two or more liens, the principal of the junior liens gradually escalated from 21.4 percent of assessed property values in 1917 to a peak of 46.1 percent of assessed values in 1925. Between 1917 and 1924, the average amount of the sum of the two liens was 85.4 percent of the assessed property values. Between 1925 and 1930, the sum averaged 109.1 percent of the assessed property values.

The roles of debt-fueled construction and durable goods booms were mentioned in the early literature, but received limited attention in subsequent accounts of the Depression. Persons (1930) attributed the boom to excessive lending on real estate and consumer durables, and Fisher (1933) outlined a theory of the impact of deflation on debt, but during sixty postwar years of relatively stable domestic financial markets their concerns faded. Now that the pattern has been repeated several times over the past twenty years in developed countries such as Japan, Finland, and Sweden, and more recently in the United States, United Kingdom, Spain, and several other European countries, it is easier to appreciate a more universal role for the impact on the

14. Some mortgages issued in 1928 would have been refinanced from earlier purchases, and the assessed value may have been from a previous year. Even so, according to the price series in appendix C in Grebler, Blank, and Winnick (1956), the average price of homes was almost unchanged between 1920 and 1928. Table 3.2 also shows that average assessed values for mortgages recorded in Franklin County were very consistent between 1923 and 1929, with one brief blip in 1924. Consequently, the fact that not all assessed values were current probably would not have affected this measure of the loan-to-value ratio much. And the level of the loan-to-value ratio from mortgage recordings in Franklin County is also consistent with those reported in the Financial Survey of Urban Housing for twenty-two cities.

economic cycle of residential construction and durable goods booms that are based on unsustainable mortgage and consumer credit expansion. This new and neglected older evidence allows economic developments from 1920 into the 1930s to be reexamined with a fresh and more accurate perspective.

3.4   Housing Sales and House Price Declines, 1926–1933

The pattern of housing market decline during the late 1920s was similar to the pattern from 2006 to 2009. A broad measure of sales volume compiled by the Federal Housing Agency (FHA) peaked in 1925 and then fell in each year from 1926 until 1933. In a pattern that has been replicated in the recent downturn, home prices began to fall after the sales volume decline.

3.4.1   Housing Sales Decline

Fisher (1951, 157–62) describes a project devised by the Division of Research and Statistics at the Federal Housing Administration to make a complete survey of deed recordings in the District of Columbia and eight US counties.[15] Figure 3.3 shows a six-month moving average of the monthly aggregated deed recordings for these nine jurisdictions from 1922 through 1940.[16]

Aside from regular seasonal variation, the series declined sharply from its peak in July 1925 until it bottomed out in February 1934. Annual deed recordings fell 64.8 percent from their annual peak in 1925 to the annual trough in 1933. Although annual peaks varied from one location to another, in six of the nine locations, annual peaks took place in 1924 (Allegheny, PA), 1925 (San Francisco, CA; Cuyahoga, OH; and Salt Lake City, UT), and 1926 (Essex, NJ, and Washington, DC).

Several years before the FHA data were collected and evaluated Vanderblue (1927b) examined the number of real estate transfers and conveyances in Miami, Orlando, and Jacksonville, Florida.[17] Real estate transfers in all three cities exhibit a similar pattern of gradual but strong growth from 1919 that continued until it reached a feverish pitch in the last three months of

15. The survey methodology is described in Works Progress Administration (1938). A deed recording is the formal record of ownership transference, whether by sale, inheritance, foreclosure, or a voluntary conveyance of property to a lender.

16. The series began in 1895 in six of the nine jurisdictions and commenced by 1898 in the other three. The series extended through 1935 in all nine jurisdictions and through 1946 in four of them. The areas covered are the District of Columbia and eight US counties. The counties and their principal cities are San Francisco (San Francisco, California); Ada (Boise, Idaho); Washoe (Reno, Nevada); Essex (Newark, New Jersey); Burleigh (Bismarck, North Dakota); Cuyahoga (Cleveland, Ohio); Allegheny (Pittsburgh, Pennsylvania); and Salt Lake (Salt Lake City, Utah). The graph in figure 3 extends beyond 1935. Fisher estimates deed recordings for several counties. These are Ada and Burleigh (1936–1940), Allegheny (1937–1940), Washoe (1939–1940), and Salt Lake (1940). See Fisher (1951, tables A1 and A2).

17. Vanderblue (1927a) describes general economic conditions in Florida from the nineties through 1926.

Fig. 3.3   Six-month moving average of deed recordings in eight counties and Washington, DC (in thousands)

1924 and the first nine months of 1925. The peak in Miami was reached in September 1925; real estate transfers had collapsed 75 percent by the time the September 1926 hurricane devastated Miami. The patterns of real estate transfers in Orlando and Jacksonville were similar: Jacksonville peaked in October 1925 and Orlando peaked in November 1925.

The Florida real estate boom was an amplified version of the more general boom throughout the country, much as the recent booms in Las Vegas, Phoenix, and Miami were amplified versions of similar booms around the country. Figure 3.4 shows that real estate transactions in Miami had increased by a factor of five in only fourteen months—from 5,000 transfers in July 1924 to 25,000 transfers in September 1925. Although the increase was remarkably rapid in Miami, its peak differed by only one month from the peak for the average of nine widely dispersed jurisdictions shown in figure 3.3.

3.4.2   House Price Movements, 1926–1933

House price data are fragmentary and obtained by a variety of methods from diverse geographical areas. Yet most show a similar temporal pattern and similar magnitudes. House prices peaked in 1926, fell moderately for at least two years, and then began a sharp decline before reaching a trough in 1933. Sales volume tracked price declines closely, as indicated by extensive data from the FHA.

Fisher (1951, 55, table 7) reviews evidence from a sample of 3 percent of urban mortgage loans in New York, New Jersey, and Connecticut compiled by the Home Owners' Loan Corporation (HOLC). This survey compared

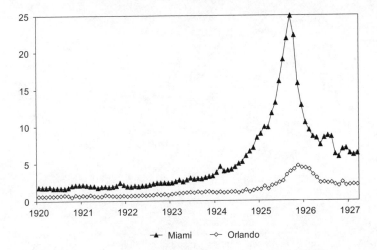

Fig. 3.4   Real estate transfers and conveyances in Miami and Orlando, Florida (seasonally adjusted, in thousands per month)

appraisal values for homeowners who were refinancing their homes in 1933 and 1934 to the purchase prices in 1925 to 1927. The median price decline between 1925 and 1933 to 1934 was 31.0 percent. For homes purchased in 1926 and 1927 the median decline to 1933 to 1934 was 26.9 percent.

The National Housing Agency used newspaper ads to compile asking prices for homes in Washington, DC, for the period from 1918 to 1948. Figure 3.5 shows a one-year moving average of these prices from 1920 through 1940.[18] The 1929 average asking price was 7.2 percent below the 1925 average asking price; by 1933 the average asking price was 26.3 percent below the 1925 average asking price. Figure 3.3 shows that, across nine jurisdictions, deed transfers fell substantially for three years before the significant decline in house prices and for four years before the stock market crash in 1929.

Grebler, Blank, and Winnick (1956, 345–49) summarize the results of a survey conducted in twenty-two cities by the Department of Commerce in 1934 and published in Wickens (1937). The survey was based on interviews of property owners who were asked (1) the current value of their property, (2) the year it was purchased, and (3) the original purchase price. The median price of single-family owner-occupied homes was determined from these survey data and this median price was used to develop an index of house prices for each year from 1890 to 1934. This series peaked in 1925. By 1929 it had fallen only 8.2 percent, but by 1933 it had fallen 30.5 percent.[19]

18. The Washington, DC monthly ask price series is provided in Fisher (1951, 53, table 6). Annual averages for the series are provided in HSUS series Dc828.

19. The survey is described in appendix C, pp. 345—348 in Grebler, Blank, and Winnick (1956). It is also available as HSUS series Dc826.

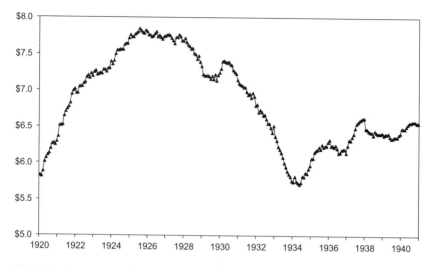

Fig. 3.5   One-year moving average of asking prices in Washington, DC (in thousands)

All three of these series show similar declines from annual peaks in 1925 to 1933. The Washington, DC, asking price series is the only monthly series, and it shows a peak in June 1926, almost a year after the sales series began to fall (although the sales series includes eight counties in addition to Washington, DC). The two series that include 1929 prices also display similar declines from the peak to 1929. Overall, given the widely different geographical coverage of these indices, and the variety of methodologies, the resulting measures of house price peaks, troughs, and percentage declines are surprisingly similar, and portray a situation in which large household home equity losses must have been widespread and severe. The price declines also demonstrate the potential for serious losses on residential mortgages.

Wickens (1941) uses census data for 1930 and data from the Financial Survey of Urban Housing for 1934 to estimate prices (table A 10) for fifty US cities. He estimates that the average value of a house fell 32.9 percent, from $6,619 in 1930 to $4,439 in 1934. He also uses 1930 census data to estimate the value of the housing stock for the entire country. The estimate of the total value of the housing stock in 1930 (from table A 2) is $122.58 billion, with owner-occupied homes valued at $64.68 billion and rented housing units valued at $57.90 billion. His table A 8 shows the value of owner-occupied housing in 1934 at $42.42 billion, and the value of rental housing as $36.75 billion. Rental unit value dropped 36.5 percent between 1930 and 1934 and owner-occupied unit value dropped 34.4 percent between 1930 and 1934. The total value of residential units fell 35.4 percent between 1930 and 1934 according to Wickens's estimates.

Table 3.3   **Cost of living and rent indices, 1921–1940**

Year	Cost of living index	Rent
1921	102.3	97.7
1922	97.4	95.9
1923	100.0	100.0
1924	101.3	106.3
1925	103.7	104.1
1926	104.3	101.3
1927	102.0	97.8
1928	100.6	93.7
1929	100.1	92.0
1930	96.7	89.5
1931	87.2	82.4
1932	77.9	72.4
1933	74.9	63.8
1934	79.4	64.8
1935	82.2	70.3
1936	84.1	77.9
1937	87.8	86.5
1938	85.7	87.0
1939	84.5	86.3
1940	87.0	86.9

Table 3.3 reproduces cost of living and rent indices for 1914 to 1941 from Colean (1944, table 41, 421). Rental price movements tracked house price movements over the course of the boom and decline, but the magnitude of the decline in rents was larger than the decline in any of the four price indices reported in this section.

Rent dropped 13.5 percent in nominal terms between 1924 and 1929; it dropped another 30.7 percent in nominal terms between 1929 and 1933. The cumulative nominal rent decline was 40.0 percent between 1924 and 1933. In real terms rent dropped 12.4 percent between 1924 and 1929 and it dropped 7.3 percent in real terms between 1929 and 1933. The cumulative real rent decline was 18.8 percent between 1924 and 1933.

Hoyt (1933, 377) finds a broadly similar pattern of rent price movements in Chicago between 1915 and 1933. His index increased from 100.0 in 1915 to 205.6 in 1925 with almost all of the increase coming between 1919 and 1924. From 1925 to 1929, the index fell 12.3 percent. It fell 39.7 percent between 1930 and 1933 to a level almost identical to its 1919 level.

It is worth noting that the nominal rent decline during the Depression period would have hurt a landlord who purchased a property with a mortgage before the property value and the rental income fell. At the same time, real rents fell much less during the Depression than real income, so that renters were also hurt between 1929 and 1933.

3.5   Mortgage Bond Defaults, Mortgage Delinquency and Foreclosure, and Unemployment

Mortgage bonds grew rapidly as a source of financing for apartment buildings and other commercial structures in the 1920s. After their spectacular rise, they had an even more precipitous collapse. In the last section, we saw that rent and residential real estate prices were falling before the general decline in 1930. It is also apparent from the data we review that rental prices fell earlier and further than purchase prices. Colean's rent index fell 11.6 percent and Hoyt's Chicago rent index fell 12.3 percent between 1925 and 1929. If these rental price strains were felt by the property owners that borrowed on mortgage bonds, then the early collapse of these bonds is understandable. The rapid accumulation of debt also had adverse consequences for households when the mortgage market collapsed from 1929 to 1931 and house prices collapsed along with it. In this section we examine the performance of mortgage bonds and the foreclosure record as indicators of the distress in the residential real estate market.

3.5.1   Mortgage Bond Defaults

The record of real estate bond issues provides a useful indication of real estate market trends. Bond issues increased rapidly, especially after 1921. The rapid growth of bond issues, their poor performance, and the pattern of early deterioration of residential mortgage bonds followed by later deterioration of commercial mortgages are all characteristics that are familiar from the recent real estate downturn. A number of studies of these developments were carried out during the depression.[20]

Data from the *Commercial and Financial Chronicle* analyzed by Johnson (1936a) show that by 1925 new real estate bond issues reached $695.8 million and accounted for 22.9 percent of corporate bond issues. As with many other series on real estate activity, the growth rate declined sharply after 1925. In 1928 real estate bonds were 1.7 percent below their peak in 1925, but then real estate bond issues began a precipitous fall. In 1929 real estate bond issues fell 51.2 percent to $333.9 million. Declines of 48.8 percent in 1930 and 32.8 percent in 1931 were followed by a virtual cessation of new issues in 1932 when newly issued bonds fell 96.8 percent. Johnson found that total real estate bond issues between 1919 and 1933 amounted to $4,114.9 million.[21] For the period from 1919 to 1931, Johnson found data on the performance of 1,090 bond issues that exceeded one million dollars, with

---

20. For an interesting history of real estate bonds, see Boysen (1931), who discusses the development of real estate bonds issued on Chicago apartment buildings starting in 1901.

21. Goldsmith (1955) estimates that the total of outstanding real estate bond issues reached $6,500 million in 1931. The large difference between their figures is most likely attributable to the fact that Goldsmith provides an estimate, whereas Johnson counts them from contemporary records. Goldsmith's estimate is provided in Grebler, Blank, and Winnick (1956, table L-2).

Table 3.4   **Defaults on Chicago real estate bonds, 1925–1934**

Year	Number of defaults	Amount (thousands) ($)	Cumulative defaults ($)	Percent defaulted (%)
1925–1928	7	8,275	8,275	1.66
1929	22	29,320	37,595	7.55
1930	50	64,095	101,690	20.42
1931	104	162,116	263,806	52.97
1932	67	146,725	410,531	82.54
1933	20	38,003	448,534	90.17
1934	5	22,706	471,241	94.74

a total issuance of $2,684 million. He evaluated bond performance by year of issue and classified them into one of three categories: called, matured, and outstanding. Bonds outstanding in 1936 were further separated into those that were current and meeting all obligations and those that were not meeting obligations, or defaulted.

According to Johnson (1936b), New York accounted for 36.3 percent of the bonds issued; 25.9 percent were issued on Chicago real estate. Koester (1939a, 1939b) evaluates the performance of 285 Chicago real estate bonds issued between 1919 and 1930. The market grew rapidly from the first issue for $1 million in 1919, doubling approximately every year until 1925, when the growth slowed and eventually peaked at $109,305,000 in 1928. Koester examined 338 mortgage bonds compiled by Moody's that amounted to $546,983,500. Detailed information was available on 302 of these bonds with a total issue amount of $536,478,500.[22] Of these 302 issues, 285 issues totaling $497,391,000 had a corporate structure with bonds and equity. Koester restricted her analysis to this pool with a homogeneous legal organization. Some moderate losses on these bonds appeared between 1925 and 1928. By the end of 1930, more than one-fifth of the bonds were in default, in advance of the banking and monetary crises of 1931. (See table 3.4.)

Apartment and apartment hotels defaulted earlier than hotel and office buildings. Office bonds had the best record, yet even their record was terrible: 87.7 percent of the office building bonds were in default by the end of 1934. The cascade of defaults on these bonds, from apartments to commercial real estate, is consistent with other aspects of the transmission of the downturn from households to businesses. Koester (1939b) examined prices for these Chicago real estate bonds and found that the basic price patterns conformed to the pattern of defaults through much of the downturn. Prices of bonds on apartment hotels fell earliest and furthest; apartment and hotel bonds fell

22. All of the excluded issues were under $475,000. Public price and performance data on these bonds were incomplete, probably because the bonds were closely held.

almost as much. Commercial property bonds and office building bonds fell least, but even so, the declines were dramatic. When apartment hotel bonds reached their minimum price in July 1933, they traded at 8.2 cents on the dollar. Apartment bonds reached their minimum of 11.36 cents on the dollar in January 1934. Office bonds fared the best of the five categories, but even they traded at only 13.0 cents on the dollar at their minimum in January 1934. Recovery of bond prices was limited even by the end of the price series Koester evaluated in January 1939. Between July 1933 and January 1939, the highest average price for any of the categories was 31.93 cents on the dollar for commercial buildings in January 1937. The high level of defaults and the low prices indicate extensive losses on the Chicago real estate bonds.

Johnson (1936b) analyzed the performance of bonds issued between 1919 and 1931 in nine cities, including Chicago. His sample of Chicago bonds differed only slightly from the sample analyzed by Koester. He found that in 1936 the recoverable value of Chicago real estate bonds was 39.0 cents on the dollar.

3.5.2   Mortgage Delinquency and Foreclosures

As in the recent debacle, mortgage delinquency was a significant factor in the depression. Wickens (1941, table D 44, 284) reports that in a survey of over 30,000 homeowners in fifty-two cities, 41.9 percent of respondents were behind in their mortgage payments on January 1, 1934. The distress was not confined to low-valued homes. The rate of delinquency among homeowners with homes valued over $15,000 was, at 41.8 percent, almost identical to the average for the full sample. The frequency of delinquency among owners of rental properties was, at 45.7 percent, even higher. The situation in some cities was dire. In Cleveland, 61.9 percent of homeowners and 66.0 percent of the owners of rental housing were delinquent. These delinquent payments must surely have generated problems with banks' incomes and their liquidity position.

Wickens (1941, table D 9, 215) also reports the percentage of mortgaged properties for owner-occupied homes (56.2 percent) and rental property owners (39.8 percent), and the average dollar amount of past due payments to lenders for delinquent homeowners ($467) and for delinquent rental property owners ($582). (Figures on delinquent payments are in table D 45 on p. 287.) Together with the number of owned and rented homes, this is enough information to estimate the total delinquent payments.[23] The results are that homeowners had about $1.16 billion of delinquent payments and rental property owners had an additional $1.31 billion in delinquent payments. These delinquent payments amounted to 10.7 percent of the $23.08 billion

---

23. Table 965, p. 886, in the 1943 edition of the *Statistical Abstract of the United States* includes the number of owner-occupied homes (10,549,972) and the number of rental homes (12,367,100) in the United States in 1930.

in nonfarm residential mortgage debt (excluding mortgage bond debt) outstanding at the end of 1933. Comparison with the current situation provides some perspective on this number. Combined with the amount of residential mortgage debt from the Federal Reserve Flow of Funds, Lender Processing Services provides enough information to develop a reasonable estimate of delinquent mortgage payments. Delinquent residential mortgage payments appear to have peaked at $85.24 billion in the third quarter of 2012. This figure amounts to only 0.9 percent of the $9,442.12 billion in mortgage debt outstanding at that time.[24] This comparison should make clear that mortgage delinquency could have been an important factor in the financial distress during the Great Depression, since its magnitude was probably an order of magnitude greater (as a percentage of outstanding mortgage debt) than it was in the recent crisis.

Unfortunately, there is no national foreclosure data until 1926. Foreclosures increased steadily from this first year through 1933 and thereafter began to decrease.[25] Foreclosures began to rise sharply before the period of rapidly falling house prices and rapidly increasing unemployment began in 1930.

For comparison, the number of foreclosures during the recent crisis peaked at 1.1 million in 2010, which would correspond to about 20.6 foreclosures per thousand mortgaged residential properties. In 2012 the rate was approximately 14.4 per thousand mortgaged residential properties. In an April 2013 *National Foreclosure Report* from CoreLogic, they estimated that 4.4 million foreclosures have been completed since September 2008. That is about 8.1 percent of the mortgaged properties at the time of the financial crisis. The rates shown in table 3.5 for the Great Depression would imply that there were about the same percentage of home foreclosures between 1929 and 1936 as there have been between 2008 and 2012. Standard & Poor's estimates that the recoverable value on the average foreclosure is about 55 percent of the loan principal. By the end of 1933, accumulated foreclosures from 1929 had reached about 5.1 percent of the properties with mortgages

---

24. From the amount of residential mortgage debt provided in the Federal Reserve Flow of Funds and the number of mortgaged properties in the LPS *Mortgage Monitor*, it is possible to determine for each quarterly reporting period the average mortgage. In the third quarter of 2012, the average home mortgage principal balance was $188,598. If we assume that the typical delinquent mortgage was a fully amortized thrity-year loan with a 6 percent interest rate, then one missed monthly payment amounted to almost exactly $600 per $100,000 principal balance. The LPS reports the number of residential mortgages thirty days past due and the number sixty days past due in its *Mortgage Monitor*. For mortgages ninety or more days past due, they report both the number of them and the average number of days past due. They also report the number of mortgaged residential properties in the foreclosure process and the average number of days that they are delinquent. From these pieces of information it is possible to estimate the number of delinquent monthly payments. For example, multiplying the number of mortgages thirty days past due by the average principal balance per mortgage and the average monthly payment on that balance yields the estimate of delinquent payments for that category of delinquency.
25. Foreclosure statistics are taken from the HSUS series Dc1255 and Dc1257.

Table 3.5   Foreclosures and foreclosure rates, 1926–1941

Year	Total foreclosures	Foreclosures per 1,000 mortgaged structures
1926	68,100	3.6
1927	91,000	4.8
1928	116,000	6.1
1929	134,900	7.1
1930	150,000	7.9
1931	193,800	10.2
1932	248,700	13.1
1933	252,400	13.3
1934	230,350	12.2
1935	228,713	12.1
1936	185,439	9.8
1937	151,366	8.0
1938	118,357	6.3
1939	100,410	5.3
1940	75,556	4.0
1941	58,559	3.4

in 1929. If lenders' losses were comparable to this, the recent estimates from Standard & Poor's losses would have been about $615 million or 2.7 percent of the residential mortgage principal outstanding at the end of 1933. Combined with losses from delinquency, the losses in the Depression would have been about 13.4 percent of mortgage loans; in the Great Recession, the figure would come to about 4.5 percent of mortgage loans. Although these are approximations, they certainly suggest that losses on mortgage lending must have been very severe and an important source of financial distress during the Depression. Moreover, foreclosure statistics underestimate both homeowner and lender distress, since many homeowners surrendered their homes before the foreclosure process was undertaken or completed. Fisher (1951, 48), citing Hoad (1942) notes that "during the eight-year period, 1931–38, 10.1 percent of all single-family homes in the [Toledo] area were foreclosed, and 9.6 percent were surrendered in lieu of foreclosure."

More disaggregated data reported in Bureau of Business Research (1943) for Franklin County, Ohio, can be used to determine which vintages of loans had the most serious foreclosure rates. Table 60 in that report shows that the percentage of mortgages resolved by foreclosure or court judgment by the end of 1937 increased monotonically from 0.5 percent in 1919 to 9.9 percent in 1928. If we assume that the hazard rate of foreclosure or court judgment was stationary for each vintage from 1917 to 1937, the percentage of loans that would go bad each year increased from 0.03 percent for those issued in 1919 to 1.09 percent for those issued in 1928. The rate then began to fall slowly to 0.66 percent by 1932. By 1934 it reached 0.04 percent per year.

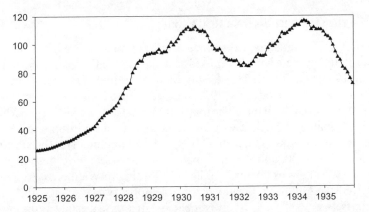

Fig. 3.6   One-year moving average of monthly foreclosures in Washington, DC

Additional evidence on the years prior to 1926 was provided by Badgley (1936), who published a monthly series on deed recordings and foreclosures from 1893 to 1936 for Washington, DC. Figure 3.6 shows a one-year moving average of Badgley's foreclosures series. It should be noted that foreclosures were increasing fastest during a period that was otherwise considered part of the economic boom, in 1927 and 1928.

In 1929 the unemployment rate was lower than in any other year in the twenties. Yet table 3.5 shows that the rate of foreclosures nearly doubled between 1926 and 1929. This result would be puzzling, but the experience of the recent housing bubble suggests a possible reason for rising foreclosures in a time of rising income and expanding employment. We have compiled much evidence that leverage was increasing as the real estate market was slowing down. Figure 3.2 shows that as late as 1928, the net increase in outstanding mortgages remained close to its peak level from 1926. Figure 3.3 shows that deed recordings in eight counties and Washington, DC, peaked in 1925 and had been falling rapidly for three years. The total number of deed recordings in 1928 was 31.4 percent below the level in 1925. Moreover, as figure 3.1 shows, new residential construction, which would absorb a large amount of new mortgage funds, was also falling by 1928. New residential construction had fallen 14.3 percent from 1925 to 1928. Yet through this developing downturn in residential construction and sales, the net flow of mortgage funds actually increased slightly between 1925 and 1928. From this it follows that the leverage was increasing as the Depression approached. It is possible or even likely that during the mid to late 1920s, underwriting standards were eroding and as house prices began to decline in 1927 and 1928, an increasing number of homeowners were unable to meet their obligations, even before the general downturn began.

3.6   Urban Bank Stress from Real Estate

Among the banks that experienced serious problems, we have some evidence that they were heavily exposed to residential real estate. According to Lucia (1985) and O'Brien (1992, 378), Bank of United States had 45 percent of its assets in real estate in 1930, compared to an average of 12 percent for other New York City banks. The final banking crisis from January to March 1933 originated in Detroit with the Guardian Union Group and Detroit Bankers Group. Union Guardian Trust had $30 million in real estate assets at the end of 1930, and it had 72 percent of its assets in real estate at the end of 1932 six weeks before it failed. According to Wigmore (1985, 437), "[w]ithin the Guardian Group as a whole approximately one-third of its total assets were in loans or investments related to real estate at the end of 1932." These figures are extremely high relative to other commercial banks. According to Grebler, Blank, and Winnick (1956, table N-10, 485), the average percentage of assets in residential mortgage loans for commercial banks in 1933 was 5.5 percent, and the average level of commercial bank lending on all real estate was only 8.7 percent.

The other main bank in the Guardian Group was the Guardian National Bank of Commerce. That bank's deposits of $198 million in December 1930 had fallen to $113.9 million when it was closed. Wigmore (1985, 438) also notes that "[t]he banks in the Detroit Bankers' Co. had over 40 percent of their assets in real estate loans or investments at the end of 1932, although their emphasis on individual home mortgages had produced a more sound portfolio." The largest bank in the Detroit Bankers' Group was the First National Bank of Detroit, which had deposits of $398.8 million when it closed.[26] In Senate hearings in late January 1934, Ferdinand Pecora quotes from the bank examiner's report of September 25, 1931, on the condition of the First National Bank of Detroit.[27]

> This report reflects a very unsatisfactory condition, showing classified loans and doubtful paper aggregating approximately the surplus and profit of the bank, without taking into consideration a large amount of slow assets. This condition has been brought about by two major causes, namely, the general business depression, and the shrinkage in the inflated value of real estate, and poor management.
>
> In the first instance Detroit has suffered along with other large cities from the depression, and more particularly because of the slowing down of the motor industry. The city has a large floating population, relying to a great extent on this one industry for its income. When this source of

26. For the final report on the condition of the First National Bank of Detroit, see table 36 in the *Eightieth Annual Report of the Comptroller of the Currency* (1942).

27. Stock Exchange Practices. Hearings before the Committee on Banking and Currency. Part 11, Detroit Bankers Company, January 24 to February 1, 1934. Washington, DC: US Government Printing Office, 1984.

income is materially reduced, all other branches of business are to some extent affected.

This condition has been reflected to a very marked degree in the value of real estate. Real estate values of 2 years ago have been cut in half, with little activity on this basis. Large buildings have not shown any market whatever. Foreclosures and receiverships are numerous.

From this quote it appears that the First National Bank of Detroit was also heavily invested in real estate, so the two largest banking conglomerates in Detroit, where the final banking panic of January to March, 1933 incubated, were both fragile institutions with large real estate portfolios.

Dolbeare and Barnd (1931) compared the condition of ten banks that failed in the summer of 1929 with a group of eight banks that survived into 1931. The successful banks were chosen first from among the strongest Florida state banks. Eight of the failed banks were chosen because they were similar in size and located in the same cities as successful banks in the study, and two failed banks were chosen because they were similar in size to other successful banks in the study. Characteristics of the failed and successful banks are compared at call dates in June and December of each year from June 1922 to December 1928. Two comparisons stand out. The real estate loans of failed banks on average grew 288.1 percent between June 1924 and December 1925. The real estate loans of the successful banks grew by 40.0 percent on average between June 1924 and December 1925. The volume of real estate loans as a percentage of assets averaged 12.3 percent in the failed banks and 15.2 percent in the successful banks during the boom period. Although the failed banks had fewer real estate loans as a percentage of assets, the real estate loans of failed banks grew much faster during the bubble period than the real estate loans of successful banks. Failed banks also grew much faster during the boom. On average deposits in failed banks grew by 220.7 percent whereas deposits in successful banks grew only 90.6 percent. Total loans of failed banks also grew faster during the boom period, 166.0 percent versus 56.6 percent, but most other characteristics of the two groups were similar. Loans as a percentage of total assets averaged 57.4 percent in the failed banks versus 56.0 percent in the successful banks during the boom period. During the boom period, cash as a percentage of total assets averaged 29.4 percent in the failed banks versus 32.4 percent in the successful banks. Deposits as a percentage of total liabilities averaged 89.0 percent in the failed banks versus 90.1 percent in the successful banks during the boom period. These results leave open the possibility that it was growth of all lending that was a key factor in the failure of these banks, but it does contribute to the body of evidence that lending on real estate was risky when real estate values subsequently collapsed.

In chapter 2 of this volume, Field argues that banks' loans to brokers were probably a more serious source of losses than real estate loans. He notes the large volume of these loans and the fact that they constituted a very large share of total lending by member banks. In spite of the large amount of loans for securities purchases, evidence from loans to brokers suggests that deleveraging in this sector was conducted quickly and with minimal losses. Loans to brokers on the New York Stock Exchange peaked in October 1929 at $8.55 billion. By the beginning of December 1929 the figure had fallen by 53 percent to only $4.02 billion.[28] Through the course of this rapid deleveraging only one brokerage, Mandeville, Brooks & Chaffee, failed. Its liabilities were estimated to be $4 million to $5 million.[29] It was seven months later when the next brokerage, Woody & Co., failed with liabilities estimated at $3 million.[30] This indicates the ease with which loans on securities could be closed out, and the safety of these loans, since the bonds and equities that secured the loans could be liquidated if margin calls went unmet.

In sharp contrast to loans on securities, mortgage lending is difficult to unwind, even as collateral collapses. (See Gjerstad and Smith 2009 for an analysis of this in the collapse of the US housing market from 2007 to 2009.) We have seen in section 3.4.2 how rapidly house prices fell during the Depression, and in section 3.5.2 we noted the escalation of foreclosures. Nevertheless, the reduction of mortgage debt was slow and prolonged, not because of a lack of distress from that category of lending. We have estimated that delinquent mortgage payments in January 1934 amounted to 10.7 percent of outstanding mortgage principal, and that losses on foreclosure may have amounted to another $615 million, or about 2.7 percent of outstanding principal at the end of 1933. Residential mortgage debt outstanding (excluding mortgage bond debt) peaked in 1931 at $27.65 billion. At the beginning of 1934, when losses on mortgage lending had reached approximately 13.4 percent of outstanding loans, mortgage loans outstanding had been reduced only $4.57 billion to $23.08 billion, a decline of 16.5 percent. The process of deleveraging in the real estate market was arduous, costly, and slow. Mortgage lending continued to fall for four more years until it reached a low of $21.92 billion in 1936 and 1937. This is remarkable in view of the fact that mortgage debt outstanding in the United States has fallen during only three periods during the past 115 years: 1932 to 1936, 1942 to 1944, and (at the time of this writing) from the second quarter of 2008 through the second quarter of 2013.

3.7   Summary: Channels of Contraction

There are five primary channels through which the construction and consumer credit booms accentuated the economic cycle. The first and most direct is reduced residential construction. The second channel was the

---

28. See *New York Stock Exchange Yearbook, 1929–1930.*
29. See "Brokerage Concern Put in Receivership," *New York Times*, Nov. 19, 1929, p. 2.
30. See "Brokerage Insolvent, Face Jury Inquiry," *New York Times*, June 20, 1930, p. 17.

damage to household balance sheets from the fall in home prices, and the negative impact from damage to household balance sheets on household demand for consumer durables and nondurables. The third channel was the reduction in firms' inventories, production, and fixed investment that resulted from the household consumption decline. The fourth channel was the feedback effect from declining production and investment to declining household income, which then circled back to affect each of the first three factors. The fifth factor was the damage to banks' balance sheets, which accentuated the troubles of both firms and households when loans could not be extended or rolled over due to the need for banks to deleverage.

3.7.1   Reduced Residential Construction

In the peak year of 1925, residential construction amounted to 5.3 percent of GDP. Between 1921 and 2010, residential construction as a percentage of GDP has exceeded 5 percent in four years. These were 1924, 1925, and 1926, and later in 1950 when the stock of housing was depleted from the low level of residential construction during World War II. Even during the recent boom, residential construction reached a maximum level of only 3.8 percent of GDP in 2005. The excess supply of structures constructed during the boom had to be absorbed before the construction industry could revive, so the decline in residential construction was the first and most direct channel by which the residential real estate downturn affected economic activity.

3.7.2   Damage to Household Balance Sheets

Housing market data show that real estate prices peaked in 1925 and 1926, and then began a slow decline that gathered momentum from 1929 to 1932. Many households borrowed when house prices were at or near their peak. Referring to figure 3.2, we see that in the years 1925 to 1928 the net flow of mortgage funds held steady at their flat four year peak of about $3 billion per year. As prices slid, household wealth fell while total debt burdens not only remained high but continued to increase even as new residential construction declined rapidly. For households with much of their total wealth consumed by their down payment, the house price decline wiped out their accumulated wealth, or worse. Short loan terms were a structural feature of the mortgage market, not only in commercial bank lending, but also in residential lending. These short contract terms probably created an additional source of contraction in mortgage lending and an additional source of downward pressure on housing prices when loans that came due were not rolled over.[31] In addition to their short term, many mortgages at that

---

31. Grebler, Blank, and Winnick (1956, table 67) list average lengths of mortgage contracts for life insurance companies, for commercial banks, and for savings and loan associations from 1920 through 1947. For the period from 1920 to 1934 the average contract length for commercial banks was only 3.0 years. The averages for life insurance companies and for savings and loan associations were longer at 6.8 and 11.2 years. But these figures are the average contract

time were either nonamortizing (i.e., interest-only as in the current crisis) or partially amortizing (i.e., balloon payments if not rolled over). For the period 1925 to 1929, about 14.3 percent of mortgages issued by life insurance companies were fully amortizing; in the same period, about 10.3 percent of mortgages issued by commercial banks were fully amortizing.[32] All these loans would have involved balloon payments at the end of their term. Savings and loan associations commonly issued fully amortizing loans: 94.9 percent of their loans between 1920 and 1929 were fully amortized. By 1935 to 1939 the share of fully amortized mortgages at commercial banks had risen to 69.0 percent.

The combination of short loan terms and the use of nonamortizing loans must have exacerbated the distress of both homeowners and lenders as the Depression developed. A large fraction of borrowers would have faced the necessity to refinance sometime between 1930 and 1935, when credit market conditions were stringent. When a borrower tried to refinance after prices had fallen, lenders either had to extend a new loan with a higher loan-to-value ratio, reduce the amount of the loan, or decline to renew it. As foreclosures were rising and prices were falling after 1926, this was an unattractive proposition for lenders, even before credit market conditions began to deteriorate significantly late in 1930. The need to refinance during a period of falling home prices must have led to distress sales when homeowners were unable to find new lenders upon expiration of their existing loans. Since many loans were not amortizing, lenders risked losses on a loan when the value of a home fell below the homeowner's equity. Lost equity and the prospect of a distress sale would naturally create uncertainty among households and lead to increased precautionary savings and reduced consumption. Estimates of personal savings in Swanson and Williamson (1972, table 3) reinforce this impression: the average level of personal savings between 1929 and 1931 was 97.5 percent higher than the average level for 1926 through 1928.

An increase in precautionary savings due to household balance sheet problems leads to declining household consumption, especially of durable goods. This in turn leads to reduced production levels and reduced employment. As reduced employment adds to household distress, it reinforces both the decline in durable goods consumption and the frequency of mortgage default and distress sales of housing. Reduced consumption from lost homeowner equity, its effect on production and employment, and the contribution of reduced employment to homeowners' mortgage distress is the second channel through which a downturn in the housing market affects economic activity.

---

length when the loan was issued, so the average length remaining on the loan when the banking troubles began would have been significantly shorter and many borrowers would have been affected when banks tried to retain liquid assets by declining to roll over loans.

32. Data on amortization are reported in Grebler, Blank, and Winnick (1956, table 66, p. 231).

3.7.3   Reduction of Firms' Inventories, Production, and Fixed Investments

As demand for consumers' durables collapsed, firms reduced inventories, but when demand failed to recover quickly, demand for producers' durables also began to fall. Investment decline impacts producers of raw materials and production equipment more than any other sector.[33] The decline in the demand for residential housing and for consumer durables leads to a desire by firms to reduce inventories, production, and employment. Reduced production then leads to a decline in demand for producer durables (plants, equipment, and structures). The large collapse in consumer durable goods demand that resulted from household balance sheet problems generated the third transmission channel into the real economy when producers' durable goods investment collapsed.

3.7.4   Feedback Effect on Households' Incomes

All of these effects have a pronounced impact on production, which feeds back to cause additional problems in the labor market. Labor market problems in turn circle back to cause further problems in the housing market and reduce consumer durable goods expenditures. Compensation to employees and proprietors' real incomes fell 11.3 percent from 1929 to 1930, whereas real GNP fell only 9.5 percent. At the same time the uncertainly associated with employees' compensation grew rapidly as unemployment rose from 2.89 percent in 1929 to 8.94 percent in 1930. In 1931 the plight of employees and proprietors grew considerably worse: their real income fell 16.6 percent, far in excess of the 6.3 percent decline in real GNP. In 1932, the gap between the decline in employee compensation and proprietors' incomes grew even larger: their real income fell 24.9 percent, while real GNP fell 13.3 percent. As their incomes fell in 1931 and 1932, employees faced increasing uncertainty as the unemployment rate increased to 22.89 percent. The brunt of the Depression fell on households, and their rapidly declining incomes led inevitably to a rapid collapse of demand for the products of industry.

3.7.5   Damage to Banks' Balance Sheets

The fifth transmission channel runs directly from households and investors to bank balance sheets. We estimated in section 3.5.2 that by January 1934, delinquent residential mortgage payments reached 10.7 percent of residential mortgage debt outstanding. Once housing equity losses among some households reach the critical threshold where their equity is exhausted and borrowers with inadequate collateral default on their payments, banks

---

33. Raw material and capital equipment output declined precipitously. Steel production (HSUS series Dd399) fell 75.5 percent between 1929 and 1932 and locomotive production (HSUS series Dd429) fell 96.4 percent from 1,770 in 1926 to 63 in 1933.

accumulate further losses. Distress among mortgage holders was not limited to owner occupants; it also included rental property owners and mortgage bond holders. In the 1920s, a large fraction of residential property was rented. Rental prices fell slightly more than property values, and the average loan term on rental properties was shorter than on loans to owner occupants. Real estate bonds issued in the 1920s on large apartment buildings, hotels, office buildings, and commercial properties accounted for an increasing share of real estate financing in the 1920s, and their performance was extremely poor. Transmission of losses into banks came from all sectors of the real estate market.

All classes of lenders deleveraged sharply during the course of the Depression. There are four reasons that banks reduce their private lending during a severe downturn. When bank capital declines as a result of losses, deleveraging is the simplest and most direct way for a bank to decrease its asset-to-equity ratio. When lending declines, the bank's assets are reduced but its equity is not directly affected. This improves its equity-to-asset ratio, even in the absence of direct capital investment. A second reason for a lending reduction is that when a loan is called or not rolled over, the funds obtained can be invested in liquid assets such as Treasury securities or excess reserves with the Federal Reserve Bank, which provide protection against illiquidity in the face of depositors' demands. A third reason for deleveraging is that borrowers are scrutinized much more carefully in a downturn, since loan collateral might decline in value and investments will produce an inadequate return during a downturn much more frequently than during a boom. A fourth—and very significant—reason that bank lending will decrease is outside of the control of the banks: many sound borrowers do not have solid investment opportunities, so borrower demand for loans declines. All four of these forms of bank deleveraging have been particularly characteristic of domestic developments during the Great Recession and the slow recovery from it. Bernanke (1983) focused on a related transmission channel from failed or suspended banks to borrowers. He argued that businesses that had established relationships with a failed bank faced reduced access to capital markets. While this is true, even solvent and surviving banks reduced their lending during the Depression.

In his discussion of the consumption decline of 1930, Temin (1976) argues that the consumption decline in 1930 was large relative to declines in wealth and income, especially when compared to consumption declines in the other two interwar recessions in 1920 and 1921 and 1937 and 1938. The unemployment rate shot up from 2.9 percent in 1929 to 8.9 percent in 1930. The foreclosure rate increased from 3.6 per thousand mortgaged nonfarm homes in 1926 to 7.1 per thousand in 1929 and 7.9 per thousand in 1930. Surely the fear of losing first a job and then a home could readily lead to a sharp decline in expenditures on housing and durable goods. As household expenditures fell, production, investment, and employment fell too, and the cycle of collapse was underway.

The accumulating household balance sheet stress after 1926 did not have a visible impact on corporate profits or the value of corporate equities even as late as October 1929. The national income accounts for 1919 to 1941 in Swanson and Williamson (1972) indicate that the sum of dividends and undistributed corporate profits were higher in 1929 than in any other year between 1919 and 1940. But the capacity of households to buy the goods and services that industry produced was dependent on debt accumulation, and the capacity of households to absorb more debt was limited, hence the profits that industry had been earning would soon collapse and the value of the capital that industries had accumulated would be limited by the collapse of household demand.

During the Depression, the decline in expenditures on new residential units plus the decline in consumption accounted for 72.9 percent of the total decline in GDP.[34] This figure is striking, but it must understate the contribution of households to the contraction. Consumer durables sales fell 49.3 percent in real terms between 1929 and 1933. With such a dramatic decline in consumer durables sales, investment in plants and equipment collapsed almost completely. Nonresidential fixed investment declined 68.6 percent, which was a precipitous collapse especially in comparison with the average decline of 11.8 percent during postwar recessions and the maximum decline of 22.5 percent during the 2007 to 2009 recession.[35]

3.8   Conclusion

The evidence presented in this chapter on the Depression, combined with the evidence from Gjerstad and Smith (2012) and Buchanan, Gjerstad, and Smith (2012) on the Great Recession, indicates that our two most severe financial crises and our two most persistent economic downturns of the past century both followed large declines in the value of residential real estate prices. It is possible that some other factor caused the downturns in residential real estate prices, the financial crisis, and the prolonged recession, but we have also described a direct mechanism by which residential real estate losses are transmitted to the financial sector, and we have indicated why the losses to households suppress consumption, especially of durable goods, and how suppressed consumption reduces capacity investment by firms.

In the Depression, as in the Great Recession, the deterioration of the resi-

---

34. This figure is calculated from NIPA table1.1.6, comparing 1929 and 1933 figures for GDP and for residential investment and personal consumption expenditures.

35. For the figures on nonresidential fixed investment and on residential investment during the Depression see footnote 9. Declines in nonresidential fixed investment in postwar recessions are taken from table 1 in Gjerstad and Smith (2012).

dential real estate market preceded the peak of the economic cycle and the broader downturn by two to three years; in both cases the damage to household balance sheets originated in residential real estate losses, and much of the damage suffered by financial sector firms resulted from transmission of households' real estate losses to financial sector firms.

This begs the question, "Why are losses on residential real estate so pernicious?" There are at least four primary reasons. First, residential real estate is illiquid, especially in a downturn when sales begin to decline. Second, it is often highly leveraged, and in the Depression we saw that mortgage credit was growing while sales and construction of new homes were falling, so leverage was increasing toward the end of the boom as prices began to fall. A third reason is that residential real estate assets are a large portion of national wealth and a large fraction of the wealth of many households, so that a downturn in residential real estate values has a substantial impact on household balance sheets and on their consumption levels, especially of durable goods and new housing assets. Finally, housing assets are immobile, so that there is no geographical redistribution of overbuilding in one area to other areas. For many real assets, redistribution is almost immediate, as with ships, airplanes, or locomotives. Even overbuilding of production capability, such as factories, would lead to a revaluation of the assets, but they would often remain utilized for export. Residential real estate is unusual in having few alternative uses when it is overbuilt. For all of these reasons, policies related to development and financing of residential real estate should be carefully considered.

References

Badgley, L. Durward. 1936. *Real Estate Transfer Index, Washington DC, 1893–1936.* Washington, DC: Division of Economics and Statistics, Federal Housing Administration.

Balke, Nathan S., and Robert J. Gordon. 1989. "The Estimation of Prewar Gross National Product: Methodology and New Evidence." *Journal of Political Economy* 97:38–92.

Bernanke, Ben S. 1983. "Nonmonetary Effects of the Financial Crisis in Propagation of the Great Depression." *American Economic Review* 73:257–76.

Boysen, Louis K. 1931. "A History of Real Estate Bonds." *Chicago Real Estate Magazine* 6 (23 May): 12–13.

Buchanan, Joy A., Steven Gjerstad, and Vernon L. Smith. 2012. "Underwater Recession." *The American Interest* May/June:20–28.

Bureau of Business Research. 1943. "Real Estate Transactions in Franklin County, Ohio: 1917–1937." Special Bulletin X-56, College of Commerce and Administration, Ohio State University.

Carney, Brian. 2008. "Bernanke Is Fighting the Last War." *Wall Street Journal,* October 18.

Colean, Miles L. 1944. *American Housing: Problems and Prospects*. New York: The Twentieth Century Fund.

Comptroller of the Currency. 1929, 1941. *Annual Report of the Comptroller of the Currency*. Washington, DC: US Government Printing Office.

Dolbeare, Harwood, and Merle O. Barnd. 1931. *Forewarnings of Bank Failure: A Comparative Study of the Statements of Certain Failed and Successful Florida State Banks, 1922–1928*. University of Florida, Business Administration Series, vol. 1, no. 1. Gainesville: University of Florida.

Fisher, Ernest M. 1951. *Urban Real Estate Markets: Characteristics and Financing*. New York: National Bureau of Economic Research.

Fisher, Irving. 1933. "The Debt-Deflation Theory of Great Depressions." *Econometrica* 1:337–57.

Friedman, Milton, and Anna J. Schwartz. 1963. *A Monetary History of the United States*. Princeton, NJ: Princeton University Press.

Gjerstad, Steven, and Vernon L. Smith. 2009. "From Bubble to Depression?" *Wall Street Journal*, April 6.

———. 2012. "At Home in the Great Recession." In *The 4% Solution: Unleashing the Economic Growth America Needs*, edited by Brendan Miniter, 50–79. New York: Crown Publishing Group.

Goldsmith, Raymond W. 1955. *A Study of Saving in the United States*, vol. 1. Princeton, NJ: Princeton University Press.

Grebler, Leo, David M. Blank, and Louis Winnick. 1956. *Capital Formation in Residential Real Estate*. Princeton, NJ: Princeton University Press.

Hoad, William M. 1942. "Real Estate Prices, A Study of Residential Real Estate Transfers in Lucas County, Ohio." PhD diss., University of Michigan.

Johnson, Ernest A. 1936a. "The Record of Long-Term Real Estate Securities." *Journal of Land and Public Utility Economics* 12:44–48.

———. 1936b. "The Record of Long-Term Real Estate Securities: By Cities of Issue." *Journal of Land and Public Utility Economics* 12:195–97.

Koester, Genevieve. 1939a. "Chicago Real Estate Bonds, 1919–1938: I. Corporate History." *Journal of Land and Public Utility Economics* 15:49–58.

———. 1939b. "Chicago Real Estate Bonds, 1919–1938: II. Market Behavior." *Journal of Land and Public Utility Economics* 15:201–11.

Kydland, Finn, and Edward C. Prescott. 1982. "Time to Build and Aggregate Fluctuations." *Econometrica* 50:1345–70.

Lucia, Joseph. 1985. "The Failure of the Bank of United States: A Reappraisal." *Explorations in Economic History* 22:402–16.

O'Brien, Anthony Patrick. 1992. "The Failure of the Bank of United States: A Defense of Joseph Lucia: Note." *Journal of Money, Credit and Banking* 24:374–84.

Persons, Charles E. 1930. "Credit Expansion, 1920 to 1929, and Its Lessons." *Quarterly Journal of Economics* 45:94–130.

Swanson, Joseph A., and Samuel H. Williamson. 1972. "Estimates of National Product and Income for the United States Economy, 1919–1941." *Explorations in Economic History* 10:53–73.

Temin, Peter. 1976. *Did Monetary Forces Cause the Great Depression?* New York: W.W. Norton and Co.

Vanderblue, Homer B. 1927a. "The Florida Land Boom." *Journal of Land and Public Utility Economics* 3:113–31.

———. 1927b. "The Florida Land Boom." *Journal of Land and Public Utility Economics* 3:252–69.

White, Eugene Nelson. 1984. "A Reinterpretation of the Banking Crisis of 1930." *Journal of Economic History* 44:119–38.

Wickens, David L. 1937. *Financial Survey of Urban Housing; Statistics on Financial Aspects of Urban Housing*. Washington, DC: US Government Printing Office.

———. 1941. *Residential Real Estate: Its Economic Position As Shown by Values, Rents, Family Incomes, Financing, and Construction, Together with Estimates for All Real Estate*. New York: National Bureau of Economic Research.

Wicker, Elmus. 1996. *The Banking Panics of the Great Depression*. Cambridge: Cambridge University Press.

Wigmore, Barrie A. 1985. *The Crash and Its Aftermath: A History of Securities Markets in the United States, 1929–1933*. Westport, CT: Greenwood Publishing Group, Incorporated.

Works Progress Administration. 1938. "Real Estate Activity Surveys: Intensive Analysis of Deeds and Mortgages Recorded in a Recent Period." WPA Technical Series. Research, Statistical, and Survey Project Circular no. 7, volume I. September 28, 1938. Washington, DC.

4

Lessons from the Great American Real Estate Boom and Bust of the 1920s

Eugene N. White

> You can have any kind of a home you want to; you can even
> get stucco. Oh, how you can get stuck-oh!
> —Groucho Marx, *The Cocoanuts* (1929)[1]

Although apparently dwarfed by the magnitude of the recent events, real estate booms and busts were not unknown in the past. Huge swings in real estate prices and construction occurred at long intervals, but they did not always spell disaster for the financial sector. Thus, an important question for today is not why there was a boom, but why its consequences were so severe for banks and other intermediaries compared to previous episodes. The 1920s, the 1980s, and the first years of the twenty-first century constitute the three great real estate events of the last one hundred years. Focusing on the 1920s is useful; for although many analysts of the current crisis maintain that its dimensions are unique, the overlooked twenties has surprisingly similar characteristics yet there was no banking crisis.

Complicating the analysis of current events are the many potential factors given for the boom. A short list of major contenders would include: (a) the

Eugene N. White is Distinguished Professor of Economics at Rutgers University and a research associate of the National Bureau of Economic Research.

For their comments and suggestions, I would especially like to thank Lee Alston, George Berry, Michael Bordo, Price Fishback, Richard Grossman, Kris Mitchener, Carolyn Moehling, John Landon-Lane, Hugh Rockoff, Kenneth Snowden, Peter Temin, and the participants of seminars at the Bank of England, Columbia University, the Federal Reserve Bank of Philadelphia, the Federal Reserve Bank of St. Louis, the Free University of Brussels, the German Historical Institute (Washington, DC), the Harvard Business School, Université Paris X Nanterre, the NBER Summer Institute, Rutgers University, the Universitat Pompeu Fabra, the University of Oslo, and the XVth World Economic History Conference, Utrecht. For acknowledgments, sources of research support, and disclosure of the author's material financial relationships, if any, please see http://www.nber.org/chapters/c12797.ack.

1. In popular culture, the 1920s real estate boom is remembered in the Marx Brothers' 1925 musical *The Cocoanuts*, which became the 1929 movie by the same name. In one scene in the film, Groucho Marx is an auctioneer of Florida land of questionable value.

Federal Reserve's excessively easy monetary policy; (b) the "Greenspan put"; (c) the failure of bank supervision; (d) moral hazard from "too big to fail" and deposit insurance; (e) deregulation of banking (notably the end of the Glass-Steagall Act); (f) the failure of rating agencies; (g) the excessive growth of Fannie Mae and Freddie Mac; (h) legislation promoting affordable housing; (i) international imbalances, notably high savings rates in China and East Asia; (j) unregulated derivatives markets; (k) greedy/predatory lenders; and (l) greedy/ignorant borrowers. These factors are used to structure my inquiry into the real estate boom of the twenties, which displayed many similar characteristics, including surging housing starts, strong regional elements, and financial innovation. Most elements blamed for the current crisis were present: weak supervision, securitization, and a fall in lending standards. The relatively more extreme character of these factors in the early twenty-first century, emphasizes the absence of policy and regulatory incentives for banks in the 1920s to take on more risk and increase their leverage.

Two monetary factors, often cited as central to the current crisis, were present in the 1920s. First, there was a "Greenspan put" that reduced money market volatility and the likelihood of a panic. Secondly, there were low interest rates that potentially provided fuel for the surge in building. However, alternative monetary policies, as defined by Taylor rules, would not have been enough to halt the boom. Whatever impetus came from these and other factors, banks were sufficiently well-capitalized and remained prudent lenders. Consequently, a drop in residential real estate prices constituted little threat to their solvency; and the storm passed without bringing down the financial system.

4.1   Why Was the 1920s Real Estate Bubble Forgotten?

Few economists have taken note of this early real estate bubble, perhaps because it was followed and obscured by the Great Depression. However, the wild boom in Florida did draw Galbraith's attention in *The Great Crash* (1954). He saw the rise and fall of Florida real estate as a classic speculative bubble: "The Florida boom was the first indication of the mood of the twenties and the conviction that God intended the American middle class to be rich."[2] Conceding that there were elements of substance, Galbraith viewed it as based on the self-delusion that the Florida swamps would be wonderful residential real estate. In spite of the fact that he saw the Florida land boom as a harbinger of the stock market bubble, Galbraith failed to recognize that it was a nationwide event.[3] How well the real estate boom

2. Galbraith (1954, 6).
3. In his stylized outline of financial crises, Kindleberger (1978) identifies a land boom, cresting in 1925, as preceding the stock market boom of 1928 to 1929, but does not provide further commentary.

of the 1920s was forgotten by economists is revealed in the first edition of Shiller's *Irrational Exuberance* (2000), where it is not even mentioned. Only in his 2007 presidential address to the Eastern Economic Association did Shiller shift his focus from equity to real estate markets. Yet Florida rates only a brief mention, and he describes the collapse as the result of a change in investor psychology prompted by the surprise increase in the supply of properties.

The more general collapse of residential investment and housing prices was, however, recognized by contemporaries. For example, Simpson (1933) found that there was an excessive expansion of residential construction in 1920s Chicago, abetted by an unholy alliance of real estate promoters, banks, and local politicians. In Cook County, he claimed that there were 151,000 improved lots and 335,000 vacant lots in the bust year of 1928, estimating it would take until 1960 to sell these properties based on his projection of future population growth. He considered Chicago to be an important example of the bubble, although Florida was the most conspicuous. Yet, beyond bewailing current conditions, Simpson provided few statistics and confounded the problems of the real estate bust with the Great Depression.

Early post–World War II research was focused on the recovery from the Depression. Morton (1956) and Grebler, Blank, and Winnick (1956) and others did not isolate the collapse of the 1920s from the Great Depression and treated it as one blur. Their implicit belief was that the New Deal reforms of banking and mortgage finance resolved most of the problems with real estate in the 1930s—thus the boom and bust of 1920s did not require special attention as a separate issue.

The only modern Great Depression study where there was a suggestion that the real estate collapse in the mid-1920s played a role in the Depression's onset was Temin's *Did Monetary Forces Cause the Great Depression?* (1976). Temin found that aggregate investment began to decline autonomously before 1929 and that the driving factor was the fall in construction after 1926, although he did not tie this to the demise of the residential housing boom. Two histories (Vickers 1994; Frazer and Guthrie 1995) provide details on the Florida boom but treat it as an isolated phenomenon. In a more recent national study, Field (1992) saw the general building boom of the 1920s as creating major problems for the economy. He identified a residential boom peaking in 1925, "a smaller orgy of apartment building" cresting in 1927, and a central business district upswing continuing through 1929. Yet, his emphasis was not on a bubble with excessive aggregate investment but on the consequences of unplanned and unregulated development that later blocked the recovery of existing subdivisions because it raised the transaction costs associated with titles and tax liens. Given this general amnesia, the first task of this chapter is to describe the dimensions of the national residential real estate boom that swept the country.

4.2   Measuring the Residential Housing Boom of the 1920s

Like the current boom and bust, the housing bubble that peaked in the mid-1920s primarily involved residential housing. In a decade of almost steady growth, the behavior of residential construction stands out among other macroeconomic aggregates, peaking in the middle of the decade and collapsing well in advance of the Great Depression. Figure 4.1 plots residential housing starts for the boom of the 1920s and the contemporary period.

The early series begins in 1889, the first year for when there is national data; it attains a peak in 1925 that was not surpassed until 1949. The contemporary series is noticeably more volatile, particularly in the 1970s and 1980s, when swings in inflation and interest rates buffeted the housing markets. In contrast, price stability of the gold standard period kept mortgage rates in Manhattan between 5 and 6 percent for the whole era, except for World War I.[4] As the population of the country was considerably smaller ninety years ago, the level of housing starts was lower, but the run-up during the booms is of the same magnitude. If 1920 and 2000 are considered baseline years, the boom of the twenties added 2.6 million units while the boom of the first decade of the twenty-first century added 1.3 million units, with starts 690,000 and 500,000 higher in the final years relative to the initial years.

Not all construction flourished during the boom of the 1920s, and residential housing dominated other types of construction expenditures. Whereas business construction, "other private construction," in figure 4.2, had been the largest component of construction in the pre–World War I era, residential construction surged ahead, more than doubling in importance. Business construction returned to prewar levels in the twenties, but the value of residential construction greatly exceeded its 1914 levels.

The subsequent stock market boom of 1928–1929 offers another useful comparison for measuring the magnitude of this surge in residential housing. Figure 4.3 depicts the value of new residential construction and the value of new stock issues, revealing the double real estate–stock market bubble of the 1920s, another parallel to the end-of-century double dotcom–real estate boom, but with the order reversed. Housing market run-ups are typically slower and smoother than in equity markets, but both experienced rapid upswings and quick declines. The peak in housing was reached when there was almost $10 billion in new residential construction for the two years 1925 and 1926, equaling the $10 billion absorbed by new securities issues in 1928 and 1929.

The thorniest problem encountered in measuring the real estate boom of the 1920s is the absence of an adequate housing price index. As is well

4. Grebler, Blank, and Winnick (1956, table 0-1).

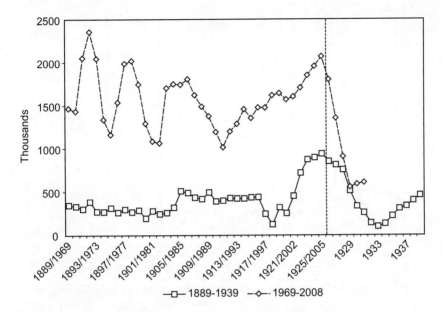

Fig. 4.1   Residential housing starts, 1889–1939 versus 1969–2011

Sources: Carter et al. (2006, series Dc510); *Economic Report of the President* (2009, table B-56).

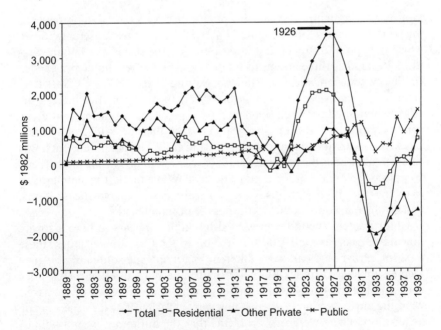

Fig. 4.2   Net real construction expenditures, 1889–1939

Source: Carter et al. (2006, series Dc87-90, series Cc66).

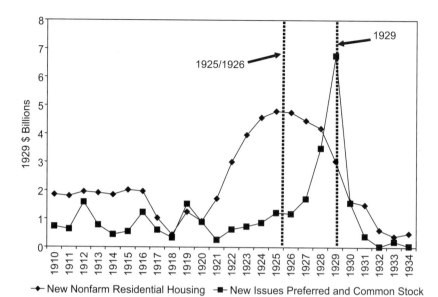

Fig. 4.3   Real new housing and new stocks issues, 1910–1934
Sources: Carter et al. (2006, series Cj835 and 836, new residential construction, series Dc257 for 1915–1939); and Grebler, Blank, and Winnick (1956, table B-5).

known, even contemporary housing price indices vary considerably depending on their construction.[5] Figures 4.4 and 4.5 report two different indices, which may point to upper and lower limits on the size of the bubble. Figure 4.4 examines three booms using the Case-Shiller real home price index (Shiller, www.econ.yale.edu/~shiller/). Setting 1920, 1984, and 2001 (five years before the price peaks) as the base years for three separate indices, the relative magnitude of each boom can be appreciated. In the current cycle, prices jumped 50 percent in five years to reach their peak in 2006. By this index, the 1920s does not appear to be as big as the current boom, but it was certainly as large as the boom in the 1980s with national housing prices rising 20 percent before declining over 10 percent. While modest by comparison to today, the eighties were disastrous for real estate in the Northeast, Texas, and California, contributing to the demise of many banks.

Unfortunately, the index presented by Shiller appears to have a strong downward bias for the 1920s. Grafted on to the Case-Shiller index, these data for earlier years are very different in origin. The source of this pre-Depression national index is Grebler, Blank, and Winnick (1956). This series is based on a 1934 survey of owners in twenty-two cities who were asked what the current value of their home was and what it cost in the year of acquisition. There were two problems that the authors were not able to

5. See, for example, OFHEO (2008).

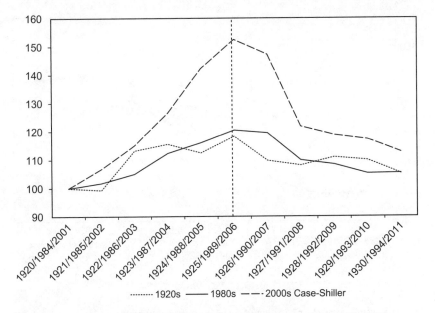

Fig. 4.4   The Case-Shiller index of real estate prices, 1920–1930, 1984–1994, 2000–2011

Source: Robert Shiller, www.econ.yale.edu/~shiller/.

address. First, the year-to-year volatility increases dramatically for the early years of the index, a feature that does not match the smooth movement of contemporary indices. This phenomenon may be attributable to the smaller and smaller number of observations in each year for houses that were purchased twenty, thirty, or forty years before 1934. Secondly, if foreclosures or abandonment of property were more common for owners who had bought late in the boom at high prices, the peak of the boom would be underestimated. The size of this potential downward bias is difficult to assess in the absence of sufficient additional national or regional data.

Florida, which may have had the biggest boom and crash in the twenties, has no housing prices index. One of the few available local series is the median asking price of single family homes in Washington, DC, which was not considered part of the boom regions.[6] Real prices of these homes rose 38 percent from 1920 to the peak, dropping by nearly 10 percent before 1929.[7] A rise of this magnitude alone would place the twenties as the second greatest real estate boom of the last one hundred years.

A superior hedonic real estate price index for Manhattan was recently

6. Carter et al. (2006, series Dc828).
7. The only other indexes are three-year moving averages for Cleveland and Seattle, while this averaging would tend to reduce the peaks, the Cleveland index still climbed 30 percent and the Seattle index 16 percent. (Grebler, Blank, and Winnick 1956, table C-2).

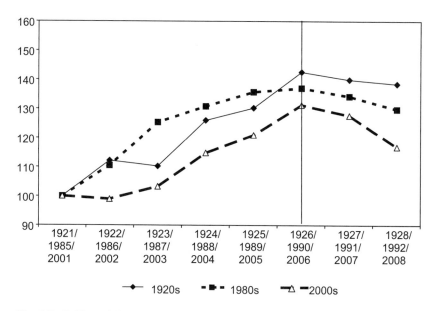

Fig. 4.5   Indices of the real value of a newly constructed house

Sources: Carter et al. (2006, series Dc257, value of new housing units, and series Dc520, number of new housing units started); *Economic Report of the President* (2009, table B-55, value of new residential housing units, and table B-56, new housing units started).

Note: All housing values are converted into real values using the Consumer Price Index. The value of a newly constructed house is equal to the value of new housing units divided by the number of new housing starts.

developed by Nicholas and Scherbina (2011) for 1920 to 1939. For this critical market, prices rose 54 percent between the fourth quarter of 1922 when the postwar recession ended and the second quarter of 1926, the acknowledged peak, before falling 28 percent to a low point in the second quarter of 1928. Their index also throws some light on real estate's potential path of recovery, had the Great Depression not hit the market a second time. By the third quarter of 1929, the market had fully recovered, probably benefitting from the stock market boom on Wall Street.

Figure 4.5 shows an index for the value of newly constructed homes that is comparable across all three booms. The real value of a newly constructed house is obtained by dividing the real value of all new housing units by the number of new housing starts. By this measure, the three booms enjoyed rises of 43 percent, 37 percent, and 31 percent during the five years before the peaks in 1926, 1990, and 2006. The most recent boom is smaller here than when measured by the Case-Shiller index because it focuses on new construction; and there was a greater rise in price of existing homes in established urban areas where urban amenities and constraints on development contributed to the boom (Glaeser, Gyourko, and Saks 2005). Combined with the regional real estate prices and the surge in starts, this evidence reveals that the boom was not confined to Florida. The Case-Shiller index appears to seriously underestimate its magnitude and the additional data suggest that the 1920s boom rivaled the early twenty-first century boom in some dimensions.

4.3   A Post–World War I Catch-Up?

The underlying macroeconomic conditions for the 1920s and the early twenty-first century also share some common characteristics.[8] Unemployment was low and growth was good. Likewise there had been a reduction in inflation. The great moderation in inflation after World War I, when the Federal Reserve took an activist role, attempting to lean against the prevailing macroeconomic winds, suggests that its role in the housing market requires close inspection. Just as critics today have blamed the Fed for firing up the boom, the Fed of the twenties may have contributed to the earlier jump in real estate prices if it had an excessively easy monetary policy or increased risk taking by reducing the fear of a panic. Yet, before turning to the role of the Fed, there are two other fundamentals that need to be accounted for: international imbalances and the post–World War I recovery of residential construction.

The enormous financing needs of World War I crowded out nonessential investment and consumption as resources were transferred to the government. Repressed demand helped to fuel the postwar boom in goods and inventories, but demand for housing was also constrained.[9] To examine the possibility that the upsurge in home construction in the mid-1920s was only a catch-up, I provide some forecasts of what would have happened if World War I had not occurred. After first differencing to ensure the stationarity of the variables, I regressed housing starts and the real value of construction on real GDP, population, and the Manhattan mortgage rate for the years 1889 to 1914.[10] The exercise is similar to Taylor's (2009) counterfactual analysis for the recent period.

The actual and predicted out-of-sample values for housing starts and the value of new construction are plotted in figures 4.6 and 4.7. The results diminish substantially the appearance of a bubble in the aggregate data. Housing starts and the value of new construction would have followed slow-

---

8. A factor commonly cited as a cause of the recent real estate boom is international imbalances, propelled by high savings rates in China and elsewhere in Asia that have led to the purchase of US government and agency securities. The opposite environment prevailed in the 1920s, as the United States had just switched from being a major net debtor to a major net lender. Whereas in 1908 foreign investments of $6.4 billion far exceeded the $2.5 billion of US investments abroad, by 1924 these had swung to $3.9 billion and $15.1 billion, respectively. This accelerating flow of American funds abroad was not sufficient to contain the boom, though it may have slowed it down.

9. For details on World War I finance, see Edelstein (2000) and Rockoff (2012)

10. The series are from Carter et al. (2006, series Dc510, Dc522), and Grebler, Blank, and Winnick (1956, table O-1).

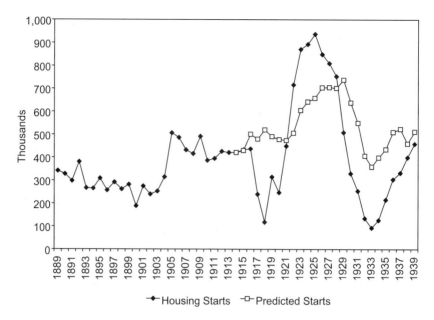

Fig. 4.6   Actual and forecast residential housing starts, 1889–1939
Source: Carter et al. (2006, series Dc510) and the text.

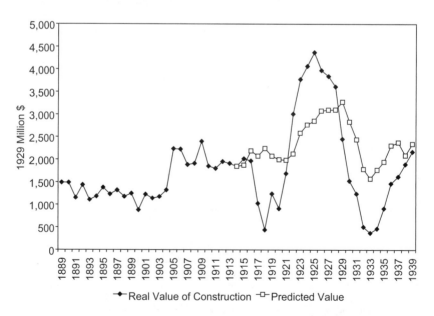

Fig. 4.7   Actual and predicted value of real new residential construction, 1889–1939
Source: Carter et al. (2006, series Dc522) and the text.

paced growth without the war and increased later as real incomes grew faster, until halted by the Great Depression. While predicted values are below their actual levels in the 1920s, the predicted wartime levels are higher. If we consider the deficit in housing starts during World War I, defined as 1917 to 1920, there were 1,049,000 starts that never materialized. In contrast there were 1,306,000 starts in excess of the predicted during the early twenties. The difference, 256,000, might be considered as a measure of the "bubble." While this may seem small, it is two-thirds of the annual average starts for 1900 to 1917. If we examine the value of new construction, there was a shortfall of $4.9 billion during the years 1917 to 1920 and "excess" construction of $7.3 billion during the boom years of the 1920s. Given that the average real value of construction was $1.8 billion for 1900 to 1917, a difference of $2.9 billion suggests that there was more to the boom than a simple postwar recovery.[11]

4.4   Was the Federal Reserve Responsible for the Boom?

Could the Federal Reserve have been responsible for this residual surge in construction? There are two channels through which the Fed could have driven activity higher: (a) a promise by the central bank to prevent a financial crisis, and (b) keeping interest rates abnormally low.

The promise that the central bank will prevent a financial crisis is often called the "Greenspan put." This phrase was coined after the 1998 collapse of Long-Term Capital Management when it was believed that the then chairman of the Federal Reserve Board, Alan Greenspan, would lower interest rates whenever necessary to preserve stability capital markets forgoing price stability. Because this appeared to guarantee an orderly exit of sellers, he was criticized because the moral hazard of such a policy would encourage excessive risk taking, thereby contributing to a boom. In addition to observers on the street, some academics (see Miller, Weller, and Zhang 2002) argue that this policy was at least partially responsible for the subsequent dotcom boom.

A version of this "Greenspan put" may have emerged in the 1920s because the establishment of the Federal Reserve System substantially reduced the threat of crises and panics by changing the stochastic behavior of interest

---

11. Some observers argued that the spread of the automobile that furthered suburban expansion may have been a new fundamental. To approximate the effects of the automobile and suburbanization in the 1920s, I added a variable, the miles of streets and roads under control of the states, to the regressions (Carter et. al. 2006, series Df184). However, this series only begins in 1904. Given the paucity of observations before 1914, it was not possible to obtain meaningful estimates for out-of-sample forecasts, so the estimated coefficients for a full sample of 1904 to 1939 were used. The coefficient on the variable for roads for the regressions with housing starts and the value of construction was insignificant. There may also be some reason to doubt that suburbanization was responsible for the housing boom. In the absence of the automobile, there could just as easily have been a greater housing boom in the central cities substituting for suburban growth and overcoming the wartime housing deficit.

rates. As is well known, the Fed was founded in response to the Panic of 1907 and charged in the Federal Reserve Act of 1913 to "furnish an elastic currency." The Fed considered it a central obligation to eliminate the seasonal strain in financial markets, as the first *Annual Report* emphasized "its duty is not to await emergencies but by anticipation, to do what it can to prevent them."[12] Miron (1986) documented that the Federal Reserve promptly carried out policies that reduced the seasonality of interest rates. Because panics occurred in periods when seasonal increases in loan demand and decreases in deposit demand strained the financial system, accommodating credit to seasonal shocks reduced the potential of a crisis. Comparing 1890 to 1908 and 1919 to 1928, Miron found the standard deviation of the seasonal for call loans fell from 130 to 46 basis points, with the amplitude dropping from 600 to 230 basis points.[13] This reduction of seasonality in interest rates lowered the stress on the financial system, leading Miron to conclude that it had eliminated banking panics during the period 1915 to 1929. Most striking was the absence of a panic during the severe recession of 1920 to 1921. Both the timing in the decline of seasonality and the role of the Fed have been challenged, but Miron's basic results have been upheld.[14] By reducing the volatility of the financial markets, the Fed may have induced additional risk taking, contributing to the real estate boom of the mid-twenties.[15]

In addition to a "Greenspan put," the Fed has been attacked for lax monetary policy in the years preceding the 2008 crisis. John Taylor (2009) has been one of its leading critics. Instead of adhering to policies that match a Taylor rule, as it had in the prior twenty years, he has argued that beginning in 2001 the Fed kept the federal funds rate far below what a Taylor rule would require. The result was that there "was no greater or more persistent deviation of actual Fed policy since the turbulent days of the 1970s," fueling the housing boom of the early twenty-first century. In response, Greenspan argued that although mortgage rates had been tightly correlated with the federal funds from 1971 to 2002, this relationship "diminished to insignifi-

12. Federal Reserve Board, *First Annual Report of the Federal Reserve Board* (1914, 17).

13. During World War I, the Fed ceded control of the level of interest rates to the Treasury, which wanted to ensure that it could float bonds at low nominal rates. Nevertheless, the Fed first began to dampen seasonals in 1915 by rediscounting bills backed by agricultural commodities at preferential rates, continuing this program until 1918. Gaining control over its discount rate in 1919, the Fed acted more directly. A measure of the Fed's intervention was its credit outstanding. Over the period 1922 to 1928, Miron (1986) calculated that there was an increase in the level of reserve credit outstanding over the seasonal cycle of 32 percent or approximately $400 million per year at a time when New York City banks' loans totaled $6 billion.

14. See Clark (1986), Mankiw, Miron, Weil (1987), Barsky et al. (1988), Fishe and Wohar (1990), Kool (1995), and Caporale and McKiernan (1998).

15. The Fed may also have induced more risk taking by providing banks near the brink of failure with loans from the discount window, contravening the rule that a central bank should lend only to illiquid not insolvent banks. In 1925, the Federal Reserve estimated that 80 percent of the 259 national banks that had failed since 1920 were "habitual borrowers." These banks were provided with long-term credit. A survey in August 1925 found that 593 member banks had been borrowing for a year or more and 293 had been borrowing since 1920 (Schwartz 1992).

cance" during the boom. Greenspan asserted that global forces were behind this change over which the Fed had little control (Greenspan 2009).

Taylor might have levied the same criticism against the Fed in the 1920s. To measure whether monetary policy was easy or tight, I apply similar Taylor rules to the Federal Reserve in the 1920s.[16] The Taylor rule is linear in the interest rate and the logarithms of the price level and real output. Using the inflation rate and the deviation of real output from a stochastic trend renders the two variables stationary. The result was a linear equation:

(1) $$r = (r^* + \pi) + h(\pi - \pi^*) + gy,$$

where r is the short-term policy interest rate, r^* is the equilibrium rate of interest, π is the inflation rate and π^* is the target inflation rate, and y is the percentage deviation of real output from trend. The policy response coefficients to inflation and the output gap are $(1 + h)$ and g, with the intercept term being $r^* - h\pi^*$. If h is greater than zero, then the policy rate will rise, not decline, in response to an increase in inflation.

Taylor's original formulation (Taylor 1993) had the federal funds rate adjusted in a fixed response to changes in inflation and the gap in real GDP, which fairly accurately described the then recent policy actions of the Federal Reserve. Even though there was no central bank or instrument like the federal funds rate, Taylor (1999) extended his model to earlier periods. For a period like late nineteenth-century America, which operated under a gold standard without a central bank, there still should have been a relationship between short-term interest rates and inflation. If a shock induced inflation in the United States, the price-specie-flow mechanism would have produced a balance-of-payments deficit with consequent losses of gold, a decline in the money stock, and a rise in interest rates. Similarly, rising real output would have increased the demand for funds and raised interest rates.

In a simple OLS estimate of his equation for the gold standard era, Taylor (1999) found low positive coefficients for inflation and the output gap.[17] If once the Fed was established, it played by the "rules of the game" and "leaned against the wind," the operation of the adjustment mechanism should have been reinforced and the response coefficients in the Taylor equation should be larger. Taylor did not follow his empirical investigation of the pre-Fed era with one for the 1920s. Instead, he lumped the twenties

16. More generally, Taylor (1999) viewed his work as focusing on the short-term interest rate side of monetary policy, rather than the money stock side. Instead of the quantity equation that had informed Friedman and Schwartz's (1963) analysis of American monetary history, Taylor formulated his monetary policy rule that was derived from the quantity equation.

17. Taylor (1999) estimated equation (1) using ordinary least squares with the commercial paper rate for the years 1879 to 1914, with inflation measured as the average inflation rate over four quarters. He did not correct for serial correlation, allowing for the possibility that monetary policy mistakes were serially correlated. He pointed out that serial correlation was high under the gold standard, and hence the equations fit poorly and his t-statistics are not useful for hypothesis testing.

and the thirties together and dismissed the Fed's efforts to find an effective rule in the interwar period because of its disastrous performance during the Great Depression. In contrast, Orphanides (2003) offers a more positive Taylor rule assessment of the Fed's actions in the 1920s, but his is a narrative appraisal.

To characterize Fed policy in the 1920s and examine counterfactual policies, I have estimated a Taylor equation for the late nineteenth and early twentieth centuries. Table 4.1 reports the estimates for a Taylor equation on quarterly data for the last years of the classical gold standard 1890 to 1914 and for the interwar gold standard, 1922 to 1929. The war years and the postwar boom and bust of 1915 to 1921 are omitted because the Fed was not free to operate as an independent central bank but instead served the interests of the Treasury. For 1890 to 1914, the interest rate is the time rate for brokers' loans, rather than the commercial paper rate used by Taylor. The market for brokers' loans was larger than for commercial paper and more closely approximates the market for federal funds as banks often parked excess funds in this market. Using the commercial paper rate or the call rate on brokers' loans did not substantially alter the results. The gross national product (GNP) data were obtained from Balke and Gordon (1986), and the output gap as the percentage deviation of real output from the trend is extracted by a Hodrick-Prescott filter.[18] The inflation rate is derived from Balke and Gordon's GNP deflator.

The first two rows of table 4.1 report the results for the Taylor equation under the classical gold standard, where the instrumental variables are the second lags on inflation, the output gap, and the time rate. These regressions produce fairly consistent results, recalling that with the lagged dependent variable the estimated coefficients are $(1 - \rho)\beta$. Hence the constant is an interest rate of approximately 4 percent. Once adjusted for this factor, the coefficients on inflation and the output gap are in the vicinity of 0.10 to 0.20, and thus smaller than the coefficients for the last twenty years of the twentieth century when the coefficient on inflation was well over one and on the output gap, somewhat under one, implying that the Fed was pursuing a stable policy. The results are similar to Taylor's (1999) and reflect the behavioral relationships in the absence of a central bank.

Taylor equations are first estimated for 1922 to 1929 using the time rate for brokers' loans. In contrast to Taylor's glum assessment, these results suggest that the Fed acted appropriately, as Friedman and Schwartz (1963) have argued. The response coefficients for inflation and the output gap are positive and significant. Furthermore, they appear to be of an appropriate magnitude once they are adjusted for the presence of the lagged depen-

18. The Hodrick-Prescott filter is used to estimate the trend from 1890.1 to 1930.2. Covering a longer period causes a sharp decline in the trend in 1929 because of the persistence of the Great Depression, creating a huge and unrealistic output gap for 1929.

Table 4.1   Taylor equation estimates

		Constant	Inflation	Output gap	Lagged dependent variable	Lagged excess interest seasonal	Adjusted $R2$
Time rate OLS	1890.1–1914.4	2.657*** (0.416)	0.084** (0.037)	0.069* (0.038)	0.360*** (0.094)	—	0.231
Time rate IV	1890.1–1914.4	2.727*** (0.442)	0.139 (0.107)	0.065* (0.039)	0.331*** (0.109)	—	0.214
Time rate OLS	1922.1–1929.4	0.642 (0.576)	0.179*** (0.058)	0.149*** (0.051)	0.896*** (0.113)	—	0.678
Time rate IV	1922.1–1929.4	0.695 (0.583)	0.147** (0.070)	0.128** (0.058)	0.881*** (0.114)	—	0.675
NYFDR OLS	1922.1–1929.4	0.708 (0.599)	0.054 (0.035)	0.031 (0.031)	0.838*** (0.146)	—	0.548
NYFDR IV	1922.1–1929.4	0.846 (0.644)	0.035 (0.046)	0.018 (0.038)	0.801*** (0.159)	—	0.544
NYFDR OLS	1922.1–1929.4	.0130 (0.662)	0.049 (0.034)	0.015 (0.031)	0.981*** (0.162)	-0.409* (0.229)	0.581
NYFDR IV	1922.1–1929.4	0.227 (0.685)	0.035 (0.042)	0.005 (0.036)	0.956*** (0.169)	-0.416* (0.230)	0.578

Note: Instruments are second lags on inflation, the output gap, and the time rate. Standard errors are in parentheses.
***Significant at the 1 percent level.
**Significant at the 5 percent level.
*Significant at the 10 percent level.

dent variable. The coefficient on inflation has a value greater than one. Of course, the Fed did not operate directly in the brokers' loan market or the commercial paper market, instead its instrument was the discount rate, buttressed by open market purchases and sales. The next two equations apply the same model with the Federal Reserve Bank of New York's discount rate as the dependent variable. Unfortunately, the discount rate was changed infrequently, leading policy to look particularly feeble unless one views its impact through the brokers' loan market where it was apparently robust.

While Taylor's equations capture the focus of contemporary policy, they do not include a measure of the seasonal problems that Miron showed were a vital component of Fed policy. To correct this omission, I include a variable for excess seasonality. Using the time rate, I constructed a centered moving average that deseasonalized the data. Taking the absolute value of the difference between the actual values and the deseasonalized values, I obtained a measure of the degree of seasonality (Wilson and Keating 2002). Although the Fed certainly would have responded more quickly if its efforts to reduce seasonality appeared weak, I include the lagged value of the difference between the time rate and the centered moving average as a measure of the response of the Fed to excess seasonality. In the last two regressions this variable has a negative and significant coefficient, suggesting that it is capturing an important feature of Fed policy even on a quarterly basis. If there was an excessive seasonal in the interest rate, the Fed intervened to reduce it.

By these simple measures, Fed policy in the 1920s appears to have been largely run in accordance with the "rules of the game" while lowering the risk of a panic. This "new regime," appearing in the 1920s, should have increased investor confidence by reducing inflation risk and panic risk. These estimates show that Fed policy moved in the right direction but the question remains as to whether policy was too loose or too tight. To address the counterfactual question of whether the Fed should have conducted policy differently in the 1920s, I apply some simple Taylor rules that have been invoked to judge recent Fed policy.

The first simple Taylor rule is Taylor's original rule with the policy response coefficients set equal to 0.50. The second rule sets the coefficient on the output response at 1.0 (Taylor 1999). When applied to the second half of the twentieth century, they show that the Fed funds rate was particularly low in the late 1960s, the 1970s, and possibly the late 1990s. In figure 4.8, these two rules are applied to the 1920s, omitting World War I when the Fed purposely kept rates low. It is important to note that the Taylor rule is being applied here when there is no target rate of inflation π^*, as in equation (1). The gold standard promised long-term price stability at the expense of short-term price volatility. In this case, the implicit inflation rate target is zero. The Fed funds rate real rate is assumed in the Taylor rule to be 2.0 percent. However, this value cannot be used for the earlier periods because the real rate for the time rate on brokers' loans was higher because they had more risk. The

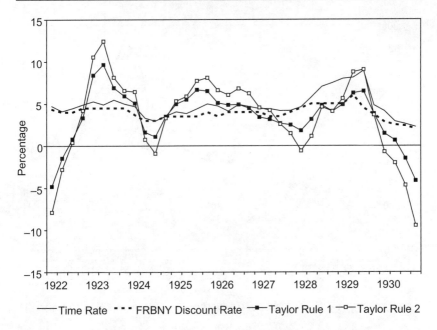

Fig. 4.8   Taylor rules and the rate of interest, 1922–1930

nominal rate averaged 5 percent for 1922 to 1929, but was closer to 4 percent before the stock market bubble of 1928 to 1929 distorted it (Rappoport and White 1994). Taking into consideration a zero inflation rate target, the real rate of interest was 4 to 5 percent. A value of 4 percent is used to construct figure 4.8, though a 5 percent value yielded similar results.

The Taylor rules have a greater amplitude than the time rate or discount rate, suggesting that that Fed policy, while appropriate, was not sufficiently vigorous. Of course, the rule is not a precise formulation of policy as it would sometimes dictate negative rates of interest.[19] Could the Fed have pursued even stronger policies in the 1920s? What is the importance of the gap between the actual interest rates and the counterfactual Taylor rates? Taylor (1999) found that policy was first too loose in the early 1960s when the gap between the federal funds rate and Taylor rule 1 was at 2 to 3 percent for three and a half years. Then, in the late 1960s to the late 1970s, it rose to 4 to 6 percent creating the "Great Inflation." Taylor's counterfactual for 2001 to 2006 pointed to a policy gap as great as 3 percent. Taylor rules in figure 4.8 suggest that policy should have been eased more quickly during the severe contraction of 1920 to 1921. It was too easy in the following boom and too tight in the short recession that followed. For the housing market,

19. Taylor (1999, 338n13) recognized this problem for analyzing alternative policy in the 1960s.

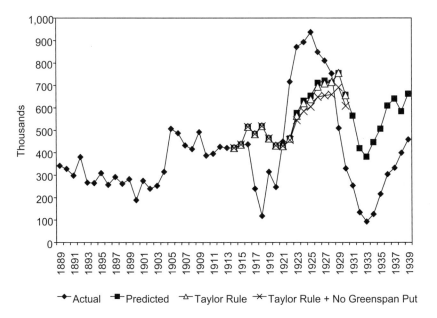

◆ Actual   ■ Predicted   △ Taylor Rule   ✕ Taylor Rule + No Greenspan Put

Fig. 4.9   The effects of alternative monetary policies on housing starts

it appears that policy eased considerably beginning in 1925 and remained loose through 1926 with the gap between the market rate and the counterfactual, peaking at 2 percent for Taylor rule 1 and staying above 2 percent for Taylor rule 2 from 1925.2 through 1926.3. These years were crucial for the housing boom and suggest, at least by the measure of the early 1960s, that the magnitude of the error was substantial and may have contributed to igniting a housing boom.

What impact could different monetary policies have had on the housing boom of the 1920s? Figure 4.9 shows the actual and predicted movements in housing starts depicted in figure 4.6. The only difference is that the predicted housing starts use the time rate on brokers' loans rather than a mortgage rate. The results differ very little but permit an exercise in counterfactual monetary policy.[20] The first question is what would have happened to housing starts if monetary policy had followed Taylor rule 1. The effect of the policy is measured as the difference between predicted housing starts and the Taylor rule. As is evident, the higher interest rates during the boom that the Taylor rule would have required would have had scant impact on housing starts.

The effects of abandoning the Greenspan put are greater, as seen in figure

20. As already noted, mortgages rates during the 1920s were quite flat and apparently unresponsive to the fluctuations in short rates. For the twenty-first century bubble, this phenomenon was also noted by Taylor (2007) who attributed it to perceived changes in the responsiveness to inflation in short rates. In the 1920s, long-run inflation would have been checked by the gold standard and thus have steadied longer rates.

4.9 with a line that combines the effect of the Taylor rule plus the Greenspan put. This effect is measured by forecasting out of sample, using a regression that adds the excess seasonality variable. In the forecast, the excess seasonality of the pre-Fed era, averaging 0.74 is substituted for the actual values that averaged 0.25 in the 1920s. The results of this exercise show that if the Fed had allowed seasonal rates to fluctuate as they had before 1914 there would have been a reduction in starts. Over the period 1922 to 1926, this "put" combined with tighter Taylor rule policy would have lowered housing starts by 196,000. The excess housing starts—the difference between the actual and predicted starts—was 1,306,000 for these years, suggesting that a different policy would have had little effect. If on the other hand, one believes that the higher postwar housing were mostly a catch-up from the wartime deficit, then there were only excess housing starts of 256,000. A reduction of 196,000 starts would have virtually eliminated this excess, suggesting that a different policy could have limited the extremes of the boom.

Of course, Federal Reserve policy in the 1920s was not focused on the housing markets. The alternative policy suggested previously would have been a radical departure from the mandate given in the Federal Reserve Act, and no one suggested that it should abandon its established policy. Even if the Fed had wanted to include the housing market in its policy deliberations, there were no national indices, as there were for industrial production. The Federal Reserve was more focused on short-term rates, which it could directly influence and whose importance was validated by the real bills doctrine that emphasized the centrality of short-term finance (Friedman and Schwartz 1963; Meltzer 2003; Wicker 1966; Wheelock 1991). Longer-term interest rates that played a role in the housing market drew far less attention than brokers' loan and related short-term rates that influenced the stock market boom. Centered in New York, the capital markets captured the concern of the Fed, but the housing market still had strong regional elements, yielding a more complex and less easily interpreted picture. Thus, the more realistic counterfactual of following a Taylor rule but not eliminating the put leaves a substantial housing boom.

4.5   A Reduction in Lending Standards?

A decline in lending standards, leading to an expansion of the mortgage market, is often cited as an important contributing factor in the boom of the early twenty-first century and the collapse of the financial sector. The expansion of mortgage credit in the 1920s was also facilitated by a loosening of lending standards with aggressive new intermediaries increasing their market share. Although the evidence for the twenties is fragmentary, there appears a more modest drop in lending standards for mortgages held by financial institutions.

The real estate boom of the 1920s saw an upswing in mortgage financing, fostered by the expansion of new entrants into the business. Mortgage fund-

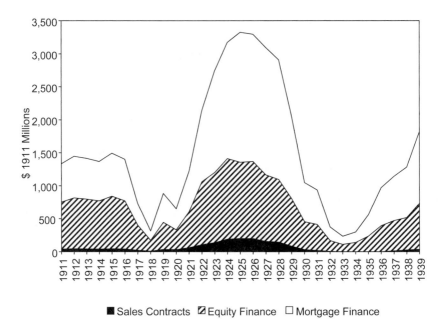

■ Sales Contracts   ▨ Equity Finance   ☐ Mortgage Finance

Fig. 4.10   Sources of funding for residential construction, 1911–1939
Sources: Grebler, Blank, and Winnick (1956, table M-1).The values are deflated by the Consumer Price Index. Carter et al. (2006, series Cc1).

ing, which had accounted for less than 45 percent of residential construction finance before World War I, rose to nearly 60 percent at the height of the boom. Depicted in figure 4.10, this change shows the rise in the real funding of residential construction by source. Mortgages, which had constituted less than half of funding in the prewar years, supplied over $2 billion of the $3.3 billion in financing for 1926.

One force behind the increase in mortgage finance was the shift in the sources of finance. Mortgage funding by source is shown in figure 4.11. Noninstitutional lending—friends, family and private local individuals—had been slowly declining since the turn of the century when it had accounted for over half the market. In the boom it fell further from 42.2 to 37.1 percent between 1920 and 1926. Mutual savings banks, which had been the largest source of institutional lending before the First World War, saw their share shrink from 19.5 to 17.6 percent over the same period. The more aggressive lenders gained ground in this short period, with commercial banks expanding from 8.8 to 10.8 percent, insurance companies from 6.2 to 8.1 percent, and savings and loans associations from 20.4 to 23.2 percent. These three innovators expanded their total mortgages by 76, 79, and 62 percent in these six years.[21]

21. Information on the sources of mortgage funding is found in Carter et al. (2006, series Dc903–928).

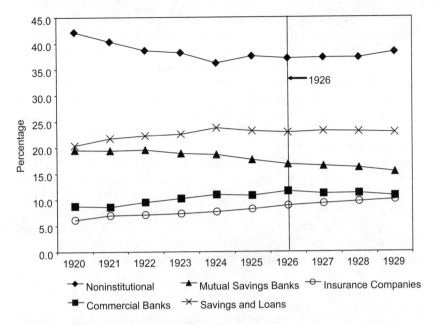

Fig. 4.11   Shares of mortgages lending by source
Source: Carter et al. (2006, series Dc907-911).

Before reviewing the available data on how the terms of mortgages changed, it is important to note that the long-term fixed interest amortized mortgage that became a standard in the early post–World War II era was uncommon before the Great Depression. Most mortgages were short-term, many had only partial or no amortization with very low loan-to-value ratios, and balloon mortgages were not uncommon. Thus, the heterogeneous contemporary mortgage market resembles more its pre-Depression ancestor than the market in the first three to four decades after World War II when there was a greater standardization.

The only detailed source of data for mortgage contracts in the 1920s is Morton (1956), who drew upon samples of loan portfolios for several hundred financial institutions. Of course, these were institutions that had survived the ravages of the Great Depression and presumably had followed more conservative practices than those that disappeared. Yet, even taking into account this survivor bias, the changes in lending for the three fastest-growing mortgage lenders appear to be far from reckless.

Commercial banks eased terms, letting their nonamortized loans increase from 41 to 51 percent in the loans sampled for 1920 to 1924 and 1925 to 1929, while the share of fully amortized loans dropped from 15 to 10 percent. The average contract length was approximately three years. Thus, the most common loans at commercial banks were nonamortized "balloon" mortgages of short duration. From the lenders' point of view these were hardly risky loans as the loan-to-value ratios averaged just above 50 percent.[22]

Although often termed savings and loan associations, the pre-Depression building and loan associations had both professional full-time firms and part-time associations that pooled members' weekly or monthly dues to lend to members to buy homes. Many of the latter were managed by real estate professionals and builders who had conflicts of interest. In contrast to commercial banks, amortized loans dominated the portfolios of building and loan associations, constituting 95 percent of the mortgages sampled. The contract lengths were almost all under fifteen years, with a mean length of eleven years. The B&Ls were one of the market innovators, developing low down payment mortgages. One product was the "Philadelphia Plan" where a B&L would issue a second amortized mortgage for 30 percent of the property value after the borrower had a first, interest only loan from a bank or other intermediary for 50 percent of the value. Eventually, the B&Ls began to issue both mortgages, even though some in the industry raised concerns about the increased risks to borrower and lender (Snowden 2010). These "affordable" products enabled the B&Ls to grab a greater market share during the boom.

Insurance companies offered a more varied mix of loans than either B&Ls or commercial banks in the 1920s, giving 20 percent nonamortized loans in the first half of the decade and 24 percent in the second half. Less than 20 percent of these mortgages were fully amortized. Contract length for loans from insurance companies averaged six years but had greater variance than other institutions with 20 percent lasting zero to four years, 51 percent five to nine years, and 26 percent ten to fourteen years.

As most observers noted, interest rates for mortgages were relatively "sticky"—moving very little over long periods of time—in comparison to other long term interest rates, such as bond yields. Grebler, Blank, and Winnick (1956) provide some data on interest rates by cities shown in figure 4.12. The first series for Manhattan was taken from the *Real Estate Analyst*. The authors composed the second series from the *Real Estate Record and Guide*, where the interest rates were weighted by the dollar value of all reported loans for March, July, and November. Similar data were available for the Bronx, which they considered to be almost entirely residential real estate and hence a better reflection of that market. Lastly, the authors compiled the St. Louis series from the *Real Estate Analyst* and the *St. Louis Daily Record*, which they believed was primarily for one-to-four family home mortgages.[23]

---

22. It is very conservative compared to the norms of the past three decades. From 1980 to 2007, the loan-to-value ratios for conventional single-family mortgages varied between 73 and 79 percent (Joint Center for Housing Studies of Harvard University 2008, table A-3).

23. Grebler, Blank, and Winnick (1956) also report a Chicago series from the graphs in Homer Hoyt's *One Hundred Years of Land Values in Chicago* (1933). They regarded Hoyt's rates as crude approximations for the value of property in the central business district. The Chicago series is not reported here as its value seems dubious given that reported rates remained fixed for decades then experienced huge jumps.

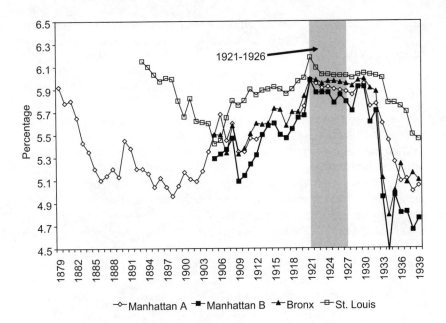

–◇– Manhattan A –■– Manhattan B –▲– Bronx –□– St. Louis

Fig. 4.12   Mortgage rates by city, 1879–1939
Source: Grebler, Blank, and Winnick (1956, table O-1).

Three facts emerge from figure 4.12. First, St. Louis rates are higher, perhaps reflecting high regional premiums. Second, and most importantly, rates were relatively more volatile in the years before the founding of the Fed, a fact which is consistent with the behavior of short-term rates. The 1920s appear to be remarkably stable with very little movement in Manhattan, the Bronx, or St. Louis. Third, the mild decline in rates shown in the national sample contract data reported by Morton (1956) is also present for the city-level data. Overall, the impetus to a real estate boom in the 1920s from a reduction in the level of mortgage rates seems minor, given the very small declines and the lower rates that persisted before the founding of the Federal Reserve. However, if stability was a spur to the boom, as the econometric evidence suggests in the previous section, then the 1920s market had a new stimulus.

While it is difficult to draw a definitive conclusion from this admittedly patchy data, the changes in lending standards and mortgage rates in the 1920s seem quite modest, except perhaps for the building and loan associations. It is unlikely that the expansion of mortgage lending exposed financial intermediaries to significant risk because of the very conservative loan-to-value ratios, typically of 40 or 50 percent. Even with a loan-to-value ratio of 20 percent, the B&Ls seem relatively cautious, though their contemporaries thought they were taking excessive risks. In general, even though housing prices fell significantly, there was little potential for a financial crisis after 1926 because mortgages originated and held by financial institutions only carried a modest risk, barring an unforeseen cataclysm such as the Great Depression. The real estate collapse that followed 1926 did not fall into that category, as the market showed some signs of recovery in 1929.

4.6   Reckless Securitization?

The 1920s also witnessed a wave of securitization of residential and commercial mortgages.[24] Real estate bonds were issued against single large commercial mortgages or pools of commercial or real estate mortgages. Single-property bonds financed construction of commercial buildings, notably offices, hotels, apartments, and theaters, in major cities. Figure 4.13 shows the annual increases in outstanding mortgage debt and real estate bonds. Although mortgage debt approximately doubled between 1922 and the peak, the growth of real estate bonds is impressive, with residential bonds representing a key component.[25] The experience of this bond market parallels the contemporary development of subprime securities. Both constituted modest but important shares of the market and both had much more dismal investment outcomes than mortgages directly held by financial intermediaries.[26]

Critical to the development of the real estate bond market was New York State's legalization of private mortgage insurance in 1904, after which securitization blossomed in the state. Title and mortgage guarantee companies were permitted to offer insurance not just against a defect in a land title but also against the nonpayment of mortgages. These companies began to originate and sell mortgages, servicing them after sale. In a development similar to the contemporary role of Fannie Mae and Freddie Mac, these firms provided explicit default insurance policies, promising purchasers that they would have a default-free income stream from investing in participation certificates in mortgage pools. In the absence of a secondary market, the bond houses offered to repurchase the securities, in effect giving a put to their customers. These policies were apparently unhedged and concentrated risk in the originating companies, subsequently contributing to widespread failures.

To protect the buyers, title and mortgage insurance companies were required by law to maintain a reserve fund, expressed as a percentage of their capital and surplus rather than the volume of their outstanding insurance commitments. They were thus constrained more by their reputation than regulation to set aside sufficient reserves. Transparency was limited

24. This description draws heavily on Snowden's (1995) history of American mortgage securitization.

25. The aggregate figures for mortgage debt and real estate bonds omit many small issues that began to flood the market in 1925, which in itself was an indicator of the boom. See Fisher (1951).

26. For instance, Alt-A and subprime mortgages each constituted 13 percent of the total new mortgage-backed securities in 2006. See Coval, Jurek, and Stafford (2009), Gorton (2008), and Mayer, Pence, and Sherlund (2009).

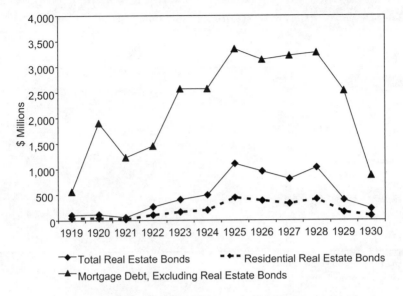

Fig. 4.13   Increases in the outstanding mortgage debt and real estate bonds, 1919–1930
Sources: Grebler, Blank, and Winnick (1956) and Carter et al. (2006, series Dc904-906).

as the companies served as their own depositories and could substitute new loans for the original mortgages. There were claims that companies had loans on foreclosed land and poorly appraised properties. According to Snowden (1995), New York regulators were overwhelmed and did not examine whether the loan-to-value ratio was the legal 50 percent; they simply accepted the claimed value. Yet, investors purchased these bonds reassured by insurance, approval of the regulators, and favorable assessments by rating agencies. In addition, Snowden (1995) concluded that the single-property real estate bonds were—evaluated by rating agencies, including Moody's—not subject to stringent standards.[27] Apparently, the public did not even take into account observable features of the bonds and mispriced risk. In an econometric examination of a sample of 125 real estate bond prospectuses, Goetzmann and Newman (2010) found that investors did not demand default or term premia but relied on the reputation of the bond houses that managed the issues, leading the authors to view investors in real estate bonds as exceedingly optimistic.

The development of these opaque securitized mortgages appears to be a precursor of growth of the securitized subprime mortgages in the early twenty-first century. Like the subprime mortgages, where quality declined rapidly with vintage, the quality of the real estate bonds rapidly deteriorated

27. See Koester (1939, 49) for details.

Table 4.2   Performance of real estate bonds, 1919–1931

Year	Number of issues	Value millions ($)	Percent not meeting contract
1919	13	31.2	1.9
1920	19	48.2	20.8
1921	13	24.2	29.8
1922	62	137.8	27.6
1923	67	165.4	41.8
1924	96	197.7	50.9
1925	178	483.6	58.3
1926	177	431.3	68.0
1927	163	379.2	72.1
1928	209	519.0	77.0
1929	62	176.3	75.7
1930	23	77.2	57.4
1931	8	12.9	27.1

Source: Johnson (1936, table II).
Note: The source omits all bonds issued under $1 million.

as the boom progressed (Wiggers and Ashcraft 2012). Johnson (1936) examined the fate of commercial real estate mortgages over $1 million, by year of issue. His data for 1919 to 1931 is presented in table 4.2, which shows the number and value of issues per year and whether the bonds met their contractual obligations. It should be remembered that while the residential market peaked in 1926, the commercial market continued to flourish through the rest of the decade. Interpretation of the table is made more difficult by the Great Depression, which independent of the bubble's collapse, caused borrowers to fall into arrears and default. Nevertheless, as the number of issues rose sharply from 1923 to 1926, the long-term performance of the bonds deteriorated sharply. Wiggers and Ashcraft (2012) provided new data that shows this deterioration was in evidence before the Depression. Drawing upon a sample of 3,800 bonds, they estimated the cumulative default rates of bonds issued between 1920 and 1932. For 335 bonds issued in 1923 and 331 issued in 1924 there were cumulative three- and five-year default rates of 0 and 0.5 percent for 1923 and 2 and 5 percent for 1924. Moving into the boom years of 1925 and 1926, there were 528 and 512 bonds issued with three- and five-year cumulative rates of 4.4 and 11 percent for 1925 and 3 and 18.9 percent for 1926.

More detail is available for the important Chicago market, which shows a similar picture. Using data from Moody's 1936 edition of *Banks, Insurance, Real Estate and Investment Trusts*, Koester (1939) identified the 285 largest issues that raised $536.5 million. Twenty-eight percent were for apartments, 22 percent for apartment hotels, 10 percent for hotels, 21 percent for office buildings, and the remainder miscellaneous. Most of the issues—190

($264.9 million)—were underwritten by real estate specialists, with invest-ment bankers offering 50 issues ($160.0 million) and banks or their securi-ties affiliates serving forty-five issues ($72.5 million). Defaults first began to appear in 1925. Between 1925 and 1928, seven issues representing $8.3 mil-lion defaulted, rising to twenty-two issues in 1929, whose face value was $29.3 million. By 1931, 69 percent of all bonds were in default; and finally 95 percent in 1936. Although the Great Depression wrought havoc on this market, a surprising 10 percent of bonds representing 7 percent of aggre-gate value defaulted during a period of healthy economic growth. For the United States as a whole, it is estimated that 60 percent of all mortgages were in arrears and one-third of all loans defaulted in the 1930s, leading to the ruin of the guarantee companies that had provided the insurance (Snowden 1995).

Like the contemporary subprime issues (Gorton 2008), there was ini-tially no market for single-property mortgages, and an attempt to create an exchange failed; instead, a market was maintained by the originating houses that initially promised to repurchase the securities from investors. The market for single-property mortgages was ephemeral, with the first bond house failing in 1926. Yet, the key difference with the early twenty-first century is that these securitized mortgages were held primarily by investors, not financial institutions; thus, unlike today, the bust in the real estate bonds did not produce bank insolvencies. National banks appear to have held little or no real estate bonds. Most of the securities in their portfolio were issued by the federal government and averaged about 10 percent of assets during the 1920s. The remainder was primarily state and local government bonds, and these accounted for only 2.5 percent assets, risking at the very most 20 percent of capital. For the same period, state banks held 6.5 of their assets in US government bonds and 3.3 in state and local securities, the latter accounting for 52 percent of capital. Thus, banks held very few risky real estate bonds in their portfolios.[28]

4.6 Riskier Banks?

While there were changes in the quality of assets, the overall risk to which financial institutions were exposed during the 1920s needs to be assessed. Risk taking by financial institutions in the boom of 2000 to 2006 was cloaked by use of off-balance sheet operations, but these were nonexistent in the 1920s.[29] Therefore, movements in the capital-to-asset ratios should capture much of financial institutions' exposure to risk. However, there were two features of banking in this era that need to be considered first—the de-

---

28. These statistics are calculated for the years 1922 to 1928, when there is relatively little variation. See Carter et al. (2006, series Cj158, Cj169, Cj212, and Cj225).

29. For a detailed description of the contemporary off-balance sheet activities of financial institutions, see Pozsar et al. (2012).

velopment of universal banking, and the general rule of double rather than simple limited liability for shareholders.

Some observers have blamed the recent banking collapse on the abandonment of the Glass-Steagall Act and the re-emergence of universal banking in the United States.[30] Given the passage of the Gramm-Leach-Bliley Act in 1999 that allowed the formation of Financial Holding Companies, combining commercial banking, investment banking, and insurance, the timing seems correct, although the barriers between these industries had been slowly eroding since the late 1980s (Crockett et al. 2003). The Glass-Steagall Act of 1933 was originally inspired by the alleged excesses of the earlier form of universal banking in the 1920s where commercial banks entered investment banking via securities affiliates. This episode was intensively investigated before the passage of the 1999 act, and the evidence revealed that the allegations made in Congress and in the popular press were not true for the industry as a whole. In fact, pre–Great Depression universal banks issued less risky securities that had fewer defaults than stand-alone investment banks (Kroszner and Rajan 1994, 1997; Puri 1994). Universal banks were not more risky than stand-alone commercial banks and relatively fewer failed during the Great Depression (White 1986). Furthermore, most of these securities affiliates were started after the real estate boom ended and as the stock market boom heated up, focusing their activities on corporate and sovereign debt rather than real estate bonds.

Banks in the 1920s differed significantly from early twenty-first century banks because they typically did not have simple limited liability (Grossman 2001). Instead, double liability was the rule, where shareholders were held liable equally and ratably. National banks had double liability, where each shareholder was "liable to the amount of the par value of the shares held by him, in addition to the amount invested in such shares." The potential effect of inducing shareholders to increase their efforts to control risk taking and monitor management was well understood. For state-chartered banks, all but about ten states had adopted double liability by the 1920s. The remainder had single, triple, or individually determined liability. For the national banks, Macey and Miller (1992) found that recovery rates from shareholders averaged 51 percent in the pre-FDIC era and concluded that double liability made shareholders more cautious and willing to intervene. Consequently, troubled banks preferred a voluntary liquidation, rather than waiting for an involuntary insolvency. Bank assets were transferred to new investors without a costly bankruptcy proceeding and assessment, leaving creditors and depositors paid in full. Examining the period 1892 to 1930, Grossman (2001) found that on average there were fewer bank failures, less risk taking,

---

30. As an example of the popular belief that repeal of Glass-Steagall contributed to the recent crisis, see Sanati (2009).

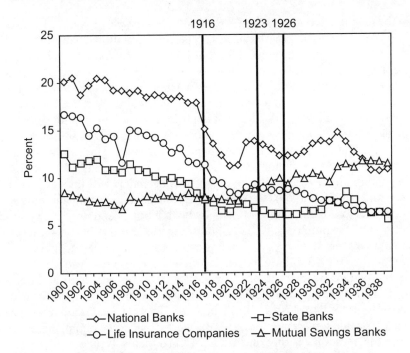

Fig. 4.14   Capital-asset ratios for selected financial intermediaries, 1900–1940
Source: Carter et al. (2006, series Cj217, Cj236, Cj159, Cj175, Cj362, Cj374, Cj741, and Cj750).

and higher capital-to-asset ratios in states where there was double or multiple liability.[31] Overall, the different liability rules of the 1920s seem to have improved the quality of corporate governance.

Figure 4.14 presents the capital-to-asset ratios for several institutions for 1900 to 1940. There were no federal or state capital-asset requirements in this era, thus the ratio should capture bankers' decisions. Commercial banks were the dominant institution with 63 percent of the assets of all financial intermediaries in 1922. This share was almost evenly divided between national banks, which were typically larger and more diversified, and state banks that were often very small. Mutual savings banks had 9 percent and life insurance companies nearly 12 percent of all assets in 1922. Savings and loans had 4 percent of assets but unfortunately there is no data on their capital for this period (Goldsmith 1958).

The figure shows the long decline in the capital-to-asset ratios that began

---

31. In later research, Grossman (2007) found that in the nineteenth century rapidly growing states on the frontier tended to adopt single liability to encourage the growth of banking while double liability was adopted in states where the banking sector was more developed.

in the nineteenth century.[32] Yet, even in 1916, on the eve of America's entry into World War I, the ratio stood at 17.8 percent for national banks, 8.3 percent for state banks, 7.8 percent for mutual savings banks, and 11.5 percent for insurance companies. By contemporary standards this would be considered a very well-capitalized industry. Part of this high level reflected the need to reassure depositors, who were unprotected by deposit insurance; but it also was indicative of the fact that many banks were small, undiversified, single-office operations requiring higher levels of capitalization.

World War I produced an abrupt departure from the gradual downward trend, with the ratio falling to 11 percent for national banks and 6 percent for state banks by 1920. The source of this decline is well known (Friedman and Schwartz 1963). To fund the war, the federal government induced the banks to expand their portfolios by buying bonds and providing loans secured by the purchase of bonds. Following the severe 1919 to 1921 recession, banks raised the ratio by holding asset growth in check and increasing capital. From 1923 to 1926, the capital-asset ratio resumed its decline with asset growth driving down the ratio. Suggestively, this ratio halts at the end of the real estate boom in 1926 only to rise again when banks were faced with the prospect of large losses in the depression. This aggregate data hints that banks became somewhat more risky during the real estate boom, but leaves open the question whether the bust threatened their solvency.

The most detailed data available on the threat to solvency from a decline in the value of real estate loans is for national and state banks. While their capital decisions were not constrained by regulations, their portfolios choices were. The National Banking Act of 1864 had imposed severe limitations on mortgage loans for national banks. Outside the central reserve cities of New York, Chicago, and St. Louis, banks were allowed to grant loans up to five years' maturity on real estate provided that each loan was worth less than 50 percent of the appraised value of the land. Furthermore, total real estate loans could not exceed 25 percent of a bank's capital (White 1983). In 1920, national banks held only 1.7 percent of their assets in real estate loans, but by 1926 this had risen to 5.4 percent. Driving this change was an increase in total mortgage loans from $371 million in 1922 to $725 million in 1926. In this latter year, national banks had a total loan portfolio of $13.3 billion and capital of $3.1 billion so that real estate loans equaled 23 percent of capital, just below the legal limit of 25 percent. The low degree of leverage ensured that even a complete loss on these real estate loans could have been easily absorbed by capital. Actual losses were relatively modest. Net loan losses in 1926 were $109 million and totaled $50 million in 1927, lower than the $118 million average annual losses for 1921–1925. The burden of these losses was,

---

32. Berger, Herring, and Szëgo (1995) chart the decline in commercial banks' capital-to-asset ratios and blame its long-term decline on the National Banking Act protections for national bank notes and the Federal Reserve's actions as a lender of last resort.

of course, not equally distributed. National bank failures had risen because of the post–World War I agricultural problems, with annual suspensions climbing from 21 in 1921 to 123 in 1926, but they declined in 1927 and 1928 to 91 and then 51 (Board of Governors 1943). If real estate losses from the bust had been severe, one would have expected an increase rather than a drop. Furthermore, most failures were in agricultural areas, unaffected by the boom in residential real estate (Alston, Grove, and Wheelock 1994).

More difficulties might have been expected for state banks because state regulations on real estate were weaker. The only survey of state regulations that is proximate in time is Welldon (1909), a decade and a half earlier. However, since state regulations changed slowly and there was a tendency to weaken rather than to strengthen them (White 1983), it should be a fairly accurate guide for the 1920s. Welldon found that only twelve states imposed any restrictions on commercial banks, and most rules tended to be weak. California and North Dakota limited real estate loans to first liens. Ohio and Texas restricted real estate loans to 50 percent of all assets, while South Carolina and Wisconsin set a limit of 50 percent of capital and deposits. The only strict states were Michigan, where real estate loans could not exceed 50 percent of capital, and New York, where rural banks could not have real estate loans in excess of 15 percent of assets and city banks in excess of 40 percent.

In general, real estate loans bulked much larger in the portfolios of state banks. They accounted for 14 percent of assets and 23 percent of all loans on the eve of the boom in 1922. State banks' real estate loans rose from $3.3 billion in 1922 to $5.1 billion during 1926, reaching 16 percent of assets and 27 percent of all loans. In the few states that regulated these loans, some state banks may have reached their legal limits, but most seem to have been well below them. Unlike national banks, real estate loans did exceed capital. In 1926, they were two and a half times capital for all state banks. Clearly, substantial losses on these loans could have produced widespread bank insolvencies.

Nevertheless, state banks do not seem to have taken on much more risk than national banks. The pattern of bank suspensions was no different from the national banks for these more numerous and smaller institutions (There were 21,214 state banks and 8,244 national banks in 1922). Suspensions rose from 409 banks in 1921 to a peak of 801 in 1926, which historians have attributed to the postwar collapse of agricultural prices (Wheelock 1992a). The real estate bust should have added to their woes, but instead suspensions fell to 545 in 1927 and 422 in 1928 (Board of Governors 1943, table 66). Commercial banks were clearly not endangered by the collapse of the real estate bubble in spite of the expansion of mortgage lending. They remained prudent, limiting the share of real estate loans in their portfolios and demanding substantial collateral.

Life insurance companies were among the more aggressive lenders in the

1920s. Mortgages as a share of assets rose from 36 percent in 1922 to 43 percent in 1926. Large losses here could certainly have driven these companies into insolvency as their capital-to-asset ratios were 8.2 percent in 1922 and 7.8 percent in 1926 (Carter et al. 2006, series Cj741, Cj744, and Cj750). While there is less data on these institutions, there is no record of any major insurance company failures in the 1920s and they appear to have been quite profitable. Data is also limited for savings and loan associations. Mortgage loans constituted 90 percent of their assets in 1922 and 92 percent in 1926. Similarly, there is no record of any uptick in S&L failures and unlike commercial banks, the number of savings and loan associations continued to grow through 1927 (Carter et al. 2006, series Cj389, Cj390, and Cj391).

Mortgage loans were central to the mission of mutual savings banks and constituted 92 percent of their loans and 43 percent of their assets in 1922. These institutions lost market share and appear to have adhered to their traditional lending standards, even though their real estate lending jumped from $2.7 to $4.3 billion. At the peak of the boom in 1926, these loans represented 95 percent of loans and 52 percent of assets (Carter et al. 2006, table Cj362–374). In spite of this apparently high level of exposure, only two mutual savings banks failed in the 1920s, one in 1922 and one in 1928 (Board of Governors 1943, table 72).

Taking this information together, it is hard not to reach the conclusion that financial institutions remained prudent lenders even as they expanded their loans to home buyers, regardless of whether they had strict limits on real estate like national banks or minimal regulations like state banks. They had adequate collateral and capital to meet substantial potential defaults; and their shareholders, generally subject to double liability, may have monitored management more carefully. This picture stands in stark contrast to the experience of recent years when financial institutions became increasingly leveraged with more and more risky assets both on and off their balance sheets.

4.7   State Deposit Insurance

In the 1920s, the federal government provided few incentives to banks to take more risk, though the Federal Reserve's policy of reducing seasonal interest rate volatility appears to have induced additional risk taking and may have expanded real estate lending. Yet, compared to today when depositors are provided with high levels of explicit deposit guarantees and implicit 100 percent insurance from the "too big to fail" doctrine, broad government protections that create risk-taking incentives were absent. There was no federal deposit insurance to induce morally hazardous behavior by banks. Several states had experimented with deposit insurance for state banks after the panic of 1907. All were very rural states, and most bank failures in the

1920s (79 percent) were in rural areas (Alston, Grove, and Wheelock 1994), while the banks most deeply involved in the housing boom of the twenties were not insured and were located primarily in urban areas.

However, these state experiments provide considerable evidence that deposit insurance may create a dangerous moral hazard. Using individual bank data for Kansas in the twenties, where state deposit insurance was voluntary, Wheelock (1992a) found that the balance sheets of insured banks exhibited greater risk taking, and that insured banks were more likely to fail than noninsured banks. By the simplest test, the capital-to-asset ratio was significantly lower for insured banks compared to uninsured banks, averaging 11 percent and 14 percent respectively.[33] County-level data revealed that deposit insurance did not prevent bank failures in counties suffering from the greatest agricultural distress in the 1920s (Wheelock 1992a). More generally, state-level banking data suggests that state deposit insurance induced rural banks to increase risk as their net worth declined (Alston, Grove, and Wheelock 1994).

Contemporary analysts and even many legislators understood the problems generated by deposit insurance and generally assessed these experiments as failures.[34] In contrast to today, where deposit insurance is viewed as politically sacrosanct, the none-too-successful state experience may have quashed enthusiasm for deposit insurance at the federal level until the Great Depression. While deposit insurance induced rural banks to expand and take risks and added to their probability of failure, it was absent for most urban banks focused on residential lending, playing little role in the real estate booms of the 1920s.

4.8   The Role of Bank Supervision

For the recent real estate boom, there are claims that bank supervision failed either to detect the deterioration of banks' balance sheets and/or showed forbearance in disciplining excessively risky institutions (National Commission 2011). Similarly, in the 1920s, financial institutions may also have taken more risk and expanded their real estate lending if the examination and supervision policies of the Office of the Comptroller of the Currency (OCC), the Federal Reserve, and the state bank regulators had weakened. Although there is scant secondary literature on the general quality of bank supervision in the 1920s, there are allegations that it failed in certain

33. These ratios are calculated from Wheelock (1992a, table 1).

34. Following the panic of 1907, seven states (North Dakota, South Dakota, Kansas, Nebraska, Oklahoma, Texas, and Mississippi) established deposit guarantee funds. Several produced extraordinary examples of unchecked morally hazardous behavior. For the debates on deposit insurance see Flood (1991) and Calomiris and White (1994). The state-operated deposit insurance systems are analyzed in White (1983), Calomiris (1990), and Wheelock (1992a).

boom regions. These charges and supervisory performance can be partly evaluated with data from the Office of the Comptroller of the Currency, which was responsible for supervision of national banks.[35]

Supervision of financial institutions can be evaluated by its three basic components—disclosure, examination, and enforcement. First, disclosure aims at inducing banks to provide uniform information to the public that will allow depositors and other creditors to determine the safety of the bank. In the pre–deposit insurance era, disclosure was regarded as essential to keep the public informed. In 1869, Congress required the Comptroller of the Currency to call for a minimum of five reports of condition, or "call reports," with three surprise dates of the comptroller's choosing. The random choice of dates was aimed at preventing window dressing of data. However, banks generally dislike disclosing information because they claim that it reveals proprietary information. Thus, the second supervisory activity—examination—permits government officials to perform a more detailed and confidential examination of the bank's condition, in addition to determining whether it is meeting regulatory requirements. Last, if a bank is deficient, the bank supervisors may impose some penalty to bring the bank back into compliance. In the 1920s, if a bank's capital was discovered to be impaired and stockholders' contributions, sales of stock, or unassisted mergers failed to remedy the deficiency, the examiners would order the board of directors to close the bank (Jones 1940). Very generally, comptrollers repeatedly stressed that their job was to reinforce the operation of the market by ensuring disclosure and promptly closing insolvent institutions (Robertson 1968).

The 1920s witnessed a change in the quality of disclosure. The Federal Reserve Act of 1913 gave the Board of Governors the power to demand reports and examine member banks (Kirn 1945), but the OCC initially carried out examination of state member banks in addition to national banks. When Comptroller Williams requested a sixth report and more detailed information, he provoked a flood of complaints from the banks. As a consequence of this uproar and the inequality between the requirements imposed on national and state member banks, the 1917 amendment to the Federal Reserve Act ordered state member banks to make their reports of condition to their Federal Reserve Bank. Additionally, the minimum number of call reports was reduced to three, rather than the five required of national banks. Furthermore, the power to set call dates was transferred to the board.

This regime shift was not complete until Williams left office in late 1921, beginning a weakening of the disclosure process. In 1922, the number of call reports fell back to five; in 1923, it dropped to four and remained at that level for 1924 and 1925. There is no comment about this change in the

35. For the Great Depression, Mitchener (2005, 2007) has studied the effectiveness of state agencies in preventing bank failures. He found that when state supervisors were granted longer terms of office and sole chartering authority they misused this authority, while sole authority to liquidate banks brought about quicker resolutions with less spillover to other institutions.

Annual Reports of the Comptroller of the Currency or the Federal Reserve Board or in the *Federal Reserve Bulletin,* but in the boom year of 1926, there were only three call reports—one for April 12, June 30, and December 3. In 1927, the board called for four reports, a number it adhered to in subsequent years. The reduction in reports suggests that the Fed was under pressure from the national banks to reduce their reporting and put them on a par with state member banks. If so, this is an example of the "competition in laxity" between state and federal regulators that had led to a reduction of capital and reserve requirements in the late nineteenth and early twentieth centuries (White 1983) and that, combined with "regulatory arbitrage," continues to bedevil contemporary American regulators. Alternatively, the Fed may have been alarmed by the condition of some banks, given that real estate values had begun to decline. The decision to skip the October 1926 call may have been made to give banks time to raise capital or make other adjustments.

Conversely, the record of bank examination reveals no such obvious deterioration and may have improved in some dimensions. All national banks had been examined twice yearly since 1898 (Kirn 1945). These examinations were intended to be unanticipated in order to provide the comptroller with a true picture of the condition of national banks and their compliance with regulations. It was well known that this surprise element had been undermined by the incentives from the compensation of examiners. Paid a fixed fee for each bank examined, officials minimized travel costs. The appearance of an examiner at one bank heralded an imminent visit at nearby banks. The new Federal Reserve regime improved examination by eliminating this incentive. Examiners were put on a salary and their expenses were paid. In addition, they were provided with assistants to handle the minor details of examination. (OCC 1919). Although the comptroller was initially responsible for examining state member banks, the 1917 amendment transferred this power to the Federal Reserve banks that organized their own examination departments.[36] The OCC reorganized its examiners in 1915 by Federal Reserve District and established a chief national bank examiner with responsibility for all examiners in the district. The resources available to the comptroller under this new regime remained roughly steady. Between 1923 and 1929, revenue, primarily from examination fees, varied between $2.1 and $2.4 million.[37] To examine the roughly eight thousand banks, the OCC employed only slightly more than two hundred examiners. Overall, the supervisory regime had a relatively light hand and relied heavily on the discipline of the market. While the number of banks per examiner was stable, real assets per examiner increased by 20 percent, which must have added to the examiners' workload, with no compensating increase in resources for

---

36.State banks complained about bearing the cost of state examinations in addition to those of the Fed, though the board could accept state examinations in lieu of additional federal ones (Kirn 1945, 164).

37. Office of the Comptroller of the Currency, *Annual Reports,* 1922–1929.

the agency. If there was a problem, it was that the agency was revenue constrained and could not readily respond, given its fee structure.

Although there was a nationwide real estate boom, Florida was singled out for reckless banking and a failure of bank supervision (Vickers 1994; Frazer and Guthrie 1995). Entry into Florida banking had been constrained by the refusal of the OCC to approve any new national charters between 1907 and 1921. This changed when the banker-developers Wesley D. Manley and James R. Anthony Jr. persuaded Florida's Senator Duncan U. Fletcher to intervene with the comptroller on their behalf. By merger and de novo charter, they assembled a chain of sixty-one national and state banks by 1925. At the state level, Anthony developed close ties to Florida comptroller Ernest Amos, who offered charters, easy supervision, and control of receiverships in exchange for campaign funds and unsecured bank loans for real estate speculation. Insider lending was widespread and often exceeded legal limits. State examiners winked at these activities, and the public was largely kept in the dark.[38]

This closely intertwined and sometimes corrupt relationship between developers, bankers, and regulators kept failed banks open. The Florida State comptroller's 1926 report concealed the deteriorating condition of the banks—notably the insolvent Palm Beach Bank and Trust Company. At the federal level, the national bank examiner found the Palm Beach National Bank to be insolvent in February 1926, but his superiors prevented its closure. At the same time, the Federal Reserve Bank of Atlanta, whose governor, M. B. Wellborn, was an intimate of Manley and Anthony, made a loan to this bank equal to 87 percent of its capital. News that one of the Manley-Anthony development companies was insolvent triggered a run on its allied banks on June 21, 1926. The bank's closure sparked a general run on the bank chains in both Florida and Georgia, with widespread failures. The regional interest rate shock to the South uncovered by Landon-Lane and Rockoff (2007) was no doubt a consequence of this disaster. Yet the panic did not spread to all Florida or all regional banks, as depositors appear to have been sufficiently well informed to distinguish between the solvent and insolvent institutions.

Overall, the OCC, which most contemporary observers conceded was the best bank regulatory agency, did not noticeably respond to the real estate boom. It garnered no additional resources, nor did it redirect its existing funds or manpower to increase supervision of rapidly expanding banking systems in hot regional markets. It may even have mildly encouraged the boom by easing entry into banking. More seriously, state supervisors such

38. In contrast to the abysmal performance by state regulators, the Atlanta District of the OCC did not reduce its oversight. Florida had one examiner, stationed in Jacksonville who later moved to Lakeland, perhaps reflecting the shift of population and activity southward. Yet, the OCC faced the same problem in the Atlanta District and Florida as it did nationally as the size of banks was quickly increasing

as those in Florida may have been co-opted by land promoters and allowed the creation of house-of-cards banking chains. Crucially, however, these failures did not imperil the whole of the banking system, which remained sufficiently well capitalized to withstand the fall in the value of real estate.

4.9   Foreclosures and Home Ownership

While there was no banking collapse in the twenties, the effects of the post-1926 collapse of the housing market show up in the foreclosure data. Unfortunately, there are no national foreclosure statistics before 1926. The only available series that covers the 1920s is the foreclosures completed during the year per thousand nonfarm real estate mortgages for 1926 to 1941, displayed in figure 4.15. After the real estate market began to decline in 1926, foreclosures steadily increased every year through the shock of the Great Depression. However, there was an extraordinary rescue of the mortgage market by the federal government during the Depression, which included the creation of the Home Owners' Loan Corporation in 1933 (Courtemanche and Snowden 2011). As a consequence, foreclosures during the Depression years may be misleadingly low. Nevertheless, the foreclosure rate in the mid-1920s is much higher than the early post–World War II period when the series briefly was continued from 1950 to 1968.

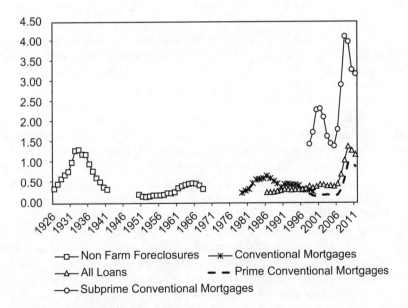

Fig. 4.15   Foreclosures (percent), 1926–2011

Sources: Carter et al. (2006, series Dc1257, Dc1283); US Department of Housing and Urban Development (2008, 2011).

For later years, a straightforward comparison is difficult because the non-farm foreclosure series was discontinued and replaced with a series that records the number of foreclosures begun during a year, instead of the number completed. Thus, the series are only roughly similar. The creation of Federal Housing Authority (FHA) and Veterans Administration (VA) insurance programs complicate comparisons further. The series "All Loans" includes foreclosures on "Conventional," VA, and FHA mortgages. "Conventional Prime" and "Subprime Conventional" foreclosures are a subcategory of conventional foreclosures. Attempting to hold the type of loan constant for comparisons, one should probably exclude subprime mortgages because they expanded the mortgage market and increased the risk of foreclosure. In spite of all of these qualifications, only prime conventional mortgages foreclosure rates remained at midcentury levels until the crisis hit in 2008. All rates suggest that rates were relatively high through the 1980s and 1990s, taking off to Great Depression levels beginning in 2007. The similarity of all but subprime foreclosure rates after 1926 and after 2008 points to a key difference: who held troubled mortgages. Even though housing prices sagged and foreclosure rates doubled between 1926 and 1929, 1920s banks, unlike their early-twenty-first-century descendants, were saddled with only modest losses from their small mortgage portfolios that were manageable with low leverage. However, this comparison does raise the broad question why rates may have been relatively high, even on conventional mortgages, in the prosperous and tranquil last decade of the twentieth century and then soared on all categories.

Part of the answer certainly lies in the huge increase in home ownership and government-induced changes in mortgage characteristics that occurred in the second half of the twentieth century. Compared to post–World War II mortgages, the typically short-term, high loan-to-value ratio mortgages issued during the 1920s were less likely to produce large losses, ensuring that financial intermediaries could survive a drop of 10 or 20 percent in the value of the collateral. The other factor was the ability of households to sustain their mortgage payments. Compared to today, the mortgage market in the twenties provided funds to a very different pool of households. Figure 4.16 reports the home ownership rates. Unfortunately, until 1969 this data is only available every ten years from the census. Nevertheless, the graph reveals a striking post–World War II jump.

At the beginning of the twentieth century, 47 percent of households owned their own homes. This proportion drifted down slightly in the next two decades then rose during the housing boom of the twenties, only to drop sharply during the Depression. Yet these movements are dwarfed by the post–World War II rise, assisted by federal policies such as the establishment of the Federal Housing Administration (FHA), Fannie Mae, and Freddie Mac. By 1970, a plateau was reached with nearly 65 percent of the households owning their own homes. The second secular rise began in the

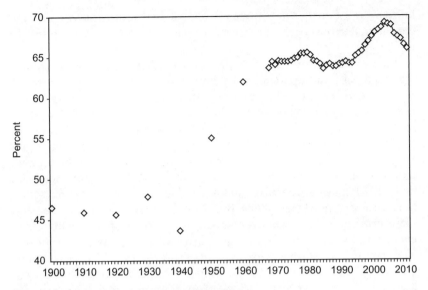

Fig. 4.16   Home ownership rates, 1900–2011
Sources: Carter et al. (2006, series Dc781 and Dc761); US Census Bureau, Housing Vacancies and Homeownership (2008, table 14, www.census.gov).

1990s, when new federal efforts to make mortgages attractive to previously ineligible households took effect. Unfortunately, the current crisis revealed that many individuals who obtained mortgages had a minimal capacity to make mortgage payments and a high propensity to default. The lower levels of home ownership in the 1920s suggest that higher risk households did not have access to mortgages and did not participate in the boom. This difference appears to be borne out by the higher levels of foreclosures in the late twentieth century, levels that even in prosperous times greatly exceeded foreclosure levels during the 1920s and 1930s.

4.10   The Boom and Bust in Retrospect

In the search for explanations of the joint real estate–banking collapse of 2007 to 2008, a comparison with the 1920s is instructive. Even though the dimensions of the residential housing bubbles were similar, the bust in the twenties did not undermine the banking system or derail the economy. Many of the alleged causes of the recent disaster were also in evidence in the 1920s. There appears to have been an easing of monetary policy by the Federal Reserve, an equivalent of the "Greenspan put," and unresponsive or complacent bank supervision at the federal and the state levels. Bank lending standards declined, and the high risk in the booming securitized mortgage industry went undetected by the rating agencies or by an optimistic public lulled by use of opaque securitized instruments. All of these factors certainly contributed to the boom, but they were not enough to undermine the banking system.

What was absent in the 1920s were policies that induced banks to take increased risks. In the twenties, there was no federal intervention in mortgage markets. Far more households rented; and the boom only increased home ownership from approximately 45 to 50 percent of households, while the early twenty-first century boom drove up home ownership from 65 to 69 percent. Because it provided new mortgages to home owners with significantly lower incomes and wealth, many features of the recent boom were more extreme, even if they are not easily quantifiable. While contemporaries in the 1920s may have decried buildings and loan associations' innovations that permitted mortgagors' effective down payments of only 20 percent, these terms appear conservative compared to zero down payment loans that characterized some mortgages in the early twenty-first century. Similarly, while securitized mortgages in the twenties obscured some of the risk present in a pool of mortgages, there was more risk to be hidden in subprime loans and hence the greater degree of complexity of more recent securitized products. This higher level of risk is apparent in the aggregate foreclosure rates of recent stable economic times that often exceeded the foreclosure rates of the post-1926 bust and the Great Depression.

Furthermore, in the 1920s, bankers were not tempted by moral hazard from deposit insurance or the too big to fail policy to take more risk on or off their balance sheets. In fact, the general imposition of double liability on bank stock may have induced bank managers, subjected to greater monitoring by shareholders, to reduce risk taking. However, this is not to say that the regulations governing the banking system of the 1920s made it particularly resilient to shocks. The dominance of small, undiversified single-office banks translated shocks from the post–World War I collapse in agricultural prices and the Great Depression into waves of bank failures.[39]

Yet, faced with incentives set by the market and government policies, banks and other financial institutions in the 1920s remained prudent, modestly lowering lending standards and increasing their holdings of mortgages. When the bust came, large losses did not accrue to them; and the most risky securitized mortgages were held by investors, not leveraged financial institutions. Banks and other intermediaries that had participated in the boom survived until the Great Depression unexpectedly hammered the banking system and home owners, causing the housing boom and bust of the 1920s to fade from sight.

---

39. For discussions of these issues see, for example, White (1983), Wheelock (1992a, 1992b), and Mitchener (2007).

References

Alston, Lee J., Wayne A. Grove, and David C. Wheelock. 1994. "Why Do Banks Fail? Evidence from the 1920s." *Explorations in Economic History* 31:409–31.

Balke, Nathan S., and Robert J. Gordon. 1986. "Appendix B Historical Data." In *The American Business Cycle: Continuity and Change*, edited by Robert J. Gordon, 781–850. Chicago: University of Chicago Press.

Barsky, Robert, N. Gregory Mankiw, Jeffrey Miron, and David Weil. 1988. "The Worldwide Change in the Behavior of Interest Rates and Prices in 1914." *European Economic Review* 32 (5): 1123–54.

Berger, Allen N., Richard J. Herring, and Giorgio P. Szëgo. 1995. "The Role of Capital in Financial Institutions." *Journal of Banking and Finance* 19:393–430.

Board of Governors of the Federal Reserve System. 1943. *Banking and Monetary Statistics, 1914–1943*. Washington, DC: BOGFRS.

Calomiris, Charles W. 1990. "Is Deposit Insurance Necessary?" *Journal of Economic History* 50:283–95.

Calomiris, Charles W., and Eugene N. White. 1994. "The Origins of Federal Deposit Insurance." In *The Regulated Economy: A Historical Approach to Political Economy*, edited by Claudia Goldin and Gary D. Libecap, 145–88. Chicago: University of Chicago Press.

Caporale, Tony, and Barbara McKiernan. 1998. "Interest Rate Uncertainly and the Founding of the Federal Reserve." *Journal of Economic History* 58 (4): 1110–7.

Carter, Susan B., Scott S. Gartner, Michael R. Haines, Alan L. Olmstead, Richard Sutch, and Gavin Wright, eds. 2006. *Historical Statistics of the United States: Earliest Times to the Present*. Millennial edition. Cambridge: Cambridge University Press.

Clark, Truman. 1986. "Interest Rate Seasonals and the Federal Reserve." *Journal of Political Economy* 94 (1): 76–125.

Courtemanche, Charles, and Kenneth A. Snowden. 2011. "Repairing a Mortgage Crisis: HOLC Lending and Its Impact on Local Housing Markets." *Journal of Economic History* 71 (2): 307–37.

Coval, Joshua, Jakub Jurek, and Erik Stafford. 2009. "The Economics of Structured Finance." *Journal of Economic Perspectives* 23 (1): 3–26.

Crockett, Andrew, Trevor Harris, Frederic S. Mishkin, and Eugene N. White. 2003. *Conflicts of Interest in the Financial Services Industry: What Should We Do About Them?* Geneva: International Center for Monetary and Banking Studies.

Economic Report of the President. 2009. Washington, DC: Government Printing Office.

Edelstein, Michael. 2000. "War and the American Economy in the Twentieth Century." In *The Cambridge Economic History of the United States: The Twentieth Century*, vol. III, edited by Stanley L. Engerman and Robert E. Gallman, 329–405. Cambridge: Cambridge University Press.

Federal Reserve Board. 1915–1929. *Annual Reports*. Washington, DC: Government Printing Office.

Field, Alexander J. 1992. "Uncontrolled Land Development and the Duration of the Depression in the United States." *Journal of Economic History* 52 (4): 785–805.

Fishe, Raymond P. H., and Mark Wohar. 1990. "The Adjustment of Expectations to a Change in Regime: Comment." *American Economic Review* 80 (4): 968–76.

Fisher, Ernest M. 1951. *Urban Real Estate Markets: Characteristics and Financing*. New York: National Bureau of Economic Research.

Flood, Mark D. 1991. "The Great Deposit Insurance Debate." *Federal Reserve Bank of St. Louis Review* 74:51–77.

Frazer, William, and John J. Guthrie Jr. 1995. *The Florida Land Boom: Speculation, Money and the Banks.* Westport, CT: Quorum Books.

Friedman, Milton, and Anna J. Schwartz. 1963. *A Monetary History of the United States 1867–1960.* Princeton, NJ: Princeton University Press.

Galbraith, John Kenneth. 1988[1954]. *The Great Crash: 1929.* Boston: Houghton Mifflin Company.

Glaeser, Edward L., Joseph Gyourko, and Raven Saks. 2005. "Why Have Housing Prices Gone Up?" NBER Working Paper no. 11129, Cambridge, MA.

Goetzmann, William N., and Frank Newman. 2010. "Securitization in the 1920s." NBER Working Paper no. 15650, Cambridge, MA.

Goldsmith, Raymond W. 1958. *Financial Intermediaries in the American Economy since 1900.* Princeton, NJ: Princeton University Press.

Gorton, Gary. 2008. "The Subprime Panic." NBER Working Paper no. 14398, Cambridge, MA.

Greenspan, Alan. 2009. "The Fed Didn't Cause the Housing Bubble." *Wall Street Journal*, March 11.

Grebler, Leo, David M. Blank, and Louis Winnick. 1956. *Capital Formation in Residential Real Estate: Trends and Prospects.* Princeton, NJ: Princeton University Press.

Grossman, Richard S. 2001. "Double Liability and Bank Risk Taking." *Journal of Money, Credit and Banking* 33 (2, part 1): 143–59.

———. 2007. "Fear and Greed: The Evolution of Double Liability in American Banking, 1865–1930." *Explorations in Economic History* 44:59–80.

Hoyt, Homer. 1933. *One Hundred Years of Land Values in Chicago.* New York: Arno Press.

Johnson, Ernest A. 1936. "The Record of Long-Term Real Estate Securities." *Journal of Land and Public Utilities Economics* 12:44–8.

Joint Center for Housing Studies of Harvard University. 2008. *The State of the Nation's Housing.* Cambridge, MA: Fellow of Harvard College.

Jones, Homer. 1940. "An Appraisal of the Rules and Procedures of Bank Supervision, 1929–1939." *Journal of Political Economy* 48 (2): 183–98.

Kindleberger, Charles P. 1978. *Manias, Panics, and Crashes: A History of Financial Crises.* New York: Basic Books.

Kirn, Brian A. 1945. *Financial Reports of American Commercial Banks.* Washington, DC: The Catholic University of American Press.

Koester, Genevieve. 1939. "Chicago Real Estate Bonds, 1919–1938: I Corporate History." *Journal of Land and Public Utilities Economics* 15:49–58.

Kool, Clemens J. M. 1995. "War Finance and Interest Rate Targeting: Regime Changes in 1914–1918." *Explorations in Economic History* 32 (3): 365–82.

Kroszner, Randall S., and Raghuram G. Rajan. 1994. "Is the Glass-Steagall Act Justified? A Study of the U.S. Experience with Universal Banking Before 1933." *American Economic Review* 84 (4): 810–32.

———. 1997. "Organization, Structure, and Credibility: Evidence from Commercial Bank Securities Activities before the Glass-Steagall Act." *Journal of Monetary Economics* 39 (3): 475–516.

Landon-Lane, John, and Hugh Rockoff. 2007. "The Origin and Diffusion of Shocks to Regiona Interest Rates in the United States, 1880–2002." *Explorations in Economic History* 44 (3): 487–500.

Macey, Jonathan R., and Geoffrey P. Miller. 1992. "Double Liability of Bank Shareholders: History and Implications." *Wake Forest Law Review* 27:31–62.

Mankiw, N. Gregory, Jeffrey A. Miron, and David N. Weil. 1987. "The Adjustment of Expectations to a Change in Regime: A Study of the Founding of the Federal Reserve." *American Economic Review* 77 (3): 358–74.

Mayer, Christopher, Karen Pence, and Shane M. Sherlund. 2009. "The Rise in Mortgage Defaults." *Journal of Economic Perspectives* 23 (1): 27–50.

Meltzer, Allan H. 2003. *A History of the Federal Reserve,* vol. 1, 1913–1952. Chicago: University of Chicago Press.

Miller, Marcus, Paul Weller, and Lei Zhang. 2002. "Moral Hazard and the U.S. Stock Market: Analyzing the 'Greenspan Put.'" *Economic Journal* 112 (478): 171–86.

Miron, Jeffrey A. 1986. "Financial Panics, the Seasonality of the Nominal Interest Rate and the Founding of the Fed." *American Economic Review* 76 (1): 125–40.

Mitchener, Kris James. 2005. "Bank Supervision, Regulation, and Instability During the Great Depression." *Journal of Economic History* 65 (1): 152–85.

———. 2007. "Are Prudential Supervision and Regulation Pillars of Financial Stability? Evidence from the Great Depression." *Journal of Law and Economics* 50 (2): 273–302.

Morton, J. E. 1956. *Urban Mortgage Lending.* Princeton, NJ: Princeton University Press.

National Commission on the Causes of the Financial and Economic Crisis in the United States. 2011. *The Financial Crisis Inquiry Report.* Washington, DC: Government Printing Office.

Nicholas, Tom, and Anna Scherbina. 2011. "Real Estate Prices during the Roaring Twenties and the Great Depression." UC Davis Graduate School of Management Research Paper no. 18-09.

Office of the Comptroller of the Currency. 1918–1929. *Annual Reports.* Washington, DC: OCC.

Office of Federal Housing Enterprise Oversight. 2008. "Revisiting the Differences between the OFHEO and S&P/Case-Shiller House Price Indices: New Explanations." January.

Orphanides, Athanasios. 2003. "Historical Monetary Policy Analysis and the Taylor Rule." *Journal of Monetary Economics* 50 (5): 983–1022.

Pozsar, Zoltan, Tobias Adrian, Adam Ashcraft, and Hayley Boesky. 2012. "Shadow Banking." Federal Reserve Bank of New York Staff Report no. 458. February.

Puri, Manju. 1994. "The Long-Term Default Performance of Bank Underwritten Security Issues." *Journal of Banking and Finance* 18 (2): 397–418.

Rappoport, Peter, and Eugene N. White. 1994. "Was the Crash of 1929 Expected?" *American Economic Review* 84 (1): 271–81.

Robertson, Ross M. 1968. *The Comptroller and Bank Supervision: A Historical Appraisal.* Washington, DC: Office of the Comptroller of the Currency.

Rockoff, Hugh. 2012. *America's Economic Way of War: War and the U.S. Economy from the Spanish American War to the Persian Gulf War.* Cambridge: Cambridge University Press.

Sanati, Cyrus. 2009. "10 Years Later, Looking at Repeal of Glass-Steagall." *New York Times,* November 12.

Schwartz, Anna J. 1992. "The Misuse of the Fed's Discount Window." *Federal Reserve Bank of St. Louis Review* 74 (5): 58–69.

Shiller, Robert J. 2000. *Irrational Exuberance,* 1st ed. Princeton, NJ: Princeton University Press.

Simpson, Herbert D. 1933. "Real Estate Speculation and the Depression." *American Economic Review* 23 (1): 163–71.

Snowden, Kenneth A. 1995. "Mortgage Securitization in the United States: Twentieth Century Developments in Historical Perspective." In *Anglo-American Financial Systems,* Michael D. Bordo and Richard Sylla, 261–98. New York: Irwin.

———. 2010. "The Anatomy of a Residential Mortgage Crisis: A Look Back to the 1930s." NBER Working Paper no. 16244, Cambridge, MA.

Taylor, John B. 1993. "Discretion Versus Policy Rules in Practice." *Carnegie-Rochester Conference Series on Public Policy* 39:195–214.

———. 1999. "A Historical Analysis of Monetary Policy Rules." In *Monetary Policy Rules*, edited by John B. Taylor, 319–48. Chicago: University of Chicago Press.

———. 2007. "Housing and Monetary Policy." Symposium on Housing, Housing Finance and Monetary Policy, Jackson Hole, Wyoming, September. Proceedings, Federal Reserve Bank of Kansas City, 463–76.

———. 2009. "The Financial Crisis and the Policy Responses: An Empirical Analysis of What Went Wrong." NBER Working Paper no. 14631, Cambridge, MA.

Temin, Peter. 1976. *Did Monetary Forces Cause the Great Depression?* New York: W.W. Norton & Company.

U.S. Census Bureau. www.census.gov.

Vickers, Raymond B. 1994. *Panic in Paradise: Florida's Banking Crash of 1926*. Tuscaloosa: University of Alabama Press.

Welldon, Samuel A. 1909. *Digest of State Banking Statutes*. Washington, DC: National Monetary Commission.

Wheelock, David C. 1991. *The Strategy and Consistency of Federal Reserve Monetary Policy, 1924–1933*. Cambridge: Cambridge University Press.

———. 1992a. "Deposit Insurance and Bank Failures: New Evidence from the 1920s." *Economic Inquiry* 30:530–43.

———. 1992b. "Monetary Policy in the Great Depression: What the Fed Did and Why." *Federal Reserve Bank of St. Louis Review* March/April:3–28.

White, Eugene N. 1983. *The Regulation and Reform of the American Banking System 1900–1929*. Princeton, NJ: Princeton University Press.

———. 1986. "Before the Glass-Steagall Act: An Analysis of the Investment Banking Activities of National Banks." *Explorations in Economic History* 23 (1): 33–55.

Wilson, J. Holton, and Barry Keating. 2002. *Business Forecasting*. Boston: McGraw Hill.

Wicker, Elmus R. 1966. *Federal Reserve Monetary Policy, 1917–1933*. New York: Random House.

Wiggers, Tyler, and Adam B. Ashcraft. 2012. "Defaults and Losses on Commercial Real Estate Bonds during the Great Depression Era." Federal Reserve Bank of New York Staff Report No. 544, February.

II

A Closer Look at the Interwar Housing Crisis

5

The 1920s American Real Estate Boom and the Downturn of the Great Depression
Evidence from City Cross-Sections

Michael Brocker and Christopher Hanes

Prior to the early twenty-first century there were several regional real estate booms in American history, but the only one that appears to have spread across most of the country occurred in the mid-1920s. In popular memory and some academic accounts (e.g., Shiller 2005), the real estate boom of the 1920s was concentrated in Florida. But as Frederick Lewis Allen (1931) observed in *Only Yesterday*, his history of the decade:

> [E]specially during its middle years, there was a boom in suburban lands outside virtually every American city . . . the automobile played its part . . . by bringing within easy range of the suburban railroad station, and thus of the big city, great stretches of woodland and field which a few years before had seemed remote and inaccessible. Attractive suburbs grew with amazing speed . . . The old Jackson farm with its orchards and daisy-fields was staked out in lots and attacked by the steam-shovel and became Jacobean Heights or Colonial Terrace or Alhambra Gardens, with paved roads, twentieth-century comforts, Old World charm, and land for sale on easy payments. (285–86)

The mid-1920s house-building boom was accompanied by rising house prices, increased home ownership rates, and financial innovations that boosted the supply of credit to real estate developers and house buyers (White, chapter 4, this volume; Snowden 2010). It was also accompanied

Michael Brocker contributed to this chapter while he was an undergraduate at the State University of New York at Binghamton and independently of his current employer. Christopher Hanes is professor of economics at the State University of New York at Binghamton.

Thanks to Price Fishback, Kenneth Snowden, and David Wheelock for comments and data, and to Eugene White and participants in the 2011 Cliometrics Conference for comments. For acknowledgments, sources of research support, and disclosure of the authors' material financial relationships, if any, please see http://www.nber.org/chapters/c12798.ack.

by an unprecedented increase in the volume of mortgage debt, which some viewed as "evidence of a fundamental revision in home owners' and probably lenders' attitudes toward mortgage indebtedness" (Grebler, Blank, and Winnick 1956, 164). In the country as a whole, construction and house prices peaked in 1925 and fell off steadily over the late 1920s. With the onset of the Great Depression in 1930, the decline in house prices accelerated and many mortgages went into default. To contemporaries, consequences were obvious:

> From 1930 to 1934, . . . the value of . . . residential property fell about one-third . . . The important role real estate values play in the economy is most clearly evident at such times. Not only the owners of real estate and the holders of real estate mortgages but also bank depositors and other persons whose savings are committed to financial institutions having substantial real estate investments may feel directly or indirectly the effects of radical fluctuations in real property prices. The disturbing effect of interrupted financing, of fluctuations in income from real property and hence in its value and salability, inevitably makes less secure the status of financial institutions and of their owners and depositors. (Wickens 1941, 1–2)

Looking back on the real estate boom of the 1920s, economists have grappled with two questions: Did it contribute to the depth of the Great Depression? Was it the result of an irrational "bubble" in residential real estate? Both questions remain open.

In the 1930s, many economists hypothesized that 1925 had been the peak of a long-swing "building cycle," independent of business cycles and of longer frequency. The business cycle depression after 1929 was deeper, they argued, because it took place during the building cycle's downswing. The hypothesis of an independent building cycle did not survive examination (Hickman 1974), but economists have continued to look for ways that the 1920s real estate boom could have depressed real activity in the 1930s. Obviously, a plunge in house prices as big as that after 1929 could depress aggregate demand. Declining house prices cause defaults on mortgage debt as home owners abandon negative equity properties or are unable to refinance balloon payment mortgages (Elul et al. 2010). Mortgage defaults damage the balance sheets of exposed financial intermediaries, choking off credit supply. Declining house prices also hinder lending by devaluing potential borrowers' collateral, and perhaps decrease consumer spending through "wealth effects" (Mishkin 1978; Case and Quigley 2008). But it is not clear that the 1920s boom was responsible for any portion of the house price declines and foreclosures after 1929. They could have been entirely a consequence, not an additional cause, of a cyclical downturn. Aggregate output and employment continued to grow for years after the house market's 1925 peak. Indeed, few economists have argued that the boom contributed to the Depression through the wealth and financial effects of house price declines and foreclosures.[1] Instead, they have considered the possibility that the boom left behind an overhang of excess housing (overbuilding, Gordon 1951; Bolch, Fels, and McMahon 1971) or an unwieldy layout of streets and land parcels (Field 1992) that depressed investment in housing capital, specifically in the 1930s.

The boom in house markets around 1925 looks like a classic bubble: excessive investment in a class of assets, driven by unreasonable expectations that the assets will continue to appreciate. But in this case, as in others, it is hard to rule out the possibility that a historical peak in asset prices reflected expectations that were rational *ex ante*, even though they were not fulfilled *ex post*. Economists still debate whether the stock market boom that ended in 1929 was a bubble (White 2006). Most booms are coincident with developments in financial markets or technology that could plausibly raise "fundamental" values of the assets in question. The mid-1920s house boom is no exception. Automobiles, for example, were a new technology that doubtless affected demand for single-family houses around cities. Imagine trying to guess at automobiles' ultimate effect on suburban real estate, based only on information available in 1925. You might conclude that the house prices of 1925 had outrun fundamentals. But you could not be very sure about it.

As other contributions to this volume attest, the experience of the early twenty-first century has revived interest in the 1920s. This is not only because the 1920s may help us understand the early twenty-first century, but because the growing body of research on the early twenty-first century provides new ways to approach the 1920s. A common approach in research on the post–World War II era is to examine cross-sectional variation across local housing markets such as metropolitan areas. Across the peak of the early twenty-first-century boom, around 2006, prices and construction across metro areas displayed in extreme form a pattern that had been seen in the smaller regional cycles of the postwar era. In the run-up to the peak some metro areas experienced persistently higher rates of increase in house prices, year after year, accompanied by relatively high rates of construction. In the bust, house prices fell most in metro areas that had experienced the greatest price increases and construction in the boom. Theoretical models of local housing markets suggest these patterns are easy to explain as the result of a nationwide bubble that was stronger in some localities than others. It is generally accepted that the post-2006 bust contributed to the "Great Recession," which followed close at its heels (the National Bureau of Economic Research [NBER] dates the cyclical peak at December 2007) through financial channels and perhaps wealth effects.

In this chapter we examine cross-sectional data on residential construction, house prices, and other variables across American cities in the 1920s and the downturn of the Great Depression. We find that cities that had

---

1. The argument of Gjerstad and Smith (chapter 3, this volume) is a rare, brave exception.

experienced the biggest house construction booms in the mid-1920s, and the highest increases in house values and home ownership rates across the 1920s, saw the greatest declines in house values and home ownership rates after 1930. They also experienced the highest rates of mortgage foreclosure in the early 1930s. These patterns look very much like those around 2006. They are consistent with a bubble. They show that the effects of the mid-1920s boom on house markets were still present as of 1929. They suggest that, in the post-1929 downturn of the Great Depression, house prices fell more and there were more foreclosures because the 1920s boom had taken place.

5.1   House Markets in Theory

In the context of house markets, most economists define a bubble as a situation in which prices are elevated by expectations of future increases in prices, and the expected level of future prices is inconsistent with a rational view of the economy.[2] To identify a bubble, it may be necessary to specify what a rational view would be, based on a theoretical model. Most models depict two features of housing markets. First, a house is a long-lived asset, a claim to the stream of future services (net of maintenance) provided by the house. Second, housing markets are fundamentally local, the flip side of local labor markets, because a person must live within commuting distance of his job.

In simple models, capital markets are perfect and owner-occupied houses are the same as units available on a rental market. Thus, house prices are determined by the real interest rate, expectations of future rents, the covariance of rents with returns on other assets such as stocks, and tax treatment of home ownership. More complicated models allow for capital market imperfections, so that house prices are also affected by the state of institutions supplying credit to house buyers, potential buyers' wealth, and their ability to insure against income shocks (Himmelberg, Mayer, and Sinai

2. Economists have developed models of "rational" bubbles, in which expectations are rational but the price of an asset exceeds its "fundamental" value; that is, the present value of the future benefits from owning the asset apart from any price appreciation (such as dividends on a stock). Glaeser, Gyourko, and Saiz (2008) explain that rational bubbles cannot arise in housing markets because the long-run supply of housing is not fixed. In a rational bubble, an asset's price can remain above its fundamental value forever, validating the expectations that support the bubble. To make this true, first, the rate of increase in the price times the probability that the bubble will continue for one more period must equal the real interest rate, so that people are willing to hold the bubbled asset. Second, the real interest rate in the economy must be lower than the rate of general rate of economic growth in real income and wealth (the economy must be "dynamically inefficient"), so that the future value of bubbled assets remains within future generations' buying power. A rational bubble cannot arise on an asset that has an ordinary upward-sloping long-run supply curve because the continuously rising price of the asset would call forth the production of more and more units, whose value would eventually exceed future generations' buying power.

2005; Favilukis, Ludvigson, and Van Nieuwerburgh 2010). Glaeser and Gyourko (2009) note that owner-occupied housing may have different characteristics from rental housing, so that the value of the future service flow from an owner-occupied house is an implicit rent related to, but not exactly the same as, observable market rents. To generalize, in models without bubbles the price of a house is determined by rational expectations of its future implicit rents (net of maintenance and accounting for tax treatment) interacting with capital market imperfections as well as the term structure of real interest rates on safe liquid assets.

Rents or implicit rents are determined in local markets by local supply and demand. Local demand increases with local population and household income. Some models (e.g., Adam, Kuang, and Marcet 2011) also allow for variations in the utility derived from housing services, relative to other consumption goods. Local supply is determined by past construction. Because construction takes time, supply is fixed in a short run. In the long run, housing is supplied at the cost of construction. Local population and income are endogenous as households migrate across localities to maximize utility and employers migrate to maximize profit.

Construction cost is the sum of the price of local land and the cost of producing a structure from capital and labor (similar to a manufactured good). The price of local land may increase with the quantity of local housing units in a way that varies across local markets. Thus, the long-run supply of housing in a local market may be less than perfectly elastic, with different elasticities across markets, even if the cost of a structure per se is the same in all locations.

Households migrate in response to local real wages and "consumption amenities;" that is, characteristics of a locality that affect residents' happiness at a given real wage. The price level in the real wage denominator varies across locations only due to differences in housing costs (other consumption goods are tradable across localities), so real wages are relatively low if housing costs are high relative to wages. Employers—at least the ones that produce for national (or international) markets—migrate in response to local nominal wages and "production amenities" that affect production or transportation costs. Some production and consumption amenities are exogenous (e.g., weather). Some are due to more or less exogenous institutional factors (e.g., state government quality). Some are affected by the size of the population or employer base (e.g., congestion costs, thick-market externalities).

In the long-run equilibrium, depicted in models following Roback (1982), nominal wages are relatively high in locations with good production amenities (which compensate for high local labor costs). Rents are high relative to nominal wages in locations with good consumption amenities (which compensate for low local real wages). Thus, rents are relatively high in localities with good production amenities (which raise local wages *and* rents) and/or good consumption amenities (which raise rents relative to wages). Relative house prices reflect rents.

Models of short-run fluctuations in local housing markets build on this structure. They add passing shocks to financial factors (e.g., real interest rates) and local supply or demand (e.g., temporary fluctuations in local population or incomes) that disturb the long-run equilibrium. There may also be changes from time to time in the exogenous components of local amenities, or the functional relation between endogenous amenities and the size of the local population. The response of prices and construction to shocks and their paths back to equilibrium depend partly on the nature of expectations, as current prices capitalize expected future rents, and expected future price increases raise current housing demand.

Two models of short-term fluctuations *without* bubbles are Van Nieuwerburgh and Weill (2010) and Glaeser et al. (2011). In these models, expectations are rational, so prices respond immediately to any predictable movement in rents. In response to shocks with statistically predictable outcomes for rents, house prices jump upon receipt of the news, then move gradually to the long-run equilibrium as factors such as construction and migration come into play.

Models with bubbles incorporate some form of nonrational expectations. There is no generally accepted alternative to rational expectations. But for house markets Case and Shiller's (1989, 2003) view is prominent. They argue that bubbles can be set off by initial price increases due to "fundamental factors" such as "demographics, income growth, employment growth, changes in financing mechanisms or interest rates, as well as changes in locational characteristics," interacting with short-run fixed supply (2003, 337). Observed price increases create irrational expectations of future increases. As expected future price increases boost current demand, they cause self-confirming increases in current prices in a feedback mechanism, but only up to a point. "Longer-run forces that come into play tend eventually to reverse the impact of any initial price increases and the public overreaction to them" (338). Construction increases supply, and employers and households migrate away from high-cost areas. When prices fail to increase as expected, the bubble ends.

Glaeser, Gyourko, and Saiz (2008) present a model of local housing markets with bubbles that is partly consistent with Case and Shiller's view. In the model, people irrationally expect an observed rate of price increase in the previous period to continue forever. As higher prices call forth greater supply, the rate of price increase slows. Eventually "beliefs revert to rationality and the equilibrium returns to the rational expectations equilibrium with, of course, an extra supply of housing," which tends to depress rents and hence house prices in the aftermath of the bubble (202). The model lacks one element emphasized by Case and Shiller: bubbles are not set off by price increases due to fundamental factors, but to an equal, exogenous increase in expected future prices that hits all markets. The subsequent evolution of prices and construction varies across markets because markets have different supply elasticities. In the boom, areas with more elastic supply see more construction but smaller price increases. When the bubbles burst, one possible outcome is that areas that had experienced more construction during the boom suffer greater price declines.

Adam, Kuang, and Marcet (2011) present another model of bubbles in local house markets supported by a feedback mechanism between experienced price increases and expected future price increases. (The localities in this model are meant to depict various national housing markets rather than areas within a country, so there is no migration between localities: the long-run steady state is determined just by preferences for housing and construction. But that does not matter for the point here.) The model is closer to Case and Shiller's view in that bubbles are set off by initial price increases due to fundamentals. Fundamentals include a real interest rate common to all markets, and idiosyncratic, local shocks to preferences that affect individual markets. A decrease in the real interest rate tends to set off a bubble in all localities, but a bubble may not develop in localities where the housing price had been falling for local reasons. Bubbles are bigger where prices had already been rising for local reasons. During the boom, localities with bigger bubbles experience greater price increases and also more construction.

5.2 Patterns in Postwar Data on Local Markets

For the postwar era, annual data on housing construction and prices are available for Census Bureau metropolitan areas, which correspond well to local housing markets in models as they are defined on the basis of observed commuting patterns. For construction most studies rely on Census Bureau estimates of housing starts. These are based on reports from municipalities on the number of construction permits, adjusted by Census Bureau estimates of the time lag between permit issuance and the beginning of construction, the fraction of permitted structures never built, and construction in municipalities that do not require permits. Multifamily structures are aggregated with single-family houses by counting each separate apartment as one unit.

With respect to prices, one must keep in mind the difference between prices in actual sales and peoples' estimates of the price a house *could* fetch if it were put on the market. For most wealth and financial effects, potential-sale estimates are more important than actual sale prices. For wealth effects, what matters are home owners' estimates. For financial intermediaries possibly exposed to mortgage debt, what matters are estimates of financial-market participants and depositors. Estimates of potential prices may deviate from actual sale prices if only because (at least until recently) there was little freely available information about house sale prices in a locality (Shiller 2005, 26).

For some years of the postwar era, measures of actual sale prices can be compared with home owner's estimates of their homes' potential sale prices, gathered by surveys. Studies find that home owners generally overestimate the price of their houses, but changes in home owners' estimates are strongly correlated with changes in actual sale prices (Kiel and Zabel 1999; Bucks and Pence 2006).

Most recent research has relied on measures of actual sale prices. Simple averages of sale prices reflect the characteristics of houses put on the market in a period, as well as changes in the price of a house of given quality. To focus on the latter, "repeat-sale indices" use prices of the same structures sold in different years. The well-known Case-Shiller series cover just a few metro areas. For cross-sectional analysis, many studies rely on the repeat-sale indices published by the Federal Housing Finance Agency (FHFA, formerly OFHEO), which are limited to sales financed by agency-insured mortgages but cover nearly all metro areas.

Prior to the national boom and bust of the early twenty-first century, research had found two strong patterns in metro-area sale prices: short-run "momentum" and long-run "mean reversion." In the short run, from year to year, the rate of change in an area's price index shows strong serial correlation: if an area's price level rises relatively fast in one year, it is likely to rise relatively fast in the following year. But in the long run, across five or ten years, an area's price level reverts to the previous trend (Kodrzycki and Gerew 2006; Glaeser, Gyourko, and Saiz 2008). Case and Shiller (1989, 2003) argue that short-run serial correlation in house price increases is evidence for bubbles: under rational expectations any predictable movements in future (implicit) rents should be immediately, not gradually, capitalized in prices. This argument is supported by Glaeser et al. (2011), who find that their rational expectations model can generate mean reversion, but not serial correlation in metro areas' house price changes.

The national boom and bust of the early twenty-first century was an extreme example of price momentum followed by mean reversion. In the early twenty-first century, indices of sale prices for the United States increased rapidly, year after year. Construction rates were also very high. Construction (nonfarm housing starts) peaked in 2005. House prices peaked in mid-2006 (Case-Shiller) or early 2007 (FHFA). Both construction and prices fell off after that. Prices fell fast through 2008, then leveled off or continued to fall at a much slower rate. The national nonfarm home ownership rate rose and fell with construction and prices, peaking in 2006 (Haughwort, Peach, and Tracy 2009). Mortgage deliquency and foreclosure rates increased in the bust (US Department of Housing and Urban Development 2011, 81–82).

The magnitude of the boom varied across metro areas. During the boom, the rate of price increase was persistently higher in some areas. At least in the later years of the boom, metro areas with the highest rates of price increase tended to have the highest rates of housing starts. In the bust, these boom cities saw the greatest house price *declines*. Thus, a metro area's rate of housing starts during the boom was *positively* related to its rate of change in house prices during the boom, *negatively* related to its rate of change in house prices during the bust (Mayer and Pence 2008; Goetzmann, Peng, and Yen 2012; Carson and Dastrup 2013; Abel and Deitz 2010). Mortgage default rates in the bust reflected price declines: they were higher in metro areas where house prices fell more, controlling for local unemployment and the prevalence of subprime mortgages (Furlong 2008; Elul et al. 2010).

The relationships between boom construction and price changes in the early twenty-first century are key to our assessment of the 1920s, so we take a look at them here. For comparison with the 1920s, it is better to look at raw permits than estimates of starts. Like starts, permits peaked in 2005. To scale permit counts to the size of the metro area we divide them by the number of metro-area housing units counted in the 2000 census. Table 5.1 shows results of regressing changes in the log of FHFA metro-area price indices on permit rates in boom years. For panel A, the left-hand-side variable is the change in log price indices across the bust from 2006 to 2008. Column (1) gives the coefficient from regressing these price changes on permits issued in the year 2000. For column (2), the RHS variable is permits in 2001, and so on across the table. The negative coefficients indicate that house prices fell more in metro areas that had more boom-year permits. For panel B, the LHS variable is the change in the log of the price indices in the boom from 2004 to 2006. The positive coefficients show that price changes in the boom years were positively related to permits. We would like to know whether the patterns in table 5.1 also held for home owners' estimates of potential sale prices, but we have found no home owners' estimates from the middle of the first decade of the twenty-first century for a large enough set of metro areas to allow for cross-sectional analysis.[3]

It would be too much to claim that the patterns in table 5.2 are evidence of bubbles. But they are certainly easy to account for as the result of bubbles. The positive correlation between construction and price increases across metro areas during the boom is consistent with a bubble set off by a general positive fundamental demand shock, magnified or muffled by local fundamental demand shocks as in the model of Adam, Kuang and Marcet (2011). The negative correlation between boom construction and price change in the bust would result from the effect of bubble-created supply on prices as the model of Glaeser and Gyourko (2009).

---

3. From 1985 to 1995 the Census Bureau's American Housing Survey collected such data for forty-one metro areas annually. Until 2004, the metro-level data were collected semiannually. Since then, due to budget cuts, the AHS has collected data for just a handful of very large metro areas in scattered years (http://www.census.gov/hhes/www/housing/ahs/datacollection.html).

Table 5.1   Changes in house prices around 2006

A. Bust

	Permit rate in year					
	2000 (1)	2001 (2)	2002 (3)	2003 (4)	2004 (5)	2005 (6)
Price change 2006–2008	−5.809 [1.143] 0.00	−5.095 [1.073] 0.00	−5.069 [0.968] 0.00	−4.247 [0.473] 0.01	−4.395 [0.704] 0.00	−3.595 [0.614] 0.00
Number obs.	260	260	260	260	261	261
R2	0.09	0.08	0.10	0.03	0.13	0.12
	1984	1985	1986	1987	1988	1989

B. Boom

Price change 2004–2006	3.347 [0.751] 0.00	3.336 [0.697] 0.00	3.596 [0.623] 0.00	3.886 [0.533] 0.00	3.406 [0.442] 0.00	3.336 [0.370] 0.00
Number obs.	260	260	260	260	261	261
R2	0.07	0.08	0.11	0.17	0.19	0.24

Notes: Metropolitan areas: (MSAs); LHS variable: change in log house price, FHFEO index; Permit rate: residential building permits (houses and apartments)/housing units in 2000 census. Coefficient, [Standard error], *p*-value.

5.3   Data from the 1920s and 1930s

For the 1920s and 1930s, cross-sectional data on housing markets are few and far between. In this section, we describe the nature and sources of the data we have found. We do not have data on actual house sale prices. We do have city or metro-area averages of home owners' estimates of the potential sale values of their homes from a few years: 1920, 1930, and 1934. We have home ownership rates from the same years. Starting in the early 1930s, we have annual data on foreclosure rates by county. From within the 1920s, we have annual counts of residential construction permits by city. Our data on prices and home ownership rates in 1920 and 1930 are from the decennial census, and thus cover nearly all cities. Our data on construction permits cover a large sample of cities. Our data on foreclosures, house values, and home ownership rates from within the 1930s are for smaller samples, but they overlap the cities covered by the building permit data to an adequate degree.

With the data we have, we can observe the cross-sectional relation between construction in the 1920s boom and two elements of house market distress in the downturn of the Great Depression: foreclosure rates, and price declines as perceived by home owners. We can also observe the relationship between

Table 5.2   **Changes in average estimated values of single-family owner-occupied houses**

City	Average value ($)		Percent change
	1930	1934	
Portland, ME	6,875	5,453	−20.7
Providence, RI	6,981	5,370	−23.1
Austin, TX*	4,918	3,779	−23.2
Topeka, KS	4,176	3,203	−23.3
Waterbury, CT	8,995	6,822	−24.2
Baton Rouge, LA*	5,449	4,124	−24.3
Boise, ID*	4,463	3,323	−25.5
Salt Lake City, UT	4,566	3,398	−25.6
Peoria, IL	6,168	4,590	−25.6
Worcester, MA	8,144	6,038	−25.9
Hagerstown, MD*	6,709	4,973	−25.9
Butte, MT	3,254	2,412	−25.9
Fargo, ND*	6,561	4,850	−26.1
Saint Paul, MN	5,604	4,142	−26.1
Minneapolis, MN	6,346	4,643	−26.8
Sioux Falls, SD	5,218	3,744	−28.2
Columbia, SC	6,617	4,730	−28.5
Saint Joseph, MO	4,419	3,153	−28.6
Indianapolis, IN	5,985	4,238	−29.2
Richmond, VA	7,197	4,967	−31.0
Des Moines, IA	5,026	3,458	−31.2
Portland, OR	5,004	3,434	−31.4
Springfield, MO*	4,172	2,863	−31.4
Cleveland, OH	9,684	6,596	−31.9
Wheeling, WV	5,026	3,411	−32.1
Lincoln, NE	5,583	3,775	−32.4
Racine, WI	7,224	4,863	−32.7
Casper, WY*	3,684	2,455	−33.4
Sacramento, CA	5,803	3,837	−33.9
Jackson, MS	5,535	3,652	−34.0
Pueblo, CO	2,884	1,889	−34.5
Erie, PA	7,905	5,127	−35.1
Kenosha, WI	8,140	5,249	−35.5
Oklahoma City, OK	5,871	3,773	−35.7
Atlanta, GA	6,701	4,288	−36.0
Binghamton, NY	8,232	5,240	−36.3
Jacksonville, FL	6,128	3,890	−36.5
Trenton, NJ	6,360	4,029	−36.7
Wichita, KS	4,649	2,938	−36.8
Greensboro, NC*	7,432	4,663	−37.3
Seattle, WA	5,166	3,086	−40.3
Little Rock, AR	5,533	3,280	−40.7
Phoenix, AR	7,080	4,175	−41.0
Dallas, TX	5,973	3,422	−42.7
Lansing, MI	6,192	3,545	−42.7
Paducah, KY*	3,780	2,124	−43.8
Syracuse, NY	10,340	5,580	−46.0
San Diego, CA	6,747	3,583	−46.9
Birmingham, AL	5,662	2,939	−48.1
Wichita Falls, TX*	5,364	2,574	−52.0

*No construction permit data

construction, perceived values and home ownership rates across the 1920s as a whole, that is from 1920 to 1930.

5.3.1 Residential Construction Permits in the 1920s

Today's estimates of housing starts evolved from a program begun by the Bureau of Labor Statistics (BLS) in the early 1920s. In 1920, the BLS began to collect information from municipalities on issued residential building permits. Localities reported not just the number of structures permitted, but the "number of families provided for" in each structure. From 1921 through the end of the decade, data were collected from over 250 municipalities. Over later decades the BLS program was expanded to cover more municipalities and eventually taken over by the Census Bureau, which developed methods to estimate starts as distinct from permits. From the 1920s there are no city-level estimates of starts, but BLS publications from the era (e.g., US BLS, 1925) give for each city the number of permits issued in a year, separately for single-family houses and multifamily structures. They aggregate multifamily structures by the number of families provided for, which is close to the definition of a housing unit in postwar housing-start estimates.[4]

Standard historical estimates of nonfarm housing starts for the 1920s and 1930s are based on these permit data. The top two lines of figure 5.1 plot estimates of single- and multifamily starts, separately, from 1900 through 1940 (Carter et al. 2006, series Dc510, 511). According to these estimates, both types of construction rose from the early 1920s to the mid-1920s. They followed different paths after that. Construction of single-family houses, specifically, appears to have boomed in the middle of the decade, peaking in 1925 and falling off sharply in 1926. Multifamily starts, on the other hand, remained high through 1928. Many studies of the 1920s boom have identified the late 1920s as the time of a separate boom in apartment buildings motivated by "speculation on quick capital gains" (Hickman 1960, 319). "White elephant apartment buildings, poorly located and with low occupancy rates, figure prominently in journalistic accounts of the boom and are certainly a feature of the late 1920s" (Field 2011, 279).

Kimbrough and Snowden (2007) use the city-level permit data as indicators of construction to examine the relation between 1920s construction and 1930s construction across cities. They calculate the total number of permits, aggregating single- and multifamily structures, for each city in three-year spans: 1921 to 1923, 1924 to 1926, and 1927 to 1929. They find that the issuance of permits in the 1930s, controlling for population and other city characteristics, was strongly related to the stability and timing of permit issuance across the 1920s. Cities where permit rates fluctuated more within the 1920s—that had more pronounced peaks—and that peaked in 1924 to 1926 rather than 1927 to 1929, tended to issue fewer permits in the 1930s.

---

4. Kenneth Snowden kindly provided us with these data.

Fig. 5.1   Housing construction and house prices, 1900–1940 (annual)

Permits are not the same as starts, of course, even apart from the lag between permit issuance and the beginning of construction. Many permitted projects are abandoned, especially, perhaps, around the peak of a boom. Also, permit counts reported by municipalities do not directly measure construction outside city limits, which was an important component of the 1920s boom (US BLS 1925, 4).

However, we believe the permit counts are the *only* reliable cross-sectional data on single-family house markets from within the 1920s. Our other data are from the beginning or the end of the decade, or within the 1930s. We use the 1920s permit counts to look for patterns analogous to the ones in table 5.1. We think of permits as an indicator of the relative magnitude of the mid-1920s boom across cities. For that purpose, the difference between permits and starts may be not a big problem. In boom cities, perhaps, an especially large fraction of mid-1920s permits were abandoned. But that would only make permit counts a better indicator of the degree a city was affected by the boom.

5.3.2   Data from the Decennial Census

To scale the number of permits to a city's size, we need a measure of the number of housing units in a city at the beginning of the 1920s. Censuses of this era did not count housing units,[5] but they did count families. A census

---

5. Census publications give counts of "dwellings," but a multiunit structure was counted as just one dwelling.

family was a group of people who shared housekeeping. The number of census families was not the same as the number of housing units, on any definition. It was, at best, an indicator of the number of *occupied* units, but it could also differ from the number of occupied units. Some units held more than one family—"doubling up." Boarding houses and apartment hotels, two types of housing common in the 1920s, were hard to categorize. Instructions to census enumerators make it clear that these were important practical problems for census counts.[6] However, the number of census families appears to be the best available estimate of the number of units in a city, and has been used as such by many studies (e.g., Wickens and Foster 1937). We will scale permit counts to the number of census families in a city in 1920 for most of the results we present. We will also look at the relationship between permit counts over the 1920s and the change in the number of census families in a city from 1920 to 1930.

Along with the number of families, census publications give home ownership rates and home owners' value estimates in 1920 and 1930. In 1920, a special census survey of nonfarm households in many cities of the United States asked a respondent to report whether he owned his home. If the answer was yes, he was asked whether his dwelling was mortgaged. If his dwelling was mortgaged, he was asked for the amount of the mortgage and an estimate of the price the home would fetch if sold. Owner-occupants of multiunit structures such as duplexes and three-deckers were asked to prorate the structures' potential sale price down to the fraction of the structure occupied by the owner. Owners free of mortgages were *not* asked to report values. Published results of this survey (US Census Bureau 1923) give numbers of renters and home owners in a city in 1920. Results also give average estimated selling prices of owner-occupied homes in a city, including units within multifamily structures, for mortgaged structures only.

In 1930 a family reported whether its home was owned or rented. Renters reported the rent bill. Home owners were asked to estimate the potential sale price of the home. As in 1920, owner-occupants of multifamily structures were expected to prorate the value of the entire structure down to the fraction they occupied. A census official later admitted that "this point was unfortunately not covered in the printed instruction pamphlet [for census takers]. Because of this there are doubtless some cases in which the owner returned the entire value of the structure rather than only that part which he

---

6. Instructions for census enumerators are available at the Minnesota Population Center, Integrated Public Use Microdata Series [IPUMS] website (http://usa.ipums.org/usa/voliii /inst1930.shtml). The 1930 instructions, for example, contain this: "*Families in hotels.* All of the persons returned from a hotel should likewise be counted as a single 'family,' *except* that where a family of two or more members (as a husband and wife, or a mother and daughter) occupies permanent quarters in a hotel (or an apartment hotel), it should be returned separately, leaving the 'hotel family' made up principally of individuals having no other family relations. The distinction between an apartment house and an apartment hotel, and in turn between an apartment hotel and a hotel devoted mainly to transients, will often be difficult to establish."

occupied as a residence" (Wickens 1941, 18, footnote 3). Census publications give median, not average, estimated selling prices of owner-occupied homes in a city, including units within multifamily structures. Unfortunately, the 1930 census collected *no information at all about mortgages.* So figures from the 1930s census are for mortgaged and nonmortgaged structures *together.*

Standard historical estimates of nonfarm home ownership rates for the United States are based on these census data. These estimates show that something unusual happened over the 1920s: the national rate, which had fallen from 1890 to 1920, reversed its downward trend and rose from 1920 to 1930—similar, of course, to the increase in ownership rates over the early twenty-first century boom. From 1930 to 1940, the home ownership rate fell again (Carter et al. 2006, series Dc729, Dc713).

From city-level figures, we calculate home ownership rates as owned units in ratio to owned plus rented, excluding homes of unknown tenure. Over 250 of the cities covered by the construction permit data are covered by the census as well. Across these cities, we can observe the relationship between 1920s permits and changes in home ownership rates from 1920 to 1930. We will also use census data to observe the relationship between permits and the change in house values from 1920 to 1930, subject to a caveat we will detail later.

5.3.3   Data from within the Great Depression

Foreclosures

In most states, records of foreclosures are kept by county governments. In the mid-1930s, the Federal Home Loan Bank Board (FHLB) began to collect reports on the number of residential foreclosures filed or completed from about seventy-five urban counties; that is, counties with most of their population in cities (Federal Home Loan Bank Board 1936, 231). For a few cities the county was contiguous with the city limits but for most the county, and hence the foreclosure counts, covered a larger area. The numbers include foreclosures on multifamily dwellings, which may have been more than 20 percent of the total.[7] For about seventy counties, annual data are available beginning with 1932 and for the single year 1926. For 1927 to 1931, the FHLB collected data from only thirteen counties. Data through 1937 were published in Federal Home Loan Bank Board (1938, 191).

The standard annual estimate of nonfarm foreclosure rates in the United States (Carter et al. 2006, series Dc1257) was derived from these data. Figure 5.2 plots the series (fraction of mortgaged structures), which of course begins with 1926. It also plots Weir's (1992) annual series for the (nonfarm, civilian, private-sector) unemployment rate. There is no telling whether the

---

7. According to the FHLB (1938, 191), "approximately 80 percent of all foreclosures are on 1-to-4 family dwellings." That means less than 80 percent were on single-family houses.

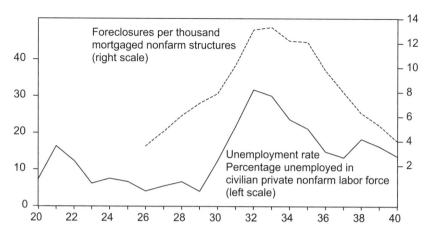

Fig. 5.2   Unemployment and foreclosure rates, 1920–1940 (annual)

foreclosure rate was much higher in the late 1920s than it had been during the boom, but it increased every year from 1926 to 1929, despite a stable, low unemployment rate. The foreclosure rate rose sharply after 1930 and peaked in 1933.

We use the foreclosure data county by county. To get a foreclosure rate, we divided foreclosure numbers by the number of dwellings—single-family houses *plus* multifamily residential structures (with each multifamily structure counted just once)—in the county (or other matching municipal unit) from the 1930 census. Almost sixty of the counties covered by the foreclosure data in 1926 and beginning with 1932 contain cities covered by the construction permits data. Across these years and counties, we can observe the cross-sectional relationship between foreclosure rates and 1920s permits.

The Financial Survey of Urban Housing and the Real Property Inventory

The most important data for our study come from surveys carried out by federal employees in early 1934: the "Financial Survey of Urban Housing" and the "Real Property Inventory." The Real Property Inventory was directed by the Census Bureau. It covered sixty-four cities. In some cities the survey extended to suburban areas outside the city limits, and published data are for the metropolitan area. It collected information mainly about the physical characteristics of the housing stock, but also recorded information about ownership. The survey was meant to cover all states, so it included some very small cities (such as Butte, Montana) from states without big cities. It did not include any of the really large cities of the day (New York City, Chicago, Philadelphia). The largest city covered was Cleveland, Ohio. None of the cities was a suburb or satellite of a larger city (with the possible exception of St. Paul, Minnesota). None was in the New York City metropolitan region (northern New Jersey, western Connecticut, downstate New York). Wickens (1937, table I) gives figures on the number of tenants and owners found in surveyed cities in the Real Property Inventory. From these figures we calculate home ownership rates as from census data. Forty-three of the cities covered by these data are also covered by the construction permit data. For these cities, we can observe the relationship between permit counts and changes in home ownership rates from 1930 to early 1934.

The associated Financial Survey of Urban Housing collected further information about housing finance and economic status of occupants in most of the cities covered by the Real Property Inventory. Complete data were collected from fifty-two cities. For six of these (Providence, RI; Cleveland, OH; Wheeling, WV; Atlanta, GA; Birmingham, AL; Seattle, WA; and San Diego, CA) the survey covered areas outside the city limits. Information was collected from owner-occupants, tenants and landlords, by mail and by agents' visits to homes. An owner-occupant was asked to report the "estimated market value of this property as of January 1st" 1930, 1933, and 1934, and a great deal of information about mortgage debt. He was also asked to report the year he had bought the property and what he paid for it. A renter was asked to report annual rental bills for 1929, 1932, and 1933. All subjects were asked to report household annual income in 1929, 1932, and 1933.[8]

Grebler, Blank, and Winnick (1956) constructed an annual index of single-family house prices for 1890 to 1934 from the home owners' retrospective reports of purchase prices in the twenty-two largest cities of the Financial Survey. This has become the standard house price index for the United States in the era (used by Shiller [2005] among others, and discussed by Fishback and Kollmann, chapter 6, this volume). The bottom line in figure 5.1 plots the index. Like single-family house starts, the house price index peaks in 1925. It falls about 6 percent from 1925 to 1930 and another 20 percent from 1930 to 1934. White (chapter 4, this volume) argues that this index may underestimate the actual level of house sale prices reached around 1925 because it does not include prices of houses that were lost by their owners between 1929 and 1934: "if foreclosures or abandonment of property were more common for owners who had bought late in the boom at high prices, the peak of the boom would be underestimated." The index may be reliable, however, with respect to the *timing* of the peak. The only other time series on single-family house prices from the 1920s, which are city-specific indexes for Cleveland, Seattle (Grebler, Blank, and Winnick 1956, 350), and Washington, DC (Fisher 1951), all peak in 1924, 1925, or 1926.[9]

To observe city-level changes in house values we use another set of figures derived from the 1934 survey. For a study published as Wickens (1941),

8. The exact questions asked in the Financial Survey are reproduced in Wickens (1937).
9. Nicholas and Scherbina (2010) show that prices of Manhattan real estate, dominated by the apartment market, of course, dipped in 1927 but rose to another peak in 1929.

researchers connected with the 1934 survey attempted to estimate the change in the value of residential real estate in the United States from 1930 to 1934. As part of this effort, they created estimates for survey cities of the average value of owner-occupied single-family houses, as reported by owners, in January 1934 and 1930 (table A10, 97). For 1934 the researchers used both the Financial Survey and the Real Property Inventory (78). For 1930 they used data from the 1930 census rather than the retrospective reports of 1930 house values from the 1934 survey, perhaps because other work with the survey data had suggested the retrospective values were biased downward (Wickens 1941, 36). To create figures that exactly matched what they had from 1934—averages, not medians, for single-family houses only, including areas outside city boundaries for the six metropolitan areas—they retabulated punch card records from the 1930 census (32, 77, 78). They were able to do this for fifty cities.

Table 5.2 shows the estimates city by city. Values fell less than 25 percent in cities such as Providence, Topeka, and Austin. The greatest declines, about 50 percent, occurred in cities including Wichita Falls, Birmingham, and San Diego. The average decrease in values in these fifty cities, weighted by 1930 population, was 33 percent. For comparison, the decline in the overall Case-Shiller repeat-sale index from July 2006 to the end of 2008 was about 27 percent. (Relative to wages or other prices, house prices fell much more after 2006.)

We believe these estimates are the best available city-by-city estimates of changes in house values in the downturn of the Great Depression. Of course, they are not actual sale prices. Even as measures of changes in the perceived market value of a given house, they are less than perfect. They must also reflect changes between 1930 and 1934 in the stock of owner-occupied single-family houses in a city. There may have been little change over 1930 to 1934 in a city's total house stock, because there was very little construction (see figure 5.1), but there must have been changes in the distribution of the housing stock between owner occupancy and rental or vacancy.

The forty cities covered by these estimates are also covered by the building permits data. For these cities, we can observe the relationship between house value decline in the downturn of the Great Depression and 1920s permits. Fortunately, though the sample is small, it appears to be representative of the United States with respect to the timing of house permits in the 1920s boom. Figure 5.3 plots index numbers of permits for single-family houses for these forty cities, and for all cities. Both sets of cities peaked in 1925. Importantly, though total single-family permits in the forty cities peaked in the mid-1920s, that was not true for each city. In about half of the cities, there were more single-family permits in the early (1921 to 1923) or late (1927 to 1929) 1920s. Figure 5.4 plots index numbers for multifamily units. Here the forty cities were not typical of the United States, which makes sense, since they did not include the big, apartment-dominated cities of the day such as New York City and Chicago.

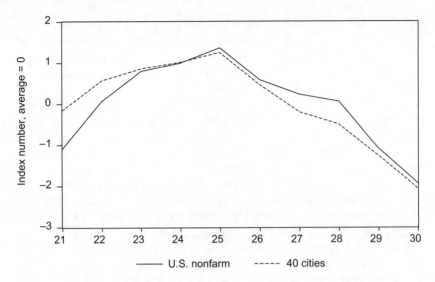

Fig. 5.3   Residential building permits, single-family houses, 1921–1930

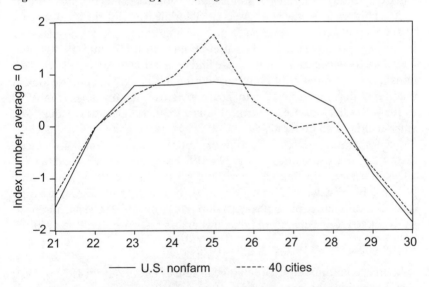

Fig. 5.4   Residential building permits, multifamily units, 1921–1930

5.4   Results

To observe relations between a city's participation in the 1920s boom and other variables, we run many cross-sectional regressions with permit counts on the right-hand side, scaled to 1920 census families and with control variables as appropriate. (Results were similar if we scaled permits to 1930 census families.) Following Kimbrough and Snowden, we average annual permit counts up to three-year intervals: the early 1920s (1921 to 1923), the mid-1920s (1924 to 1926), and the late 1920s (1927 to 1929). Some kind of aggregation across years is necessary because there is strong collinearity between permit counts for individual years. But we distinguish between single-family and multifamily structures.

When we put the change in a city's number of census families from 1920 to 1930 on the left-hand side, we find the change in census families was positively related to permit counts over the 1920s as a whole and to permits within most intervals of the 1920s. But the change in census families was peculiarly *un*related to single-family house permits in the mid-1920s. It was also unrelated to multifamily permits in the late 1920s, the period often identified as an apartment boom. These patterns may indicate that cities with more boom-period permits experienced some combination of especially high growth in vacancy rates and especially high rates of permit abandonment.

Next, using the sample of forty cities from the Financial Survey, we put the 1930 to 1934 change in the average house value on the left-hand side. We find average perceived house values fell more from 1930 to 1934 in cities that had experienced high rates of single-family house permits during the mid-1920s. This remains true when we control for measures of the local severity of the Depression—changes in family income, changes in retail sales—or for changes in average rents. The pattern holds *only* for the mid-1920s boom years and for *single-family* houses: we find no relation to early- or late-1920s house permits, or to multifamily permit rates. Using census data, we look at the change in values from 1920 to 1930 and across the entire span from 1920 to 1934. Results indicate that from 1920 to 1930, average house values *rose more* in cities with high rates of mid-1920s house permits.

The foreclosure data, which combine houses and multifamily structures, show that foreclosure rates over 1932 to 1934 were positively related to mid-1920s house permits and also positively related to late-1920s multifamily permits. Finally, we find that mid-1920s house permits were negatively related to the change in home ownership rates from 1930 to 1934, and positively related to the change in home ownership rates from 1920 to 1930.

5.4.1   Changes in Census Families 1920–1930

In an accounting sense, the change in census families from 1920 to 1930 was determined by construction of new housing units over the entire decade, changes in rates of vacancy and doubling up, changes in municipal boundaries, destruction of old structures, breakup of single-family houses into apartments, and errors in the census count. Permits measure just one of these determinants, construction, and measure that imperfectly because some permits are abandoned.

Table 5.3 shows correlations between the 1920 to 1930 change in the log of census families in a city, and the city's permit counts scaled to the number of 1920 census families in the city. Panel A is for the 254-city sample of all cities in the permit data and the 1920 census. Panel B is for the sample of

Table 5.3 **Correlations between construction permits and changes in census families**

A. 254 cities

		House permits			Multifamily permits	
	ΔLn(Families) (1)	1924–1926 (2)	1921–1923 (3)	1927–1929 (4)	1924–1926 (5)	1921–1923 (6)
Houses 24–26	0.73					
Houses 21–23	0.68	0.79				
Houses 27–29	0.71	0.69	0.51			
Multifam. 24–26	0.46	0.14	0.13	0.03		
Multifam. 21–23	0.47	0.13	0.25	0.10	0.59	
Multifam. 27–29	0.58	0.28	0.24	0.28	0.80	0.52

B. 40 cities

		House permits			Multifamily permits	
	ΔLn(Families) (1)	1924–1926 (2)	1921–1923 (3)	1927–1929 (4)	1924–1926 (5)	1921–1923 (6)
Houses 24–26	0.69					
Houses 21–23	0.70	0.79				
Houses 27–29	0.84	0.71	0.70			
Multifam. 24–26	0.27	0.43	0.36	0.18		
Multifam. 21–23	0.36	0.10	0.22	0.10	0.47	
Multifam. 27–29	0.54	0.38	0.42	0.73	0.40	0.23

forty cities also covered by the 1930 to 1934 value data. Looking down the first columns, one sees that in both samples growth in the number of census families was strongly correlated with permit counts of every period. The second columns show that mid-1920s single-family permits were strongly correlated with single-family permits in the other two periods. The last rows show that late-1920s multifamily permits were strongly correlated with multifamily permits in other periods. Correlations were much weaker between single- and multifamily permits.

Table 5.4 shows results of regressing the change in families on permit counts, for both samples. Estimated coefficients would be close to one if all permitted projects were carried out and construction was uncorrelated with the other factors affecting the change in families. Coefficients could be less than one if some permitted projects were abandoned, but abandonment rates were uncorrelated with permit counts. Results in columns (1) and (2), which aggregates permit counts across the decade as a whole, seem to match this pattern.

But results in columns (3) and (4), with permit counts divided into the early, mid, and late 1920s, do not. For the larger sample in column (3), two coefficients are not significantly different from zero: the coefficient on mid-1920s house permits, and the coefficient on multifamily permits in the late 1920s. This is true even though the simple correlations between these variables and the change in families is positive (as indicated in table 5.2). Coefficients on other periods' permits are significant and larger in magnitude than their counterparts in column (1). For the smaller sample in column (4), coefficient values are similar to column (3) but none is significantly different from zero—no surprise given the high correlations apparent in table 5.3. When multifamily permits are excluded from the right-hand side in column (5), coefficients for early- and late-1920s house permits are significant at conventional levels and larger than one, while the coefficient on mid-1920s house permits is not significantly different from zero.

Statistically, these results mean that across cities the change in families was positively related to permit counts *outside* the boom periods. But the change in families was positively related to boom-period permits—mid-1920s for houses, late 1920s for multifamily—only to the degree that boom-period permits were positively correlated with other periods' permits. To put it another way, the change in families was positively related to the portion of variation in boom-period permits that was correlated with other periods' permits (which boosts the other periods' coefficients in columns [3], [4], and [5]). The extra variation in permit counts across cities specific to the boom periods was unrelated to the growth in family count across the 1920s.

Given the factors making up the change in families, this means cities where permit counts were especially high during the booms, relative to permit counts in other periods, must have experienced some combination of the following: high rates of permit abandonment, increases in vacancy rates, destruction of old housing, decreases in doubling up, less breakup of houses

Table 5.4   **Change in city census families, 1920–1930**

Sample:	254 cities (1)	40 cities (2)	254 cities (3)	40 cities (4)	40 cities (5)
Coeffs.					
Houses 21–29	0.971 [0.142] 0.00	0.789 [0.142] 0.00			
Multifam. 21–29	0.751 [0.053] 0.00	0.716 [0.121] 0.00			
Houses 24–26			−0.736 [0.570] 0.20	−0.789 [0.129] 0.54	−0.508 [0.765] 0.51
Houses 21–23			1.953 [0.451] 0.00	1.496 [1.475] 0.32	2.259 [0.700] 0.00
Houses. 27–29			2.233 [0.540] 0.00	3.988 [2.273] 0.09	2.685 [1.323] 0.05
Multifam. 24–26			1.081 [0.479] 0.02	1.424 [1.574] 0.37	
Multifam. 21–23		1.263	0.692 0.00	[0.344] 0.79	[2.579]
Multifam. 27–29		0.084	−2.301 0.87	[0.500] 0.13	[1.477]
R^2	0.97	0.85	0.97	0.88	0.78
R bar 2	0.97	0.84	0.97	0.86	0.77

Notes: Coefficient, [White robust SE], p-value.

into apartments, less expansion of municipal boundaries, and census counts erroneously low in 1930 or erroneously high in 1920.

Of the items on this list, two stand out as likely correlates of boom-period permits: permit abandonment and vacancy. According to Frederick Lewis Allen (1931), vacant buildings and abandoned projects were conspicuous in the late 1920s:

> 1928 or 1929 . . . many suburbs were plainly overbuilt: as one drove out along the highways, one began to notice houses that must have stood long untenanted, shops with staring vacant windows, districts blighted with half-finished and abandoned "improvements." (287)

5.4.2   Changes in House Values 1930–1934

Table 5.5 shows results for changes in values from 1930 to January 1934. Column (1) shows results with single- and multifamily permit rates on the right-hand side. Column (2) includes only house permits. Either way

Table 5.5   Changes in house values 1930–1934, 40 cities

Coeff. on	(1)	(2)	(3)	(4)	(5)	(6)	(7)	(8)	(9)
Houses 24–26	−2.126	−2.206	−2.141	−2.131	−2.346	−2.610	−2.511	−2.079	−2.515
	[0.982]	[0.784]	[0.875]	[0.579]	[0.845]	[0.993]	[0.608]	[0.590]	[0.620]
	0.04	0.01	0.02	0.00	0.01	0.01	0.00	0.00	0.00
Houses 21–23	−0.134	−0.126	−0.347	−0.487	−0.437	0.359	0.069		
	[1.190]	[1.176]	[1.060]	[1.079]	[1.119]	[1.105]	[1.136]		
	0.91	0.92	0.75	0.65	0.70	0.75	0.95		
Houses 27–29	−0.767	−1.179	−0.278	−0.745	0.735	0.612	−0.007		
	[1.612]	[0.964]	[1.695]	[0.913]	[1.654]	[1.932]	[0.957]		
	0.64	0.23	0.87	0.42	0.66	0.75	0.99		
Multifam. 24–26	−0.786		−0.666		−1.166	−0.669			
	[1.542]		[1.523]		[1.530]	[1.780]			
	0.61		0.67		0.45	0.70			
Multifam. 21–23	0.465		−0.879		1.068	−1.467			
	[1.392]		[1.259]		[1.740]	[1.365]			
	0.74		0.49		0.54	0.29			

	(1)	(2)	(3)	(4)	(5)	(6)	(7)	(8)	(9)
Multifam. 27–29	−0.972 [2.029] *0.74*		−0.997 [2.275] *0.66*		−1.258 [2.052] *0.54*	−1.060 [2.398] *0.66*			
House 21–23+ 27–29								−0.745 [0.961] *0.44*	0.808 [1.182] *0.50*
Multifam. 21–29								−2.459 [1.816] *0.18*	−2.926 [1.884] *0.13*
ΔIncome tenants			0.299 [0.135] *0.04*	0.263 [0.127] *0.05*				0.290 [0.128] *0.03*	
ΔRetail sales					0.288 [0.115] *0.02*				
ΔRents						0.356 [0.122] *0.01*	0.310 [0.100] *0.00*		0.346 [0.120] *0.01*
R bar 2	0.32	0.38	0.40	0.43	0.41	0.44	0.46	0.45	0.49

Notes: Coefficient, [White robust SE], *p*-value.

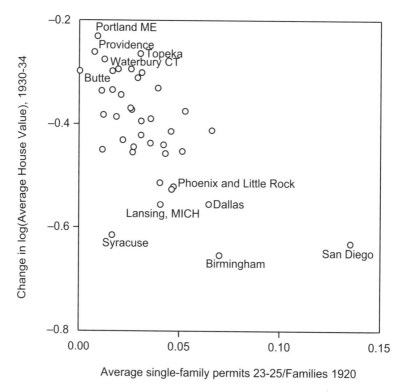

Fig. 5.5   Change in average house values 1930–1934 and mid-1920s house permits

coefficients on 1924 to 1926 house permit rates are negative and significantly different from zero at conventional levels. Coefficients on multifamily permits, and on house permits in the early or late 1920s, are *not* significantly different from zero. Figure 5.5 is a scatterplot that shows the negative correlation between the change in house values and the mid-1920s house permit rate.

Many studies of postwar data find that metro-area house prices are affected by exogenous shocks to growth in local employment, personal income per capita, and unemployment rates, presumably through demand (Case and Shiller 2003). It is important to control for such variables here. Unfortunately, there are no data on local unemployment rates from around 1933 but the Financial Survey itself gives good measures of income changes in reported household incomes for 1930 and 1933. The published survey results (in Wickens 1941) give incomes for home owners and tenants separately. We use tenants' income for the results we present, in case home owners' own income changes biased their assessment of house values or vice versa, but all results were very similar if we used the change in owners' income. As an alternative measure of local economic conditions, we use the change in retail sales from 1929 to 1933 for the county containing the city. These are the same data used by Fishback, Horrace and Kantor (2005). The original sources for the data give retail sales for cities as well, but the county data are a better match for the results on foreclosure rates that we will present later. Adding these variables to the RHS, in columns (3), (4), and (5), makes little difference to the building permit coefficients. Coefficients on income change and retail sales are both positive and significantly different from zero, as one would expect.

Recall that the 1934 survey asked tenants to report rental bills in 1933. The same researchers who estimated the change in single-family house prices to January 1934 also estimated the change in a city's average rents from 1930 to 1933, using the survey data for 1933 and retabulated 1930 census records (Wickens 1941, table B-8, 125). For columns (6) and (7) we add the change in average city rents to the RHS. The coefficient on the change in rents is positive, indicating that, as one would expect, house values fell more in cities where rents fell more. But the coefficient on mid-1920s house permits is still positive, significantly different from zero, and even larger in magnitude than in columns (1) through (5).

None of our results show a significant relation between the 1930 to 1934 change in house values and permits for multifamily units, or permits for houses outside the mid-1920s. To make sure that this is not just because of collinearity between those variables, in columns (8) and (9) we combine all multifamily units into one variable and do the same for early- and late-1920s house permits (the sum of permits 1921 to 1923 and 1927 to 1929, in ratio to 1920 census families). Coefficients on these variables are still not significantly different from zero.

5.4.3   Changes in House Values 1920–1930 and 1920–1934

Next we examine how mid-1920s house permits were related to changes in average values from 1920 to 1930, and over the entire span from 1920 to 1934. There is an important caveat for the results for 1920 to 1930, but together with the results for 1920 to1934 they indicate that boom cities saw bigger increases in average values from 1920 to 1930. The caveat is that we cannot make a perfect match between the data for 1920 and 1930. The 1920 figures are averages for owner-occupied units including the owner's portion of multifamily structures, *excluding* structures that were not mortgaged (recall owners without mortgages were not asked to report house values). Published 1930 census figures also include the owner's portion of multifamily structures, but include mortgaged structures, and are medians not averages. Researchers for the 1934 survey calculated 1930 figures for most survey cities that are a better match for the 1920 data: *averages* for cities (not metropolitan areas), apparently by retabulating census punch cards (Wickens 1941, table A-6). But they could not exclude nonmortgaged structures

Table 5.6   Changes in house values 1920–1930 and 1920–1934

| | 1920–1930 | | | | 1920–1934 | |
| | 45 cities | | 254 cities | | 42 cities | |
Coeff. on	(1)	(2)	(3)	(4)	(5)	(6)
Houses	5.353	4.167	3.614	4.145	2.122	1.631
24–26	[2.185]	[1.738]	[1.420]	[1.355]	[1.268]	[1.045]
	0.02	0.02	0.01	0.00	0.10	0.13
Houses.	−6.107	−5.060	−4.215	−3.946	−5.796	−5.337
21–23	[2.310]	[2.111]	[1.223]	[1.229]	[1.451]	[1.319]
	0.01	0.02	0.00	0.00	0.00	0.00
Houses.	−0.749	0.005	−1.441	−1.936	−3.359	−1.291
27–29	[3.638]	1.666	[0.797]	[0.773]	[2.505]	[1.141]
	0.84	1.00	0.07	0.01	0.19	0.26
Multifam.	−3.198		2.635		0.659	
24–26	[3.338]		[0.761]		[1.887]	
	0.34		0.00		0.73	
Multifam.	5.674		0.331		3.144	
21–23	[5.362]		[0.370]		[2.782]	
	0.30		0.37		0.27	
Multifam.	1.418		−0.208		3.876	
27–29	[4.483]		[0.721]		[3.487]	
	0.75		0.77		0.27	
R bar 2	0.04	0.09	0.16	0.06	0.32	0.34

Notes: Coefficient, [White robust SE], *p*-value.

from the averages, because the 1930 census collected no information about mortgages. This may be a problem. In the 1934 survey, average values were higher for mortgaged houses. If that was also true in 1930, and if the fraction of mortgaged houses in 1930 was larger in cities that had more mid-1920s single-family permits, then there will be a positive bias to any estimated relation between mid-1920s permits and the change in values from 1920 to 1930.

Subject to this caveat, the data indicate that mid-1920s house permits were positively related to the change in house values across 1920 to 1930. Table 5.6, columns (1) and (2) show results from the better data for the 1934 survey cities. Columns (3) and (4) show results from the published 1930 census medians, which give a larger sample. Generally, the coefficient on mid-1920s house permits is positive and significantly different from zero.

For 1934 there are figures for survey cities that exactly match 1920 data. Wickens (1941, table D-7) gives average values in surveyed cities (excluding outlying areas) for *mortgaged* owner-occupied units (including multifamily structures) only. The last two columns of table 5.4 show results of regressions with the 1920 to 1934 change on the LHS. The coefficients on early-1920s permits are significantly negative but the coefficients on mid-1920s permits are positive and not significantly different from zero. Thus, there is no indication that boom cities' house values *rose less* from 1920 to 1934. Since we know that boom cities' values *fell more* from 1930 to 1934, it seems safe to conclude that boom cities saw greater increases from 1920 to 1930.

Of course, the change in a city's average home value from 1920 to 1930 must have been affected by changes in characteristics of the stock due to net construction. If newly built houses were generally priced higher than old ones, average values would rise more in cities with more construction, whether or not construction was associated with differences in prices of given houses. But this *cannot* account for the apparent relation between mid-1920s permits and the 1920 to 1930 change in average values. Houses built in the late 1920s were even newer, yet coefficients on late-1920s permits are *not* positive.

Finally, we want to know whether the change in house values 1930 to 1934 was actually related to 1920s house construction, or to the change in house values 1920 to 1930, or to both. To do this, we must change the specification a bit. Our measures of house values in 1930 may be affected by unaccounted-for factors (such as measurement errors) absent from our 1934 measures. If we simply added the change in values 1920 to 1930 to the RHS of the specification for table 5.3, corresponding to:

$$\text{Ln}(P_{1934}) - \text{Ln}(P_{1930}) = \text{Constant} + \beta\,[\text{Ln}(P_{1930}) - \text{Ln}(P_{1920})] + \ldots,$$

then such factors would tend to create a negative estimate for β even if the "true" β were zero. Thus we instead estimate:

$$\text{Ln}(P_{1934}) = \text{Constant} + \gamma 1\,\text{Ln}(P_{1930}) + \gamma_2\,\text{Ln}(P_{1920}) + \ldots,$$

which means: $\gamma_1 = 1 + \beta$ $\gamma_2 = -\beta$. If the true value of β is zero, the estimated coefficient on 1920 values (γ_2) should be close to zero and the estimated coefficient on 1930 values (γ_1) should be close to one. If the true value of β is between zero and negative one, the estimated coefficient on 1920 values should be positive, and the estimated coefficient on 1930 values should be about equal to one *minus* the coefficient on 1920 values.

Results in table 5.7 indicate the change in values 1930 to 1934 was related to *both* mid-1920s construction and the value change from 1920 to 1930. In all columns, the LHS variable is the log of 1934 single-family house values we have been using all along. For columns (1) and (2), the 1930 number is the average value of single-family houses, which is the best match for the 1934 number but a worse match for the 1920 measure (which is city only, includes owners' portion of multifamily, mortgaged only). For columns (3) and (4), the 1930 number is the one that best matches the 1920 number (city only, including owners' portion of multifamily, mortgaged and nonmortgaged). Either way, the coefficient on 1920 values is positive (significantly different from zero except in column [1]) and the estimated coefficient on 1930 values should be about equal to one *minus* the coefficient on 1920 values. The estimated coefficient on mid-1920s house permits is still negative.

Table 5.7   **Changes in house values 1920–1930 and 1920–1934 and 1920s construction permits**

Coeff. on	40 cities			
	(1)	(2)	(3)	(4)
1930 value matching	0.796	0.773		
1934 measure	[0.097]	[0.084]		
	0.00	0.00		
1930 value matching			0.644	0.625
1920 measure			[0.111]	[0.110]
			0.00	0.00
1920 value 0.147	0.169	0.336	0.348	
	[0.104]	[0.085]	[0.130]	[0.125]
	0.15	0.05	0.01	0.01
Permits houses	−2.870	−2.697	−2.944	−2.788
24–26	[0.515]	[0.482]	[0.650]	[0.595]
	0.00	0.00	0.00	0.00
ΔIncome tenants	0.242		0.167	
	[0.135]		[0.157]	
	0.08		0.30	
ΔRetail sales		0.328		0.277
		[0.089]		[0.113]
		0.00		0.02
Rbar 2	0.92	0.94	0.88	0.89

Notes: LHS variable: Ln (1934 house value). Coefficient [White robust SE], *p*-value.

5.4.4   Foreclosures

Recall that foreclosure counts include foreclosures on multifamily structures. Some of the counties covered by the foreclosure data contained more than one city covered by the building-permit data: for these we aggregated the cities' permits. To control for local economic conditions we add the change in county retail sales 1929 to 1933 to the RHS. The FHLB foreclosure data include New York City and a number of its New Jersey suburbs; we exclude these from our regression samples since we have no sensible definition of "local economic conditions" for such places. On the same grounds we exclude Camden, New Jersey, (a suburb of Philadelphia). A number of states had more than one county included in the foreclosure data. State laws (such as, in the early 1930s, foreclosure moratoriums, Wheelock [2008]) are a potentially important factor affecting foreclosure rates, given economic local conditions. Thus, it may be appropriate to cluster standard errors at the state level.

In table 5.8, columns (1) and (2) show results for the average foreclosure rate 1932 to 1934, with and without clustered SEs. The coefficient on mid-1920s house permits is positive and significantly different from zero, indi-

Table 5.8   **Foreclosure rates**

	1932–1934 Clustered SE		1926	1935–1937
	(1)	(2)	(3)	(4)
Counties	58	58	58	57
Coeff on.				
Houses	0.74	—	−0.01	0.15
1924–26	[0.34]	[0.30]	[0.04]	[0.22]
	0.04	0.02	0.87	0.49
Houses	−0.64	—	0.01	−0.32
1921–23	[0.35]	[0.37]	[0.05]	[0.28]
	0.08	0.09	0.87	0.26
Houses	−0.61	—	0.00	−0.13
1927–29	[0.26]	[0.26]	[0.04]	[0.17]
	0.03	0.02	0.93	0.44
Multifam.	0.05	—	−0.04	0.06
1924–26	[0.43]	[0.41]	[0.05]	[0.28]
	0.91	0.91	0.41	0.84
Multifam.	−0.39	—	0.05	0.10
1921–23	[0.24]	[0.28]	[0.06]	[0.29]
	0.12	0.17	0.44	0.74
Multifam.	1.32	—	0.04	0.20
1927–29	[0.52]	[0.50]	[0.07]	[0.38]
	0.02	0.01	0.53	0.60
ΔRetail sales	−0.05	—	0.00	−0.04
1929–33	[0.02]	[0.02]	[0.00]	[0.02]
	0.02	0.03	0.18	0.04
R^2	0.35	0.35	0.10	0.13

Notes: Coefficient, [White robust SE], *p*-value.

cating that boom cities saw higher foreclosure rates in the downturn. The coefficient on late 1920s multifamily permits is also significantly positive. Foreclosure rates for 1926, in column (3), and 1935 to 1937 in column (4), appear unrelated to any of the permit variables.

Only fifteen counties in the foreclosure data contain cities covered by the 1934 survey, so we cannot very well estimate the relation between foreclosures and house value changes from 1930 to 1934. But figure 5.6 is a scatterplot of these counties' average foreclosure rates from 1932 to 1934 against changes in house values for the survey cities they contain. The obvious negative relation indicates that foreclosure rates were higher in counties where city house values fell more.

5.4.5   Home Ownership Rates

Changes in home ownership rates should reflect the relative frequency of foreclosures and distressed sales. Assuming a family is unlikely to buy an-

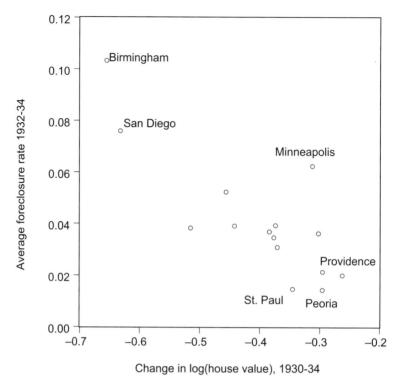

Fig. 5.6   Foreclosure rates 1932–1934 and change in average house values 1930–1934

other house shortly after a foreclosure or distressed sale, and some degree of persistence in residence in a city, cities that experienced higher rates of distressed sales and foreclosures over 1929 to 1933 would show greater decreases in home ownership rates from 1930 to 1934.

In table 5.9, columns (1) through (5) show results of regressing changes in ownership rates from 1930 to 1934 on various combinations of 1920s construction permits and changes in income or rents from 1930 to 1934. Coefficients on mid-1920s house permits are generally negative: in the 1929 to 1933 downturn, home ownership rates fell more in cities that had boomed in the mid-1920s. Figure 5.7 is a scatterplot that shows the negative correlation between the change in the home ownership rate from 1930 to 1934 and mid-1920s single-family permits. As the stock of structures was more or less fixed over 1930 to 1934, this correlation indicates that over the 1929 to 1933 downturn boom cities saw more conversions of formerly owner-occupied units to rental or vacancy.

Was the change in the home ownership rate actually related to 1920s permits, or to the 1930 to 1934 change in house values? Because the home own-

Table 5.9   Changes in home ownership rates

| | 1930–1934 | | | | | | 1920–1930 | | 1920–1934 |
	(1)	(2)	(3)	(4)	(5)	(6)	(7)	(8)	(9)
Cities	40	40	40	40	43	43	254	43	43
Coeffs.									
Houses 24–26	−68.722	−82.164	−67.002	−79.406	−68.907	−64.385	83.588	120.928	52.021
	[39.656]	[33.177]	[33.606]	[29.516]	[33.235]	[23.283]	[32.565]	[44.364]	[57.053]
	0.09	0.02	0.05	0.01	0.04	0.01	0.01	0.01	0.37
Houses 21–23	−24.080	−7.204	−17.139	−2.760	−2.766		−114.328	−139.575	−142.341
	[35.500]	[30.943]	[41.595]	[34.552]	[41.574]		[31.800]	[41.201]	[64.595]
	0.50	0.82	0.68	0.94	0.95		0.00	0.00	0.03
Houses 27–29	−47.411	−15.353	−17.139	13.491	−34.419		−35.990	−35.419	−69.838
	[63.891]	[53.310]	[41.595]	[44.433]	[39.349]		[39.164]	[45.046]	[51.288]
	0.46	0.78	0.68	0.76	0.39		0.36	0.44	0.18
Multifam. 24–26	35.336	50.247							
	[39.816]	[43.712]							
	0.38	0.26							
Multifam. 21–23	35.336	−0.336							
	[39.816]	[47.583]							
	0.381	0.99							
Multifam. 27–29	63.071	60.947							
	[93.484]	[69.544]							
	0.50	0.39							
ΔIncome tenants	4.058		5.441						
	[5.319]		[5.293]						
	0.45		0.31						
ΔRents		10.029		11.016					
		[4.594]		[4.941]					
		0.04		0.03					
ΔHouse value 30–34						8.495			
						[5.352]			
						0.12			
R bar 2	0.39	0.48	0.37	0.47	0.39	0.40	0.09	0.20	0.19

Notes: Coefficient, [White robust SE], p-value.

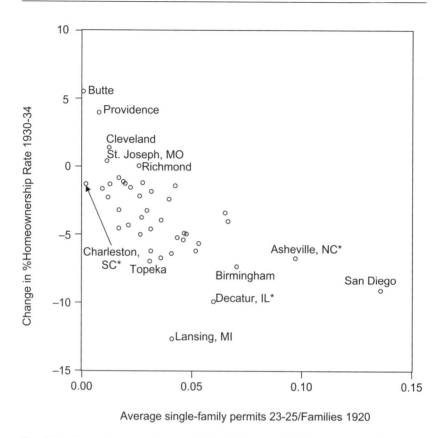

Fig. 5.7   Change in ownership rate 1930–1934 and mid-1920s house permits

ership data are for survey cities, we can check. For column (6), RHS variables were mid-1920s house permits rates and the 1930 to 1934 change in house values. The coefficient on permit rates is significantly different from zero and about the same as in the other columns. The coefficients on the value change from 1930 to 1934 are not significantly different from zero. Apparently it was really a city's participation in the mid-1920s boom, not the change in house values that was related to the change in the home ownership rate.

Columns (7) and (8) show results for change in home ownership rates from 1920 to 1930. Here the coefficient on mid-1920s house permits is positive and significantly different from zero, showing that boom cities saw greater *increases* in home ownership across the 1920s. With the change 1920 to 1934 on the LHS, in column (9), the coefficient on mid-1920s permits is positive but not significantly different from zero.

5.5   Remaining Questions

Clearly, a city's participation in the mid-1920s house boom was strongly related to the degree of distress in its house market after 1930. But what was the mechanism linking the mid-1920s boom to house market conditions after 1929? And why did those particular cities boom in the mid-1920s?

5.5.1   What Was Different about Boom Cities in 1929?

In 1930, the peak of the single-family house boom was four or five years in the past. Why did the cities that had boomed then experience higher fore-closure rates and greater decreases in perceived house values in the Great Depression? What was different about boom cities as of 1929? Research on postwar house markets suggests some possibilities. In the aftermath of local booms in the postwar era, asking prices of home owners attempting to sell their houses have exhibited "downward stickiness," falling much slower than prices in realized sales, while the number of housing units for sale and the average time a unit remains on the market increase (Genesove and Mayer 2001; Case and Quigley 2008). Benitez-Silva et al. (2010) find that a home owner overestimates the value of his house more if he bought the house at a time of rising house prices, mainly because he overestimates subsequent capital gains.

Perhaps house prices were also subject to downward stickiness in the late 1920s. If so, then as of 1929 home owners' estimates of potential sale prices could have been higher, relative to actual sale prices, in mid-1920s boom cities. House markets in these cities would more likely be in a state of dis-equilibrium, with asking prices unusually high relative to selling prices and larger numbers of houses on the market, unsold, for longer. As overestimates dissipated after 1929, perhaps especially fast in response to the conspicuous events of the Depression, perceived values would fall farther in boom cities because they had been further above equilibrium in 1930. If this hypothesis is correct, as of 1929 boom cities should have tended to have higher fractions of houses for sale, longer average times on the market, and higher ratios of home owners' estimates to actual sale prices. Unfortunately, we have not found data on such variables from around 1929.

Another mechanism apparent in postwar data is interaction between shocks to a local house market and the degree to which home owners in the market are already leveraged. In data from 1984 to 1994, Lamont and Stein (1999) found that house values were more sensitive to changes in per capita income in metropolitan areas where home owners reported especially high ratios of mortgage debt to house values. Perhaps home owners in mid-1920s boom cities were more leveraged as of 1929, and that magnified the effect of the cyclical downturn on those cities' house markets. Also, in the late 1920s many mortgages were outright balloon loans with maturities as short as five years (White, chapter 4, this volume). Perhaps in boom cities more balloon mortgages came due in 1930 to 1933—about five years after the boom. According to Hickman (1960, 323) "after the boom collapsed many a borrower was unable to refinance his mortgage balance when it came due. Foreclosures and distress sales would have been fewer . . . during the early 1930s had mortgages been fully amortized."

Unfortunately, we have found no cross-sectional data on home owners' mortgage debt around 1929. As we have noted, the 1930 census collected no information about mortgage debt. The 1934 Financial Survey gathered extensive data from home owners on their mortgage debt at the time of the survey. It also asked about their mortgage debt back in 1930. We have calculated home owners' leverage (mortgage debt as a fraction of mortgaged homes' values, or as a fraction of all homes' values) in our cities in 1920, and in 1930 based on the retrospective data from 1934 home owners. We have found no relation between these variables and 1920s permits, changes in house values, or ownership rates. But 1934 home owners were a select group. They had survived the wave of foreclosures in 1932 and 1933. There is no telling what we would find if we had information about leverage of *all* home owners in 1930, including those who lost their homes before 1934.

5.5.2   What Was Different about Boom Cities in the Early 1920s?

Models of house markets discussed previously imply that a general increase in house prices and building can be caused by decreases in real interest rates, innovations that loosen credit supply in imperfect financial markets, and factors that increase the utility people derive from a unit of housing. Under rational expectations, price increases at the inception of a boom reflect forecasts of shocks' effects on (implicit) rents in the long run, when the building supply response is complete. In models with bubbles, people incorrectly extrapolate experienced price increases into expectations of the future, with feedback to current prices, so fundamental shocks that would tend to raise a market's prices can cause bigger price increases and more building than would occur under rational expectations, until the bubble bursts.

With or without bubbles, a general shock can cause some local markets to boom more than others as the shock interacts with localities' preexisting characteristics. Shocks that change the nature of local amenities, or the functional relation between population size and endogenous amenities, can boost some localities' rank in the long-run structure of relative house prices. Empirical studies of postwar housing markets have found that financial innovations in mortgage credit raised house prices more in localities where credit had been especially restricted before due to a lack of local lending institutions or low wealth of potential borrowers (Mian and Sufi 2010; Favara and Imbs 2011). Studies have examined the possibility that relative house prices in hot localities were raised by the technological innovation of air conditioning, which raised the amenity value of their climates (Biddle 2012). In the early twenty-first century price increases were larger relative to growth in housing supply in metropolitan areas where local government regulations restricted land development (Saks 2008; Gyourko, Saiz, and Summers 2008) or geography restricted the marginal supply of buildable land (Saiz 2010).

The house-building boom of the 1920s has been attributed to automobiles; low, stable, real interest rates; new types of financial intermediaries that supplied more credit to home buyers and builders; and a lack of house building during the First World War that left housing supply below equilibrium at the start of the 1920s (White, chapter 4, this volume). The last factor cannot explain the mid-1920s: a supply snapback should be associated with *falling* prices. But the others would tend to raise prices as well as construction. Automobiles, that is to say the decreasing cost of quality-adjusted automobiles and the development of supporting infrastructure, meant a decrease in the cost of a key complement to single-family detached houses, individual transportation. In a model that does not include transportation explicitly, the spread of automobiles would correspond to an increase in the utility of services from a single-family house.

Automobiles and 1920s financial innovations could have affected house prices in some cities more than others. Along with raising the utility of single-family houses, automobiles must have changed the functional relation between local population and amenities through the nature of congestion costs. The rise of an earlier transportation technology, railroads, had clearly reordered local amenities since the early nineteenth century as it reduced the value of proximity to navigable water (Glaeser and Kohlhase 2004). The new mortgage institutions of the 1920s, building and loan associations and mutual savings banks, grew faster in some regions at least partly due to differences in state regulations; perhaps more importantly, they appeared in regions where mortgage credit was relatively restricted prior to the 1920s (Snowden 2003).

For us, the question is whether there are measures of cities' characteristics as of, say 1920, that have strong predictive value for cross-sectional variations in mid-1920s single-family permit counts, particularly the component that is orthogonal to permit counts in other periods. So far, we have not found any such data. Further research on regional aspects of 1920s mortgage finance institutions may bear high returns here.

5.6   Conclusion

In conclusion, we review what we have found in the data, then pull together an interpretation—a story of what happened in American housing markets across the 1920s and in the downturn of the Great Depression.

From 1920 to 1930, home ownership rates and home owners' estimates of house values rose more in cities that issued especially large numbers of single-family house building permits in the boom years of the mid-1920s. But these cities did not experience especially high growth in the number of census families. In the early years of the Great Depression, these cities saw bigger declines in home ownership rates and in home owners' estimates of house values. They saw higher rates of foreclosure.

Our interpretation is that in the early 1920s some set of fundamental shocks, perhaps including the development of automobiles and new mortgage finance institutions, tended to raise house prices and construction in some cities more than others. By the mid-1920s differences between cities were being reenforced by a feedback mechanism of irrational expectations in a bubble. After 1925 the bubble burst. Prices and construction began to fall. In cities where prices and construction had most outrun fundamentals, prices had the farthest to fall, and many building permits were abandoned (which helps account for the absence of a relation between mid-1920s permits and growth in census families).

In 1929, house markets in the cities that had boomed in the mid-1920s were still in disequilibrium. In these cities vacancy rates were high (which also helps account for our results on census families) and home owners' estimates of potential sale prices were high relative to actual sale prices (so they were still high relative to 1920 prices, whether or not actual sale prices were still high relative to 1920 prices). Home owners in these cities may have had more mortgage debt, on average, and more balloon mortgages about to come due.

Then the Depression hit. As home owners' overestimated values were corrected, perceived values fell more in former boom cities. Actual sale prices may have fallen more, too, as sticky asking prices became unstuck and a backlog of sellers who had been holding out for above-market prices gave in. As the general decline in income interacted with relatively high leverage, rates of foreclosure and distress sales were higher in former boom cities, and home ownership rates fell more.

This story fits the evidence, but we admit it is long on speculation. We have hopeful, perhaps irrational expectations that it will be validated by future research. In any case, our evidence shows that cities more affected by the residential real estate boom of the mid-1920s suffered greater declines in perceived house values and higher foreclosure rates during the Great Depression. Thus, they tend to support a view that the 1920s real estate boom contributed to the Great Depression through wealth and financial channels.

References

Abel, Jaison R., and Richard Deitz. 2010. "Bypassing the Bust: The Stability of Upstate New York's Housing Markets During the Recession." *Federal Reserve Bank of New York, Current Issues in Economics and Finance* 16 (3): 1–7.

Adam, Klaus, Pei Kuang, and Albert Marcet. 2011. "House Price Booms and the Current Account." NBER Working Paper no. 17224, Cambridge, MA.

Allen, Frederick Lewis. 1931. *Only Yesterday*. New York: Blue Ribbon Books.

Benitez-Silva, Hugo, Selcuk Eren, Frank Heiland, and Sergi Jimenez-Martin. 2010. "How Well Do Individuals Predict the Selling Prices of their Homes?" State University of New York at Stony Brook. Working Paper, March.

Biddle, Jeff E. 2012. "Air Conditioning, Migration, and Climate-Related Wage and Rent Differentials." *Research in Economic History* 28:1–41.

Bolch, Ben, Rendigs Fels, and Marshall McMahon. 1971. "Housing Surplus in the 1920s?" *Explorations in Economic History* 8 (3): 259–83.

Bucks, Brian, and Karen Pence. 2006. "Do Homeowners Know Their House Values and Mortgage Terms?" Working Paper, Federal Reserve Board of Governors, January.

Carson, Richard T., and Samuel R. Dastrup. 2013. "After the Fall: An Ex Post Characterization of Housing Price Declines Across Metropolitan Area." *Contemporary Economic Policy* 31 (1): 22–43.

Carter, Susan B., Scott S. Gartner, Michael R. Haines, Alan L. Olmstead, Richard Sutch, and Gavin Wright, eds. 2006. *Historical Statistics of the United States: Earliest Times to the Present*. Millennial edition. Cambridge: Cambridge University Press.

Case, Karl E., and John M. Quigley. 2008. "How Housing Booms Unwind: Income Effects, Wealth Effects, and Feedbacks through Financial Markets." *European Journal of Housing Policy* 8 (2): 161–80.

Case, Karl E., and Robert J. Shiller. 1989. "The Efficiency of the Market for Single-Family Homes." *American Economic Review* 79 (1): 125–37.

———. 2003. "Is There a Bubble in the Housing Market?" *Brookings Papers on Economic Activity* 2003 (2): 299–362.

Elul, Ronel, Nicholas Souleles, Souphala Chomsisengphet, Dennis Glennon, and Robert Hunt. 2010. "What 'Triggers' Mortgage Default?" *American Economic Review* 100 (2): 490–4.

Favara, Giovanni, and Jean Imbs. 2011. "Credit Supply and the Price of Housing." Discussion Paper no. 8129, Center for Economic Policy Research, July.

Favilukis, Jack, Sydney C. Ludvigson, and Stijn Van Nieuwerburgh. 2010. "The Macroeconomic Effects of Housing Wealth, Housing Finance, and Limited Risk-Sharing in General Equilibrium." NBER Working Paper no. 15988, Cambridge, MA.

Federal Home Loan Bank Board. 1936. *Review* April, 2 (7).

———. 1938. *Review* February 4 (5).

Field, Alexander J. 1992. "Uncontrolled Land Development and the Duration of the Depression in the United States." *Journal of Economic History* 52 (4): 785–805.

———. 2011. *A Great Leap Forward*. New Haven, CT: Yale University Press.

Fishback, Price, William Horrace, and Shawn Kantor. 2005. "The Impact of New Deal Expenditures on Local Economic Activity: An Examination of Retail Sales, 1929–1939." *Journal of Economic History* 65 (1): 36–71.

Fisher, Ernest M. 1951. *Urban Real Estate Markets: Characteristics and Financing*. New York: National Bureau of Economic Research.

Furlong, Fred. 2008. "Drivers of Subprime Mortgage Delinquencies and Foreclosures." In *Synopses of Selected Research on Housing, Mortgages and Foreclosures*. Working Paper, Federal Reserve System, September.

Genesove, David, and Christopher Mayer. 2001. "Loss Aversion and Seller Behavior: Evidence from the Housing Market." *Quarterly Journal of Economics* 116 (4): 1233–60.

Glaeser, Edward L., and Joseph Gyourko. 2009. "Arbitrage in Housing Markets." In *Housing Markets and the Economy,* edited by Edward Glaeser and John Quigley, 113–47. Cambridge, MA: Lincoln Institute of Land Policy.

Glaeser, Edward L., Joseph Gyourko, Eduardo Morales, and Charles G. Nathanson. 2011. "Housing Dynamics." Working Paper, Society for Economic Dynamics.

Glaeser, Edward L., Joseph Gyourko, and Albert Saiz. 2008. "Housing Supply and Housing Bubbles." *Journal of Urban Economics* 64:198–217.

Glaeser, Edward L., and Janet Kohlhase. 2004. "Cities, Regions and the Decline of Transport Costs." *Papers in Regional Science* 83 (1): 197–228.

Goetzmann, William N., Liang Peng, and Jacquelin Yen. 2012. "The Subprime Crisis and House Price Appreciation." *Journal of Real Estate Finance and Economics* 44 (1–2): 36–66.

Gordon, Robert A. 1951. "Cyclical Experience in the Interwar Period: The Investment Boom of the Twenties." In *Conference on Business Cycles,* Universities-National Bureau, 163–214. New York: National Bureau of Economic Research.

Grebler, Leo, David M. Blank, and Louis Winnick. 1956. *Capital Formation in Residential Real Estate: Trends and Prospects.* New York: Princeton University Press.

Gyourko, Joseph, Albert Saiz, and Anita Summers. 2008. "A New Measure of the Local Regulatory Environment for Housing Markets." *Urban Studies* 45 (3): 693–729.

Haughwort, Andrew, Richard Peach, and Joseph Tracy. 2009. "The Homeownership Gap." Federal Reserve Bank of New York. Staff Report no. 418, (December).

Hickman, Bert G. 1960. *Growth and Stability of the Postwar Economy.* Washington, DC: Brookings.

———. 1974. "What Became of the Building Cycle?" In *Nations and Households in Economic Growth*, edited by Paul David and Melvin Reder, 291–314. New York: Academic Press.

Himmelberg, Charles, Christopher Mayer, and Todd Sinai. 2005. "Assessing High House Prices: Bubbles, Fundamentals, and Misperceptions." *Journal of Economic Perspectives* 19 (4): 67–92.

Kiel, Katharine A., and Jeffrey E. Zabel. 1999. "The Accuracy of Owner-Provided House Values: The 1978–1991 American Housing Survey." *Real Estate Economics* 27 (2): 263–98.

Kimbrough, Gray, and Kenneth Snowden. 2007. "The Spatial Character of Housing Depression in the 1930s." Working Paper, University of North Carolina at Greensboro, August.

Kodrzycki, Yolanda, and Nelson Gerew. 2006. "Using State and Metropolitan Area House Price Cycles to Interpret the U.S. Housing Market." Federal Reserve Bank of Boston. Public Policy Briefs 06-1, (October).

Lamont, Owen, and Jeremy C. Stein. 1999. "Leverage and House-Price Dynamics in U.S. Cities." *RAND Journal of Economics* 30 (3): 498–514.

Mayer, Chris, and Karen Pence. 2008. "Subprime Mortgages: What, Where and to Whom?" Federal Reserve Board of Governors. FEDS Working Paper no. 2008-29.

Mian, Atif, and Amir Sufi. 2010. "The Great Recession: Lessons from Microeconomic Data." *American Economic Review* 100 (2): 1–10.

Mishkin, Frederic S. 1978. "The Household Balance Sheet and the Great Depression." *Journal of Economic History* 38 (4): 918–39.

Nicholas, Tom, and Anna Scherbina. 2010. "Real Estate Prices During the Roaring Twenties and the Great Depression." Harvard Business School. Working Paper, (January).

Roback, Jennifer. 1982. "Wages, Rents and the Quality of Life." *Journal of Political Economy* 90 (4): 1257–78.

Saiz, Albert. 2010. "The Geographic Determinants of Housing Supply." *Quarterly Journal of Economics* 125 (3): 1253–96.

Saks, Raven. 2008. "Job Creation and Housing Construction: Constraints on Metropolitan Area Employment Growth." *Journal of Urban Economics* 64 (1): 178–95.

Shiller, Robert J. 2005. *Irrational Exuberance,* 2nd edition. Princeton, NJ: Princeton University Press.

Snowden, Kenneth. 2003. "The Transition from Building and Loan to Savings and Loan." In *Finance, Intermediaries, and Economic Development*, edited by Stanley L. Engerman, Philip T. Hoffman, Jean-Laurent Rosenthal, and Kenneth L. Sokoloff, 157–206. Cambridge: Cambridge University Press.

———. 2010. "The Anatomy of a Residential Mortgage Crisis: A Look Back to the 1930s." NBER Working Paper no. 16244, Cambridge, MA.

US Bureau of Labor Statistics. 1925. *Building Permits in the Principal Cities of the United States in 1923. Bulletin 368.* Washington, DC: GPO.

US Census Bureau. 1923. *Mortgages on Homes: A Report on the Results of the Inquiry as to the Mortgage Debt on Homes other than Farm Homes at the Fourteenth Census, 1920. Census Monograph II.* Washington, DC: GPO.

US Department of Housing and Urban Development. 2011. *U.S. Housing Market Conditions, Historical Data* 2011:1.

Van Nieuwerburgh, Stijn, and Pierre-Olivier Weill. 2010. "Why Has House Price Dispersion Gone Up?" *Review of Economic Studies* 77:1567–606.

Weir, David R. 1992. "A Century of U.S. Unemployment, 1890–1990: Revised Estimates and Evidence for Stabilization." *Research in Economic History* 14:301–346.

Wheelock, David C. 2008. "Changing the Rules: State Mortgage Foreclosure Moratoria During the Great Depression." *Federal Reserve Bank of St. Louis Review* November:569–84.

White, Eugene N. 2006. "Bubbles and Busts: the 1990s in the Mirror of the 1920s." In *The Global Economy in the 1990s: A Long-run Perspective*, edited by Paul W. Rhode and Gianni Toniolo. Cambridge: Cambridge University Press.

Wickens, David L. 1937. *Financial Survey of Urban Housing: Statistics on Financial Aspects of Urban Housing.* Washington, DC: United States Department of Commerce, GPO.

———. 1941. *Residential Real Estate: Its Economic Position as Shown by Values, Rents, Family Incomes, Financing, and Construction Together with Estimates for All Real Estate.* New York: National Bureau of Economic Research.

Wickens, David L., and Ray R. Foster. 1937. *Non-Farm Residential Construction, 1920–36.* NBER Bulletin 65, (September). New York: National Bureau of Economic Research.

6

New Multicity Estimates of the Changes in Home Values, 1920–1940

Price Fishback and Trevor Kollmann

The boom and bust in housing during the early twenty-first century has led to renewed interest in the boom and bust in housing between 1920 and 1940. Numerous people have been clamoring for comparisons of the booms and bust in the housing markets in the two periods. In this volume Alex Field, Eugene White, and Steve Gjerstad and Vernon Smith have provided careful analyses to meet this call, based on currently available data. Accurate comparisons of housing markets require good measures of home ownership, homebuilding, and housing prices. In this chapter, we provide new estimates of home values that help to better elucidate the trajectory of prices for the critical years of 1920 to 1940.

Unfortunately, current multicity estimates of the changes in nominal housing values for the period are based on series designed for long-run comparisons. Leo Grebler, David Blank, and Louis Winnick (GBW; 1956, 342–356) created two series, one adjusted for depreciation and another unadjusted, that covered twenty-two cities from 1890 through 1934. They created the series as a robustness check for their estimates of building costs over time. Both series have received a great deal of attention because they

Price Fishback is the Thomas R. Brown Professor of Economics at the University of Arizona and a research associate of the National Bureau of Economic Research. Trevor Kollmann is a lecturer in economics at the School of Economics, Finance, and Marketing at RMIT University.

We would like to thank Andra Ghent, Keoka Grayson, Chris Hanes, Shawn Kantor, Jonathan Rose, Ken Snowden, and Eugene White for their advice on the chapter. The research in the chapter was funded by grants SES-1061927, SES-0921732, and SES 0617972 from the National Science Foundation. Any opinions expressed do not represent the attitudes or opinions of the National Science Foundation. For acknowledgments, sources of research support, and disclosure of the authors' material financial relationships, if any, please see http://www.nber.org/chapters/c12800.ack.

are reported in the past two *Historical Statistics of the United States.*[1] In *Irrational Exuberance* Robert Shiller (2005) extended the series to 1953 by splicing a time series of average asking prices in five major cities onto the unadjusted GBW series. This Shiller-GBW hybrid series is now widely cited in papers, in the press, and on the Internet because it has been combined with the modern Case-Shiller/S&P Repeat Sales Price Index to provide a continuous series from 1890 to the present.

As the GBW series are meant to both provide annual estimates and to be consistent across long time periods, the scholars creating them did not use a great deal of information that is available from other sources for specific time periods. Currently, the two GBW series suggest conflicting stories about the path of nominal housing values during the 1920s housing boom. The unadjusted series combined into the Shiller-GBW hybrid has housing values in 1920 that were 7.3 percent *higher* than in 1930, while the GBW adjusted series has values that were 6.5 percent *lower*; therefore, they describe drastically different pictures of growth rates in nominal housing prices during the 1920s. During the New Deal period from 1934 to 1940, the only multicity series commonly used is the Shiller-GBW hybrid series. It suggests a very strong recovery by 1940 of housing values to 95 percent of the level seen in 1930. Recent hedonic price indices created for Manhattan by Tom Nicholas and Anna Scherbina (2013) raise some doubt about that figure because they find housing values in 1939 that are roughly 70 percent of the 1930 level and New York City is among the five cities in the Shiller-GBW hybrid.

We investigate the changes in housing values in cities between 1920 and 1940 using a variety of alternative sources: the mortgage census of 1920, the family census of 1930, the housing census of 1940, Home Owners' Loan Corporation (HOLC) surveys of real estate professionals, results of housing inventories performed under New Deal works projects for over one hundred cities, and archival information from the financial housing surveys performed by the Civil Works Administration and used by GBW that allows us to more than double the number of cities in the GBW index. To check for robustness, we compare the new estimates to the Bureau of Labor Statistics (BLS) estimates of the rent Consumer Price Index (CPI) and the values of building permits per family taken care of.

We find that all nominal housing value series show a strong decline between the late 1920s and the early 1930s. However, there are sharp differences between the Shiller-GBW hybrid and the rest of the series circa 1920 and 1940. All of the series except the Shiller-GBW hybrid imply that housing values in 1920 were well below the 1930 value and thus imply much stronger growth rates in housing values during the 1920s housing boom. Only the Shiller-GBW hybrid predicts a strong recovery in housing values

---

1. See US Bureau of the Census (1975, series 259 and 260, 647) and Snowden (2006, series Dc826 and DC827, 4–515).

to within 5 percent of the 1930 level in 1940. All of the other series suggest that nominal housing values in 1940 remained at least 18 percent below the 1930 values and several series suggest that values lurched downward between 1933 and 1940.

In addition, we compare the boom and bust in housing values in the early twenty-first century with the 1920 to 1940 period, showing changes in nominal housing values, housing values adjusted for CPI inflation, and housing values relative to income. In all comparisons, the rise in housing prices during the early twenty-first century was dramatically more rapid than in the 1920s boom. After 2007 the nominal and inflation-adjusted national median values reported by all home owners fell sharply but not to the year 2000 levels. However, nominal and real sales price indices suggest that actual sale prices have fallen back to the year 2000 level.

The comparisons of the two busts are complicated by the major deflation between 1929 and 1933 and the huge drop in per capita incomes during that period. Both the nominal and inflation-adjusted series show that housing values reported by all home owners had fallen below their 1922 levels by 1940. If the experience in the Depression were repeated over the next few years, which is a big if, home owners face the scary prospect that nominal and real home values might well continue to stay well below the year 2000 level or even fall. On the other hand, the affordability of housing rose sharply in both periods as housing prices fell and incomes grew.

6.1   The Existing Multicity Estimates

Currently there are two multicity time series that are being used to describe how home prices and housing values changed between 1920 and 1940. The coverage is limited and the focus of each series is on developing consistent annual series that run from 1890 to the present. The estimates that have received the most attention come from a time series reported by Robert Shiller (2005) in *Irrational Exuberance*. Between 1920 and 1940 the series splices together two time series: a series of home prices unadjusted for depreciation reported by Grebler, Blank, and Winnick for 1890 through 1934 and a series of median home asking prices for 1934 through 1953.

For the period from 1890 through 1934, Grebler, Blank, and Winnick (1956, 342–356) used information for twenty-two cities from Wickens ([1937, table 3] for each city). This information comes from a series of surveys conducted by the Civil Works Administration in the winter of 1934 in 64 cities.[2] Each

---

2. The surveys were conducted in two ways, by visits from personal enumerators and a survey handed out and then returned by mail. "A house-to-house canvas was made of all occupied residential properties within the boundaries of every tenth block in larger cities and every seventh block within smaller cities. Where necessary to insure sampling of all important areas, additional blocks, chosen by informed local agencies, were also covered by the enumerators." Surveys for a separate sample were distributed and to be returned by mail to four out of every

home owner was asked the original cost of the home in the year the home was purchased, as well as the owner's assessment of the current sale price he might anticipate receiving for the home. GBW then used this information to construct a set of home price indices for single-family homes for each of the cities and then aggregated them. They provided a raw set of estimates and then reported a set of estimates that took into account an annual compound depreciation rate of 1 3/8 percent in the homes that they based on a careful analysis of other data (GBW, appendix E). Their discussion suggests that they felt that the adjusted estimates were more accurate. They pointed out that their unadjusted estimates for Cleveland and Seattle showed a much smaller rise in prices in the 1920s than three-year moving averages of prices paid for newly constructed one-family homes developed by Frank Garfield and William Hoad for the same cities.[3] This finding was consistent with their expectation that the unadjusted series biased downward the home price rise.

In a sense the GBW indices are similar to a repeat sale price index because the owners reported their estimated 1934 sale value and the price they paid in the year they purchased the home. Shiller likely chose the unadjusted GBW index because it is most like the repeat sales index that he and Karl Case have developed for the modern period. The argument for the repeat sales index is that quality is held constant because the same house is being evaluated in the earlier and later period. However, if the service quality of the home is depreciating with wear and tear over time, the home being evaluated in 1934 is of lower quality relative to the home when it was first purchased. The diminution of quality is greater the longer the gap between the date of purchase and the time of evaluation in 1934. Had the home kept the same quality over time, its value in 1934 would have been higher than a depreciated home in 1934, and therefore, if the price index is not adjusted for depreciation, the growth in prices for homes of the same quality will be underestimated. The reverse holds if home owners made improvements between the date of purchase and 1934. These problems led GBW to create the second index in which they made estimated adjustments for the net effect of improvements and depreciation.[4]

Since the GBW index ended in 1934, Shiller spliced in new information for the years 1935 through 1953. Shiller (2005, 269–70) reports that the home price index for 1934 through 1953 is a simple average over five cities of median home asking prices advertised in newspapers for Chicago, Los

nine remaining blocks. The combined totals of returned surveys covered about 15 percent of all families in the cities included in the survey (Wickens 1937, xv–xvi).

3. Garfield and Hoad (1937) used the underlying information from the CWA surveys of Cleveland and Seattle that allowed them to focus on newly constructed costs of purchase of one-family wood homes with five or six rooms.

4. The indices also suffer from measurement error that likely arises because in many cities the purchase date for roughly half the homes was more than a decade earlier and it relied on the home owner having an accurate impression of the selling price of the home in 1934, a year in which very few homes were selling.

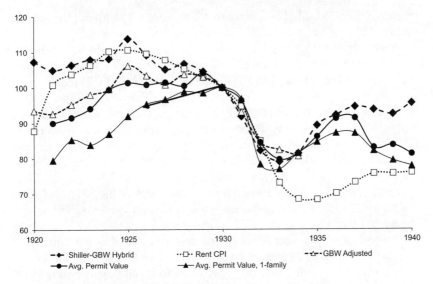

Fig. 6.1 Multicity estimates of housing values, prices, and rents
Note: 1930 value = 100.

Angeles, New Orleans, New York, and Washington, DC. For all but Washington, DC, students used microfilmed newspapers from the Yale University Library and collected "approximately thirty prices for each city and year." The information for Washington, DC for 1934 to 1948 data came from a median asking price series collected by E. M. Fisher (1951), which is also reported separately as series Dc828 in the millennial edition of the *Historical Statistics* (Snowden 2006, 4–515). Shiller notes that "the median series does not make any attempt to correct for home quality change," unlike the modern series that he and Karl Case developed. "Improvements in home size and quality give median home prices an upward bias, and this is why [he] avoided using median prices outside the 1934–53 interval."

Figure 6.1 shows the paths followed by the Grebler, Blank, and Winnick (GBW) adjusted series and the Shiller-GBW hybrid series. Figure 6.1 also includes three additional series for comparison. The first two are the "average value of residential building permits per family taken care of" for 257 cities: (a) all types of housing and (b) one-family houses. This is a rough estimate of what builders considered a likely value of the new building, but does not include the value of the lot. The third is the rent portion of the Urban Consumer Price Index, representing the rents paid by tenants in thirty-two cities. Rents generally tend to move in the same direction as housing values; of the 394 counties with over 50,000 people in 1930, less than 1 percent experienced a change in median rents between 1930 and 1940 that moved in the opposite direction of the change in median home values, while the correlation weighted by population was 0.36. All series are indexed so that the 1930 value equals 100.[5]

All the series show a peak in values sometime in the mid to late 1920s. The average permit value series both peak around 1929 and 1930, while the Shiller-GBW hybrid, the GBW adjusted and the rent CPI reach peaks in 1925, ranging from 6.2 to 13.7 percent higher than the 1930 price. One potential reason for the difference in the timing of the peak for permit values and for the remaining series is that the permit values likely do not incorporate the value of the lot on which the building is located. All five series hit troughs between 1933 and 1935 that are about 19.4 to 26.7 percent below the 1930 price.

On the other hand, there are distinct differences at the 1920 and 1940 endpoints. By using the unadjusted GBW series, the Shiller-GBW hybrid shows that housing prices in 1920 were 7.3 percent *higher* in 1920 than in 1930 while all of the other series on the graph suggest that housing prices and rents were 6.5 to 20 percent *lower* in 1920 or 1921 than in 1930.

The Shiller-GBW hybrid index also leads to much higher estimates of the recovery to 1940 in home prices than the other series, as it reaches 95 percent of the 1930 value, 21 percent above the trough in 1933. In contrast, the rent CPI and the average values of building permits in 1940 were at most 82 percent of their 1930 value.

6.2   Single-City Indices

As might be expected, the multicity indices disguise a great deal of variance in the experiences across the country. Figure 6.2 plots the Shiller-GBW hybrid and the GBW adjusted indices against the Garfield-Hoad indices for prices of new single-family homes in Cleveland and Seattle, two of the twenty-two cities underlying the GBW indices up to 1934. The Fisher asking price series for Washington, DC, and a new hedonic price index series for Manhattan created by Tom Nicholas and Anna Scherbina are added since Washington, DC, and New York City were two of the five cities used by Shiller to create the hybrid index after 1934.[6] All of the series peak sometime

---

5. Both measures of the average value of building permits per family provided for come from US Bureau of Labor (1941b, 16) and then were indexed so that the 1930 value equals 100. Measures were provided for one-family units and for multifamily units. The CPI rent index is from US Bureau of Labor (1941a) and adjusted so that the 1930 value equaled 100.

6. Tom Nicholas and Anna Scherbina (2013) created a price index for real estate transactions for Manhattan between 1920 and 1939. For each month they collected thirty prices from real estate transactions and ran a pooled hedonic regression and employed time dummies to capture the change in price adjusted for the features of the housing over time. Unlike the other series, the Manhattan series includes some commercial buildings and a number of multifamily tenements that included stores on the first floor. They control for these features with their hedonic regressions with dummy variables for the presence of a store on the first floor, although they do not provide separate estimates without these groups. As a contrast, in the estimates of home values used later, home owners were expected to provide values for only the residential part of the

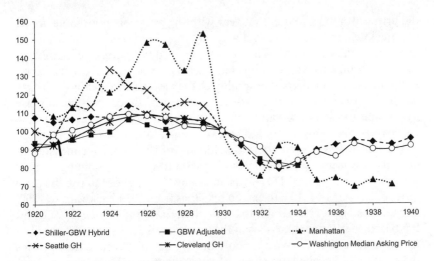

Fig. 6.2   Time series of housing price estimates for different cities

during the 1920s although the timing varies such that Seattle peaks in 1924 and Manhattan in 1929 while the rest peak around 1925. They all hit troughs in the early 1930s, although the Manhattan series bounces upward in 1933 and 1934 before dropping again.

Once again, the series differ sharply at the 1920 and 1940 endpoints. The Shiller-GBW hybrid and Manhattan indices are well above 100 in 1920 even though Manhattan is not among the cities in the Shiller-GBW hybrid until after 1934. The Cleveland, GBW adjusted, and Washington indices are all well below 100, although Washington is not among the cities in the Shiller-GBW hybrid index at that time. In 1939, the Manhattan index is well below the Shiller-GBW hybrid and the Washington, DC, asking price index.

6.3   How Well Does the GBW Series Match a Regular Resale Price Series?

There are flaws in all of the extant methods for calculating the value of homes. The ideal would be to survey all home owners and for them to all fully understand the market and how it responds to quality changes each year. Many studies use prices or reported values as dependent variables in hedonic house price regressions that hold various attributes constant. The modern Case-Shiller resale price index methodology uses comparisons *each year* on

---

building if there was a store present. The Cleveland and Seattle series were created by Garfield and Hoad (1937) using unpublished information for the CWA survey that Grebler, Blank, and Winnick used. They focused on new one-family homes with six rooms and used the answers to the same questions about cost of homes at the time of purchase used by Grebler, Blank, and Winnick. Fisher (1951) collected asking prices for Washington, DC homes.

the prices of homes sold in that year with the prices of those same homes the previous time they were sold in an attempt to hold quality constant by focusing on the same home. Their methodology description discusses extensively the problems with quality changes between sales of the same home. Arguing that the likelihood of quality change is much greater as the length of time between sales rises, they use econometric methods that typically give less weight to each observation as the gap in time between prior sale and resale rises (S&P Dow Jones Indices 2013).

The information necessary to develop any of these accurate measures is not currently available without devoting several years to examining original sources at the city level. This problem is why Shiller chose to use the price series developed by GBW to extend his series from 1934 backward to 1890. The GBW series is comparable to the modern Case-Shiller index in one way. It is based on value comparisons of the same homes across time. The similarity stops there. The GBW series does not use actual recorded transactions prices. Instead, it calculates an index with value 1 in 1934 from the ratio of the average of the survey respondents' remembered cost of purchase in year 1934-t (C_{1934-t}) to the respondent's estimate of the home value in 1934 (V_{1934}). $GBWI_{1934-t} = C_{1934-t}/V_{1934}$. This information is available for homes surveyed *only for the year 1934*.

In contrast, a regular resale price index for this time period would have the same type of current and past price transaction information for homes sold in *every year*, not just 1934. This is important because it provides many more estimates of the relationship across years between prices, and allows a regular price series to pick up changes in prices for homes that are sold multiple times over the period studied. The Case-Shiller methodology also estimates discount factors for resale pairs to control for the time value of money when the time between sales is longer than a period. To control for the likelihood that the quality of homes changes more as the time gap (k) between sale and resale lengthens, the methodology estimates generalized least square weights that ultimately put less weight on resales as the time between sale and resale lengthens.

Note the differences. First, the unadjusted GBW index has no adjustment for changes in quality of the same house over time and cannot use any type of weighting scheme for earlier years because its ratio of the price in year t to the 1934 value is the index value for that year. This is why Grebler, Blank, and Winnick (1956) proposed their index adjusted for depreciation of the quality of the house over time.

Second, because the regular resale price index has information on current sales from every year, it captures price changes for homes that resell multiple times and thus captures many more price comparisons over shorter spans of time when the home quality is more likely to be the same. To show how the absence of information on multiple sales of the same home can skew the GBW index, consider the following example. There are two sets of homes, each composing half of the sample. The A half of all homes were purchased in 1920 for 100 and then were not sold before 1934 when they were then valued at 100. The B half of homes were purchased in 1920 for 90 and then resold in 1927 for 110. This second group of homes was not resold again until 1934 and then had an average value of 100. Finally, had the A homes been sold in 1927, their price would have been the same 110 as for the B homes that did sell then. In this case the true value price index would rise from 95 in 1920 to 110 in 1927 before declining again to 100. On the other hand, the 1920 GBW index estimate of 100 overstates the true home price in 1920 because it misses the information on the resale of the B homes that were resold in 1927. The bias can go in the opposite direction as well.

The point here is not that the GBW unadjusted index should not be used at all. It provides a first look at the relative prices across time. However, when they created the index, Grebler, Blank, and Winnick (1956) provided an alternative index that they thought more accurately reflected adjustments for quality. So the question becomes which index is more consistent with the patterns seen in other imperfect estimates of housing values over the same period.

We offer a series of estimates based on comparisons of home values between census years and in inventory surveys over the period as robustness checks. Alex Field (chapter 2, this volume) has shown us that comparisons of census survey estimates of home values in 1920 and 1930 will likely overstate the rise in quality-adjusted housing prices because over 30 percent of the 1930 housing stock was composed of new housing units that were likely of higher quality than the existing units. In comparisons of census estimates for 1930 and 1940, the direction of the bias is uncertain. Approximately, 2.5 million new homes were added to the nonfarm housing stock. These were likely to have the new technological amenities, but the low incomes of the 1930s might have led to smaller homes. Alex Field has estimated that roughly 1.8 million housing units that were vacant or abandoned in 1930 were back in the housing stock in 1940, which would have lowered average quality. On the other hand, average quality would have been raised by the funds provided by the Home Owners' Loan Corporation to improve the quality of roughly 400,000 homes and low interest rates on 2.3 million Title I repair and reconstruction loans guaranteed by the Federal Housing Administration (Fishback, Rose, and Snowden 2013; Federal Housing Administration 1940, 3).

6.4   Alternative Estimates of Housing Values

The advantage of each of the series discussed in sections 6.1 and 6.2 is that they have values each year over an extended period of time. However, they generally are very limited in the number of cities covered. To complement and potentially replace these series, we show the results of comparisons at key points in time during the period 1920 through 1940. We use two sets of data to examine the changes in home values over the period. The first set are based on reports by home owners of the sale value of their homes in the 1920, 1930, and 1940 censuses and in a series of surveys of the housing inventory undertaken by the Civil Works Administration and over 110 other cities during the mid-1930s. The second are based on reports by real estate agents to the Home Owners' Loan Corporation of the minimum and maximum sale values in all of the neighborhoods within over one hundred cities of homes for key years between 1929 and 1939.

6.4.1   An Index for Average Home Values in 1920, 1930, 1933, 1934, and 1940

Constructing a consistent index for housing prices requires information reported on the same basis for the same types of homes and information reported for the same sets of geographic areas. We construct an index for home values for 1920, 1930, 1933, 1934, and 1940 from average values for nonfarm owner-occupied mortgaged homes using information from the 1920 and 1940 censuses and from the reports on housing values in 1930, 1933, and 1934 from a financial survey performed by the Civil Works Administration in 1934.

The 1920 census conducted a mail survey of mortgage holders, asking for the "market value of the home on January 1, 1920 (amount for which the home could be sold within a reasonable time)" and reported average values for 273 cities (US Bureau of the Census 1923, 18,173–8).[7] The 1930 census report on families reported median housing values and the distribution of

---

7. As seen in the text, the Financial Housing Survey in 1934 and the 1930 and 1940 censuses all explicitly stated in their instructions that the value of the lot (what the census termed as real estate) was included in the value. The mortgage census volume (US Bureau of the Census 1923) never explicitly makes the statements that the value of the lot is included, although statements throughout the text suggest that it is, and E. M. Fisher (1951, 51) later treats estimates of average values for 1920, 1930, and 1940 as comparable except for the fact that the 1920 estimates were for mortgaged homes. Sales of homes and the mortgages for homes, particularly one-family homes, typically included the real estate beneath it, and the question in the survey asked about the value at which the home could be sold within a reasonable time. Statements in the original report suggest that the writers believe the value of the lot (real estate) to be included in the average values. For example, in comparing differences in the rise in average values across cities between 1890 and 1920, the report stated that "the high average values in the rapidly growing cities were partly due to the expected rise in real estate values which has since taken place" (US Bureau of Census 1923, 69). The statement referred to 1890 values, which the census compared directly with 1920 values in several tables without further comment. The census reported that the average value of homes had not risen nearly as fast as the rise in real estate prices, building costs, and interest rate on other securities. They argued that this "seems to indicate that there has been an increase in the ownership of smaller homes," which would have come about because declines in the size of the home offset the rise in these other factors in determining the value (43). As can be seen, the later censuses and the Financial Housing Surveys were more careful in their wording in the instructions. To the extent that respondents did not include the value of the lot in their sale value of the homes, a rise in values between 1920 and 1930 is overstated.

housing values for owner-occupied homes but did not specify the mortgage status or report average values, so the information is not directly comparable with the 1920 information. Fortunately, the Civil Works Administration (CWA) in 1934 performed a financial housing survey in sixty-four cities spread across the country and reported information on the average value of mortgaged owner-occupied properties for forty cities that overlap with the 273 cities from the 1920 census. The CWA survey asked owners to provide an "estimated market value of the property" on January 1 of the years 1930, 1933, and 1934. Values were "understood as the estimated market values reported by the owners" and "not assessed valuations." The values also included the cost of the lot or site (Wickens 1937, xxv, xxvi). We located handwritten summary tables for sixty-one of the sixty-four cities surveyed by the CWA at the National Archives Branch in Missouri in a group of boxes under an entry titled "Drugstore Survey, St. Louis, MO 1926–1927." The summary tables provided average values for owner-occupied properties, owner-occupied properties free of mortgage, and owner-occupied properties that were mortgaged.[8] Separate averages were reported in each category for single families as well. Wickens (1937) presented most of this information from these handwritten tables for twenty-two of the cities. Grebler, Blank, and Winnick (1956, 344–358) then used information on the cost of the house at the time of purchase for those twenty-two cities to construct the housing price index that Shiller used for his home price series from 1890 through 1934. Wickens (1941) later reported some of the information on values for the original twenty-two and an additional thirty cities, which were used by Michael Brocker and Chris Hanes (chapter 5, this volume) for their analysis of the determinants of the rise and fall in housing values.[9]

The 1940 census surveyed home owners as to their mortgage status and the "value of an owner-occupied home," which represented "the amount for which the dwelling unit, including the land as belongs with it, would sell under ordinary circumstances—not at forced sale. If the owner-occupied unit is in a structure that contains more than one dwelling unit, or if part of the structure is used for business purposes, only that portion occupied by the owner and his household" is considered (US Bureau of the Census 1943, 4). Volume IV of the housing census on mortgages reported the average value

8. The tables were unnumbered but were titled "Value and Debt Status of Urban Residential Property, by Type of Dwelling: Mortgaged Properties and Properties Free of Mortgage, and Owner Occupied with and without Rental Parts, January 1, 1930, 1933, and 1934." From that information we collected the information on all owner-occupied properties, owner-occupied properties that were mortgaged, and owner-occupied properties that were free of mortgage for each of the three years. We collected the same information for one-family homes as well.

9. Wickens ([1937], xxvi, and tables 5, 8, 31, 32, 33 for each city) reported values of owner-occupied properties and values of owner-occupied mortgaged properties for each of the twenty-two cities but did not include all of the detail found in the handwritten tables. Wickens (1941, table A10) later reported information on average values of owner-occupied one-family nonfarm homes for fifty cities, which included the twenty-two from the 1937 volume.

of properties for owner-occupied mortgaged one-family properties for 185 cities with more than 100,000 people (US Bureau of the Census 1943, vol. IV, part 1, 80, 88–9). Volume II of the housing census also reported averages for all owner-occupied homes for all cities and towns in tables 21 and 23 for each state (US Bureau of the Census 1943).

From this information we construct a spliced index for the average value of owner-occupied mortgaged homes (AVOOMS) with values of 100 for 1930 for the 40 cities for which information was reported in the sources covering 1920, 1930, 1933, 1934, and 1940. The AVOOMS index is created by splicing together two overlapping series with the 1930 value equal to 100: a series for the average value of owner-occupied mortgaged homes (AVOOM) for 1920, 1930, 1933, and 1934, and a series for the average value of one-family mortgaged owner-occupied (AVOOM1F) for the years 1930, 1933, 1934, and 1940.

To develop the 1920 value of the index, we used city averages for owner-occupied mortgaged homes from the 1920 census and for 1930 from the CWA study. We calculated the ratio of the average value in 1920 (AV_{i20}) to the average value in 1930 (AV_{i30}) for each city i and then calculated a weighted average across cities using the number of families in owner-occupied homes in 1930 (N_{i30}) in each city as the weight.

$$\text{AVOOM Index}_{20} = (\Sigma \, (AV_{i20}/AV_{i30}) * N_{i30})/\Sigma \, N_{i30} * 100.$$

All other indices that were built up from individual cities are constructed with the same procedure. In the 1920 to 1940 period the number of owner-occupied homes in 1930 in each city is used as the weight. For the early twenty-first century we use the number of owner-occupied homes in the year 2000 for each city as the weight.

Since the 1940 census reported average values for owner-occupied mortgaged homes for only one-family dwellings, we created a separate (AVOOM1F) index for 1930, 1933, 1934, and 1940 using the CWA information and the 1940 census information for those types of homes. The AVOOM and AVOOM1F indices in table 6.1 use information from forty cities that have 715,328 owner-occupied homes in 1930. As shown in the bottom of table 6.1, the cities include 1 of the 10 largest cities, 14 of the top 50, 27 of the top 100, and 36 of the top 200. We developed the spliced AVOOMS by calculating the AVOOM/AVOOM1F ratio for 1930, 1933, and 1934 and then calculating the average of the three ratios. The AVOOM and AVOOM1F indices were so close together that the average ratio was 0.99957. We then multiplied the average ratio by the AVOOM1F values for 1933, 1934, and 1940 to get the spliced index for the average value of owner-occupied mortgaged homes (AVOOMS) in table 6.1. The values underneath the index values are standard deviations of the indexes across cities using the number of nonfarm home owners as a frequency weight.

Table 6.1 Housing value indices for the average value of owner-occupied mortgaged properties, 1920, 1930, 1933, 1934, and 1940

Year		AVOOM	AVOOM1F	AVOOMS	5GBW hybrid	GBW unadjusted	GBW adjusted	Cities used by Grebler, Blank, and Winnick		
								AVOOMS	AVOOM1F	AVOO
1920	Mean	86.1	n.a.	86.1	107.3	107.3	93.5	84.4	n.a.	n.a.
	Std. Dev.	12.3						12.6		
1930	Mean	100.0	100.0	100.0	100.0	100.0	100.0	100.0	100.0	100.0
	Std. Dev.									
1933	Mean	82.6	82.5	82.6	79.1	79.1	82.4	82.2	82.2	82.1
	Std. Dev.	3.9	4.1					3.6	3.7	3.8
1934	Mean	79.2	79.3	79.2	81.4	81.4	80.6	78.7	78.8	78.5
	Std. Dev.	4.4	4.5					3.9	4.1	4.2
1940	Mean		73.6	73.6	95.6	n.a.		71.2	n.a.	70.0
	Std. Dev.		10.7					10.0		12.9
Number of cities		40	40	40	22 [1930–1934] or 5 [1934–1940]	22	22	20	22	22
Number of families in 1930 in cities		715,328	715,328	715,328	497,329 [1930–1934] or 807,944 [1934–1940]	497,329	497,329	491,552	497,329	497,329
Top 10		1	1	1	3	1	1	1	1	1
Top 50		14	14	14	5	12	12	12	12	12
Top 100		27	27	27		18	18	18	18	18
Top 200		36	36	36		20	20	20	20	20

Sources: AVOOM stands for average value of mortgaged owner-occupied homes. The 1F refers to one-family homes. The index uses only cities with information in all three sources. The average values of mortgaged owner-occupied homes were reported for 1920 by the US Bureau of the Census (1923, 18, 173–78) and for 1930 in handwritten tables from the US Bureau of Foreign and Domestic Commerce (undated). The average values of mortgaged one-family owner-occupied homes were reported for 1930, 1933, and 1934 by the US Bureau of Foreign and Domestic Commerce (undated) and for 1940 by the US Bureau of the Census (1943, vol. IV, part 1, 80, 88–89). The Shiller-GBW hybrid adjusted for inflation is graphed by Shiller (2005, 36) and was downloaded from http://www.econ.yale.edu/~shiller/data.htm on April 24, 2012. From 1920 through 1934, it is the same as the Grebler, Blank, and Winnick (GBW) unadjusted index. The GBW adjusted and unadjusted indices are from Grebler, Blank, and Winnick (1956, 342–356) and are reported as series Dc826 and Dc827 by Snowden (2006, 4–515).

Note: 1930 value = 100.

6.4.2   Comparisons of Indices for 1920 through 1934

The AVOOMS index in 1920 contrasts sharply with the Shiller-GBW hybrid index, while resembling more closely the rent CPI and the GBW adjusted index. The AVOOMS index in table 6.1 rises from 86.1 in 1920 to 100 in 1930. This rise differs quite a bit from the decline from 107.3 to 100 in the Shiller-GBW index, which is the unadjusted GBW index until 1934. Meanwhile, the rise is more consistent with the rises seen in figure 6.1 from 87.8 to 100 by the CPI rent index, from 93.5 to 100 in the GBW adjusted index, from 90 to 100 in the average value of all residential permits, and from 79 to 100 in the average value of single-family building permits. The rise in the AVOOMS may have been greater than for the GBW adjusted index in part due to a rise in the average quality of the housing stock, which would have occurred if the rise in quality of newly built housing from improvements like running water and electricity was not offset by a decline in size because the new home owners had on average lower incomes than existing home owners.

Between 1930 and 1934 all of the indexes show sharp drops in prices in the first four columns of table 6.1. The AVOOMS index falls to 82.5 in 1933 and then 79.3 in 1934. Meanwhile, both the Shiller-GBW hybrid and the GBW unadjusted index fall to 79.1 and 81.4, because they are identical from 1920 through 1934. Note that the GBW index adjusted for depreciation falls to similar levels of 82.4 in 1933 and 80.6 in 1934 because the adjustments for depreciation diminish markedly as the series comes to an end in 1934. The CPI rent index falls even more than the other series to a low of 68.6 in 1934.

The relationships between the GBW adjusted and unadjusted indices and the AVOOMS index can be investigated further because the indices share twenty of the twenty-two cities used by the GBW indices. Casper, Wyoming, and Reno, Nevada, are the missing cities. We can also construct AVOOM1F and an index for the average value of owner-occupied homes (AVOO) using all twenty-two cities from the GBW index for the years 1930, 1933, and 1934. Grebler, Blank, and Winnick (1956, 344–358) developed their series as a check on the estimates of construction costs that stretched back to 1890. With the information from the CWA surveys, the only way to achieve this goal was to use the information that owners reported on the prices they paid for the homes at the time of purchase, which included homes that had been purchased in the 1890s. As a result, they ignored the information in the CWA surveys in which home owners separately reported their own estimates of value as of 1930 and 1933.

In the right portion of table 6.1, the 1920 value for the AVOOMS index is 84.4 for the shared twenty cities. This value looks more like the GBW adjusted index of 93.5 than the unadjusted GBW index of 107.3. In 1933 and 1934 all of the indices are more similar ranging from 79.1 to 82.1 for 1933 and 78.5 to 81.4 in 1934. The AVOOMS, AVOOM1F, and AVOO are no farther apart than 0.3 index points from each other in either year, while the GBW unadjusted and adjusted indices are within 3 index points. The underlying information in each series has flaws. The GBW series rely on memories of purchase prices paid at the time of purchase over an extended period of time and needs to be adjusted for depreciation, while the AVOOMS relies on owners' perceptions of the market price of their homes in 1934, 1933, and 1930.

6.4.3   Comparisons of Indices for 1940

The AVOOMS in table 6.1 also contrasts sharply with the Shiller-GBW hybrid in 1940. The AVOOMS suggests that home prices fell by 7.2 percent from 1934 to 1940 to a level that was only 73.6 percent of the 1940 level. The Shiller-GBW hybrid index suggests a strong rise that brought housing prices back within 5 percent of the 1930 values. Given that the 1934 to 1940 portion of the Shiller-GBW hybrid was composed of asking prices, it might be that sellers were far more optimistic than most home owners as to the rise in prices over time. It should be noted, however, that the Manhattan hedonic sale price index constructed by Nicholas and Scherbina (2013) also shows a drop from the 1933 and 1934 prices that left the actual 1939 sale prices approximately 30 percent lower than in 1930.

6.5   Expanding the Coverage of Cities Using Medians for the Period 1930 to 1940

One limitation of all of the indices discussed so far is their limited coverage of cities. The AVOOMS index has the broadest coverage but it covers only forty cities. The coverage can be expanded a great deal for the period 1930 to 1940 using the 1930 and 1940 census reported values and a greatly expanded set of cities in 1934, 1935, and 1936 for which housing inventory surveys were conducted. This requires a shift from average to median values because the census did not report averages for cities in 1930 but did report medians. The housing inventory surveys generally did not report averages or medians but did report distributions of values by value categories. We used a formula for calculating medians using the distributions of values that led to estimated medians that were very close to the 1930 and 1940 reported medians and thus appears to be useful for calculating medians for the 1934, 1935, and 1936 housing inventory surveys. See appendix A for the method used and a discussion of the comparability of the housing value categories.

One advantage of following this median approach with the data from the census and housing inventories in the 1930s is that we can use similar methods to estimate median values for the period 2000 to 2010 for reports of housing values in the 2000 census, and in the American Community Survey from 2003 through 2010 and thus make comparisons between the earlier and later periods using the same type of data (see figure 6.3). The 2000 census

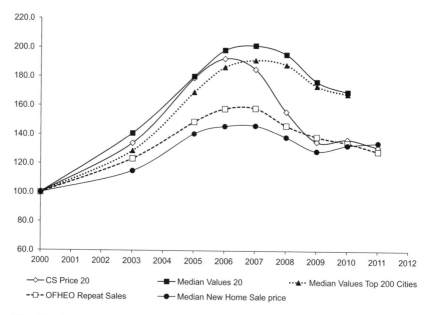

Fig. 6.3   Median values and various sale price indices from 2000 to 2011
Note: 2000 value = 100.

and ACS asked home owners to report values in categories and not as a continuous measure, so we use the same methods for estimating medians in the modern era as in the 1930s. Even though there are other modern measures of housing value in the form of resale prices of the same homes and median sale prices of new homes, such measures are not currently readily available for the 1930s. The use of median values for the reported sale values of all owner-occupied homes including those not for sale can be used in both time periods. The disadvantage is that we are relying on self-reported estimates and not actual transaction prices in both periods. The estimates of changes over time should therefore be consistent as long as the biases from such self-reported estimates are consistent over the time frame examined.

The resulting means of the cities for which there are median values for owner-occupied (MVOO) homes are reported in table 6.2. The goal is to show differences across time within the same sets of cities. Comparisons are also included using median for the AVOOMS index and the Shiller-GBW hybrid indices. All of the indices in table 6.2 indicate a sharp drop in home prices between 1930 and the mid-1930s. For the 181 cities with median values in 1930, sometime in the mid-1930s, and 1940 the MVOO index is 76.0 for the mid-1930s and then drops further to 62.8 by 1940. For the 94 cities reporting in 1934 the index fell to 79.7 in 1934 and further to 62.8 in 1940. The 47 small cities that performed inventory surveys for 1935 experienced an even larger drop to 64 by 1935 and then fell to 63.5 by 1940. Forty more

Table 6.2 Indexes based on median values of owner-occupied homes in 1930, 1934, 1935, 1936, and 1940 for different samples of cities

Year		Median index for cities reporting in							Other indexes		
		1930 & 1940	Mid-1930s	1934	1935	1936	Shiller (1934–1940)	AVOOMS	Used by GBW	Shiller-GBW	AVOOMS
1930	Mean	100	100	100	100	100	100	100	100	100	100
	std. dev.										
1934–1936	Mean		76.0								
	std. dev.		14.9								
1934	Mean			79.7				80	77.8	81.4	79.3
	std. dev.			14.7				14.6	13.5		
1935	Mean				64.0					89.3	
	std. dev.				11.6						
1936	Mean					67.9				92.2	
	std. dev.					9.5					
1940	Mean	62.2	63.5	62.8	63.5	66.9	54.6	64.5	63.5	95.6	73.6
	std. dev.	10.2	9.0	9.5	8.2	6.3		8.2	8.1		
Coverage of cities											
Number of cities		978	181	94	47	40	5	40	22	5	40
Number of families		5,871,658	1,824,940	1,326,971	196,742	301,227	807,944	715,328	497,329	807,944	715,328
Number of cities in											
Top 10		10	3	3	0	0	3	1	1	3	1
Top 50		50	25	20	0	5	5	14	12	5	14
Top 100		100	50	37	4	9		27	18		27
Top 200		200	80	56	12	12		36	20		36

Sources: Information on median values for each city in 1930 and 1940 comes from the US Bureau of Census (1943, vol. II, parts 1–5, table 24 for each state). Information on median values was calculated from distributional information reported by Wickens (1937), the US Bureau of Foreign and Domestic Commerce (undated), and Stapp (1938). Weighted means and standard deviations use as weights the number of families owning and occupying nonfarm homes who reported home values in the city in 1930 from the US Bureau of the Census (1933, 60, 73–81, tables 7, 21, and 23 for each state).

Note: 1930 value = 100.

cities that did inventories in 1936 reported a drop to 67.9 by 1936 and then to 66.9 by 1940. The AVOOMS index follows a similar path, dropping to 79.3 percent of the 1930 level in 1934. After 1934 it continues to drop but only to 73.6 percent by 1940. When the median index is used for the forty AVOOMS cities, the drop to 80 in 1934 is almost the same as for the medians for more cities. The median index for the forty AVOOMS cities drops to 64.5 in 1940, which is similar to the drops seen for the other median indexes. The difference in the drops for the averages and the medians suggests that the prices for higher-valued homes were recovering better in the late 1930s than for the lower valued homes.

As was the case for comparisons of the AVOOMS with the Shiller-GBW hybrid, there is a sharp contrast between the picture drawn by the Shiller-GBW hybrid and the median indices in the late 1930s. The Shiller-GBW hybrid index shows that asking prices in 1940 were 95 percent of the 1930 level. An index of median home values based on the 1930 and 1940 censuses for the same five cities shows a value of 58.9 when it is not weighted by the number of home owners, and 54.5 when it is weighted. In essence, these cities fared much worse than the vast majority of cities because the median index for 1940 relative to 1930 values ranged from 62 to 67 percent for the largest 978 cities, including these five. The median value reported for Washington, DC, in the census in 1940 was 81.9 percent of the 1930 value, roughly 9 percent lower than the 91.2 percent value for asking prices reported in the *Historical Statistics*. This implies that the gap between the changes in asking prices and census-reported values was much larger for New York, Chicago, New Orleans, and Los Angeles, the other four cities in Shiller's index. The 1940 values in those cities in the bottom of table 6.3 ranged from 45 to 58 percent of the 1930 value. The twenty-two cities examined by Grebler, Blank, and Winnick fared somewhat better than the five cities examined by Shiller. Their 1940 median values were 63.5 percent of the 1930 values.

The coverage is largest for the census years 1930 and 1940. Information on medians and value distributions for 978 cities includes all of the cities with more than 2,500 population in the United States and many smaller towns and cities. For each of the cities in 1930 and 1940 the census either directly reported the median value or the distribution of values across categories from which we could calculate a median value. For each city we calculated the ratio of the median value in 1940 to the median value in 1930 to create an index with 1930 = 100. Then we calculated means and standard deviations, unweighted and weighted by the number of families owning homes and reporting values in 1930, for different combinations of cities. For all 978 cities with 5.9 million families reporting values in 1930, the weighted median value in 1940 was 62.2 percent of the 1930 value. Table 6.3 also contains comparisons of the averages across different rankings of cities in terms of families reporting. Home values fell the most in the largest ten cities in the country. The weighted index shows that the 1940 values were 54.7 percent of the 1930 values in the top ten cities, which accounted for roughly one-fourth

Table 6.3   **1940 Median index values of owner-occupied homes, averaged across cities**

		Unweighted	Weighted by the number of families owning homes in 1930	Number of families in 1930 covered
All	Mean	65.5	62.2	5,871,143
	std. dev.	11.4	10.2	
Top 10	Mean	56.0	54.7	1,476,142
	std. dev.	5.8	5.7	
Top 20	Mean	61.8	58.0	1,960,161
	std. dev.	9.9	8.8	
Top 30	Mean	63.7	59.4	2,300,426
	std. dev.	9.6	9.3	
Top 40	Mean	62.9	59.5	2,543,589
	std. dev.	8.8	9.0	
Top 50	Mean	62.8	59.7	2,732,899
	std. dev.	9.0	9.0	
Top 100	Mean	62.9	60.3	3,345,022
	std. dev.	9.7	9.4	
Top 200	Mean	62.7	60.6	4,043,384
	std. dev.	9.7	9.4	
Top 300	Mean	63.2	61.0	4,487,624
	std. dev.	9.8	9.5	
Shiller 5 cities	Mean	58.9	54.6	807,944
	std. dev.	13.7	8.7	
GBW cities	Mean	65.7	63.5	497,329
	std. dev.	9.0	8.2	
Specific cities				
Washington, DC		81.9		46,208
Cleveland		53.1		80,047
Seattle		72.8		49,874
New York		57.1		341,491
Chicago		45.2		257,923
New Orleans		53.0		30,264
Los Angeles		57.7		132,058

Sources: US Bureau of the Census (1943, vol. II, parts 1–5, table 24 for each state). Weighted means and standard deviations use the number of families owning and occupying nonfarm homes who reported home values in the city in 1930 from the US Bureau of the Census (1933, 60, 73–81, tables 7, 21, and 23 for each state).
Note: 1930 value = 100.

of the households among the 978 cities. The standard deviation across this group of cities was also low at 5.57. As more and more cities are included in the index, the 1940 value rises relative to the 1930 value so that with all cities included the weighted average shows that 1940 values were 62.2 percent of the 1930 values with a standard deviation of 10.2.

The situation looks the same whether using averages or medians for the values reported in 1930 and 1940. The focus has been on medians because the family census of 1930 did not report averages.[10] From the Integrated Public Use Microdata Series (IPUMS) data sets downloaded from Ruggles et. al. (2010) we calculate averages and medians for eighty-nine cities in both 1930 and 1940. The eighty-nine cities account for about 2.9 million families in 1930. The number of cities is limited to eighty-nine due to limits on local geographic coding of cities in the 1940 IPUMS sample. Using the medians, the weighted averages across cities showed that housing values in 1940 were 59.5 percent of the 1930 value, while using averages for the cities, the values in 1940 were at 55 percent of the 1930 value.

In sum, comparisons of housing values using census data for 1930 and 1940 show a dramatic decline in housing values of over 40 percent for the decade. This is a sharp contrast to the limited data on median housing asking prices for the five large cities used by Shiller in his housing index.

6.6   HOLC Values from 1929 through 1938 Reported by Real Estate Professionals

An alternative set of information on housing prices is available from surveys of neighborhoods performed by the Home Owners' Loan Corporation between 1935 and 1939. The surveys asked local real estate professionals with working knowledge of the neighborhoods to provide information on a variety of features of the neighborhoods, including estimates of the range of housing values and the changes in those values over time within the neighborhoods for up to three kinds of housing. In establishing the range the real estate experts gave a "low-end" and "high-end" price for the typical homes in the neighborhood. We have compiled information for eighty-three cities that allow comparisons between prices circa 1929 and the early 1930s (1932 through 1936). For eighty-eight cities comparisons can be made between 1929 and 1937 to 1938. Table 6.4 shows the comparisons when values for multiple years are grouped and for each specific year with the number of cities and coverage of home owner households in each comparison. In all cases the index is set such that the 1929 value is equal to 100.

The HOLC data show an even sharper drop in home values between 1929 and the early 1930s than the Shiller-GBW hybrid index or the census housing inventory information. In table 6.4, the lowest that the Shiller-GBW hybrid dropped was to 75.7 percent of the 1929 level in 1933, while the low-end price home values reported to the HOLC dropped to an average of 65.8 percent of the 1929 level across the years 1932 to 1936. The drop was greatest at almost 40 percent for the five cities reporting information for 1929 and 1934. Table 6.5 shows that the drop from 1929 to the early to mid-1930s was even greater for the high-end price homes. The average across cities for the

---

10. Wickens (1941) calculated averages for 1930 from census figures on the housing distribution data by making assumptions about the distributions within each category.

Table 6.4 Home value value indices for low-range homes based on reports by real estate experts for neighborhoods, 1929–1938

Year		Both	1932	1933	1934	1935	1936	1937	1938
1932–1936	Mean	69.7							
	std. dev.	20.4							
1937–1938	Mean	79.5							
	std. dev.	19.0							
1932	Mean		65.5						
	std. dev.		10.3						
1933	Mean			65.8					
	std. dev.			9.4					
1934	Mean				62.8				
	std. dev.				5.7				
1935	Mean					73.3			
	std. dev.					34.7			
1936	Mean						71.6		
	std. dev.						8.7		
1937	Mean							76.6	
	std. dev.							8.8	
1938	Mean								70.3
	std. dev.								19.4
Number of cities		82	18	13	5	19	19	66	23
Number of families		1,335,384	1,714,43	1,765,43	3,848,01	1,644,87	2,807,61	8,695,64	6,413,26
Top 10		3	0	0	1	0	1	2	1
Top 50		15	1	1	2	2	6	10	8
Top 100		33	5	5	2	8	9	22	14
Top 200		62	13	8	5	13	16	48	20

Source: Home Owners' Loan Corporation (no date). All means and standard deviations are weighted by the number of home owners reporting values of homes in the city in the 1930 census.

Note: 1929 value = 100.

Table 6.5   Home value indices for high-range homes based on reports by real estate experts for neighborhoods, 1929–1938

Year		Both	1932	1933	1934	1935	1936	1937	1938
1932–1936	Mean	62.6							
	std. dev.	13.1							
1937–1938	Mean	75.0							
	std. dev.	29.0							
1932	Mean		65.1						
	std. dev.		14.3						
1933	Mean			58.5					
	std. dev.			10.3					
1934	Mean				58.2				
	std. dev.				1.8				
1935	Mean					66.7			
	std. dev.					26.2			
1936	Mean						67.0		
	std. dev.						11.9		
1937	Mean							78.8	
	std. dev.							80.4	
1938	Mean								77.7
	std. dev.								40.5
Number of cities		82	18	13	5	19	19	66	23
Number of families		1,335,384	1,714,43	1,765,43	3,848,01	1,644,87	2,807,61	8,695,64	6,413,26
Top 10		3	0	0	1	0	1	2	1
Top 50		15	1	1	2	2	6	10	8
Top 100		33	5	5	2	8	9	22	14
Top 200		62	13	8	5	13	16	48	20

Source: Home Owners' Loan Corporation (no date). All means and standard deviations are weighted by the number of home owners reporting values of homes in the city in the 1930 census.

Note: 1929 value = 100.

high value homes over the period 1932 to 1936 was 62.1 percent of the 1929 values with lows around 58 percent in 1933 and 1934.

Later in the decade the HOLC data suggests that housing prices recovered somewhat but nowhere nearly as much as the Shiller-GBW hybrid index suggests. The HOLC data in tables 6.4 and 6.5 show that housing values in 1937 and 1938 had recovered to around 75 to 79 percent of the 1929 level for the high-end homes and 70 to 79 percent of the 1929 level for the low-end homes. In contrast, the Shiller-GBW hybrid suggests a recovery to around 90 percent of the 1929 level. However, this contrasts with the continued drop in housing prices shown by the census housing inventory indices, which had fallen to less than 67 percent of the 1930 value, which likely was lower than the 1929 value.

6.7   Adding an Estimate for a 1920 Median

Thus far, we have not included a measure of medians that includes 1920 because the 1920 census did not report the medians for all owner-occupied homes. The AVOOMS index for average values of mortgaged owner-occupied homes is useful but it only covers forty cities when comparing 1920 to 1930 and 1940. As a robustness check on the AVOOMS index, we have developed an alternative estimate based on comparing the average prices of mortgaged homes for the 273 cities reported in 1920 to the median price of all homes in 1930. This comparison has the advantage in that it includes all of the top eighty cities in terms of number of home owners in 1930 and 183 of the top 200, and covers 4.8 million homes in 1930. It has the disadvantage that the ideal comparison would be between the median value of owner-occupied homes in 1920 and the median value of owner-occupied homes in 1930. We can estimate a median value of owner-occupied homes in 1920 by assuming that the ratio of the median value of owner-occupied homes to the average value of mortgaged owner-occupied homes in 1930 is the same as in 1920 and then multiplying the 1930 ratio by the 1920 average value of mortgaged owner-occupied home.[11]

Using data for fifty-two cities covering 758,000 homes in the CWA 1934 survey, we calculated a 1930 ratio for the median value of all owner-occupied homes to the average value of mortgaged owner-occupied homes of 0.9235 with a standard deviation of 0.09. The unweighted average was 0.922. We then multiplied the 0.9235 ratio by the average value of owner-occupied mortgaged homes in 1920 to obtain an estimate of the median value of all owner-occupied homes in 1920 in each city.

Table 6.6 shows the estimated indices for median values for 1920, 1930,

11. If the distribution of housing values became more skewed toward high value homes between 1920 and 1930, then the ratio of median to mean values in 1930 might have been lower than in 1920. This would lead to an underestimate of the true median in 1920 after multiplying the 1930 median/mean ratio by the 1920 mean.

Table 6.6   Indices of the mean of city median estimates for different city groupings, 1920–1940

| | | AVOOMS | Shiller-GBW hybrid | GBW adjusted | 1920 Census | Median Estimates for cities with values in | | |
						1920 census and 1934 inventories	Cities for AVOOMS	Rent CPI
1920	Mean	86.1	107.3	93.5	81.5	83	86	88.8
	std. dev.	12.3			14.1	11.4	11	12.12
1930	Mean	100.0	100.0	100.0	100.0	100.0	100.0	100.0
	std. dev.							
1933	Mean	82.5	79.1	82.4				72.1
	std. dev.							9.5
1934	Mean	79.3	81.4	80.6		79.3	80.0	67.9
	std. dev.					13.4	14.6	9.2
1940	Mean	73.6	95.6		60.9	62.6	64.5	76.3
	std. dev.				9.6	9.1	8.3	5.4
Number of cities		40	5*	22	273	75	40	32
Number of 1930 families		7,153,28	8,079,44*	4,973,29	4,282,297	1,270,107	7,153,28	2,123,992
Top 10		1	3*	1	10	3	1	9
Top 50		14	5*	12	49	19	14	25
Top 100		27		18	97	32	27	29
Top 200		36		20	184	56	36	31

Sources: See text and notes to tables 6.1–6.5. All means and standard deviations are weighted by the number of home owners reporting values of homes in the city in the 1930 census.

Note: 1930 value = 100.

*These numbers reflect the coverage of the Shiller asking price index for five cities from 1934 through 1940. The period 1920 through 1934 covers the same cities as the GBW adjusted index.

1934, and 1940 using different groupings of cities and offers comparisons with the AVOOMS and Shiller-GBW hybrid and GBW adjusted indices. When all 273 cities from the 1920 census reports are included, the estimated median home value in 1920 is 81.5 percent of the 1930 value, rises to 100 in 1930, and then drops to 60.9 percent in 1940. We can add a 1934 median estimate for seventy-five cities for which information was reported in 1920, 1930, 1934, and 1940. For just those seventy-five cities the median index rises from 83 in 1920 to 100 in 1930, falls to 79.3 in 1934, and then 62.6 in 1940. For the forty cities included in the AVOOMS index, the median index and AVOOMS indices track pretty closely. They both move from 86 in 1920 to 100 in 1930, to around 79 or 80 in 1934, and then fall off further by 1940. The median index drops substantially more by 1940 than does the AVOOMS. Given how well the AVOOMS tracks the median measure for the forty cities, it seems reasonable to think that the differences between the median indices for the forty cities and the 273 cities are based on the selection of the cities. Since the median index covers nearly all of the largest cities and a much larger share of the population base, the median index might well give a more accurate picture of the nationwide change in housing values over time.

The indices based on home prices reported by home owners in the censuses of 1920, 1930, and 1940 look quite different from the Shiller-GBW hybrid index. The census reports suggest that home values rose between 1920 and 1930 rather than the fall described by the Shiller-GBW index. The GBW adjusted index more closely matches the census information. In the 1930s all measures agree that there was a significant drop in housing prices between 1929 and 1930 and the middle 1930s. But the measures diverge again thereafter. The Shiller-GBW asking price measures suggest a rise in prices that almost reached the 1930 level, while the remaining measures all suggest that home values in the late 1930s remained 26 to 40 percent below the 1930 values.

6.8   When and How High Was the Peak Home Value in the 1920s?

Currently, there are five multicity indices that describe or might proxy the path of housing values during the 1920s: the GBW adjusted and unadjusted series, the rent CPI, the average value of all building permits per family taken care of, and the average value of one-family building permits. The two most closely aligned with our AVOOMS are the unadjusted and adjusted series created by Grebler, Blank, and Winnick (1956) with home owners reporting values at various points in time. We can improve on the GBW series by adding an additional thirty-one cities to the twenty-two cities that they used. The information for the additional cities comes from the handwritten tables derived from the CWA financial survey of 1934 and found in the US Bureau of Foreign and Domestic Commerce Record Group at the National Archives. We follow Grebler, Blank, and Winnick's methods in constructing the index. For example, to create the unadjusted index for the year 1920 for each city, we divided the average "cost of purchase of homes" bought in 1920 from the survey and divided by the average "value of the homes" the home owner reported for January 1, 1934 for that same group of homes. To match all of our other comparisons, we then indexed the series so that the 1930 value in the city was equal to 100.[12] We then aggregated across cities in two ways: an unweighted average across cities and a weighted average using the number of families in owner-occupied homes reporting values in the 1930 census. To create a series adjusted for depreciation, we followed Grebler, Blank, and Winnick by using a 1 3/8 percent compounded annual depreciation rate.

The original GBW series and the new GBW-style series using different weighting schemes are reported in table 6.7 along with the number of cities covered and the number of families in those cities reporting values for owner-occupied homes in the 1930 census. In comparisons of the unadjusted series, the new weighted series starts 1.6 points lower than the original GBW unadjusted series, hits a peak that is 0.5 points higher in 1925, and then falls to a trough in 1933 that is 2.3 points higher. For the series adjusted for depreciation, the new weighted series starts 1.5 points lower than the original GBW series in 1920, hits a peak in 1926 that is 4 points higher, and then hits a trough in 1933 that is 4.2 points higher than the trough in 1934 for the original GBW adjusted series.

Another way to use the new series is to use the information to interpolate between the benchmark estimates for the AVOOMS for forty cities for the years 1920, 1930, 1933, 1934 and the benchmarks for forty-six cities using the median estimates for 1920, 1930, and 1934.[13] We interpolate for each city individually and then aggregate across cities. Consider the interpolations for the AVOOMS using the new adjusted series as an example. We start with the benchmark values for 1920, 1930, 1933, and 1934. We then create ratios of the AVOOMS to the new GBW-style adjusted series in each of those years. For the period between 1920 and 1930 we used a straight-line interpolation to create interpolated ratios for each year. To get the value for 1921 we then multiply the interpolated ratio by the new adjusted GBW-style value in 1921; similar calculations were made for 1922 through 1939. A similar process was used to obtain values for 1931 and 1932.[14] This method was used for all other

12. Our calculations for Seattle and Cleveland exactly matched those reported by Grebler, Blank, and Winnick (1956).

13. We can create the AVOOMS interpolated series for up to forty-five cities if we stop in 1934. The requirement to have a value for 1940 from the census drops five cities that are all outside the top one hundred cities in terms of population. The number of families in 1930 lost is 21,536. The difference in the index is at most 0.4 in any one of the years. We reported the AVOOMS for forty cities only to save space.

14. The following was the formula used, with the number referring to the year, the ratio is R, AV is the AVOOMS index and AS is the adjusted series. We calculated $R20 = AV20/AS20$ and $R30 = AV30/AS30$. For 1921 the ratio is $R21 = R20*0.9 + R30*0.1$, and the 1921 interpolated value (IAV21) is $IAV21 = R21*AS21$.

interpolations. We then aggregated across cities using weighted averages with the number of families in owner-occupied homes reporting values in the 1930 census as the weights.

We have interpolated the AVOOMS and the median series using both the new unadjusted series and the new adjusted series. The two AVOOMS series in table 6.7 show that there is not much difference in the values that are interpolated by the adjusted and those interpolated by the unadjusted series for the 1920s, as they are never more than 0.4 points apart. When the time series are forced to match the benchmarks in 1920 and 1930, the main differences come in the timing and the size of the peaks and both the unadjusted and adjusted time series have peaks at roughly the same time.

In addition to the AVOOMS and median series, we have included the Shiller-GBW hybrid, the rent CPI, and the average values of building permit series in table 6.7 so that it is easy to compare all rises and falls in housing values. Many of the series also appear in figure 6.4. Table 6.7 also includes 1940 values for the series that have values in that year. All of the series show a peak in housing values in 1925 or 1926 with the exception of the average values for building permits, which peak in 1929 and 1930. The largest growth rate in value between 1920 and the peak is 26 percent for the rent CPI, followed by the AVOOMS and median indices at around 21 or 22 percent. The smallest growth is 3.6 percent for the unweighted new series and only 6 percent for the original GBW unadjusted series and the Shiller-GBW hybrid.

The largest decline in value between the peak in the 1920s and the trough after 1930 is a 38.6 percent decline for the median series from a peak of 104.9 in 1926 to a low of 64.4 in 1940. This is rivaled by the drops for the rent CPI of 38 percent from the peak of 110.7 in 1925 to the bottom of 68.6 in 1934. Both AVOOMS series fall roughly 30 percent from peaks above 105 in 1926 to a low of 73.6 in 1940. The Shiller-GBW hybrid also falls about 30 percent from a peak of 113.8 in 1925 to a bottom of 79.1 in 1933. The smallest declines are the falls of around 21 percent for the new adjusted series for fifty-three cities from peaks in 1925 to troughs in 1933.

The bottom line for all of the series is that they all peak sometime between 1925 and 1930, and they all fall sharply by 20 to 30 percent by around 1933 or 1934. The differences lie in the estimates of the rise from 1920 to the peak and the changes in prices after 1934. The indices based on the unadjusted GBW methods, including the Shiller-GBW hybrid all start in 1920 at a level above the value in 1930 and thus end up with a relatively small rise to the peak of 3 to 8 percent between 1920 and the mid-1920s. All of the remaining indices start at least 6.5 percent *below* the 1930 level and thus show rises to from 1920 to the 1920s peak of 13.5 to 26 percent. After 1940, the Shiller-GBW hybrid suggests a rise in home values to 95 percent of the 1930 value, while all other series show 1940 values that are 18 to 36 percent below the 1930 values.

Table 6.7 Old and new GBW-style housing value series, interpolated AVOOMS and median series, and existing series, 1920–1934, and 1940

Year	Original GBW unadjusted	New GBW-style unadjusted, unweighted	New GBW-style unadjusted, weighted	Original GBW adjusted	New GBW-style adjusted, unweighted	New GBW-style adjusted, weighted	AVOOMS interpolated with new GBW-style, unadjusted	AVOOMS interpolated with new GBW-style, adjusted, weighted	Median interpolated with new GBW-style adjusted	Shiller-GBW hybrid	Rent CPI	Average value of residential building permits	Average value of one-family building permits
1920	107.3	107.7	105.7	93.5	93.8	92.0	86.1	86.1	86.4	107.3	87.8		
1921	104.9	110.2	107.2	92.7	97.3	94.7	89.9	89.7	89.8	104.9	100.8	90.0	79.5
1922	106.4	109.4	107.8	95.3	98.0	96.5	92.5	92.2	92.2	106.4	103.8	91.6	85.3
1923	107.9	111.1	111.1	98.0	101.1	100.9	97.7	97.4	96.8	107.9	106.4	94.1	83.9
1924	108.2	111.4	112.5	99.6	104.5	103.5	100.7	100.3	99.9	108.2	110.3	99.5	86.9
1925	113.8	111.6	114.3	106.2	108.0	106.6	103.7	103.3	103.0	113.8	110.7	101.4	92.0
1926	109.2	111.3	113.5	103.4	107.1	107.4	105.5	105.1	104.9	109.2	109.6	100.8	95.4
1927	105.1	110.3	110.3	100.8	105.8	105.8	104.5	104.1	104.1	105.1	107.8	104.1	96.7
1928	106.7	109.5	109.1	103.7	106.5	106.1	104.9	104.6	104.7	106.7	105.3	100.5	98.9
1929	104.5	107.0	105.5	103.0	105.7	104.1	103.4	103.2	103.2	104.5	102.8	100.1	98.5
1930	100.0	100.0	100.0	100.0	100.0	100.0	100.0	100.0	100.0	100.0	100.0	100.0	100.0
1931	91.8	92.9	92.4	93.1	94.2	93.7	92.9	92.9	91.8	91.8	94.7	96.4	96.8
1932	82.2	83.3	83.0	84.4	85.7	85.3	84.6	84.6	82.3	82.2	85.0	84.5	78.4
1933	79.1	81.0	81.4	82.4	84.4	84.8	82.6	82.6	80.5	79.1	73.2	79.7	77.0
1934	81.4	83.7	81.9	80.6	88.5	86.6	79.2	79.2	80.4	81.4	68.6	81.5	81.5
1940							73.6	73.6	64.4	95.6	76.0	81.3	77.9
Maximum	113.8	111.6	114.3	106.2	108.0	107.4	105.5	105.1	104.9	113.8	110.7	104.1	100.0
Year of max.	1926	1925	1925	1926	1925	1926	1926	1926	1926	1925	1925	1927	1930
Minimum	79.1	81.0	81.4	80.6	84.4	84.8	73.6	73.6	64.4	79.1	68.6	79.7	77.0

	1933	1933	1933	1934	1933	1933	1940	1940	1940	1933	1934	1933	1933
Year of min.	1933	1933	1933	1934	1933	1933	1940	1940	1940	1933	1934	1933	1933
Growth rate 1920 to max.	6.0	3.6	8.1	13.5	15.1	16.7	22.5	22.1	21.4	6.0	26.0	15.7*	25.7*
Growth rate max. to min.	-30.5	-27.4	-28.8	-24.1	-21.8	-21.1	-30.2	-30.0	-38.6	-30.5	-38.0	-23.4	-23.0
Growth rate 1930 to 1933	-20.9	-19.0	-18.6	-17.6	-15.6	-15.2	-17.4	-17.4	-19.5	-20.9	-26.8	-20.3	-23.0
Number of cities	22	53	53	22	53	53	40	40	46	22	32	257	257
Families in 1930 in cities covered	4,973,29	7,612,04	7,612,04	4,973,29	7,612,04	7,612,04	7,153,28	7,153,28	7,397,53	4,973,29	2123992		
Top 10	1	1	1	1	1	1	1	1	1	1	9	10	10
Top 50	12	14	14	12	14	14	14	14	14	12	25	50	50
Top 100	13	27	27	13	27	27	27	27	27	13	29	100	100
Top 200	20	37	37	20	37	37	36	36	37	20	31	200	200

Note: 1930 value = 100.

***Significant at the 1 percent level.

**Significant at the 5 percent level.

*Significant at the 10 percent level.

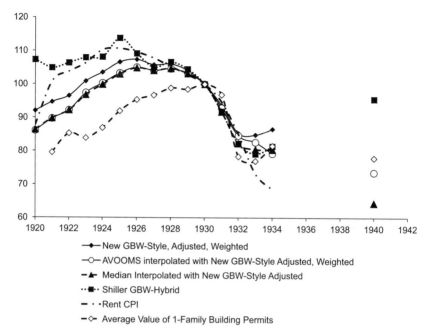

Fig. 6.4   Home value indices, 1920–1940
Note: 1930 = 100.

6.9   Comparisons to Modern Series

To make the comparisons of housing price trends across periods, we sought to use similar data and the same methods in the early twenty-first century as we used in the 1920s and 1930s. There are a number of home price and value series available in the early twenty-first century. We focus on the surveys that followed the lead of surveys in the 1920s and 1930s by asking all home owners to report the sale value of their home, whether the home was for sale or not. The census of 2000 and the American Community Surveys between 2003 and 2010 asked home owners "to estimate the full current market value of the property, including both house and land, even if the respondents owned only part of the property." "Apart from group quarters, all owner-occupied or vacant-for-sale units were covered, including mobile homes, condominiums, units with offices or businesses attached, and houses on lots of any size. For mobile homes in pre-2008 ACS and PRCS data, the value of the land was included in the value; in the 2008 ACS . . . , land value was included only if the owner of the mobile home also owned the land."

The 2000 survey and the ACS surveys asked people to report their home sale values by marking the value category for the home. As a result, the reporting of the information looks very much like the summary tables in the 1930 and 1940 censuses and in the inventory surveys in the mid-1930s. Therefore, we used the method for calculating medians that we used for the inventory surveys in the mid-1930s.

Table 6.8 shows medians indexed so that the 2000 value is equal to 100 for a variety of groupings of cities. Indexes across time were calculated for each city using the medians in that city and then were aggregated as a weighted average with the number of owner-occupied homes reporting values in 2000 as the weight. The Case-Shiller repeat sales price index for ten cities and for twenty cities receives a great deal of attention; therefore, we show the median home values for the Case-Shiller ten-city and twenty-city groupings, as well as information for the top 50, 100, 400, and all cities. Table 6.8 also contains the Case-Shiller and Office of Federal Housing Enterprise Oversight (OFHEO) Repeat Sales Indices and the Median New Home Sale Price Index for comparisons.

The rise in nominal house prices in the 2000 to 2007 housing boom far outstrips the rise in prices during the housing boom of the 1920s. All of the median values in table 6.8 peaked in 2007. The increases between 2000 and 2007 ranged from a high of 125 percent for the ten cities used in the Case-Shiller index to a low of 91.6 percent for the 400 cities with the most home owners in 2000. These growth rates are four to five times greater than the growth rates of 21 to 22 percent between 1920 and the peak in the mid-1920s shown by the AVOOMS and median indices in table 6.7. The housing value growth in the 1920s is also substantially lower than housing price growth rates shown by the sale price indices in table 6.8, which range from 46.4 percent for new home prices to 109.1 percent for the Case-Shiller ten-city index.

Arguably, the fall in nominal housing prices between 1930 and 1933 was worse than the fall in prices between 2007 and 2010. Here is a case where percentage drops do not tell the whole story. The AVOOMS and median indices in table 6.7 fell by roughly 17 to 20 percent between 1930 and 1933. The median home values in 2000 fell by 12 to 17 percent from 2007 to 2010, depending on the group of homes examined. A better comparison to the damage done to housing values is how the housing values compared to the start of the periods in 1920 and 2000. In 2010 all the housing indices show prices that are 32 to 86.8 percent *higher* than they were in 2000. In contrast, by 1933 the home values were *lower* than they were in 1920. Whereas in the Great Recession people saw part of the rise in housing values fall away, during the Great Depression, the entire rise was eliminated and housing prices fell still more. The AVOOMS and the median estimates in tables 6.6 and 6.7 show that the situation had worsened by 1940, such that home values were 14.5 to 25.5 percent lower than in 1920.

Table 6.8   Housing price indices, 2000–2011

Year	Median indices all home owners in census and American Community Surveys						Repeat sales price indices			New homes sale price	CPI housing
	All	Top 50	Top 100	Top 400	Case-Schiller 10 cities	Case-Schiller 20 cities	Case-Shiller 10 cities	Case-Shiller 20 cities	OFHEO	Median	
2000	100.0	100.0	100.0	100.0	100.0	100.0	100.0	100.0	100.0	100.0	100.0
2003	128.0	134.2	128.6	128.0	172.7	140.9	140.8	134.0	123.3	114.9	109.0
2005	169.2	174.6	170.0	169.2	201.9	180.2	194.7	179.0	148.9	140.6	115.4
2006	186.5	193.1	187.7	186.5	222.4	198.4	209.1	192.6	158.0	145.9	119.8
2007	191.6	197.3	192.5	191.6	225.0	201.6	199.8	185.2	158.3	146.4	123.6
2008	188.2	193.1	189.3	188.2	214.9	195.6	166.4	156.0	146.4	138.3	127.5
2009	173.7	176.5	174.4	173.7	193.0	176.8	144.9	135.3	138.7	128.8	128.0
2010	168.3	170.3	168.9	168.3	186.8	169.8	147.9	136.9	134.5	132.8	127.5
2011							142.8	131.6	128.7	134.5	129.2
Peak year	2007	2007	2007	2007	2007	2007	2006	2006	2007	2007	2011
Growth rate 2000 to peak	91.6	97.3	92.5	91.6	125.0	101.6	109.1	92.6	58.3	46.4	29.2
Growth rate peak to 2010	−12.1	−13.7	−12.3	−12.1	−17.0	−15.8	−29.3	−28.9	−15.0	−9.2	n.a.

Sources: Median sale values reported by all home owners created indices for medians within each city over the years with year 2000 values equaling 100 and then aggregated across cities with averages weighted by the number of home owners reporting values in the year 2000. The data come from microdata samples from the 2000 census and 2003–2010 American Community Surveys downloaded from Ruggles et. al. (2010) at www.ipums.org. The S&P/Case-Shiller Repeat Sales Price was downloaded from http://www.standardandpoors.com/indices/sp-case-shiller-home-price-indices/en/us/?indexId=spusa-cashpidff—p-us—on April 24, 2012, and the monthly data were averaged for each year. The OFHEO (Office of Federal Housing Enterprises Oversight) indices were downloaded from http://www.fhfa.gov/Default.aspx?Page=14 on April 30, 2012. The Median New Home Sales Price Index was downloaded from http://www.census.gov/const/uspricemon.pdf on May 1, 2012.

Note: Year 2000 value = 100.

6.10   Deflating the Home Price Series by the CPI and Nominal Per Capita Income

The focus has been on nominal price changes because of the difficulty in measuring nominal prices accurately; yet other prices and incomes were not standing still during these periods. Therefore, it is important to show changes in housing prices relative to all prices by deflating by the CPI. In addition, we examine the affordability of housing by dividing the indices by an index for nominal GDP per capita in the two periods.

The behavior of prices and nominal incomes were quite different during the 1920–1940 period and the early twenty-first century. The early twenty-first century was a period of mild CPI price inflation of 2.5 percent per year while nominal Gross Domestic Product (GDP) per capita grew fast enough that real per capita incomes grew through 2007 before a decline during the recession. Real per capita incomes nearly caught up to the 2007 level again in 2011. In contrast, the 1920s followed the end of a dramatic inflation during World War I. The CPI fell 20 percent between 1920 and 1922 and then fluctuated around a flat trend through 1929. The Great Depression was associated with a 25 percent drop in the CPI from 1929 to 1933. During the rest of the 1930s, there was a mild inflation of 2.7 percent per year from 1933 to 1937, followed by mild deflation from 1937 to 1939. Meanwhile, per real capita incomes fell sharply in the recession at the beginning of the 1920s, grew relatively quickly until 1929, and then fell by 30 percent between 1929 and 1933. Real income per capita did not reach its 1929 level again until 1940.

6.10.1   Adjusting for the CPI

The adjustment for CPI inflation does not change the story of housing prices in the early twenty-first century much. The rise in real housing prices from 2000 to 2006 and 2007 is dampened relative to the rise in nominal housing prices. For example, real median housing values for the top 400 cities rose only 46.9 percent in table 6.9 compared with the nominal price rise of 91.6 percent shown in table 6.7. The decline in real housing prices from 2006 and 2007 to 2010 looks worse. The median index for the top 400 cities fell 16.6 percent to 132.9. Meanwhile, the resale price indices adjusted for CPI inflation and new home sales price indices fell to roughly the same levels they had reached in 2000.

The wild gyrations in the price level in the 1920s and 1930s caused the housing prices adjusted for inflation to follow a substantially different path from nominal housing prices. Instead of rising to a peak in the mid-1920s and then declining until 1940, as the nominal housing prices did, the AVOOMS and median indices adjusted for inflation in table 6.10 and figure 6.5 rose roughly 41 percent to a peak in 1928, fell slightly to 1930, and then rose to a new higher peak in 1933. The real housing prices then declined

Table 6.9   Home value indices relative to Consumer Price Index and per capita GDP

	Home values adjusted for CPI inflation					Home prices relative to per capita GDP				
Year	Case-Shiller repeat sales, 20 cities	Median home values 20 CS cities	Median home values top 400	OFHEO repeat sales	Median new home sale price	Case-Shiller repeat sales, 20 cities	Median home values 20 CS cities	Median home values top 400	OFHEO repeat sales	Median new home sale price
2000	100.0	100.0	100.0	100.0	100.0	100.0	100.0	100.0	100.0	100.0
2003	125.4	131.8	119.7	115.4	107.5	123.3	129.6	117.7	113.4	105.7
2005	157.9	158.9	149.2	131.3	124.0	148.1	149.0	140.0	123.2	116.3
2006	164.5	169.5	159.3	134.9	124.7	151.7	156.3	146.9	124.4	115.0
2007	153.8	167.4	159.1	131.5	121.5	140.5	152.9	145.3	120.1	111.0
2008	124.8	156.4	150.6	117.1	110.7	117.2	147.0	141.5	110.0	104.0
2009	108.6	141.9	139.4	111.3	103.4	105.1	137.4	135.0	107.8	100.1
2010	108.1	134.1	132.9	106.3	104.9	103.0	127.7	126.6	101.2	99.9
2011	100.8			98.6	103.0	95.9			93.8	98.0
Year of peak	2006	2006	2006	2006	2006	2006	2006	2006	2006	2006
Growth rate 2000 to peak	64.5	69.5	59.3	34.9	24.7	51.7	56.3	46.9	24.4	16.3
Growth rate peak to 2010	−34.3	−20.9	−16.6	−21.3	−15.8	−32.1	−18.3	−13.8	−18.7	−14.1

Sources: See table 6.8. The Consumer Price Index was downloaded from the BLS website (www.bls.gov). Per capita GDP was downloaded from the Measuring Worth website (http://www.measuringworth.com/uscompare/).

Note: 2000 value = 2000.

Table 6.10   Housing values relative to CPI and GDP per capita, 1920–1940

Year	Housing values adjusted for CPI inflation					Housing values relative to GDP per capita				
	New GBW-style, adjusted, weighted	AVOOMS interpolated with new GBW-style adjusted, weighted	Median interpolated with new GBW-style adjusted	Shiller GBW-hybrid	Average value of one-family building permits	New GBW-style, adjusted, weighted	AVOOMS interpolated with new GBW-style, adjusted, weighted	Median interpolated with new GBW-style adjusted	Shiller GBW-hybrid	Average value of one-family building permits
1920	76.9	71.9	72.1	89.6		83.5	78.1	78.4	97.3	
1921	88.5	83.9	84.0	98.1	74.4	103.1	97.7	97.8	114.3	86.7
1922	96.3	92.0	92.0	106.1	85.1	108.2	103.3	103.3	119.2	95.6
1923	98.8	95.4	94.8	105.7	82.2	98.8	95.3	94.8	105.7	82.1
1924	101.2	98.0	97.6	105.7	85.0	100.7	97.5	97.2	105.2	84.6
1925	101.5	98.4	98.1	108.3	87.6	100.3	97.1	96.9	107.0	86.5
1926	101.5	99.3	99.1	103.1	90.1	96.0	94.0	93.8	97.6	85.3
1927	101.9	100.2	100.2	101.2	93.1	96.6	95.0	95.0	95.9	88.3
1928	103.3	101.9	102.0	103.9	96.3	98.0	96.7	96.7	98.6	91.3
1929	101.4	100.6	100.6	101.8	96.0	90.6	89.9	89.9	91.0	85.8
1930	100.0	100.0	100.0	100.0	100.0	100.0	100.0	100.0	100.0	100.0
1931	102.9	102.0	100.8	100.9	106.4	112.5	111.5	110.2	110.3	116.3
1932	104.4	103.5	100.7	100.6	95.9	134.4	133.3	129.7	129.6	123.4
1933	109.6	106.7	104.0	102.2	99.5	140.2	136.5	133.0	130.7	127.2
1934	108.0	98.8	100.3	101.6	101.7	123.1	112.6	114.3	115.7	115.9
1940		87.7	76.7	113.9	92.8		71.5	62.5	92.8	75.7
Max	109.6	106.7	104.0	108.3	106.4	140.2	136.5	133.0	130.7	127.2
Maximum year	1933	1933	1933	1925	1931	1933	1933	1933	1933	1933
Growth rate 1920 to max	42.6	48.5	44.2	20.9	43.0*	67.9	74.8	69.7	34.3	46.8
Growth rate 1920 to 1920s peak	34.5	41.7	41.3	20.9	34.5	29.5	32.3	31.8	22.5	

Sources: See table 6.7 for nominal values. CPI is based on 1935–1939 budgets and then adjusted so that the 1930 value equals 100. It comes from the US Bureau of Labor Statistics (1941a, 36, 44). Gross domestic product per capita (GDP per capita) is series Ca12 reported by Sutch (2006, 3–25).

Note: 1930 value = 100.

***Significant at the 1 percent level.

**Significant at the 5 percent level.

*Significant at the 10 percent level.

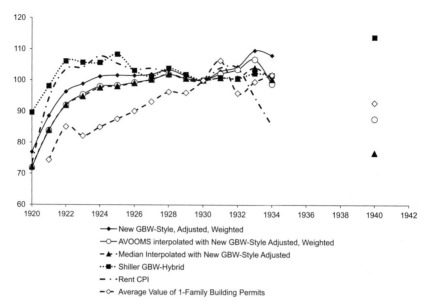

Fig. 6.5   Home values adjusted for CPI inflation, 1920–1940
Note: 1930 = 100.

to a level in 1940 that lay somewhere between the 1920 and 1922 levels.[15] Whatever home owners gained in real value after 1920, they had largely lost by 1940. The other series all follow a similar pattern of a temporary peak in the 1920s and then a higher peak around 1931, 1932, or 1933. All but the Shiller-GBW hybrid series also then experience a decline in real value. In contrast, the Shiller-GBW hybrid series rises to a new peak in 1940 that is more than 27 percent higher than the 1920 value.

15. Most studies adjust for inflation by dividing by a measure of the price level, either the Consumer Price Index or the implicit price deflator used to deflate gross domestic product. This makes perfect sense with a neutral inflation or deflation where most prices are moving in the same direction. It becomes trickier when relative prices are changing dramatically, as they did in the 1920s and 1930s and again in the early twenty-first century. Rents rose rapidly until 1925 while the prices of the rest of the goods had fallen sharply between 1920 and 1922. Between 1925 and 1933 rents fell more than the prices of the rest of the goods and rents stayed substantially lower than prices for the remaining goods for the rest of the 1930s. However, it turns out that it does not make too much difference to the index when it is deflated by either the overall CPI or by the nonrent CPI. The magnitudes are different but the same story is told. The AVOOMS home value index relative to the overall CPI rises from 71.9 in 1920 to 100 in 1930. It then rises to 106.6 because there was severe deflation during the early 1930s before falling to 98.9 and then 87.7. When the adjustment is relative to the price index for nonrent goods, the rise is from 67.9 in 1920 to 100 in 1930 to 105.5 in 1933 then a decline to 95.9 and 85.9. The median housing value estimates follow a similar path from 68 in 1920 to 100 in 1933 to 72.6 in 1940 relative to the full CPI, and from 64.3 to 100 to 71.1 relative to the nonhousing CPI.

6.10.2   Affordability: Housing Prices Relative to Income

The affordability indices show the ratio of the indices for home prices to indices for nominal GDP per capita. When the index rises, houses become more expensive relative to people's incomes. As with the adjustments for the CPI, scaling housing prices relative to incomes dampens the growth rate in relative housing prices relative to the growth rate in nominal housing prices. In the early twenty-first century, nominal median housing values for the top 400 cities rose 91.6 percent, but they rose only 47 percent faster than incomes rose during the period, as seen in table 6.9. Housing prices than fell relative to incomes afterward so that housing values relative to incomes were somewhere between the values in 2003 and 2005.

In the earlier period every series in the right side of table 9.10 and in figure 6.6 shows that housing prices rose much faster than incomes between 1920 and 1922. The houses became 23 to 33 percent less affordable in that two-year span. Incomes grew faster than housing prices until 1929 when nearly all of the indices bottom out around 89 to 93. Then, there was a large swing: housing prices fell, but incomes fell much faster. By 1933 the index had risen to over 130 in every housing value index. From the peak affordability level reached in 1929, houses had become 44 to 50 percent less affordable. For the rest of the decade every series except the Shiller-GBW hybrid shows a large drop in the index to levels that made housing 11.8 to 30.4 percent more

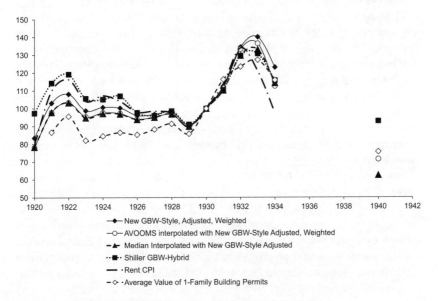

Fig. 6.6   Home values relative to GDP per capita, 1920–1940
Note: 1930 = 100.

affordable relative to income than in 1929 and 7 to 20 percent more afford-able than in 1920. In all cases incomes rose much faster than housing prices over the rest of the decade.

6.11   Conclusion

The most commonly cited time series for nonfarm home values and prices between 1920 and 1940 was created by Robert Shiller with a goal of showing long-run changes in housing prices from 1890 to the present. Shiller relied on a series developed by Grebler, Blank, and Winnick (1956) for 1890 to 1934 and then spliced in a new series based on thirty asking prices per year in five major cities to extend the series from 1934 to 1953. The emphasis on obtaining annual series that are consistent over the long run caused the scholars to avoid using information from the US censuses and other sources that would have allowed them to perform a more careful examination of the period from 1920 to 1940. In this chapter we develop a new version of the Grebler, Blank, and Winnick series for 1920 to 1934 that includes more than twice as many cities, as well as several alternative measures for changes in housing prices between 1920 and 1940 that are based on information collected from other government publications and archival sources. We then use the information to compare and contrast the changes in housing prices during the boom and bust in housing prices between 1920 and 1940 and the modern day boom and bust in the early twenty-first century.

The new indices and the Shiller-GBW hybrid indices all show that nominal housing prices fell by somewhere between 20 and 30 percent from a peak between 1925 and 1930 to a low level around 1933 and 1934. However, there is substantial disagreement about the values circa 1920 and 1940. For 1920 the Shiller-GBW hybrid suggests that housing values were 4.9 to 7.3 percent *higher* than they were in 1930, while the series based on 1920 mortgage census information, the rent CPI, average values of residential building permits and Grebler, Blank, and Winnick's preferred series adjusted for depreciation show that housing values circa 1920 were anywhere from 6.5 to 20 percent *lower* than in 1930.

For 1940 the Shiller-GBW hybrid index shows that housing prices had returned to *within 5 percent* of the 1930 value. In contrast, all of the other series have 1940 values that are *18.7 to 35.6 percent lower* than in 1930. In summary, the most commonly cited current series suggests much lower growth rates in nominal housing prices between 1920 and the mid-1920s peak than all of the other series show and a much stronger recovery after 1933 than any other series. In fact, several of the series suggest declines from 1933 to 1940 rather than recovery.

Comparisons of the booms and busts in nominal home values show that the growth in nominal home values between 2000 and 2006 to 2007 was much more rapid than in the 1920s boom. Home values fell significantly between 2007 and 2010, but nominal values remained substantially higher than in 2000. For every housing measure except the current Shiller-GBW hybrid, the situation in the 1930s will shock people in the modern era. After housing prices fell sharply between 1930 and 1933, nominal housing values failed to rebound by 1940 to anywhere near their 1930 level, nor did they reach their 1920 level. In fact, several series suggest that housing prices continued to fall until 1940.

When housing values are adjusted for CPI inflation, the growth rate in housing values is dampened between 2000 and 2006 to 2007, but it is still substantially larger than the growth in the 1920s boom. The median values reported by all home owners for the top 200 cities grew 59.4 percent between 2000 and 2006, compared with growth rates of 35 to 42 percent for similar indices in the boom period between 1920 and 1928. The bust from 2007 to 2010 shows strong declines in median real home values reported by all home owners but leave people with values at least 30 percent above the values in 2000. The changes in inflation-adjusted home values from 1928 to 1933 look quite different from the sharp declines in nominal home values because of the 30 percent deflation in all prices between 1929 and 1933. Between 1928 and 1933, inflation-adjusted home values declined for a couple of years and then rose to a new peak that was higher than the peak in the 1920s. Between 1933 and 1940 real home prices fell for every series except the extant GBW-Shiller hybrid series to levels that were between the levels seen between 1920 and 1922. If by some chance the modern era were to repeat the pattern in the 1930s, home values would continue to decline or stagnate over the next several years.

The affordability of housing was examined by comparing the ratio of home values to per capita income over time. In the early twenty-first-century boom, median housing values reported by all home owners rose 47 percent faster than income before the index fell back to a level 27 percent above the 2000 ratio. In the 1920s the sharp recession in 1921 to 1922 caused incomes to fall while housing prices were rising, leading to an early peak in 1922 in the ratio. By 1929 home price affordability had risen sharply, as nominal housing prices started declining after 1925 and per capita incomes rose. The Great Contraction caused per capita incomes to fall much more quickly than housing prices fell between 1929 and 1933, and housing became much less affordable. The situation reversed itself by 1940, causing the ratio of housing prices to incomes to fall below the ratios in 1920, so that relative to income housing was more affordable than at any time in the intervening period.

While more clearly defining the movements in housing values, the results in this chapter should not be considered the final word on the prices in the period from 1920 to 1940. Each of the series we have discussed has its own set of flaws and biases. We hope that the questions raised by the differences across series leads to additional work to collect more data from local newspapers, archives, and government records to develop additional estimates of housing prices.

Appendix A

Calculating Medians from the Reported Distributions of Housing Values

The 1940 census of housing reported median values for homes in each city for both 1930 and 1940. They also reported distributions of housing values for 1940, and the 1930 census of housing reported both medians and distributions of housing values for 1930. We also calculated medians for housing values from the distribution in the following way. The most commonly reported categories for cities in the 1930 and 1940 census and in the housing inventories were values from $1–$999, $1,000–$1,499, $1,500–$1,999, $2,000–$2,499, $2,500–$2,999, $3,000–$3,999, $4,000–$4,999, $5,000–$7,499, $7,500–$9,999, and $10,000 and over. The 1930 census also included categories for $10,000–$14,999, $15,000–$19,999, and $20,000 and over. Sixty-seven of 960 cities with information in 1930 had medians higher than $10,000, but the census reported those medians. By 1940 only 13 of 956 cities had median housing values higher than $10,000. When we calculated the medians from the distribution information, we followed a procedure similar to the following: create the cumulative distribution for the categories, pick the category in which the cumulative percentage (CPH) is higher than 50 with a top income of YH and the cumulative percentage of the next lower category (CPL) is less than 50 with a top income of YL. The formula used to calculate the median is (50-CPL)/(CPH-CPL) * (YH-YL). For example, if 46 percent of the homes were valued at $2,999 or less and 53 percent were values at $3,999 or less, the median is calculated as (50–46)/(53–46) * (3,999–2,999).

The housing inventories for 1934, 1935, and 1936 from the property inventories and the financial survey of housing in 1934 did not report median or average values, although they did report distributional information. We used the same formula for the median as described earlier. The categories used in the 1934 Financial Survey of Housing for 65 cities were $1–$999, $1,000–$1,499, $1,500–$1,999, $2,000–$2,999, $3,000–$3,999, $4,000–$4,999, $5,000–$7,499, $7,500–$9,999, $10,000–$14,999, $15,000–$19,999, and $20,000 and over. The only difference was the lack of a split at $2,500 within the $2,000–$2,999 category. Another 31 city inventories in 1934 reported information for $1–$999, $1,000–$1,499, $1,500–$1,999, $2,000–$4,999, $5,000–$9,999, $10,000–$19,999, and $20,000 and over. The estimates of the medians for these cities are therefore subject to more measurement error.

The categories for the 1935 inventories were the same as for 1930 for eleven of the forty-nine cities except the category for $1,000–$2,000 was not split at the $1,500 value. The remaining thirty-eight cities had the same categories as in 1930 except that the values from $5,000 to $10,000 were split into $5,000–$5,999, $6,000–$7,999, and $8,000–$9,999. These same categories were also used in city inventories for forty-one cities in 1936.

Appendix B

Comparability of the Surveys in 1930, 1940, and the Early Twenty-First Century

The IPUMS description of how housing values were reported in the original census manuscripts for 1930 and 1940 say that "enumerators consulted with the owners to estimate the sale value of the housing unit. For single-family, non-farm houses, the estimate included the value of the house and land. . . . For owner-occupied units that were part of a building containing other households or businesses (except a small room used by the owner for an office), the estimate included only the value of the part of the house in which the owner's household lived. For example, if the owning household of a two-family house rented half of the house to another household, only half of the house's value would have been reported. . . ." This information was downloaded from the IPUMS USA website (http://usa.ipums.org /usa-action/variables/VALUEH#comparability_tab) on April 17, 2012.

For the 2000 census and the American Community Surveys of 2003 and 2005–2010, "respondents estimated the full current market value of the property, including both house and land, even if the respondents owned only part of the property." "Apart from group quarters, all owner-occupied or vacant-for-sale units were covered, including mobile homes, condominiums, units with offices or businesses attached, and houses on lots of any size. For mobile homes in pre-2008 ACS . . . data, the value of the land was included in the value; in the 2008 ACS . . . land value was included only if the owner of the mobile home also owned the land." This information was downloaded from the IPUMS USA (website http://usa.ipums.org/usa-action/variables /VALUEH#comparability_tab) on April 17, 2012.

References

Federal Housing Administration. 1940. *Sixth Annual Report of the Federal Housing Administration For the Year Ending December 31, 1939*. Washington, DC: Government Printing Office.

Fishback, Price, Jonathan Rose, and Kenneth Snowden. 2013. *Well Worth Saving: How the New Deal Safeguarded Home Ownership*. Chicago: University of Chicago Press.

Fisher, Ernest M. 1951. *Urban Real Estate Markets: Characteristics and Financing*. New York: National Bureau of Economic Research.

Garfield, Frank, and William Hoad. 1937. "Construction Costs and Real Property Values." *Journal of the American Statistical Association* 32 (December): 643–53.

Grebler, Leo, David Blank, and Louis Winnick. 1956. *Capital Formation in Residential Real Estate*. Princeton, NJ: Princeton University Press.

Home Owners' Loan Corporation. Area Descriptions. Records Related to the City Survey File, 1935–1940 Entry 39. Boxes 1–156. Record Group 195 Records of the Federal Home Loan Bank Board. Home Owners Loan Corporation. National Archives II, College Park, Maryland.

Nicholas, Tom, and Anna Scherbina. 2013. "Real Estate Prices during the Roaring Twenties and the Great Depression." *Real Estate Economics* 41 (Summer): 278–309.

Ruggles, Stephen J., Trent Alexander, Katie Genadek, Ronald Goeken, Matthew B. Schroeder, and Matthew Sobek. 2010. *Integrated Public Use Microdata Series: Version 5.0* [Machine-readable database]. Minneapolis: University of Minnesota.

S&P Dow Jones Indices. 2013. *S&P/Case-Shiller Home Price Indices: Methodology.* PDF from McGraw Hill Financial. Accessed June 14, 2013. http://us.spindices. com/documents/methodologies/methodology-sp-cs-home-price-indices.pdf.

Shiller, Robert. 2005. *Irrational Exuberance*, 2nd edition. Princeton, NJ: Princeton University Press.

Snowden, Kenneth. 2006. "Housing." In *Historical Statistics of the United States: Earliest Times to the Present.* Millennial edition, vol. 4, edited by Susan B. Carter, Scott S. Garner, Michael R. Haines, Alan L. Olmstead, Richard Sutch, and Gavin Wright, 481–525. Cambridge: Cambridge University Press.

Stapp, Peyton. 1938. *Urban Housing: A Summary of Real Property Inventories Conducted on Works Projects, 1934–1936.* Works Progress Administration. Washington, DC: Government Printing Office.

Sutch, Richard. 2006. "National Income and Product." In *Historical Statistics of the United States: Earliest Times to the Present.* Millennial edition, vol. 4, edited by Susan B. Carter, Scott S. Garner, Michael R. Haines, Alan L. Olmstead, Richard Sutch, and Gavin Wright, 481–525. Cambridge: Cambridge University Press.

US Bureau of the Census. 1923. *Mortgages on Homes: A Report on the Results of the Inquiry into the Mortgage Debt on Homes Other than Farm Homes at the Fourteenth Census, 1920.* Census Monographs II. Washington, DC: Government Printing Office.

———. 1933. *Fifteenth Census of the United States, 1930, Population, Volume IV: Families, Reports by States, Giving Statistics for Counties, Cities, and Other Urban Places.* Washington, DC: Government Printing Office.

———. 1943a. *Sixteenth Census of the United States, 1940. Housing, Volume II, General Characteristics: Parts 1–5.* Washington, DC: Government Printing Office.

———. 1943b. *Sixteenth Census of the United States, 1940. Housing, Volume IV, Mortgages on Owner-Occupied Nonfarm Homes, Part 1: United States Summary.* Washington, DC: Government Printing Office.

———. 1975. *Historical Statistics of the United States: Colonial Times to 1970.* Washington, DC: Government Printing Office.

US Bureau of Foreign and Domestic Commerce. Undated. Handwritten Tables from the Surveys of Urban Housing. Record Group 151, Entry 50 Records of the Drugstore Survey, St. Louis, MO 1926–1927. Boxes 245–264. National Archives, Missouri Branch.

US Bureau of Labor Statistics. 1941a. *Changes in Cost of Living in Large Cities in the United States, 1913–1941. Bulletin No. 699.* Washington, DC: Government Printing Office.

———. 1941b. *Building Construction, 1941. Bulletin No.713.* Washington, DC: Government Printing Office.

Wickens, David. 1937. *Financial Survey of Urban Housing.* US Bureau of Foreign and Domestic Commerce. Washington, DC: Government Printing Office.

———. 1941. *Residential Real Estate: Its Economic Position As Shown by Values, Rents, Family Incomes, Financing and Construction, Together with Estimates for All Real Estate.* New York: National Bureau of Economic Research.

7

The Prolonged Resolution of Troubled Real Estate Lenders during the 1930s

Jonathan D. Rose

7.1 Introduction

Building and loan associations (B&Ls) were an important source of residential real estate loan funds during the interwar period. This chapter studies how one set of particularly troubled B&Ls in Newark, New Jersey, slowly unwound their obligations over the late 1930s and 1940s, following financial shocks which included credit losses on foreclosed real estate and demands for withdrawals from investors.[1]

Key to this story is the absence of contractual or statutory mechanisms that could have forced resolution more quickly. To prevent some B&L investors from withdrawing at 100 cents on the dollar while leaving losses for

Jonathan D. Rose is an economist in the Division of Monetary Affairs at the Board of Governors of the Federal Reserve System.

The views expressed here are solely the responsibility of the author and should not be interpreted as reflecting the views of the Board of Governors of the Federal Reserve System or of anyone else associated with the Federal Reserve System. I thank Price Fishback, Andra Ghent, Ken Snowden, Eugene White, and seminar participants at the NBER Conference on Housing and Mortgage Markets in Historical Perspective and at Yale University. For acknowledgments, sources of research support, and disclosure of the author's material financial relationships, if any, please see http://www.nber.org/chapters/c12799.ack.

1. The focus on B&Ls in the mid-Atlantic region in this chapter is deliberate, as B&Ls were unusually numerous prior to the Depression in this region, with roughly 500 based in Newark alone, and the 1930s recovery of these institutions was remarkably prolonged compared to the national pattern. Of an estimated 12,000–13,000 B&Ls active across the country in 1930, more than 4,000 were located in Pennsylvania and about 1,500 in New Jersey. The activity in Maryland is not well documented as B&Ls were wholly unregulated in that state until the 1940s, but crude estimates suggest around 1,000 to 1,500 associations. The focus on New Jersey is due to its superior data, and the subfocus on Newark is due to the rich history of the 499 B&Ls, most very small, that operated in that city. The B&Ls in this region lagged the pattern of recovery typical for B&Ls in most of the country, where closures and reorganizations were largely finished by 1939.

remaining investors, New Jersey legislators and jurists revised statutes and issued new legal interpretations that allowed B&Ls to restrict withdrawals until loss reserves were established. However, establishing such reserves often took years, and in the interim B&Ls had no clear path for achieving consensus over whether to realize losses and how to allocate losses once realized. These associations struggled for a decade to find such consensus and unwind their obligations.

In response, a secondary market for B&L liabilities, known as shares, emerged in the mid to late 1930s.[2] This was a market-based resolution mechanism that allowed shareholders to exit their associations, though at steep losses. Similar markets existed in many major cities and were an important feature of the Depression experience for those who accumulated savings through B&Ls.

Importantly, this secondary market was also credited for helping clear the housing market. Buyers of discounted shares subsequently used those shares to purchase real estate from B&Ls at the much higher book value of the shares. The B&Ls preferred these transactions to cash sales if the book value of the shares exceeded the cash price a property could command, as this allowed the association to avoid realizing some losses on its books. Therefore, it was possible for both the buyer and seller of real estate to be better off by exchanging real estate for shares rather than cash because of the loss previously borne by the original holder of the shares.

The median trading price of B&L shares in Newark was low, about forty cents on the dollar of book value during 1939 and 1940. The pattern of market prices across associations is consistent with the primacy of withdrawal considerations, as investors took the largest discounts on shares of associations that were least able to pay withdrawals. In contrast, solvency characteristics have less explanatory power.

The secondary market began to fade in the second half of 1940 as more formal resolutions picked up. The Newark industry was reduced from 499 associations in 1930 to 55 associations in 1945. From 1938 to 1940, a wave of associations exited heavily through voluntary liquidations and state seizures. These associations tended to have larger holdings of foreclosed real estate, to be less profitable, and to have relatively heavier discounts of their shares on the secondary market. In 1942 and 1943 another wave of associations went through reorganization. The main reorganization strategy involved spinning off bad assets (foreclosed real estate, delinquent loans) into separate bad banks, receiving a liquidity infusion from the Reconstruction Finance Corporation (secured by the bad assets) to satisfy unpaid withdrawals, and qualifying for insurance by the Federal Savings and Loan Insurance Cor-

2. Much of the country's B&Ls operated mainly with equity shares. Despite being equity, these shares were subject to withdrawal like deposits. Some states, including Ohio and California, allowed B&Ls to explicitly accept deposits or instruments similar to certificates of deposit.

poration. The RFC cash was critical to addressing the persistent maturity mismatch, and the wartime economic expansion also contributed to the liquidation through higher real estate prices.

The late timing of these resolutions significantly lags the pattern characterizing commercial banks and some (but not all) B&Ls in other parts of the country (See Richardson [2007] for commercial banks and Ewalt [1962] and Snowden [2003] for B&Ls). The slow resolution of these institutions also relates to a literature, traditionally in the context of commercial banks, regarding depositors' access to funds during downturns (Anari, Kolari, and Mason 2005; Rockoff 1993; Kaufman and Seelig 2002). B&L liabilities have not historically been considered part of the core money aggregates and, in fact, appear to have become less money-like during the height of B&L troubles. Lack of access to savings in B&L was a fact of life across the country during the 1930s.

7.2   Background

7.2.1   General B&L Background

Building and loan associations, the predecessors of savings and loan associations, were generally mutually owned thrift organizations that invested almost wholly in real estate loans.[3] Here I focus largely on the industry as it existed in New Jersey. There was a certain amount of diversity in B&L practices across the country, and so readers interested in a more thorough and geographically generalized discussion would find useful the information in Snowden (1997, 2003), Snowden and James (2001), Bodfish (1931, 1935), Bodfish and Theobald (1938), Clark and Chase (1925), and Ewalt (1962).

The 499 B&Ls in Newark at the end of 1930 were generally quite small, as the median number of investors was about 450 people. State law put some limit on B&L size through prohibitions against branching or the use of agents, and against loans on properties outside of New Jersey. These restrictions should not be overstated, though, because large associations did exist in the state. The West End B&L, for example, had 33,000 investors and was one of the largest B&Ls in the country.

Snowden (1997) suggests that the small traditional size of B&Ls (not just in Newark but across the country) was a choice of the associations' management (e.g., local builders) who had little desire to manage associations larger than what was necessary to provide financing for their other businesses.[4]

3. The transition to *savings* and loan terminology occurred during the 1930s and 1940s. It was partly a rebranding, but it also reflected a set of important institutional changes.
4. Along these lines, Piquet (1930) tabulates the occupations of New Jersey B&L presidents and secretaries, and finds they were most commonly builders, realtors, and insurance brokers, as well as merchants, clerks, and accountants. In this sense, the growth of the B&L industry was a development endogenous to the relative immaturity of institutional mortgage markets

Table 7.1   Aggregate balance sheet, 1930 and 1937, Newark B&Ls

Assets			Liabilities		
	1930	1937		1930	1937
Cash	1.1	1.3	Shares-installment		
Liquid investments	0.3	0.9	payments	63.1	42.5
Mortgage loans-			Shares-one payment	14.6	19.3
B&L contracts	85.6	31.4	Shares-other	0.5	1.9
Mortgage loans-other	2.0	5.5	Borrowed money	5.7	2.4
Loans on shares	2.5	0.8	Accrued dividends	14.0	5.1
Real estate owned	6.7	54.0	Reserves and		
Late share payments	1.2	3.9	unapportioned profits	1.1	22.8
Other	0.7	2.2	Other	1.0	5.9
Total	100.0	100.0	Total	100.0	100.0

Notes: The balance sheets are expressed as percentage points out of 100. Total assets were $480 million in 1930 and $298 million in 1937.

All things considered, though, the extreme preponderance of associations in Newark was a bit unusual, though shared by neighboring cities in New Jersey, Pennsylvania, and Maryland. Members held a total of about 425,000 accounts at Newark B&Ls in 1930, in a city with 444,000 people.

Table 7.1 displays the aggregate balance sheet of Newark B&Ls in 1930 and 1937.[5] Most assets were in real estate loans, primarily residential, though some associations also invested in commercial properties in the 1920s, particularly apartment buildings and some small mixed-use properties. This expansion into non-owner-occupied lending was criticized, at least in retrospect, but its extent is difficult to quantify as the published balance sheets do not separate out different types of real estate.[6] Holdings of non–real estate assets were fairly negligible prior to the Depression but became quite important by 1937.

On the liability side, New Jersey B&Ls were funded mainly by traditional

---

in late 1800s and early 1900s. Snowden (2003) rejects an alternate hypothesis that the small size of most B&Ls was chosen in order to ease peer monitoring. Larger and more geographically diverse associations had been more numerous during the late nineteenth century but many failed in a large wave during the 1890s.

5. I use data from 1930 in this example because 1930 is the first year in which reserves and unapportioned profits are reported separately from apportioned profits.

6. Some measure is available in RFC loan files, which are careful to characterize the collateral available. For example, at the West End B&L, the largest association in Newark, the majority of owned real estate parcels were traditional one-to-four family residential properties, but by value apartment buildings constituted about two-thirds of the available collateral. From a small sample of RFC loan files, apartment building loans and real estate appear to be more common at the larger associations, while the nonresidential properties held by smaller associations were mixed-use properties such as a store combined with a dwelling. At the Enterprise B&L, which is discussed later in this chapter, fifteen of eighteen real estate parcels were one-to-four family residences, and the other three were mixed-use properties.

equity shares. The resulting ownership structure was quite diffuse, motivated traditionally by mutual ideals. In an "installment" share, a shareholder committed to monthly payments, and the share would mature when those payments, combined with apportioned profits (retained earnings), reached a prefixed maturity value, typically $200 in about eleven to twelve years (roughly $2,700 today adjusted for inflation). These liabilities were meant to reduce maturity mismatch with assets, but in practice withdrawal privileges undermined the long-term nature of these shares. Other funding was also obtained with "income" shares, which were similar to certificates of deposits, as the full maturity value of an income share was paid up front and cash dividends were then paid out instead of accumulated.

7.2.2   The Depression Foreclosure Crisis

The nation as a whole experienced a severe foreclosure crisis in the early and mid-1930s. Wheelock (2008), White (2010), Courtemanche and Snowden (2010), Fishback et al. (2011), and Rose (2011) provide background on this. In general, the "double trigger" theory of borrower default emphasizes the importance of negative income shocks combined with lower property prices.[7] Both triggers were present in the 1930s. In Newark, unemployment was still about 16 percent in 1940 according to the census, and another 4 percent of the labor force was in emergency relief programs. The median value of owner-occupied housing in Newark fell to 52 percent of its 1930 level by 1940, compared to 61 percent in the country as a whole. Much of the decline likely occurred in the first few years of the decade, but even in 1939 a federal survey described real estate prices in Newark as "still shrinking from the high levels of the late 1920s."[8]

In such an environment, foreclosures mounted, and correspondingly there were very large increases in holdings of foreclosed real estate at Newark B&Ls. Table 7.1 indicates that real estate accounted for 54 percent of Newark B&L assets in 1937. The annual flow of foreclosures in Newark did not materially decrease from its peak until 1937, and were still quite elevated in 1939. Prodigious quantities of institutionally owned real estate had a persistently depressive effect on prices in the market. In 1938, a federal agency noted that, in northern New Jersey, "At least until such time as this liquidation by the B&L associations is farther advanced, there would appear to be little prospect of any improvement in prices; possibly even the contrary."[9]

---

7. See Foote, Gerardi, and Willen (2008) for a discussion of the double trigger.

8. The HOLC officials were in good position to observe these trends since they were in charge of selling their own foreclosed properties. Source: field report titled "Survey of Economic, Real Estate, and Mortgage Finance Conditions in Five Counties in Northern New Jersey," p. 11, September 30, 1939, box 48, City Survey File, Records of the Home Owners' Loan Corporation, record group 195.3, National Archives II, College Park, MD.

9. Report on Newark, NJ, p. E111, box 4, City Survey Files, Records of the Home Owners' Loan Corporation, record group 195.3, National Archives II, College Park, MD.

7.2.3   Imposition of Withdrawal Restrictions

During the 1930s, withdrawals picked up as shareholders desired access to their savings amid the weakened economy. Withdrawals gained urgency as shareholders lost confidence in their B&Ls.[10] However, many B&L members were reluctant to liquidate foreclosed real estate in order to meet other members' withdrawals, given the depressed real estate market. In addition, since B&Ls in New Jersey carried real estate at cost of acquisition rather than market value, realizing losses on real estate could possibly lead to insolvency.

These problems were without much recent precedent, as B&Ls had rarely if ever been subjected to such large withdrawals, certainly not during the prosperous 1920s. The B&L bylaws sometimes maintained two restrictions on withdrawals. The first was a requirement for advance notice, typically thirty days. Many contemporary sources note that these requirements were not enforced during the 1920s as they were unnecessary, and the subsequent enforcement during the 1930s took shareholders by surprise. The second was some sacrifice of apportioned profits. Apportioned profits typically vested at 20 percent a year, so that by the sixth year of the savings contract, no sacrifice occurred. Since apportioned profits were fairly small during the first five years, this was not much of a deterrent.

Statutory withdrawal restrictions turned out to be more important in practice. Up to the 1930s, New Jersey law held that no withdrawals could be delayed for more than six months. During that six months, withdrawals were to be paid in the order received, and no more than one half of revenue was required to be paid out. Two major changes occurred in the early 1930s, as the six-month limit threatened to send much of the industry into the hands of the court as investors sued under the six-month rule.

First, in mid-1932, the New Jersey Supreme Court ruled that even after six months, withdrawals could still be restricted, on the basis that withdrawal was a statutory privilege rather than a contractual right. The court held that the statutory privilege could be rescinded for two reasons. First, withdrawals would cause "forced sales in these times when there is no market for real estate and association mortgage assets, repayable in shares, are unsalable." Second, "the statute should not apply where the exercise of the right granted there under would disturb the financial stability of the associations or materially depreciate the value of the shares of the remaining members."[11]

A second development occurred in the legislature which, under "emergency" powers first asserted during 1933, passed a new law that allowed the B&Ls' regulator (the commissioner of banking and insurance) to restrict

---

10. As an interesting historical note, Piquet (1930) states that the 1929 stock market crash led to a small crisis of confidence in New Jersey B&Ls, sparking withdrawals and freezing up some institutions. This episode would be in line with the idea that the stock market crash was important for the uncertainty it created.

11. *Building and Loan Guide and Bulletin,* July 1932, p. 3–4.

withdrawals at his discretion. This authority was repeatedly extended until September 1940, and though the original law and its extensions were challenged many times on constitutional grounds, it appears to have never been struck down.[12]

These developments could be interpreted either as altering the rights of shareholders, or as clarifying those rights. These withdrawal restrictions were quite consistent with the preexisting idea that both profits and losses should be mutually shared across all B&L members. Shareholders would have been familiar with the concept since mutuality was a central selling point for B&Ls to their investors, a central ethos of those associations, and a key legal foundation that allowed B&Ls to avoid federal taxation. Nevertheless, no law during the 1920s allowed withdrawals to be delayed for years. Also, it was largely unanticipated that associations would be unable to agree on whether to realize losses and how to allocate those losses. That discord was a decidedly nonmutual eventuality, and obviously some shareholders were more willing to realize losses than others, as evidenced by those who sold their shares on the secondary market.

7.2.4   Fallout from Withdrawal Restrictions

Withdrawal restrictions lasted for years at many Newark B&Ls and were a disaster for shareholder relations. Comprehensive data on withdrawal restrictions are not available, but reports and examples from the period abound. As late as 1939, a Federal Home Loan Bank Board (FHLB) report noted that the "majority of the associations are still on a restricted withdrawal basis."[13] In 1940 the secretary of the New Jersey B&L League similarly stated that, prior to many reorganizations, "shareholders were being paid little or nothing, perhaps $25 a month as a necessitous case."[14]

The largest association in Newark, the West End, fits this pattern. In 1940, it had "an unpaid withdrawal list reaching several millions which hadn't been materially reduced since about 1933." Before it was reorganized, "many of the shareholders thought that it was frozen tighter than any concrete that was ever poured."[15] The RFC, considering a loan to the West End for reorganization, noted that the West End's "frozen nature has caused many shareholders to withhold their monthly payments and not reinvest their maturities, as well as to react against new shareholder investments." Of five

---

12. Eventually this was modified to stipulate that, if in each month an association used one-third of its net receipts to pay maturities or add to maturity reserves and another one-third to pay withdrawals, then shareholders were categorically barred from suing that association to seek a withdrawal.

13. Report titled "Comparison of HOLC Activities and the Building and Loan Situation with Economic, Real Estate, and Mortgage Finance Conditions in Northern New Jersey," p. 5, box 52, City Survey Files, Records of the Home Owners' Loan Corporation, record group 195.3, National Archives II, College Park, MD.

14. *Building and Loan Guide and Bulletin*, July 1940, p. 56.

15. *Building and Loan Guide and Bulletin*, February 1940, p. 49.

associations with RFC loan files between 1938 and 1941 that I have viewed, all were still restricting payment on withdrawals, and some on maturing shares.

The result was that B&Ls had "completely destroyed public confidence by restrictions on withdrawals and recapture of dividends" already by 1935.[16] In 1939, the same characterization remained: "Building and loan associations in the Northern New Jersey Area, once having resources per capita ranking among the highest in the country, today, excepting a comparatively few, are in a generally frozen condition and lack public confidence."[17]

The only solution offered by supervisors was the establishment of loss reserves. Loss reserves were important because, if inadequate, members withdrawing at 100 percent of book value would avoid incurring their share of their associations' losses. Therefore, under the new emergency powers, the state B&L regulator required strong withdrawal restrictions until adequate loss reserves were assembled. Accumulating these reserves was costly. Newark B&Ls had entered the Depression with loan loss reserves constituting less than 1 percent of liabilities. To establish new reserves, associations were required to first convert unapportioned profits, then to reclassify previously apportioned profits (kept on books until shares matured), then to further accumulate through new earnings.[18]

To establish loss reserves, associations commonly reclassified another liability item, apportioned profits, into general loss reserves. In 1935, one out of every three associations had zero apportioned profits, meaning all had been converted into reserves. Reclassification of apportioned profits was subject to return to shareholders if reserves ultimately exceeded losses, which contributed to the unwillingness of B&L managers to actually tap the loss reserves so created. As an example, table 7.9, discussed later, itemizes the loss reserves held by the Enterprise B&L in 1941; 40 percent of the loss reserves were still kept in a separate account and had not been used, having been established by recapture of apportioned profits half a decade earlier.[19]

16. Field Report titled "Summary, Survey of Essex County New Jersey," p. 1, October 30, 1935, box 48, City Survey File, Records of the Home Owners' Loan Corporation, record group 195.3, National Archives II, College Park, MD.

17. Report titled "Comparison of HOLC Activities and the Building and Loan Situation with Economic, Real Estate, and Mortgage Finance Conditions in Northern New Jersey," p. 5, box 52, City Survey Files, Records of the Home Owners' Loan Corporation, record group 195.3, National Archives II, College Park, MD.

18. This reserve building was required by order of the state regulator and was probably the most significant state-level intervention. Of course, modern accounting rules would have required even larger provisioning at earlier dates. The set of policies governing reserve building were implemented as Orders 1 and 1A, on March 14, 1933, authorized by emergency legislation passed in the preceding days. These orders were modified by Orders 3 and 3A, dating to May 23, 1933. This law was originally set to expire within one year, but was repeatedly renewed, with the last renewal that I can find preserving it until 1940.

19. The reclassification of apportioned profits was a serious blow to borrowers as well. In the traditional "pledged share" B&L loan, a borrower accumulated shares just as an investor did; when the shares matured they would be used to extinguish the full principal debts. Admittedly,

Without the discipline of meeting withdrawal demands, complying with modern accounting standards, or the guidance of an effective regulatory resolution regime, real estate liquidation and loss realization was repeatedly put off. As late as 1940, the president of the Federal Home Loan Bank of New York described Newark's B&L managers as hoping for a miracle:

> In far too many cases, the directorates of financial institutions substantially burdened with foreclosed real estate, rather than facing the facts and marketing their steadily depreciating properties at current values (writing off whatever loss may be necessary in the process) are, unconsciously perhaps, engaging in one of the biggest real estate speculations of all time. For in such cases managements are refusing to sell at current levels solely in the hope that at some future and undeterminable date they will be able to get higher prices.[20]

One B&L manager described some colleagues as "apparently waiting for the millennium to come before selling their properties. They have their eyes only on the cost."[21] These delays in loss realizations helped lead to the creation of the secondary share market, in which shareholders realized losses that associations as a whole refused to. This market is examined in the next section.

7.3   Secondary Market

In response to withdrawal restrictions, by the late 1930s it became common practice for B&L shareholders in Newark to liquidate their shares on a secondary market, though at a loss.[22]

The demand side of the share market largely consisted of people purchasing shares in order to use them as a means of payment for real estate, as Newark B&Ls sold their real estate in exchange for their own share liabilities.[23] In this section, I sketch the economics of why these transactions were

---

the mixing of a share contract on the liability side with a mortgage on the asset side is confusing. One way to think about this is to imagine a fully amortized mortgage in which a bank, rather than using the noninterest portion of the monthly payment to extinguish part of the principal debt, instead invested it in equity shares of the bank. The term of such a loan would not be fixed but rather would depend on the profitability of the institution itself; highly profitable institutions would return greater profits, allowing shares to mature faster. The opposite can happen as well, though. When apportioned profits were taken back and new profits were limited, if they existed at all, borrowers were forced to make payments for longer periods than they had anticipated. Some frustrated borrowers defaulted or moved their loans to other institutions, further depriving B&Ls of needed income.

20. George Bliss, *Newark Sunday Call*, 21 April 1940, part IV p. 10.

21. *Building and Loan Guide and Bulletin*, August 1936, p. 25.

22. For a contemporary description, see, for example, *Sunday Call* 5 January 1941, part V p. 3.

23. Real estate sales were reported as "one of the most important factors" for the "increased activity" during 1939 in this share market. Some demand for shares also came from mortgage borrowers who were able to pay some of their outstanding debts with shares in the association from which they had borrowed, but this type of exchange appears to have been clearly secondary in importance to the real estate transactions. The *Sunday Call* describe these transactions as "not nearly as frequent as real estate sales" but nevertheless there was "little doubt that they

in the interests of each party, and give special attention to how this was a market-based resolution mechanism to unwind the obligations of B&Ls.

7.3.1   Development of the Market

Market functioning was aided by so-called speculators, who helped provide liquidity, and by brokers, who intermediated between buyers and sellers.[24] Not much can be said about the speculators, but regarding brokers there is evidence of a fairly competitive market; in 1939, at least nine brokerage firms regularly advertised their services in a Newark newspaper, the *Sunday Call*. Examples of such advertisements are reproduced in figure 7.1.

The earliest hints of the B&L share market start in 1933, when the first advertisements for broker services appeared, such as in figure 7.1. It was not until 1938 that the market appears to have really matured. In 1938, managers were still uncertain how their shareholders would react to the maturing market, and whether they would have even more difficulty recruiting additional shareholders if such prospective shareholders saw their shares trading for twenty-five or fifty cents on the dollar.[25] Meanwhile, state regulators and leaders of the B&L movement saw the share market as an opportunity to liquidate the industry's real estate, and so consistently exhorted associations to exchange real estate for shares. These efforts succeeded. Over 1939, trading activity spread to the shares of more and more associations. By the end of 1939, most shareholders had become familiar with the market, how it worked, and why it existed.[26]

The market appears to have been at its most active from 1938 to 1940. Trading activity then declined in latter 1940 and especially 1941. For example, advertisements for broker services became more common in the late 1930s, peaking at about nine or more in each issue of the *Sunday Call* in 1939. Advertisements then fell to three by 1941, two in 1943, and zero in 1946. The decline in activity was generally attributed to years of real estate liquidation, which left the stock of remaining properties reduced, and to a decline in the number of shares for sale at low prices, perhaps as the most desperate shareholders had by 1941 generally sold their shares.[27]

---

have been a contributing factor in creating a market for shares of many associations" (9 July 1939, part III, p. 6).

24. The *Sunday Call* described speculators as key to maintaining liquidity for some shares with infrequent real estate sales (9 July 1939, part III, p. 6).

25. *Building and Loan Guide and Bulletin*, July 1938, p. 71.

26. *Sunday Call*, 9 July 1939, part III, page 6.

27. *Sunday Call*, 4 January 1942, part IV, p. 9. Along the same lines, in April 1941 a Federal Home Loan Bank Board document noted that "share sales are fast drying up due to absorption of cheap certificates." "Report on Newark, New Jersey" p. 7; April, 1941, box 47, City Survey File, Records of the Home Owners' Loan Corporation, record group 195.3, National Archives II, College Park, MD.

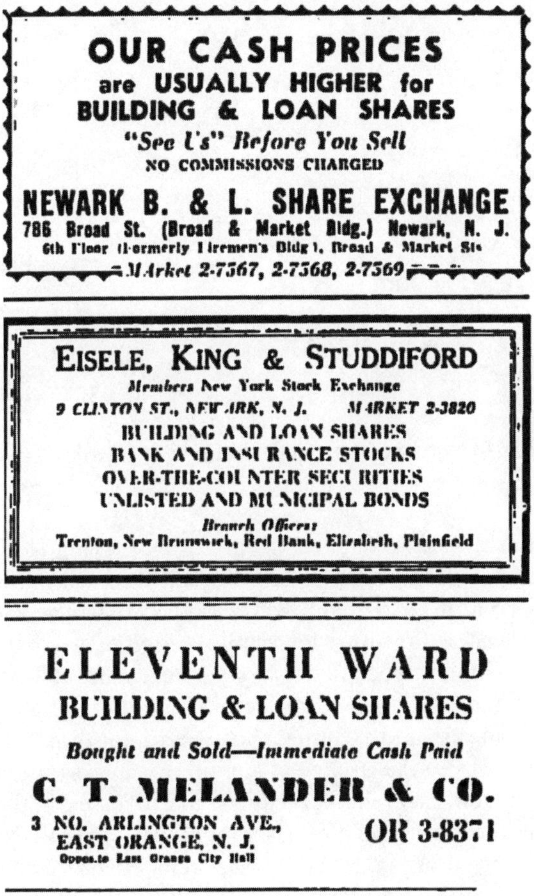

Fig. 7.1 **Advertisements for broker services for B&L share sales**
Source: Newark Sunday Call, 1 January 1939, part III, p. 5.

7.3.2 Why Did the Share Market Help Clear the Housing Market?

The share market was widely credited with helping clear the housing market. It is not immediately apparent why such a market was necessary for this purpose: clearing the housing market would presumably require prices to drop, but B&Ls always had the option of lowering their prices, and had long resisted doing so. In order for the share market to clear the housing market, it would have to provide B&Ls some benefit over a cash sale, while still lowering real estate prices for those on the demand side of the housing market.

A simple balance sheet exercise has a way of clarifying how this was possible. Suppose that an association had the simple stylized balance sheet

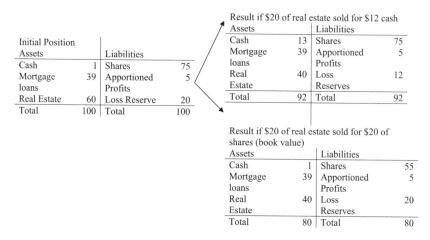

Fig. 7.2   Stylized balance sheet implications of real estate sales

depicted on the left side of figure 7.2, and it was trying to sell a piece of real estate valued on its books at $20, though the cash market price was $12. If sold for $12 in cash, loss reserves would be depleted by $8 and the association's coverage for future losses would look a bit doubtful. Alternatively, suppose that the association's shares were trading at forty cents on the dollar. A real estate purchaser might be willing to purchase, say, $20 worth of shares for $8 in cash and exchange those shares for the same parcel. Loss reserves would not need to decline at all, but it is important to realize that a loss did occur: some shareholder realized $12 in losses on their shares. At an upper limit, the real estate purchaser might be willing to exchange up to $30 of shares, since those shares could be purchased at $12, the cash market value of the property. At the lower limit, the B&L would have no incentive to accept shares with book value of less than $12.

In essence, there were two prices. The nominal price was the book value of the shares, which determined the amount of liabilities the B&L could retire. The effective price was the price of obtaining those shares, which is what really matters to the real estate purchaser. This helped clear the housing market because the effective price dropped. This is an interesting situation in which both the supply and demand sides to the real estate transactions benefited by the use of shares; the key is that these benefits originated in the loss taken by the shareholder who sold shares. By realizing a loss via the secondary share market, a shareholder essentially created a surplus that was available to two parties: the other shareholders of their B&L, and the real estate purchasers.

Contemporary sources support the idea that prices worked in this fashion. A summary of the Atlantic City share market stated this idea most starkly:

The customary method is to mark up the value of the property to a point where the discount price of the shares will result in a present day, fair cash value. For example, take the case of a piece of real estate worth $5,000 in today's market. If the shares are selling at fifty cents on the dollar, in an all share sale, the association promptly fixes the price at $10,000 irrespective of its book value or worth to them.[28]

I suspect this quote overstates the case a bit; it seems more likely that the parcel mentioned would sell for a bit less than $10,000 in the presence of transaction costs to obtain secondhand shares and some bargaining power on the side of the real estate purchaser. Other examples fit this pattern, including a case study that was discussed at length in a conference of B&L managers in mid-1938. An association was willing to sell a piece of real estate for $1,000 in cash and a $5,200 mortgage, but a second offer was made for $800 in cash and $6,700 in shares. The second offer is attractive to the real estate purchaser, since the shares were more than likely obtained for half price or less—about $3,350. The second offer is also attractive to the B&L on the supply side, since, with a nominal price of $1,300 more than the first offer, fewer losses would have to be realized by the B&L's remaining shareholders.

Another example fits the same pattern. A B&L manager described how his association had acquired a property with book value of $10,000, expected a loss on the property, and had two offers for its sale. The first was for $8,500 in cash and a mortgage, the second for $6,000 in cash and $5,000 in shares. The second offer actually gave the association the rare opportunity to record a gain on a piece of foreclosed real estate, and still involved a smaller outlay to the purchaser than the pure cash offer.[29]

As in the preceding examples, payment for real estate typically consisted of some combination of a cash down payment combined with a mortgage or with shares.[30] To be clear, if the shares were part of the transaction, they would be applied to the nominal transaction price at book value, and subsequently cancelled as liabilities. Associations considered both types of offers.

This helps articulate the sense in which the secondary share market helped associations liquidate real estate and clear the housing market. The New

28. Report on Atlantic City, pp. 28–29, box 51 City Survey Files, Records of the Home Owners' Loan Corporation, record group 195.3, National Archives II, College Park, MD.

29. *Building and Loan Guide and Bulletin*, June 1939, p. 58.

30. Some sources from the period note that these transactions were subject to the approval of the state regulator. However, the reality was that *every* real estate transaction required the approval of the state regulator—with one major caveat. The caveat is that if associations adopted a real estate classification plan that gave each parcel a grade from A to D, they were able to unload the Cs and Ds without seeking regulatory approval. It appears that regulatory approval was either easily obtained or that associations made use of this classification scheme, since the market for shares was so widespread. See *Building and Loan Guide and Bulletin*, June 1939, p. 56.

Jersey state regulator, for example, described the competitive edge of B&Ls in this manner:

> A considerable volume of sales is resulting from the use of shares in exchange for real estate. Many associations are able to secure a competitive advantage in the real estate market by this means and have thus been able to create a real estate activity which otherwise would not have existed. This has resulted in returning a considerable amount of property back to private owners thus reducing the overhang of institutionally owned real estate.[31]

This quote indicates that the cash market value of real estate was low enough that B&Ls chose not to transact; the share market helped "create" these transactions by lowering the effective prices. After all, by 1938, the real estate market was not as dysfunctional as it was in 1933; at a low enough price, a B&L would have been able to sell its real estate for cash and a mortgage, albeit at a realized loss.[32]

While lower prices helped B&Ls sell their real estate, this was not necessarily a positive development for the housing market. Working through the overhang of real estate may have boosted expectations for recovery, but in the short run this effect could easily be dominated by the cheap effective prices of B&L real estate. When households are deleveraging, fire sales of real estate can damage the ability of owner-occupants to engage in transactions of their own that might increase economic efficiency. Along these lines, B&Ls faced criticism for their sales' negative effect on market prices, as described by this Home Owners' Loan Corporation (HOLC) report:

> Building and loan associations as a whole are being charged with "dumping" of acquired properties due to their acceptance of shares at par toward purchase price of real estate, when such shares could be purchased at substantial discounts. . . . It is open to question whether it is really dumping or whether it is not merely finding levels at which business can be done.[33]

Other HOLC documents note that the HOLC was at a competitive disadvantage against B&Ls because of the low effective prices via the use of shares. The HOLC was very much in a position to know this, since it owned large amounts of foreclosed real estate and sought to liquidate those holdings.

In some sense, B&Ls' remaining shareholders gained at the expense of the shareholders that sold their shares. While the secondhand share sales were

31. *Building and Loan Guide and Bulletin*, December 1938, p. 30.
32. As a side note, the discussion highlights the difficulty of defining a singularly meaningful market price of real estate in a depressed market. Given two offers with the same nominal prices, B&Ls valued the offer with shares differently than the offer without shares. Likewise, given the same two offers, the actual cost to the purchaser changed when shares were involved.
33. Field Report titled "Survey of Economic, Real Estate, and Mortgage Finance Conditions in Five Counties in Northern New Jersey," p. 15, September 30, 1939, box 48, City Survey File, Records of the Home Owners' Loan Corporation, record group 195.3, National Archives II, College Park, MD.

voluntary and presumably Pareto improving, B&Ls used the share market to push an extra portion of their real estate losses onto the set of shareholders who had sold their shares, rather than distributing those losses equally across all shareholders. This could be interpreted as a reward for patience. Alternately, it could be interpreted as compensating the rest of the association for the cost of early withdrawals, but this is less compelling considering that withdrawal restrictions were often still in place in 1939 or 1940. In any case, the share market established a price of liquidity, which many years of history have shown can be mispriced during financial crises. Alternatively, B&L managers may have just preferred that their paper losses be realized not by the association but by shareholders on the open market.[34]

7.3.3 Secondary Markets in the Rest of the Country

Secondary B&L liability markets were common in the 1930s, though they certainly did not exist in every major city. Importantly, none of these markets existed before the Depression. Survey reports of urban real estate markets, conducted by the HOLC during the second half of the 1930s, indicate that several large cities had active B&L liability markets, including Cleveland, Columbus, Indianapolis, Milwaukee, New Orleans, and Philadelphia. The surveys indicate that liability trading also occurred in a number of other smaller cities in Alabama, Mississippi, Florida, North Carolina, Missouri, Indiana, elsewhere in New Jersey, Colorado, Texas, and California. Notably missing from these lists are all cities in New England, and some major cities with large amounts of B&L activity such as Chicago, Cincinnati, Louisville, Omaha, Pittsburgh, and St. Louis.

The share markets were a common but not uniformly prevalent feature of the Depression B&L experience. These markets generally worked to help associations dispose of real estate, but the exact mechanics differed from city to city, and few persisted into the late 1930s as Newark's did. State laws regarding withdrawals differed, as did the take-up rate of federal aid and the structure of B&L liabilities. For example, a twist in some markets was the competing interests of depositors against shareholders. Allegations of corruption seem to have been not uncommon as well, with B&L management accused of manipulating the share markets in various ways.

In the existing Depression literature I am aware of two references to sec-

---

34. As a final note, there is some indirect evidence that the secondary market was, to a degree, a substitute for more formal resolution. After associations exited, trading in their shares reportedly fell, but was not eliminated. Trading was noted as sometimes occurring in the shares both of associations in liquidation and of the various "bad bank" entities that held defaulted mortgages and real estate loans spun off during reorganizations. (See a discussion in the *Sunday Call*, 4 January 1942, part IV, p. 9.) In this data set spanning price quotes in 1939 and 1940, there were ninety-five associations that exited during those years and that had quotes available before their exits. After their exits, prices were only quoted for fifty, a bit more than half. In contrast, of the associations with share prices available and that survived to the end of 1940, about 85 percent continued to have prices quoted up until the end of 1940.

Table 7.2   Share markets in other cities

City	Date	Median	25th percentile	75th percentile	Number of quotes
Newark	Jan-39	38	30	44	164
Oklahoma City	Jan-34	40	36	50	42
New Orleans	Jan-34	40	35	48	37
San Francisco	Feb-34	51	30	60	36
Cleveland	Jan-34	52	45	57	49
Columbus	Jan-34	62	54	68	20
Milwaukee	Jan-35	78	72	83	40

Sources: Quotes are from the following sources: *Daily Oklahoman*, 7 January 1934; *New Orleans Time-Picayune*, 13 January 1934, p. 22; *San Francisco Examiner*, 6 January 1935; *Cleveland Plain Dealer*, 6 January 1934, p. 11; *Columbus Dispatch*, 7 January 1934; *Milwaukee Journal-Sentinel*, 16 January 1935, p. F1.

ondary B&L share markets. Kendall (1962) briefly notes that "some" cities developed such markets, and specifically mentions Milwaukee, reproducing an offering sheet from a brokerage in that city containing approximate market prices for the shares of ninety-six associations. Rockoff (1993) mentions that a secondary market for B&L liabilities existed in Youngstown, Ohio, as well.

Table 7.2 gives a simple comparison between shares prices of Newark B&Ls and the prices of B&Ls in a limited sample of six other cities with B&L share markets. Newark B&L quotes are roughly in the same range as those in Oklahoma City and New Orleans, but below the median prices in San Francisco, Cleveland, Columbus, and Milwaukee. Newark is somewhat of an anomaly as the first quotes available are from 1939, whereas in most other cities (except Milwaukee) the markets were at their height in the mid-1930s and no longer operating by 1939. Altogether, more research is warranted on the timing of these markets across cities, the variation in share prices across and within cities, and the existence of markets in some cities but not others.

7.4 Examining Share Prices

7.4.1 Share Price Data

Data on share prices are available from January 1939 to December 1940. The source is detailed in the appendix. Information on prices in 1938 may exist but I have not been able to obtain them. The period from 1938 to 1940 is roughly the period when historical sources indicate trading volume was at its most active. Over time, the quotes were published weekly, but short-term volatility was quite limited: most shares do not change more than a few cents over the two-year period. Of the 384 associations still active at the beginning of 1939, 60 percent have quotes available. Figure 7.3 contains a reproduction of one of the share price listings.

Building and Loan Share Quotations

Furnished by Eisele, King & Studdiford.

These quotations are for Newark associations, unless otherwise specified. All quotations are subject to confirmation.

The quotations should not be taken to represent the book value of the shares listed. They are merely approximate bid prices at which shares are currently quoted in the local market. In some cases associations expect to pay liquidating dividends in excess of the amount quoted. A bid is not an appraisal.—Editor.

Association	Bid	Association	Bid
A-1	31	Manor	27
Abington	47	Manufacturers	60
Able Old Hickory	26	Masonic	42
Acme	54	Mayflower	38
Acropolis	38	McKinley	47
Action	33	Mechanics	37
Adamant	43	Metropolitan	37
Aggressive	40	Modern	35
Alert	45	Montifiore	33
Almanac	30	Monitor	20
Amalgamated	18	Mt. Prospect	53
American	63	Mutual	48
Annexed District	45	Mt. Sinai-New Deal	30
Arrow	53	Nelson	40
Assembly	38	Newark	45
Bankers	23	New Empire	53
Barringer	43	Newstead	25
Big Brother	37	Normal	38
Bigelow New	52	North American	38
Bigelow Trust Shares	28	Novel	12
Bonded	36	O. K.	42
Branch Brook	50	Opportunity	52
Broad and Market	40	Ordway	45
Broad Street	40	Outlook	54
Buildmore	40	Owl	25
Bulwark	45	Oxford	38
Capital	47	Pacific	45
Casino	40	Paramount	45
Cedars	50	Parker	35
Central	38	Parkview	45
Century	53	Paywell	70
Charter Oak	39	Perfection	60
		Pilgrim	46
		Popular	27
		Postoffice Clfs	37
		Precise	38
		Producers	37
		Provident	42
		Public	58
		Realty	30
		Reliable	31
		Renowned	29
		Rex	40
		Rialto	33
		Roseville	33
		Sanford	45
		Savings	49
		Select	48
		Seymour	40

Fig. 7.3 Share price listing excerpt
Source: Newark Sunday Call, 23 June 1940, part IV, p. 6.

In January 1939, the median bid quote for the shares of active Newark B&Ls was thirty-nine cents. For now, the median price is noted in order to gauge the scale of losses being realized by shareholders who sold their shares. A discount to thirty-nine cents would represent a large loss for any shareholder selling at the time. Figure 7.4 displays the distribution of share prices across associations. Some sold for as little as twenty cents on the dollar, and few exceeded sixty cents.

7.4.2 Cross-Sectional Characteristics of Share Prices

On the secondary market, what should determine the discount of B&L liabilities from their book value? On the one hand, the basic solvency of the association would affect the extent to which would the book value would

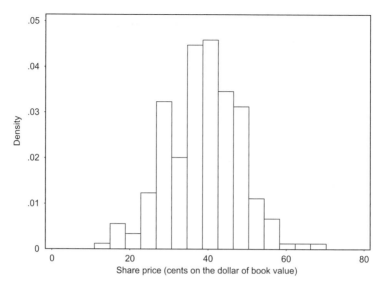

Fig. 7.4   Distribution of share prices for B&Ls active at the beginning of 1939

ever be fully paid out. On the other hand, the earnings capacity and liquidity position of an association would affect how soon those payments would come. Of course, liquidity and solvency are not wholly distinct concepts (see Carlson, Mitchener, and Richardson [2011] for example). Nevertheless, here I use those two terms in the sense of separating out the probability of being paid full book value from the timing of those payments. In general, the liquidity aspect appears to be more important for share prices.

No perfect measures of solvency or liquidity are available. Assets held in real estate and loss reserves on the liability side are the best measures of general solvency, although it would be even better to know the expected losses on the real estate assets. In terms of liquidity, one useful measure might be the size of a B&L's withdrawal list or the expected duration of a withdrawal request. These are not available in New Jersey, but they may be problematic even if they were available, since shareholders were known to not bother with requesting withdrawal if it were a fruitless exercise.

Summary statistics of available balance sheet characteristics are given in table 7.3. Some of these characteristics I will describe as being more associated with solvency, and others with liquidity. These variables essentially exhaust all available balance sheet information. Liability-side characteristics include apportioned profits per share, a dummy indicating if apportioned profits were zero, the extent of reliance on prepaid "income" shares (supposedly a relatively "hot" funding source compared to installment shares), the extent of borrowed money, and the extent of loss reserves. Asset-side characteristics include the portions of assets held in real estate, arrears, and

Table 7.3   **Summary statistics**

	1939		
	Median	Mean	Standard deviation
Liability characteristics			
Apportioned profits/shares	6.20	6.40	4.60
1(Apportioned profits = 0)		0.15	
Value of income shares/value of all shares	0.33	0.32	0.15
Borrowed money/liabilities	0.000	0.014	0.029
Reserves/liabilities	0.27	0.28	0.09
Asset characteristics			
Real estate/assets	0.48	0.48	0.18
Arrears/assets	0.013	0.040	0.069
Share of mortgages unpledged	0.43	0.44	0.28
Liquid assets/assets	0.026	0.042	0.048
Log(assets)	12.74	12.80	0.71
Lagged characteristics from 1930			
Apportioned profits/shares	12.7	12.2	4.0
Real estate/assets	0.033	0.047	0.052
log(assets)	13.39	13.41	0.73
Income shares/all shares	0.17	0.18	0.09
Borrowed money/liabilities	0.062	0.060	0.039
Reserves/liabilities	0.0056	0.0078	0.0073
Other characteristics			
Year established	1912	1911	12
1(Received RFC loan before 1935)		0.14	
1(Member of FHLB by 1936)		0.07	
1(Optional plan)		0.28	
1(Nonserial plan)		0.20	

liquid assets, respectively, the log of total assets, and the share of mortgages that are unpledged, a measure of transition away from the old B&L mortgage. Note that arrears are shareholders' obligated payments that have not been made, rather than arrears on, say, loans.[35] Lagged values of some of these liability and asset characteristics, from 1930, are also included. Finally, the year of establishment is included, as are dummy variables for whether the B&L received an RFC loan before 1935, whether it was a member of the FHLB, and whether it operated on the optional or nonserial plans (with the serial plan associations as the excluded group).[36]

35. Since the B&L loan contract used installment shares as sinking funds, arrears on loans may have been characterized in this manner as well.
36. Serial plan associations were the most traditional form, with new share investments only opening up at specified points in time, typically once a quarter. Nonserial plans allowed them to be opened at any time. Optional plan associations still used installment shares but the payments were optional (at the discretion of the shareholder) rather than required every month.

Table 7.4   **Predictors of share prices**

Dependent variable: share price

	Coeff.	SE	Coeff.	SE
Liability characteristics				
Apportioned profits/shares	0.78*	(0.15)	0.62*	(0.19)
1(Apportioned profits = 0)	−6.34*	(1.62)	−3.26***	(1.77)
Value of income shares/value of all shares			−0.54	(5.83)
Borrowed money/liabilities			−29.8	(25.8)
Reserves/liabilities			0.55	(7.37)
Asset characteristics				
Real estate/assets			−6.80	(4.29)
Arrears/assets			−30.0*	(9.23)
Share of mortgages unpledged			3.24	(2.21)
Liquid assets/assets			22.1	(17.0)
Log(assets)			−0.76	(1.84)
Lagged characteristics from 1930				
Apportioned profits/shares			0.0066	(0.23)
Real estate/assets			−3.47	(11.2)
Log(assets)			1.46	(1.87)
Income shares/all shares			−3.16	(9.91)
Borrowed money/liabilities			−0.85	(14.0)
Reserves/liabilities			−36.5	(68.9)
Other characteristics				
1(Received RFC loan before 1935)			−0.047	(0.063)
1(Member of FHLB by 1936)			−0.99	(1.47)
Year established			2.19	(2.21)
1(Optional plan)			−4.50*	(1.51)
1(Nonserial plan)			−5.01*	(1.50)
Constant	36.9*	(1.11)	123	(123)
Observations	202		202	
R-squared	0.35		0.45	

Notes: The share price is scaled between 1 and 100; that is, one unit is one cent on the dollar. Balance sheet data are from 1938. The share price is the median price quoted over 1939 and 1940 for each association. Two B&Ls that underwent reorganizations in late 1938 are excluded, as their balance sheets were highly unusual immediately after the reorganizations, with large amounts of cash that were quickly drawn down in the following months. Robust standard errors.

***Significant at the 1 percent level.
**Significant at the 5 percent level.
*Significant at the 10 percent level.

Table 7.4 reports the results of two simple ordinary least squares (OLS) regressions of the share price on these characteristics. In practice, the variables I would associate with the liquidity effect appear to dominate, but the data are not perfect and so these conclusions should be taken with that hedge.

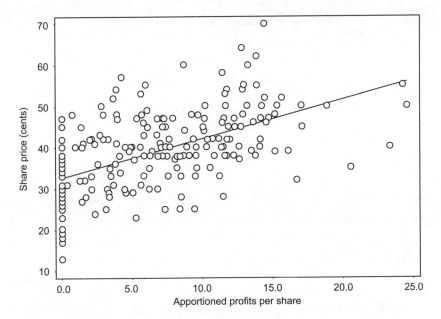

Fig. 7.5   Share prices plotted against apportioned profits per share

The apportioned profits variables dominate the results. The magnitude is about a three to four cent change in the share price for a one standard deviation change in apportioned profits, along with an additional three-cent drop in the presence of zero apportioned profits. These are reasonably strong changes given that the share prices range from about twenty to sixty cents on the dollar. The simple regression of share prices on the two apportioned profits variables itself has an R-squared of 35 percent, reported in the first column. Figure 7.5 plots share prices in early 1939 against apportioned profits per share at the end of 1938, showing the correlation.

What do apportioned profits reflect? Arguably, they are more associated with liquidity than solvency, for the following reasons. Recall that apportioned profits are dividends applied to installment shares but not distributed until those shares reach maturity value. New apportionment was severely constrained during the mid-1930s as associations were forced to build loss reserves, and existing apportionments were very often partly or wholly reclassified into loss reserves. By 1938, higher levels of apportioned profits characterized associations that no longer needed to build more loss reserves. In turn, the important point here is that withdrawals were restricted by order of the state regulator until these loss reserves were established. Consequently, associations with more apportioned profits in 1938 were quite likely to be paying larger amounts of withdrawals.

Another interpretation of the apportioned profits variables might focus on the fact that associations with more apportioned profits likely had higher

Table 7.5   Importance of dividend rates

Dependent variable: share price

	Coeff.	SE
Apportioned profits/shares	0.61**	(0.30)
1(Apportioned profits = 0)	1.6	(7.52)
Dividend rate	2.1	(1.45)
Constant	32.6	(3.5)
Observations	39	
R-squared	0.29	

Notes: The share price is scaled between 1 and 100; that is, one unit is one cent on the dollar. Balance sheet data are from 1938. The share price is the median price quoted over 1939 and 1940 for each association. The dividend rate is set to zero if no dividend had been paid in either 1937 or 1938, as the survey was done in late 1938 or early 1939. Robust standard errors.
***Significant at the 1 percent level.
**Significant at the 5 percent level.
*Significant at the 10 percent level.

dividend rates. If shares were fixed maturity bonds, then associations with lower dividend rates would likely exhibit larger discounts from par value. Of course, installment shares were distinct from bonds inasmuch as their dividends were retained rather than paid out and the maturity value was fixed rather than the maturity date, and payouts at maturity were also restricted in the 1930s. Nevertheless, it is worth trying to distinguish this yield effect from the withdrawal effect emphasized in the previous paragraph. To that end, I have a limited amount of data on dividends from a special HOLC survey of Newark B&Ls in 1938. Unfortunately, there are only thirty-nine observations in which I observe this dividend information and have share prices. There is a strong 64 percent correlation between apportioned profits per share and the dividend rate, which ranges from 0 to 5 percent. When the share price is regressed on both variables, only apportioned profits retain significance. That simple regression is reported in table 7.5, and indicates that apportioned profits are capturing something else, arguably the withdrawal situation.

Returning to table 7.4, another liquidity measure is the extent of asset holdings in cash and liquid investments. This measure of asset liquidity shows little predictive power in table 6.4, even though this would seem naturally related to the ability to pay withdrawals. However, more flexible nonlinear specifications do indicate that very low levels of asset liquidity are associated with lower share prices. For example, when a dummy for very low asset liquidity term is included (not shown, measured as less than 2.5 percent of assets in cash or liquid investments), B&Ls with near zero liquid assets had lower share prices on the order of about one to two cents, while the relationship fades for moderate and higher levels of liquidity.

It is also worth noting that large amounts of arrears were associated with lower share prices, although the magnitude is a moderate 1.5 cent change in the share price for a one standard deviation change in arrears over assets. Recall that arrears are obligated payments that shareholders have not made. This is quite an intangible and dubious asset that would have done little to improve liquidity, but likely reflects both liquidity and solvency issues.

Few other variables have much predictive power, including some variables that would seem strongly related to solvency issues. Real estate holdings do not have any conditional statistical relationship with share prices, and the result is not dependent on the linearity imposed in table 7.4, as more flexible quadratic and cubic specifications also have little predictive power (not shown). The size of loss reserves does not have predictive power, nor does the ratio of loss reserves to real estate holdings.

Altogether this evidence is consistent with a liquidity-centric story, though it is not fully able to rule out alternative stories. As one final piece of history, though, the experience of three B&Ls that experimented with real estate segregation in 1933 (discussed more in the next section regarding reorganization) is relevant. By 1938, each had zero real estate or delinquent loans, since those assets had been placed in separate bad banks, with shareholders receiving certificates of participation in those bad banks. In no way could these reorganized associations be considered insolvent, but their share prices were still trading between thirty-seven and fifty-three cents on the dollar in 1939. The real estate segregation by itself did little to solve liquidity issues, which continued to weigh on shareholders who wanted access to their investments. This anticipates one of the key features of most of the successful reorganizations of the late 1930s and early 1940s: cash loans secured by real estate, which were then used to pay withdrawals that had been restricted since 1933. This is discussed at more length in section 7.5.

These results help us understand the share market, but do not tell us much about the root of B&Ls' credit problems and why they varied across associations. Such an analysis is handicapped by a lack of data on issues such as associations' management competency, underwriting standards, types of real estate collateral and their locations, or borrower characteristics.

7.5   Formal Resolution in the Late 1930s and Early 1940s

At the end of 1930, 499 associations were operating in Newark. By the end of 1944, fifty-five associations were still active in the city. Thirty-seven associations had avoided any changes, and the other eighteen associations were all that were left of the 462 that had undergone some major structural event, including liquidation, state action, reorganization, and merger. Table 7.6 tabulates the exit process by year and type of exit.

This section examines these events, grouping them into two large waves. Relatively few structural events occurred in the early and mid-1930s,

Table 7.6   Major structural events of Newark B&Ls

Type of action	1931–1936	1937	1938	1939	1940	1941	1942	1943	1944	Total
Liquidations and bulk transfers										
Voluntary liquidation	3	14	38	32	66	34	39	11	2	239
Bulk transfers	0	0	0	1	10	8	9	18	4	50
State actions										
Conservatorship	7	0	0	0	0	0	0	0	0	7
Liquidation	5	0	0	0	0	0	0	0	0	5
Possession	8	0	1	0	20	0	0	0	0	29
Reorganizations										
With new charter	4	0	0	7	1	2	34	34	1	83
Without new charter	12	1	6	1	0	0	0	0	0	20
New or retained charters	4	0	2	3	0	0	4	5	0	18
Other										
Merged	19	0	2	2	3	1	0	0	0	27
Moved out of Newark	2	0	0	0	0	0	0	0	0	2
Total (excluding new or retained charters)	58	15	47	43	100	45	82	63	7	
Associations at end of 1930	499									
Total actions taken, above	462									
New or retained charters	18									
Associations at start of 1945	55									

Notes: The table refers to the years in which the actions were initiated. Voluntary liquidation was known to take several years, as was the liquidation of real estate spun off into bad banks during reorganization. The reorganizations took different forms, as discussed in the text. Many reorganizations also involved mergers, but I avoid double counting here: the 103 associations that reorganized consolidated into the eighteen charters indicated, but four of those (all formed in the early 1930s) exited before 1945.

especially on a per-year basis. The first large wave of resolution actions started in 1937 or 1938, and consisted mainly of closures of the institutions in the poorest condition. The second wave, particularly in 1942 and 1943, was dominated more heavily by reorganizations, made possible by a large-scale federal intervention.

7.5.1   First Wave of Exit: Liquidations and Other Closures

In the first wave, primarily during 1938, 1939, and 1940, exits were dominated by liquidations and appear to have been driven by conventional factors stemming from poor balance sheets, as well as pressure from shareholders for withdrawals as measured by share prices.

Voluntary liquidation and bulk transfer were each a voluntary choice to end the operations of an association. Discussions among B&L leaders in the late 1930s make clear that the two were considered close substitutes. In a voluntary liquidation, an association placed all of its assets into a liquidating corporation. In a bulk transfer, an association sold off some of its assets to another association, and placed the rest in a liquidating corporation. In either case, liquidation itself was not immediate but depended on the pace of real estate sales. Voluntary liquidation was far more common, particularly before 1940. After 1940, more reorganized associations were able and willing to purchase assets in bulk.

Actions by the state regulator, the Department of Banking and Insurance, were less common than liquidations. After twenty B&Ls were closed by the state in the early 1930s, one more was seized in 1938, and then twenty more in one day in April 1940. Incompetence or manifest insolvency appear to have motivated most of these actions. The seizures in 1940 were a long overdue effort to spur deeply frozen associations into formal liquidation. The commissioner of banking and insurance stated the rationale: "The problem associations, for the most part, remained apathetic . . . As time went on, it became increasingly evident that in the absence of any voluntary correction or dissolution by a substantial number of these associations, the department would be obliged to take action."[37] Nevertheless, in most cases of poor condition, B&Ls were left to build capital by slowly retaining earnings and taking back apportioned profits. Illiquidity was not countered with seizure but rather addressed through withdrawal restrictions.

To understand which characteristics were associated with the closures from 1938 to 1940, I use a probit framework in which the dependent variable is a dummy for closure, defined as voluntary liquidation, bulk transfer, or state seizure. The set of characteristics is the same set as used in section 7.4, with the addition of each association's share price.

The marginal effects and standard errors are reported in table 7.7. I first report results using data from 1937, predicting closure from 1938 to 1940 in

---

37. *Building and Loan Guide and Bulletin*, July 1940, p. 25.

Table 7.7 **Closures from 1938 to 1940**

	Closure in 1938–1940		Closure in 1940		
Dependent variable:					
B&Ls included:	All		Subset with share prices		
Vintage of data:	1937	1939	1939	1939	1939
	(1)	(2)	(3)	(4)	(5)
Share price			−0.024*	−0.018*	
			(0.0049)	(0.0066)	
Asset side:					
Real estate/assets	1.13*	0.76*		0.83**	0.87**
	(0.24)	(0.23)		(0.39)	−0.36
Arrears/assets	1.75*	1.53**		0.85	1.45***
	(0.51)	(0.60)		(0.92)	−0.84
Share of mortgages unpledged	−0.063	−0.16		−0.15	−0.18
	(0.16)	(0.11)		(0.20)	−0.2
Liquid assets/assets	−0.34	1.15***		0.73	0.67
	(0.95)	(0.63)		(1.05)	−1.04
Log(assets)	−0.51*	−0.29*		−0.16	−0.12
	(0.14)	(0.11)		(0.16)	−0.16
Apportioned profits/shares	0.012***	0.012		0.014	0.0035
	(0.0070)	(0.0079)		(0.015)	−0.014
Liability side:					
1(Apportioned profits = 0)	0.40*	0.39*		0.42*	0.43*
	(0.082)	(0.12)		(0.14)	−0.14

	(1)	(2)	(3)	(4)
Portion of shares in income shares	−0.13	0.060	−0.42	−0.44
	(0.33)	(0.27)	(0.41)	(0.39)
Borrowed money/liabilities	1.34	1.37	2.76	3.36***
	(1.12)	(1.05)	(2.07)	(1.88)
Reserves/liabilities	0.60	0.86**	0.16	0.2
	(0.56)	(0.40)	(0.60)	(0.6)
Apportioned profits/shares	0.0013	0.00027	0.026	0.023
	(0.0097)	(0.0096)	(0.017)	(0.016)
Real estate/assets	1.07***	1.06***	1.93***	1.66***
	(0.56)	(0.60)	(1.02)	(0.96)
Log(assets)	0.36*	0.25**	0.12	0.07
	(0.13)	(0.10)	(0.17)	(0.16)
Lagged from 1930				
Income shares/all shares	0.61	0.72***	1.91*	1.93*
	(0.49)	(0.41)	(0.73)	(0.69)
Borrowed money/liabilities	0.029	0.25	−0.014	0.17
	(0.77)	(0.72)	(1.26)	(1.26)
Reserves/liabilities	2.55	0.32	−15.4**	−12.4***
	(4.19)	(5.09)	(6.99)	(6.52)
Observations	427	338	169	169
Number with LHS = 1	168	96	63	63
Pseudo R-squared	0.24	0.30	0.34	0.31

Notes: Probit estimation with marginal effects displayed. The five "other characteristics" from table 7.4 are also included but not displayed here to save space. Closure includes voluntary liquidation, bulk transfer, and regulatory seizure. Robust standard errors.

***Significant at the 1 percent level.

**Significant at the 5 percent level.

*Significant at the 10 percent level.

the first column, and then using data from 1939 predicting closure in 1940 in the second column. The 1939 data are helpful for many reasons, including that the data on share prices are first available in 1939. Since share prices are not available for every association and selection may be an issue, columns (3), (4), and (5) report results using the subset of associations with share prices, first including share prices as an explanatory variable by itself, then adding the other controls, and finally without the share price.

The results are generally unsurprising insofar as they indicate that measures of balance sheet distress predict closures in this period. These results will contrast, though, with those in the next subsection in which reorganizations in 1942 and 1943 are studied instead of these closures.

In terms of credit quality, associations with relatively large amounts of real estate were strongly more likely to close in these years. A B&L with a 10 percentage point greater share of assets held as real estate in 1939 had a roughly 8 percentage point higher probability of closure in 1940. For example, at the extreme, at the end of 1939 there were seventeen associations that had more than 75 percent of their assets in real estate, and fourteen of those closed the following year.

Share prices have strong predictive power over closures as well, as associations with lower share prices were strongly more likely to close in 1940. The magnitude is roughly that every two-cent level change in the 1939 share price is associated with a 1 percentage point increase in the probability of closure. Interpreting this relationship is not necessarily straightforward. Associations with very low share prices could have had shareholders clamoring for serious action such as liquidation. However, share prices are still observed for some institutions after their closures in this period, and the prices rarely changed afterward. This indicates that the incentives of shareholders to seek liquidation to satisfy their withdrawal requests were limited, as liquidation was still protracted. Another possibility is that share prices capture a range of other unobserved characteristics that are related to viability.

As a check that the regulatory seizures are not completely driving the results, the first column of table 7.8 replicates this analysis but excludes associations that were seized by the state regulators. The coefficient on real estate decreases moderately, and the coefficient on arrears drops to nearly zero, suggesting perhaps that the state officials targeted associations with extreme values of each. A look at the data confirms that the associations seized by regulators were those at the very upper end of the distribution of real estate burdens. This indicates that the voluntary liquidations and bulk transfers were less a direct function of real estate burdens and more a function of the ability to return profits to shareholders and to allow them to sell their shares at less sacrificial prices.

Finally, the second column of table 7.8 examines closures in 1941. The characteristics that predict the 1941 closures are quite different, and this anticipates some of the results in the next section. Credit quality, share

Table 7.8 **Closures from 1938 to 1940, continued**

	Dependent variable:	Liquidation in 1940	Closure in 1941
	B&Ls included:	Subset without seizures (and with share prices)	Subset with share prices
	Vintage of data:	1939	1940
		(5)	(6)
	Share price	−0.016*	
		(0.0060)	
Asset side:	Real Estate/assets	0.63***	0.36
		(0.37)	(0.26)
	Arrears/assets	0.022	−0.76
		(0.86)	(1.21)
	Share of mortgages unpledged	−0.016	−0.26***
		(0.18)	(0.14)
	Liquid assets/assets	1.13	0.89**
		(0.94)	(0.42)
	Log(assets)	−0.12	−0.16
		(0.15)	(0.11)
Liability side:	Apportioned profits/shares	0.018	−0.0051
		(0.013)	(0.010)
	1(Apportioned profits = 0)	0.52*	−0.042
		(0.16)	(0.12)
	Portion of shares in income shares	−0.34	−0.40
		(0.41)	(0.33)
	Borrowed money/liabilities	2.15	3.40**
		(1.74)	(1.62)
	Reserves/liabilities	0.13	0.32
		(0.53)	(0.43)
Lagged from 1930	Apportioned profits/shares	0.018	−0.017
		(0.016)	(0.012)
	Real estate/assets	1.73***	−0.13
		(0.99)	(0.84)
	Log(assets)	0.058	0.052
		(0.14)	(0.10)
	Income shares/all shares	1.84*	0.12
		(0.66)	(0.50)
	Borrowed money/liabilities	0.79	0.45
		(1.23)	(0.87)
	Reserves/liabilities	−13.0***	−6.25
		(7.28)	(5.79)
	Observations	154	131
	Number with LHS = 1	48	27
	Pseudo *R*-squared	0.35	0.23

Notes: Probit estimation with marginal effects displayed. The five "other characteristics" from table 7.4 are also included but not displayed here to save space. Closure includes voluntary liquidation, bulk transfer, and regulatory seizure. Robust standard errors.

***Significant at the 1 percent level.

**Significant at the 5 percent level.

*Significant at the 10 percent level.

prices, and profitability all have little predictive power. Instead, the liquidations are generally more difficult to predict. Liquidity of assets is important, reflecting the ability to make a short-term payout during liquidation, and to some extent associations with more old style mortgages were more likely to liquidate, suggesting they were not embracing the new world of mortgage lending.

Two developments may help explain the 1941 closures. First, the buildup to World War II changed the return to liquidation, making it more attractive to all associations. A special report written by HOLC officials in August 1941 noted the remarkable changes in conditions:

> In the four month period, since the rendering of the original report covering Newark, conditions have changed materially . . . The combination of [defense orders and war contracts] has greatly stimulated employment and brought many new residents to Newark. This has had a noticeable effect upon occupancy, rents, and the sales market.[38]

These sentiments were echoed at around the same time in all of the key primary sources, including the *Sunday Call* and the *Building and Loan Guide and Bulletin*. The second development is the ongoing reorganization program. Many of the associations that reorganized in 1942 began preparations in 1941, for example, by applying for loans from the RFC. Had economic conditions not changed and had the reorganization program not developed, the fate of those associations would likely have been different.

7.5.2 Second Wave of Exit: Reorganizations

In the second wave of structural events at Newark B&Ls, primarily during 1942 and 1943, reorganization became a much more dominant choice. Of the 201 associations still active at the beginning of 1941, 145 either closed or reorganized during the subsequent two years. As a result, generally speaking, the choice for these associations was not whether to have a major structural event, but whether that event would be a complete exit or some form of reorganization.

By about 1940, the strategy for reorganization coalesced into a set of procedures with three main features:

1. An association's assets were split in two, with the good assets placed in a new association and the bad assets placed into an association whose only purpose was liquidation; that is, a "bad bank" in modern vernacular. This usually involved some form of consolidation of multiple associations in order to ensure the new association was large enough to be viable. Shareholders would be issued participation certificates in the liquidating corpora-

---

38. Report on Newark, NJ, April 1941, special addenda dated August 1941, box 47, City Survey Files, Records of the Home Owners' Loan Corporation, record group 195.3, National Archives II, College Park, MD.

tion and shares in the new association, which together would have face value equal to the old shares.[39]

2. Most of the new associations required infusions of liquidity in order to meet pent-up demand for payments on withdrawals or matured shares. This liquidity came in the form of a loan from the Reconstruction Finance Corporation (RFC), or possibly an investment in shares by the Home Owners' Loan Corporation (HOLC). The RFC loan was secured first by the real estate held in the liquidating association and second by a general lien on all of [both] associations assets; the RFC cash would be placed in the new association.

3. The new association qualifies for insurance from the Federal Savings and Loan Insurance Corporation.

Altogether, 103 associations went through reorganization, though not all using the exact set of the aforementioned procedures. Those procedures were not fully formulated until 1939, and they were implemented most heavily in 1942 and 1943, with sixty-eight associations reorganizing in those years. The hiatus during 1940 and 1941 was largely due to demands by the federal agencies involved that any further reorganizations be part of a comprehensive program for the closure or rehabilitation of *all* troubled B&Ls in Newark, a large task that required careful planning and some legislative accommodation.[40] Newark was joined by several other cities in requiring this "community program." Similar community programs were conducted in Philadelphia, New Orleans, Milwaukee, Baltimore, Chicago, and Altoona, PA.[41] Uniquely dysfunctional was the state of New Jersey, though, with twenty separate community programs of its own.[42]

According to data on RFC activities available at the National Archives, the large majority of loans were approved in 1941 and 1942 and dispensed in the subsequent year. The records indicate fifty-nine loans were approved by the RFC to Newark B&Ls between 1938 and 1943, totaling $13.7 million. In comparison, all Newark B&Ls had $51 million in assets at the end of 1943.

The core of the postwar savings and loan industry in Newark belonged to fourteen consolidated associations that emerged from this reorganization

39. Associations also had the option of writing down shareholder's capital during the reorganization. It is unclear how many or if any associations in Newark exercised the option.

40. The FSLIC also insisted on having the ability to be a joint receiver with the state regulator in case of an insured association's failure, and the FHLB insisted on having a law allowing for easier conversion into federal charters. Both of these required legislative fixes, and those actions are actually somewhat remarkable given the extreme resistance to the federal program demonstrated in New Jersey during the 1930s.

41. These programs were partly done for the sake of the industry itself. Federal officials, however, emphasized their necessity so that the reorganized and insured institutions would not be put at risk by the continued presence of frozen institutions. See the annual reports of the Federal Home Loan Bank Board in 1938–1939 (p. 107), 1939–1940 (p. 107), and 1940–1941 (p. 120).

42. See *Federal Home Loan Bank Review*, November 1943, p. 33.

Table 7.9   **Example of asset segregation**

	Old association	New association	Liquidating association
Assets			
Mortgage loans	$96,181	$23,506	$72,676
Real estate	179,007	0	179,007
HOLC bonds	4,525	4,525	0
Cash on hand and in banks	35,028	103,528	4,500
Total	$314,741	$131,559	$256,183
Capital and Liabilities			
Shares	$178,336	$124,835	$53,501
RFC loan	0	0	73,000
Reserves—established prior to recapture of profits	25,341	0	25,341
Reserves—established by recapture of profits	54,761	0	54,761
Reserves—established after recapture of profits	55,957	6,693	49,263
Other	347	30	317
Total	$314,741	$131,559	$256,183

Notes: This is the asset segregation plan adopted by the Enterprise B&L of Newark, which received a $73,000 loan from the RFC for reorganization. The data reflect Enterprise's condition in April 1940 when it first approached the RFC. Reorganization was ultimately executed in early 1942.

process. All but two were formed by associations that were approved for loans by the RFC. After resisting this outcome for nearly a decade, the core of Newark's thrift industry now offered accounts that were insured by the Federal Savings and Loan Insurance Corporation, were free of the burden of foreclosed real estate, and were relatively large, professionally managed, with permanent offices. In 1950, when the troubles of the 1930s were finally just memories, the fourteen reorganized associations held 92 percent of Newark B&L assets. In comparison, the 103 associations that, through reorganizations and asset transfers, were consolidated into these fourteen had controlled only 42 percent of Newark B&L assets in 1930.

Asset segregation and liquidity infusions were both critical. Table 7.9 helps to elucidate this, by showing the reorganization plan of the Enterprise B&L. According to RFC loan files, Enterprise sent 80 percent of its assets to the liquidating association. Altogether, Enterprise did not have a very large core business worth preserving, which is why ten other Newark associations simultaneously reorganized with Enterprise in the same manner, forming the Penn Savings and Loan Association.

With a large RFC loan to fund Enterprise's liquidating association, 70 percent of the share liabilities were put in the new association (a bit more than typical). The B&L managers learned to expect withdrawals of about 30 percent of new associations' share liabilities in the first few months, which would be met with the RFC cash.[43] Indeed, the RFC loan file notes that

43. *Building and Loan Guide and Bulletin*, February 1940, p. 15.

Enterprise's withdrawals were still restricted, and outstanding withdrawal requests totaled about 12 percent of share capital in 1941. In addition, while Enterprise's reserves were quite large relative to real estate, 40 percent of those reserves had been created in 1933 by recapture of profits, and so were specially earmarked for return to shareholders if managers could avoid tapping them.

Without the RFC loan, Enterprise would not have been well positioned to solve its withdrawal problem. As an illustration, there were fifteen Newark associations that experimented with asset segregation in 1933, but the three consolidated associations that resulted had difficulty gaining traction because their liquidity positions were essentially unchanged.[44] Their balance sheets indicate they were chronically short on liquid assets post-reorganization; two of three never had more than 2.5 percent of their assets in cash or securities. Two eventually voluntarily liquidated, and the third liquidated via bulk transfer of assets to one of the new federally insured associations. As noted in the previous section, their shares were still traded in the secondary market in 1939, at around fifty cents on the dollar. With this experience in mind, after the first version of the new reorganization strategy was presented at the state B&L convention in 1937, the most important question involved liquidity:

> What of these liabilities which are our real headaches, our unpaid maturity list? . . . Where do we get the money to pay off the withdrawals and the maturities? How can we continue as a going concern, simply by the bookkeeping operation of transferring some bad assets from one association to another, or from one account to another in the same association?[45]

Asset segregation was not a panacea, but it did accomplish at least two things. First, it clarified to existing shareholders the extent of their maximum potential exposure to losses on the bad assets. Second, and probably more importantly, it allowed new investors to have their capital invested wholly in good assets. It had been difficult to attract new capital into a B&L that had, say, 50 percent real estate on its books, since that capital's return would be lower than the return on the new mortgage investments it allowed.

To conclude this section, it is informative to repeat the type of analysis used in the previous section with a probit framework in which the dependent variable is a dummy for reorganization after 1941. The set of right-hand-side variables is the same. The results are reported in table 7.10. The estimation reported in the first column includes all associations active at the end of

---

44. Authority for asset segregation was always implicitly available, and was made explicit in two pieces of state legislation in the early 1930s, and then in a 1937 reorganization act, and again modified in 1939 and later. The method of segregation used in 1933 was slightly more cumbersome, as these associations were required to set up trust entities, which were liquidated by special trustees under the supervision of the state regulator. Nevertheless the mechanics were essentially identical and it is difficult to believe that the distinction between trust accounts and liquidating corporations can alone explain the long delay in asset segregation.

45. *Building and Loan Guide and Bulletin*, August 1937, p. 15.

Table 7.10   Reorganizations in the 1940s

		Dependent variable: reorganization after 1941		
B&Ls included:	All	Subset that closed or reorganized	Subset with share prices	Subset with share prices
Vintage of data	1941	1941	1941	1941
	(1)	(2)	(3)	(4)
Share price			−0.0018	
			(0.0090)	
Asset side:				
Real estate/assets	1.48*	1.63*	2.40*	2.41*
	(0.34)	(0.41)	(0.76)	(0.75)
Arrears/assets	−3.57	−3.52	−6.49***	−6.46***
	(2.31)	(2.65)	(3.36)	(3.35)
Share of mortgages unpledged	0.79*	0.91*	1.49*	1.48**
	(0.23)	(0.31)	(0.57)	(0.57)
Liquid assets/assets	3.16*	3.85*	5.57*	5.56*
	(0.70)	(0.86)	(1.11)	(1.10)
Log(assets)	0.39*	0.51*	0.89*	0.89*
	(0.084)	(0.12)	(0.21)	(0.21)
Liability side:				
Apportioned profits/shares	−0.014	−0.015	−0.016	−0.017
	(0.012)	(0.016)	(0.023)	(0.024)
1(Apportioned profits = 0)	−0.19**	−0.069	−0.17	−0.19
	(0.096)	(0.21)	(0.20)	(0.18)
Portion of shares in income shares	−0.029	0.088	−1.36***	−1.36***
	(0.40)	(0.58)	(0.80)	(0.79)
Borrowed money/liabilities	−2.94	−0.97	−3.65	−3.70
	(2.52)	(3.01)	(4.08)	(4.01)
Reserves/liabilities	−1.03***	−1.17	−2.93*	−2.93*
	(0.56)	(0.72)	(1.09)	(1.09)

Lagged from 1930:				
Apportioned profits/shares	-0.012	-0.030	-0.036	-0.037
	(0.014)	(0.019)	(0.028)	(0.028)
Real estate/assets	-0.69	-1.51	-1.37	-1.42
	(1.19)	(1.50)	(1.82)	(1.79)
Income shares/all shares	-0.56	-0.83	0.38	0.38
	(0.60)	(0.90)	(1.28)	(1.28)
Borrowed money/liabilities	-0.54	-0.85	1.09	1.11
	(1.06)	(1.48)	(2.12)	(2.11)
Reserves/liabilities	-7.90	-7.36	-3.62	-3.17
	(7.90)	(11.0)	(11.8)	(11.8)
Other characteristics				
1(Received RFC loan before 1935)	0.24	0.17	0.25	0.25
	(0.23)	(0.22)	(0.21)	(0.21)
1(Member of FHLB by 1936)	-0.074	-0.23***	-0.38*	-0.38**
	(0.12)	(0.13)	(0.15)	(0.15)
Year established	0.0085***	0.012**	0.025**	0.025**
	(0.0044)	(0.0060)	(0.0099)	(0.0098)
1(Optional plan)	-0.17***	-0.24***	-0.70*	-0.70*
	(0.100)	(0.14)	(0.14)	(0.14)
1(Nonserial plan)	-0.066	-0.096	-0.46*	-0.46*
	(0.10)	(0.14)	(0.17)	(0.16)
Observations	191	150	103	103
Pseudo *R*-squared	0.49	0.47	0.57	0.57

Notes: Probit estimation with marginal effects displayed. Robust standard errors.

***Significant at the 1 percent level.

**Significant at the 5 percent level.

*Significant at the 10 percent level.

1941, while the second includes just those that closed or reorganized, setting aside those that survived.

Naturally, associations reorganizing had large amounts of real estate, but it is interesting that they had even larger amounts than associations that liquidated during the same time period. One way to think about this is that, by the end of 1941, the associations with large amounts of real estate that had not yet liquidated were clearly looking for some way to avoid that fate. After all, the large majority of associations either closed or reorganized after 1941, so the decision for most was not whether to take some major action but the form of that action.

Larger associations were more likely to reorganize. As troubled as some of the larger associations were, their size ensured that they still had enough good assets to form the core of a new association. Smaller associations that reorganized tended to do so while merging their good assets with many other associations. Reorganizing associations also had converted almost all of their mortgages away from pledge mortgages into direct reduction mortgages, a sign that they were taking steps to embrace the modern mortgage industry.

7.6   Modern Parallels

The trading of B&L shares on secondary markets resembles practices that characterize modern closed-end mutual funds. Funds of this sort have a fixed amount of shares outstanding at any given time and do not offer to pay out withdrawals. This is advantageous to the extent that these funds are able to hold less liquid assets. In place of withdrawals, investors can trade their shares on a secondary market, typically at some discount to the net asset value of the shares. Since there is no specific withdrawal value, these funds do not "break the buck" in the same sense as money market mutual funds or B&Ls for that matter. As a thought experiment, Newark B&Ls could be thought of as having operated in a manner similar to money market mutual funds that abruptly converted into closed-end mutual funds. Ignoring the profound regulatory barriers that make such a conversion purely a thought experiment, such a move would dramatically alter the nature of investors' claims in a way that captures the important part of B&L investors' 1930s experience.

The imposition of withdrawal restrictions at B&Ls also has some parallels to developments in the auction-rate securities (ARS) market during the 2007 to 2009 financial crisis. Holders of ARS were accustomed to the option of selling their holdings if desired at periodic auctions, but became unable to do so as demand at auctions decreased in early 2008 and investment banks declined to provide backstops against auction failure. The aftermath was litigious and involved basic questions of what investors were promised, much like the questions over the obligations of B&Ls to their investors. Ultimately, after litigation by state attorneys general and federal and state regulators, some investment banks agreed to buy back ARS.[46]

Finally, focusing on the nature of financial crises at intermediaries more broadly, what these episodes have in common is the inability of these institutions, during periods of macroeconomic or financial distress, to fulfill promises that were made either explicitly or implicitly during stronger economic times. Such unfulfilled promises can create particularly persistent problems when they involve real estate assets with long durations. For example, today the resolution of representation and warranty issues related to securitization transactions continue to weigh on mortgage lenders. These issues stem from contractual agreements made during boom times that proved difficult to fulfill or unwind during postcrisis macroeconomic environments. The problem in each case is not necessarily the promise itself but rather the lack of clear provision for what to do when the promise breaks down.

7.7   Conclusion

This chapter has studied how B&Ls unwound their obligations after taking on large amounts of foreclosed real estate during the 1930s. Resolution among Newark, NJ, B&Ls was postponed as those institutions exploited the gray area between illiquidity and insolvency. After a large balance sheet shock, insolvency was given a temporal dimension, as the persistent reality of lower real estate prices was downplayed. The time horizon of a B&L as a whole did not always reflect the short-term needs of some shareholders to access their savings during the Depression. The secondary share market reflects this most starkly; illiquidity only protected the solvency of those with long time horizons, while those shareholders who sold their shares realized the steep losses others would not.

The federal government's role stands out as particularly helpful in resolving Newark B&Ls' issues. The intervention by the Reconstruction Finance Corporation starting in 1939 is notable for finally matching a patient funding source to real estate assets, and for creating a substantial amount of new liquidity for the first time in a decade. In fact, this chapter adds a new dimension to the set of federal programs described by Snowden (2003) as transforming the thrift industry during the 1930s. Snowden shows that, nationally, the future of the thrift industry lay within a new federally designed system of national charters, FHLB membership, and FSLIC insurance. New Jersey thrift leaders at first rejected each of these innovations. In 1945 there were still no federally chartered S&Ls in Newark, an anomaly. By that time, though, B&L managers and shareholders had capitulated to the comprehensive overhaul carefully designed in the late 1930s by federal authorities.

Not all federal programs had equally lasting impacts. This chapter has

---

46. See Austin (2010) for more background on the ARS market.

not discussed much the discount facilities of the Federal Home Loan Bank System or the troubled asset relief available through the Home Owners' Loan Corporation. Not many Newark associations were able to qualify for FHLB membership, and FHLB collateral requirements were stricter than those of the RFC program as those two institutions had very different structures. The Home Owners' Loan Corporation was likely more helpful with its purchases of distressed mortgage loans. However, the HOLC did not purchase the most distressed mortgages possible; rather, it purchased those that were creditworthy given restructuring.[47]

In a previous study I have suggested that the HOLC was in many ways a lenders' program, purchasing mortgages from lenders at generous terms, and I have no reason not to believe that was the case in Newark. In fact, it is sobering that, even as ambitious, large, and generous as the HOLC was, it was still insufficient to deal with problems on the scale of those at Newark B&Ls.

Appendix
Data and Textual Sources

New Jersey B&L balance sheet data were published each year in the *Annual Report of the Commissioner of Banking and Insurance*. Until 1939, these data recorded the condition as of the fiscal year-end of each association. Starting in 1939, the reports recorded the condition of each B&L on December 31st of each year. The post-1938 vintage data are preferred whenever possible for the purposes of comparability, even though most balance sheets did not change much over the course of a year as many of these associations were quite frozen.

Prices for shares on the secondary share market were published in a weekly Newark newspaper, the *Sunday Call*, as early as January 1939, and continued to be published until December 1940. Quotes may have been published in 1937 or 1938 as well, but I have not yet been able to view the newspaper in those years.

Throughout the text I make references to loans from the Reconstruction Finance Corporation to Newark B&Ls. All of this information is from the Records of the Reconstruction Finance Corporation, record group 234,

---

47. The B&Ls in Essex county held about $325 million in mortgage loans as of the end of 1933, and the HOLC purchased $45 million in mortgages from all the mortgage lenders in the county from 1933 to 1936, but it is impossible to know how much of that came from B&Ls, and Newark is most of Essex county but not all of it. While there were sizable declines in mortgage loans outstanding at B&L's during the years in which the HOLC purchased mortgages, there were similarly sized declines before and after those years as well. As far as I know, there is no comprehensive data on the amount of loans the HOLC purchased from B&Ls specifically on a city, county or state basis.

stored at the National Archives in College Park, Maryland. Basic information on the number and size of loans approved to Newark B&Ls was gathered from the "Index to Loans Made to Banks and Railroads," boxes 1–27, which is alphabetically ordered. I also make references to some loan files with more detailed information. The archives have many thousands of boxes of loan files to various types of entities, and so in practice, I have had time to view only a limited number of files. Loan files for the West End and Warranty B&L associations are stored in box 42 of the "Records of Declined and Cancelled Loans, 1932–1946" as both loans were eventually cancelled; Warranty ultimately executed a bulk transfer, whereas the West End arranged for a liquidity infusion from a source other than the RFC. Altogether, these are two of the four RFC loans to Newark B&Ls that were cancelled, out of the fifty-nine that were approved. The loan files for the Enterprise, Outlook, and Woodside B&L associations are stored, respectively, in boxes 57, 139, and 193 of the "Paid Loan Case Files, compiled 1932–1942." Note that those records are arranged in two groups, those paid before 1942 and those paid during 1942, and the box numbering restarts at 1 for loans paid during 1942. These three loans were paid during 1942.

References

Anari, A., J. Kolari, and J. Mason. 2005. "Bank Asset Liquidation and the Propagation of the U.S. Great Depression." *Journal of Money, Credit, and Banking* 37 (4): 753–73.

Austin, D. Andrew. 2010. "Auction-Rate Securities." Congressional Research Service RL34672.

Bodfish, H. Morton. 1931. *History of Building and Loan in the United States.* Chicago: United States Building and Loan League.

———. 1935. *The Depression Experience of Savings and Loan Associations in the United States.*

Bodfish, H. Morton and A. D. Theobald. 1938. *Savings and Loan Principles.* New York: Prentice-Hall.

Carlson, Mark, Kris J. Mitchener, and Gary Richardson. 2011. "Arresting Banking Panics: Fed Liquidity Provision and the Forgotten Panic of 1929." *Journal of Political Economy* 119 (5): 889–924.

Clark, Horace F., and Frank A. Chase. 1925. *Elements of the Modern Building and Loan Associations.* New York: The Macmillan Company.

Courtemanche, Charles, and Kenneth Snowden. 2010. "Repairing a Mortgage Crisis: HOLC Lending and its Impact on Local Housing Markets." *Journal of Economic History* 71 (2): 307–37.

Ewalt, Josephine H. 1962. *A Business Reborn: The Savings and Loan Story, 1930–1960.* Chicago: American Savings and Loan Institute Press.

Fishback, Price, Alfonso Flores Lagunes, William C. Horrace, Shawn Kantor, and Jaret Treber. 2011. "The Influence of the Home Owners' Loan Corporation in Housing Markets During the 1930s." *Review of Financial Studies* 24 (6): 278–307.

Foote, Christopher, Kristopher Gerardi, and Paul Willen. 2008. "Negative Equity and Foreclosure: Theory and Evidence." *Journal of Urban Economics* 64 (2): 234–45.

Kaufman, George G., and Steven A. Seelig. 2002. "Post-Resolution Treatment of Depositors at Failed Banks: Implications for the Severity of Banking Crises, Systemic Risk, and Too Big to Fail." *Economic Perspectives* (2):27–41.

Kendall, Leon T. 1962. *The Savings and Loan Business.* Englewood Cliffs, NJ: Prentice-Hall.

Piquet, Howard S. 1930. *Building and Loan Associations in New Jersey.* Princeton, NJ: Princeton University Press.

Richardson, Gary. 2007. "Quarterly Data on the Categories and Causes of Bank Distress during the Great Depression." *Research in Economic History* 25:37–115.

Rockoff, Hugh. 1993. "The Meaning of Money in the Great Depression." NBER Historical Paper no. 53. Cambridge, MA: National Bureau of Economic Research.

Rose, Jonathan. 2011. "The Incredible HOLC? Mortgage Modification During the Great Depression." *Journal of Money, Credit and Banking* 43 (6): 1073–1108.

Snowden, Kenneth A. 1997. "Building and Loan Associations in the U.S., 1880–1893: The Origins of Localization in the Residential Mortgage Market." *Research in Economics* 51 (3): 227–50.

———. 2003. "The Transition from Building and Loan to Savings and Loan, 1890–1940." In *Finance, Intermediaries, and Economic Development*, edited by Stanley L. Engerman, Phillip T. Hoffman, Jean-Laurent Rosenthal, and Kenneth L. Sokoloff. Cambridge: Cambridge University Press.

Snowden, Kenneth A., and Joshua James. 2001. "The Federalization of Building and Loans, 1927–1940: The North Carolina Experience." University of North Carolina, Greensboro. Unpublished Manuscript.

State of New Jersey Department of Banking and Insurance. Various Years. *Annual Report of the Commissioner of Banking and Insurance.*

Wheelock, David C. 2008. "The Federal Response to Home Mortgage Distress: Lessons from the Great Depression." *Federal Reserve Bank of St. Louis Review* 90 (3): 133–48.

White, Eugene. 2010. "Lessons from the Great American Real Estate Boom and Bust of the 1920s." NBER Working Paper no. 15634, Cambridge, MA.

III

Securitization in Earlier Times

8

Dutch Securities for American Land Speculation in the Late Eighteenth Century

Rik Frehen, William N. Goetzmann, and K. Geert Rouwenhorst

8.1 Introduction

Dutch investors have historically played an important role in American finance. The financiers of the American Revolution turned to the Dutch markets for loans to support their war effort and, with Hamilton's visionary restructuring of the American debt, the Dutch early faith in American promises paid off handsomely. On the heels of their successful financial investment in early US government bonds, Dutch investors in the 1790s turned their attention—and money—toward the speculative potential of the American land itself. Two of the most important foreign investments in American land development prior to the nineteenth century were the Dutch loans for the purchase of vast tracts of lots in the newly designated capital city of Washington, DC, and the Holland Land Company loans to purchase, promote, develop, and resell large sections of western New York State, with tracts that included the future Erie Canal. Both of these projects

Rik Frehen is an assistant professor in the Finance Department at Tilburg University. William N. Goetzmann is the Edwin J. Beinecke Professor of Finance and Management Studies and director of the International Center for Finance at the Yale School of Management and a research associate of the National Bureau of Economic Research.

K. Geert Rouwenhorst is the Robert B. and Candice J. Haas Professor of Corporate Finance and deputy director of the International Center for Finance at the Yale School of Management.

We would like to thank the librarians at the Stadsarchief in Amsterdam, the Gemeentearchief Rotterdam, and the Universiteit van Amsterdam archief for their assistance. We thank Frans Buelens, Ed Glaeser, Oscar Gelderblom, Kim Oosterlinck, and the participants in the 2011 NBER conference and the 2012 Conference on the History of Business and Finance at the Toulouse School of Economics for suggestions. For acknowledgments, sources of research support, and disclosure of the authors' material financial relationships, if any, please see http://www.nber.org/chapters/c12795.ack.

were financed by the public issuance of securities that traded on the Dutch capital market.

While Washington, DC's early development and the operations of the Holland Land Company have both been studied from the perspective of American economic history, few studies have taken the perspective of Dutch investors, and asked what motivated them to invest, what precedents existed for these novel and presumably highly risky ventures, how their investments fared over time, and what impact the experience had on future securitizations. The loans offer a rare opportunity to study the process of financial innovation—particularly innovation in the collateralization of real property.

In 1793 and 1794, several complex debt securities called "negotiaties" were floated in the public capital markets of Amsterdam and Rotterdam to finance the two American land projects. The Washington, DC, loans were made to the American financier James Greenleaf who had earlier been instrumental in arranging US government loans on the Dutch market. The Holland Land Company loans were made by a consortium of major Dutch merchants, many of whom had been involved in underwriting and pooling US government debt issues in the Netherlands.

The land negotiaties involved multiple forms of collateral to address different types of risks implicit in the investment, as well as legal and custodial arrangements designed to mitigate fraud and operational failure. In this chapter we examine the terms, conditions, markets, and legal framework of these securities. We document their financial precedents and show how they relied on the rapidly evolving financial institutions of the time.

Our analysis tells the story of both success and failure. The first land venture capitalized by public securities—the Holland Land Company—survived for more than half a century and generated substantial economic returns to investors; however, a structural reorganization within a decade of its creation was necessary to make it work. The second—the James Greenleaf venture to buy and develop lots in the District of Columbia, in partnership with Robert Morris and John Nicholson—ultimately defaulted and the ensuing transatlantic legal dispute over the collateral dragged on for decades. Dutch investor losses arose not only from default, but also from fraudulent manipulation by Greenleaf and ineffective protection of investor rights by the American legal system, which significantly reduced recovery from the collateral.

We argue that the restructuring of one set of securities and the failure of the other is due to the path dependency of Dutch financial innovation and the mismatch between fixed-income financing and land speculation. Although the market in late eighteenth-century Holland had apparently become comfortable with mortgage-backed securities, perhaps it should not have been. Equity finance, as opposed to debt finance, might have better served investors. Consistent with this hypothesis, we show how both firms sought to convert to equity-like financing in the years after issuance.

In particular, the Holland Land Company used a restructuring technique previously employed to provide a residual claim on assets in a closed-end portfolio. Greenleaf and his fellow entrepreneurs in the Washington, DC, enterprise, Robert Morris and John Nicholson, were deeply indebted as a result of numerous land speculations. Shortly after their Washington, DC, venture they attempted to pool their property assets and float a public offering of equity shares in the North American Land Company to American and European investors. They were unsuccessful and went to debtor's prison.

Our use of historical evidence to examine financial innovation is not new. A number of researchers have pointed out that there is much to learn about mortgage securitization from the historical mortgage market (cf. White, chapter 4, this volume; Snowden 1995, 2010; Fishback, Horrace, and Kantor 2001; Goetzmann and Newman 2010). The benefit of focusing on the late eighteenth-century Dutch market is that the process of innovation can be clearly traced in historical documents and in public security price quotations. The richness of the historical material allows us to identify specific precedents to innovation. It also allows us to observe the social and business network in which the innovations appeared and diffused.

8.2   Historical Background

Our overview of the eighteenth-century Dutch capital markets is necessarily brief and will focus on the appearance of publicly traded, collateralized financial instruments, which is the specific context in which the innovation we study appears.

8.2.1   Asset-Backed Securities

An important precedent for the American property securities studied in this chapter is a class of loans collateralized by the revenue stream of the sale of commodities. An early example is the 1659 security issued by Johan Deutz to the House of Austria, which was financed by a loan issued at 4 percent, and collateralized by a monopoly given to Deutz over the product of Austria's rich quicksilver mines. In effect, the loan was a means to secure the monopoly, rather than the principal source of profit by Deutz.[1] The demand of commodity security for a loan is not surprising in this example, but the financing of the transaction by Deutz's loan issue is noteworthy in that Deutz's credit was enhanced not only by the commodity, but his ability as a merchant to benefit from the monopoly and thus reduce the uncertainty of loan repayment.

This commodity-backed structure eventually became a standardized financial product in the Amsterdam market. In the early eighteenth century, Dutch merchants faced a competitive global market for key commodi-

1. Barbour (1950, 109).

ties from the Americas—particularly sugar and coffee. The erosion of the monopoly of the Dutch West Indies Company over Atlantic trade to the Netherlands led to the emergence of independent plantation owners in Surinam, Essequibo, and Demerary, and in certain Caribbean islands such as St. Eustacia. These independent plantations were financed with innovative securities for which the Deutz Austrian loan set a clear precedent. From 1753 to 1795 (when the Dutch relinquished sovereignty over their South American plantations), Dutch merchants floated over 240 "plantation loans" in the public markets. These were debt investments in sugar plantations of Dutch South America and the Caribbean that were collateralized by mortgages on the overseas properties (including land, slaves, and capital equipment), and the annual commodity production of the plantation.[2]

An interesting feature of plantation loans is that the merchants in the commodities trade functioned as financial intermediaries in what we might now call "structured products," which were broadly referred to as negotiaties. The merchant underwrote the issuance of the loans to the public and served as the administrator and servicer, and as the merchant for the commodities on the exchange. His compensation was a commission on sales of the plantation produce while the rest of the sale proceeds were used to service the debt. Van der Voort (1973) notes that the typical interest rate paid by the planters was 5 to 6 percent, and the rate paid to bond holders was fixed as well. The first of the plantation loans was floated by William Gideon Deutz in 1753—evidently building on his firm's knowledge and reputation from the Austrian loan. This innovation spread to other issuers. According to Van der Voort, ultimately 76 to 80 million guilders of plantation loans were issued by a large number of merchant houses and standard measures of investment safety were applied in the issuance—including a maximum loan-to-value ratio. They took many forms, and issuers would often pool the mortgages from several plantations into a single negotiatie.

A drop in commodity prices in 1771 and a financial crisis in the Amsterdam market in 1773 led to widespread defaults on plantation negotiaties, and a drop-off—though not a complete disappearance—in their issuance. Van der Voort estimates that investors suffered substantial losses, recovering only one-fourth of their capital and realizing no more than 3 percent interest. This event was undoubtedly the first mortgage-backed securities crisis. It is interesting from an institutional standpoint because it revealed to the Dutch market the potential for the failure of collateralized bonds to guarantee full or even significant recovery of capital. In addition, it caused the restructuring of fixed-income claims, including the issuance of equity-

---

2. Van der Voort (1973) is a detailed study of the Dutch plantation loans from which this discussion is taken. See the English summary pp. 218–221. A recent master's thesis in English is Hoonhout (2012). The role of the plantation loans in Dutch financial development is discussed in Rouwenhorst (2005).

like certificates. This model of converting debt to equity was evidently not limited to plantation loan defaults. A security from 1776, recently acquired for the Yale Collection of Financial History, is a receipt for a share in a Swedish iron works that had been financed by debt issuance on the Amsterdam capital market, and a reorganization of the debt claim resulted in an exchange for equity. It is not known how many such exchanges took place, but such a conversion, or at least an equity-like restructuring, would later become useful for the Holland Land Company consortium.

Rouwenhorst (2005) points out that the plantation loans also played a key role as precedents for another Dutch financial innovation of the eighteenth century—closed-end mutual funds. These were negotiaties that offered a stream of interest derived from a portfolio of traded securities. The first of these, Eendragt Maakt Magt, was a purely financial security issued in 1774 by Abraham van Ketwich. It was unrelated to the commodities trade except insofar as it held in its diversified portfolio plantation loans in Essequibo, Berbice, and Danish American islands, along with securitized Danish toll revenues, Russian and German sovereign debt, and Spanish toll revenue bonds.

These loans were not simply pass-through instruments, but fixed-income securities with a stated yield—around 5 percent in many cases. The periodic income from the underlying securities was intended to cover the stated yield. The income from the underlying securities was further expected to pay for a lottery by which random shares in the negotiatie would be retired at values above their face amount. This peculiar feature insured that the return on the pool of bonds stochastically dominated the return distribution for any single loan. As we discuss later, the closed-end fund negotiatie structure was also adapted to the financing of American land speculation.

One important difference between the plantation loans and the American land securities discussed in this chapter is that the American securities were claims on future land sales. They were not a means to finance transatlantic commodity trade, but rather were based upon the financing, development, subdivision, and resale of wilderness property. The plantation loans can be interpreted as a means for Dutch merchants to lay off the capital cost of the plantation generating profitable commodity trade. There appears to have been no reliance on future capital appreciation of the collateral as the grounds for the profitability of the investment. In the case of the Holland Land Company and the Washington, DC, loans, this was precisely the opposite. They yielded no commodities for merchants to trade, and the entirety of the expected economic benefit derived from land price appreciation. Although the American land securities used a similar structure to the plantation loans—land or mortgage-backed securitization—the fundamental nature of the underlying economic benefits differed, and thus the risk and timing of future cash flows differed.

8.2.2   Other Precedents

There are other financial precedents relevant to the issuance of securities in Amsterdam to finance American land purchases. The first is the emergence of land banks in various forms through the eighteenth century. Only a brief overview is offered here. The first land bank proposals were floated in England around the end of the seventeenth century as a means to create money out of real property. One of the early land bank theorists, John Law, regarded the scarcity of money as one of the greatest constraints to commercial development, and the reliance of European economies on the supply of New World silver as a risk to be mitigated by changing the collateral for money from precious metal to real property.

America was one of the first places to implement land banking due to the extreme scarcity of hard specie in the colonies. Beginning in South Carolina in 1712, publicly sponsored land banks—actually, more properly loan offices, since they were not deposit-taking institutions—were created by colonial governments to issue mortgages in paper currency that could ultimately be used to purchase foreclosed properties. Other colonies immediately followed suit. In Boston, a private land bank was launched. Parliament was alarmed that the currency of several colonies traded at a discount, reflecting the market perception of their risk. Among other things, the structure of the land bank system embedded conflicts of interest: local boards appraised properties and made loans. A 1738 mortgage contract for seventy-five pounds issued by the Rhode Island Colony sixth land bank is representative.[3] The twenty-five-year note at 5 percent interest was issued at a 1:2 loan-to-value ratio as determined by a panel of six trustees acting for the general assembly of the colony. The borrower, Edward Arnold, received paper notes for his pledge, which circulated in the colony. His interest payments, along with other borrowers who made up the 100,000 pound loan issue, were evidently sufficient to cover the annual colonial budget. The incentives of the colonies to operate land banks of this sort were clear. While solving the problem of scare specie, they also provided revenue for government. Related lending represented an obvious problem. Parliament outlawed land banks by 1741 and ultimately they were closed.

Land banks did not make a significant reappearance until the end of the ancient regime and the creation of France's revolutionary currency, the assignats.[4] Dutch investors in 1794 and 1795 would surely have been familiar with the French securities backed by confiscated church properties. By 1795, the assignats were virtually worthless due to excess issuance and were replaced in the following year by the mandats territoriaux, which likewise rapidly declined in value.

---

3. In the Yale Collection of Financial History.
4. Cf. White (1995).

Perhaps more relevant precedents for the American securities were early American land companies. A number of pre- and post-Revolutionary companies were formed to claim, develop, and settle western lands—the Ohio Company launched by a group of powerful Virginians being among the most well known. These firms were essentially private equity share-based companies that could conceivably have served as a model for Dutch investors as well. Livermore (1939) argues that they were innovative corporate structures in their own right. The American agent of the Holland Land Company, Theophile Cazenove, began purchasing shares in American companies in the 1790s. Besides toll and bridge companies, he bought shares in the Pennsylvania Population Company founded by Pennsylvania's comptroller general, John Nicholson, in 1792—partner to Greenleaf and Morris in the Washington, DC, venture. As such, the Dutch consortium comprising the Holland Land Company was familiar with this form of public equity, and perhaps based their own organization on it. The Holland Land Company was itself divided into transferable shares, although there is no evidence that the shares traded on public markets.

Although Dutch financiers were not known to be involved in the American land bank experiment or the French assignat system—except perhaps as speculators—these models are relevant in that they demonstrate the active use of property as collateral for publicly traded debt, whether interest-bearing securities or paper money. They indicate that securities collateralized by land were not unknown at the time of the Dutch land loans. However, while there were clear precedents for property-backed securities in the European markets in the late eighteenth century, investor experiences with them may not have been favorable.

Finally, another relevant precedent is the Landschaften of eighteenth-century Prussia studied by in this volume (chapter 9) and elsewhere by Kirsten Wandschneider. She traces the development of these land credit associations to a financial crisis in 1770 that required the restructuring of debt of the landed nobility. This was accomplished through the issuance of public bearer bonds backed by mortgages held by the Landschaften. Wandschneider likens them to modern "covered bonds," which have recently been proposed as safer alternatives to mortgage-backed debt. Undoubtedly, these were also known to Dutch financiers in the 1790s.

8.2.3   Dutch Investment in American Debt

The story of Dutch investment in the debt of the early United States is well described by Riley (2009). The first underwriters of American loans in the Netherlands were the firms of W. & J. Willink, N. and J. van Staphorst, and De la Lande and Fynje, who floated loans for the United States in 1782. These Dutch intermediaries earned commissions as high as 8 percent for the early flotations and 3 to 5 percent for later loans.

Even more profitable was the speculation on domestic debt of the United

States, which Dutch merchants bought at steep discounts at the nadir of American creditworthiness prior to Hamilton's reorganization of the debt. Over the period 1782 to 1794, Dutch speculators issued a number of negotiaties on the Dutch capital markets backed by the bonds of the United States. These American negotiaties typically paid a promised rate of interest and were secured with US securities held in trust. Riley points out that the first movers in this securitization of American debt were also major boosters of America. Pieter Stadnitski, a member of the Dutch Patriot faction ultimately aligned with the French Revolution, was not only a major purchaser and securitizer of US bonds but also an enthusiastic pamphleteer who wrote glowingly about the new American democracy and the wonderful American land. Riley calculates that Stadnitski made a killing by buying American paper at 37.5 percent of face value and selling it at 60 percent of face value to investors in his negotiaties. Investors in his funds also profited as the prices of the negotiaties rose in the Dutch market as a result of the strengthening of American finances. Stadnitski's arbitrage was rapidly imitated by other merchants and, not surprisingly, spreads narrowed.

An important feature of these American fund negotiaties is that they provided for a distribution of residual profits deriving from the purchase of US bonds at a discount. As prices of the United States' debt rose to par, the capital gain accruing to investors—even after the issuers took their cut as intermediaries—was substantial. Thus there was some "right-tail" to the distribution of expected returns to investing in the debt of the young United States. Their popularity with the Dutch public may have been due as much to this feature as to the conviction that the United States was certain to meet its obligations.

The firm of Daniel Crommelin and Sons in Amsterdam was among the several issuers of negotiaties backed by US notes. He was aided in this operation in 1794 by an American merchant from Boston, James Greenleaf. Greenleaf was married to a daughter of a member of a prominent Amsterdam banking family and served as US consul to the Netherlands. He knew the Crommelin family through their mercantile dealings in the United States. An American branch of the family was stationed in New York, where part of Greenleaf's business was also located.

8.3   Financial Innovation: American Property Securities

The rich data in Dutch archives and the considerable historical research devoted to the history of the Holland Land Company and to the early development of Washington, DC, make it possible to trace in detail the process of innovation leading to the issuance of its securities on American speculative lands. This section describes the development of these securities and their contractual details.

8.3.1   Holland Land Company Negotiaties

In 1789 a consortium of leading merchant houses formed to explore land purchases in America. The firms of Stadnitski, Van Staphorst, Van Eeghen, and Ten Cate & Van Vollenhoven had all made money buying American funds and issuing negotiaties. Perhaps equally relevant, the investors to whom they had sold negotiaties backed by American debt securities also made money. As mentioned earlier, the consortium employed an agent to travel to America, Theophile Cazenove, who scouted opportunities and began to invest the firm's capital, initially into American share companies. These included shares in the Pennsylvania Population Company and shares in the James River Company—a firm nominally headed by George Washington to improve the navigation of the James River for development of the commercial traffic into the southern Virginia piedmont. In April 1791 the Holland Land Company joint ventured with the Rotterdam firm of Van Beefting and Boom to explore sugar maple operations with the hope of establishing another source of commodity production in the American forests. Cazenove, perhaps due to his involvement with John Nicholson, also became interested in purchasing undeveloped land for division and sale to immigrants and US settlers. In December of 1792, the Dutch consortium bought 3,300,000 acres in the Genesee River valley from Robert Morris. That year the Holland Land Company was created. The five firms brought in the Van Willinks and retained Rutger van Schimmelpenninck as legal advisor.[5] The share company was formed among the participants and the shares were not publicly traded, so it was, in effect, a private equity company. The firm further formalized its structure in 1796.

The first public financing of the Holland Land Company was a subscription of negotiaties of 3,000,000 guilders floated in January 1793 on one million acres of land in the Genesee valley, which was valued (or transferred to the trustees of the negotiatie) at 1.2 guilders per acre. In addition 1,200,000 guilders in American funds was transferred to the trustees to cover the costs of paying interest over the first five years. The first issue was completely subscribed, and a second followed in June.[6]

The Holland Land Company offering was promoted by a pamphlet published by Stadnitski extolling the virtues of America, describing the particulars of the settlement process and projections about an increase in the demand for land. Evans (1924, 28) notes that Stadnitski's pamphlet

---

5. This account is taken from Evans (1924, and ff).

6. Details of the offering can be found in *Nieuwe Nederlandsche jaerboeken, of Vervolg der merkwaerdigste geschiedenissen: die voorgevallen zyn in de Vereenigde provincien, de generaliteits landen, en de volkplantingen van den staet. 1.–33. deel, 1766–98, Volume 2.* P. 1442. Also see the certificate Amsterdam City Archives, archive no. 333 "Holland Land Company," inventory no. 867 "Shares of various negotiations."

describes the speculative profits Morris himself had made—tripling his investment in a million acre purchase via a sale to the British Pultney Company. Accompanying this pamphlet were calculations of expected profits of more than 200 percent over a nine-year horizon accruing to an investment in 400,000 acres of land in the Genesee valley. Important to our analysis is that this spreadsheet, almost certainly prepared by Stadnitski for a French investment market, shows no positive cash flow for the first five years. Even in an optimistic scenario capital investment was required; hence the necessity of substituting a portfolio of US debt to address the problem of the mismatch between duration of the debt and the assets. The management fees, in addition to costs, were 1 percent for startup (up front), and .5 percent for payment of dividends.

The Holland Land Company negotiaties are puzzling in several respects. First, they did not promise any economic benefits from future land sales, other than meeting interest payments. This suggests that the market demand for the securities was not based on an expectation of speculative profits from development of the American frontier. The debt structure was clearly not due to lack of knowledge about equity financing. Cazenove was already purchasing American equity securities on the firm's behalf. Essentially the negotiatie provided leverage for the consortium to buy American lands, and a portion of their property was pledged as collateral. The Stadnitski financial forecast makes it clear that the firm understood that, even under an optimistic scenario, for the first years of operation cash flow would be negative, necessitating the inclusion of American government securities to meet promised interest payments in the first few years of operation.

Also puzzling is why Dutch subscribers to the Holland Land Company issues would take such significant risks for a relatively modest yield. It is unlikely that, in the event of default, the property in the wilderness of New York could be easily liquidated by creditors, when the borrowers were unable to do so. Perhaps the reputation of the borrowers and the recent returns to investments in American debt provided additional implicit promise of fulfillment.

Going forward, the Holland Land Company bonds met their minimal obligations by paying interest through 1798; however, land sales necessary to extend the interest payments did not materialize. In 1804 the combined cash reserves for the two loans had decreased to 520,000 Florins due to a combination of large investment in the enterprise, poor cash flows from land sales, and a high burden of interest payments.[7] As a consequence the company faced a large debt overhang, which resulted in a strong disincentive to the equity owners of the company to continue. This led to an offer of a major restructuring of the negotiaties.

7. Evans (1924, 430).

The restructuring involved a merger of the two negotiaties that was in part motivated by a conflict of interest between the two investor groups, who developed a preference for the January negotiatie over the June issue. The lands of the January negotiatie included the headquarters of the company, which caused the surrounding lands also owned by the January negotiatie to trade at a premium. The merger put the two investor groups back on equal footing. But more importantly, the complex restructuring of the negotiaties was an attempt to mitigate the debt overhang. The proposal was for a repurchase agreement to reduce the debt burden in return for an opportunity for investors to participate in the residual profits of the land sales. In particular, the company offered investors a lottery to buy back their shares at a steep discount (40 percent or 35 percent of par), but investors were not required to participate. Investors who elected to participate and whose shares were drawn by lot would receive an equity stub to share in the final distribution of the residual profits of land sales at the end of the negotiatie's term.[8] Investors who participated likely believed that their interests were better served by owners and equity holders who were granted debt relief and renewed incentives to develop lands going forward, and perhaps the prospect of some participation in the upside of the fortunes of the company after a period of disappointing results. In the end a two-thirds majority of the bondholders accepted this exchange.

Our archival study shows that the well-known merchant houses that floated the Holland Land Company were among the first subscribers to the lottery scheme. Perhaps they aimed to signal other bond holders that subscription would be to their benefit. Although it is unclear to what extent lottery subscriptions were public knowledge, making lottery subscriptions public would have both a positive and negative effect on future lottery subscriptions. On the one hand, it may serve as a validation by revealing that many of the prominent financiers have subscribed. On the other hand, once a large number of bond holders have subscribed, unsubscribed bonds may benefit from an expected drop in default risk triggered by a reduction in debt overhang.

The firm ultimately retired all 3,000 shares of the negotiatie, as planned, and in addition there was a substantial residual value. Over a twenty-year period, it made periodic payments to investors based upon land sales, which finally wound up in 1858. The amount investors received in total was 6,673,447.5 F. Evans claims that investors made a reasonable return on their investment in the long run, although this interpretation depends on selection of a risk-appropriate discount rate.

---

8. The merger agreement separately stipulated that the company might subsequently try to buy back shares below par in the open market (in which case investors would not participate in the equity residual) or at par, in which case investors would get an equity stub.

8.3.2   A Closed-End Fund Negotiatie

As part of its restructuring in 1805, the Holland Land Company also issued a closed-end fund negotiatie to raise capital.[9] To our knowledge this fund is previously unreported in the literature on the Holland Land Company. The negotiatie enumerates three different securities for lands in the state of New York—two issued by members of the Holland Land Company consortium and one by the Holland Land Company itself—presumably one of the two mortgage-backed securities discussed earlier, but perhaps alternatively a share in the consortium itself. It also lists two American land company stocks (the St. James River Company and the Pennsylvania Population Society) and a bond issue of the state of South Carolina. These securities were held in trust, and the proceeds from their interest, dividend payments, and future sales were used to benefit two classes of investors. The first class received 5 percent annual interest and were redeemed by lot. The second class received no interest payments, only the residual value from the underlying securities. This rendered the second class of investors in the negotiatie equity claimants.

This structure is interesting for several reasons. First it shows the shares in the American land companies purchased by Cazenove were ultimately monetized by the Holland Land Company through what we would today call a "structured product." Second, it indicates that the founding investors in the Holland Land Company monetized their holdings through issuance of negotiaties that were not evidently quoted on the Amsterdam exchange (as were the Holland Land Company 1793 issues). Third, it indicates that, by 1805, there was a demand for equity-like claims on American land speculation. As such, it may be further evidence of a transition to separating debt-like and equity-like financing of land ventures around this time.

8.3.3   Washington, DC, Bonds

In 1793, the success of the Holland Land Company negotiatie clearly set a precedent for James Greenleaf's loan. In that year, Greenleaf began to negotiate for the purchase of 3,000 lots in the new national city of Washington, DC, while concurrently seeking financing from his former Dutch associates using a vehicle very much like the Holland Land Company securities. As with the Holland Land Company negotiaties, this involved two types of collateral: one for the interest payments to investors and another for the assets of the negotiatie. Both were held in trust. His efforts at soliciting Dutch financing resulted in two negotiaties—one issued in Amsterdam by the firm of Daniel Crommelin and Sons and the other in Rotterdam issued by Rocquette, Elzevier, and Beeldemaker.

---

9. Amsterdam City Archives, archive no. 333 "Holland Land Company," inventory no. 867 "Shares of various negotiations."

Following the pattern of the Holland Land Company group, Greenleaf undertook this issue after purchasing property in partnership with two other investors, both major real estate speculators: Robert Morris, former superintendent of the US Treasury, and John Nicholson, former comptroller general of the Commonwealth of Pennsylvania. Neither is named in the Dutch issues, which treat Greenleaf as the sole borrower. Morris had earlier sold the land in New York to the Holland Land Company and Nicholson was involved in several land company schemes including the Pennsylvania Population Company in which the Holland Land Company principles had invested. Thus all three partners were familiar to Dutch financiers. Greenleaf purchased 3,000 lots in September of 1793, for twenty-five pounds per lot, with terms allowing him to make annual payments over the following seven years at zero interest.[10] In December, Robert Morris contracted for an additional 3,000 lots on the same terms at thirty-five pounds each. Arbuckle (1975) calculates that these 6,000 lots encompassed 42 percent of the available property in the capital city.[11] The structure of the partnership between Greenleaf, Morris, and Nicholson is unclear.

The terms of the Amsterdam loan are known from the proposal drawn up by Greenleaf and presented to the firm of Daniel Crommelin and Sons.[12] He proposed a two million guilder loan with a term of twelve years, for which he offered as collateral the 3,000 house lots purchased from the city of Washington, DC. To guarantee the interest on the loan over the first six years of the term of the loan, he offered as collateral a portfolio of US government debt and other securities. He had the right to redeem debt at face value and in so doing redeem a pro rata share of the title to the land held in trust. Thus, the initial conception of the security was strictly a debt instrument.

The exact nature of the collateral structure is interesting. The titles to the financial securities and to the real property were transferred to the trustees of the respective issues. This same structure for the Holland Land Company relied only on a notary who held the land deeds. The transfer of property deeds to Washington, DC, was documented through notarized and witnessed letters from officials in the United States. The squares in which the properties are located were concentrated in the north and east of the city, although Greenleaf's best known development is Greenleaf's Point in the city's southwest.

The trustees for the loan were Peter Godefroy, Daniel Crommelin, and Rutger Jan Schimmelpenninck. Godfrey and Crommelin were the merchant bankers issuing the bond. Schimmelpenninck was a prominent lawyer and politician who, in the year 1795, became the leader of the Patriot revolt in

---

10. Arbuckle (1975, 117).

11. Arbuckle (1975, 118).

12. Amsterdam City Archives, archive no. 654 "Archive of the Firm Daniël Crommelin and Sons, since 1859 Tutein Nolthenius and De Haan," inventory no. 106 "Letters from J. Greenleaf, received by A. Gerard, clerk of the Crommelin firm, 1973 and 1794."

the Netherlands that resulted in the Batavian Republic. He also held shares in the Holland Land Company.

The Rotterdam loan, referred to in the financial press as Rocqette, Elzevier, and Beeldemaker op gronden Washington, was issued on December 15, 1794, and was intended to be for one million guilders and pledged 1,500 house lots. It had a term of five years, a 5.5 percent interest rate, and a similar mortgage and trustee structure to the Amsterdam loan. A lottery structure of the Rotterdam loan was not tied to the value of the properties but instead simply paid a premium of face value for bondholders chosen by lot. These premia show strong similarities to modern lottery plans and were paid out conditional on full repayment by the loan according to the following structure:

- 10 premia for 100 percent
- 10 premia for 50 percent
- 20 premia of 25 percent
- 50 premia of 20 percent
- 90 premia of 10 percent
- 220 premia of 5 percent

Held open for subscription over the first several months of 1794, the loan was ultimately undersubscribed and the terms adjusted accordingly. While the issuers originally planned to raise 1,000,000 guilders in capital and connect 1,500 lots within the city of Washington, DC to the loan, market sentiment evidently only allowed them to raise 150,000 guilders and the number of lots was proportionally reduced to 225, a total of 668,250 square feet.

All lots were transferred in the names of custodians Gillis Groeneveld, Rudolph Mees, and Pieter van der Wallen van Vollenhoven and posted as collateral to the loan with an act of renunciation to protect the investors. The deeds of transfer by Sylvanus Bourne, "on behalf of the gentlemen Groeneveld, Rudolph Mees and Pieter van der Wallen van Vollenhoven" of half of the 2,632,000 square feet of lots, all within the city of Washington, DC, are deposited with the notary, as collateral for the negotiatie. These lots were bought by consul Greenleaf on July 29, 1794. Together with these deeds, the notary received all documents needed to transfer a sufficiently large portion of property in to the aforementioned custodians. Interest on the loan was 5.5 percent, secured through US sovereign debt certificates in the names of Rocquette, Elzevier, and Beeldemaker. In addition to the US debt certificates and Washington, DC, property, James Greenleaf was held personally liable for the loan.

The Amsterdam loan collected only 200,000 guilders and the Rotterdam loan collected only 150,000 guilders. The fees of the Amsterdam investment issuers are not known from the surviving documents. The so-called directors of the Rotterdam loan incurred a 1 percent setup fee and .5 percent per dividend.

The failure of the Greenleaf flotations is variously attributed to the turmoil of the Dutch politics at the time and the invasion of the country by France, but perhaps the market was simply skeptical about a security floated by an American consortium as opposed to a Dutch consortium. In addition, perhaps investors were rightly mistrustful of Greenleaf himself. Evidently Greenleaf did not share the proceeds of the Dutch loans, meager as they were, with the partnership.[13]

In all, 200 bonds were issued by Crommelin in Amsterdam with a face value of 1,000 guilders. The list of subscribers contains the names of other merchant houses of the day, including bankers. Unlike preceding US debt negotiatie issued by Crommelin with Greenleaf, there are no surviving certificates and thus they may not exist, although the legal rights of the holders are summarized in the "Nieuw Nederlandse jaerboeken" as previously indicated. From the period 1796 through 1811, the Amsterdam Pryscourant quoted bid and ask prices for the two Washington, DC, negotiaties on a regular basis.

The story of the Greenleaf, Nicholson, and Morris bankruptcies is a fascinating one that will not be recounted here. Essential to our analysis is the step they took on February 20, 1795, (the year following the loans) to launch the North American Land Company. Each partner contributed property to the company totaling 4,479,317 acres. These properties were held in trust, and shares were issued to the founders. While attempts were evidently made to float a public offering of shares in the North American Land Company in US markets and in the Netherlands, relatively few shares were issued and these evidently to creditors of the two men.[14] Greenleaf sold his shares in 1796 to his partners for $1,500,000 in notes, although he remained connected with the business of the firm for many years as it wound up. He represented its business interests after the death of his former partners. In addition, he ultimately represented the business interests of the Dutch claimants to the Washington, DC, lots.

The holders of the Dutch negotiatie expected to be shielded from the tribulations of Greenleaf and company by virtue of having title to the properties in trust, and the guarantee of the US securities to cover promised interest payments. The Dutch title to the lots was later challenged due to Greenleaf's conveyance of the titles prior to performance of his obligations to the US government. Lots were sold under the stipulation that they be built upon. This led to a protracted legal dispute, the necessity of the Dutch investors to retain counsel in America, to meet tax obligations on the lots, and to auction the properties.

Greenleaf outlived his two partners and oversaw the disposition of the assets of the North American Land Company. He continued to develop

13. Arbuckle (1975, 118).
14. Livermore (1939, 168).

property in Washington, DC, despite his bankruptcy, and ultimately built a number of houses in an area of southwest District of Columbia called Greenleaf Point, some of which still stands today.

Our archival research revealed evidence that Greenleaf took advantage of the Dutch investors on a second occasion. In the 1830s he offered his services to them as a sales agent and contracted to organize an auction of the Washington, DC, lots held in the Rocquette, Beeldemaker, and Elzevier negotiatie. He agreed with the bondholders to split the revenues from the land sales evenly. All taxes and intermediary costs were to be paid by the "Holland gentlemen," however. Greenleaf won these terms after a long negotiation. At the auction in May, 1835, Greenleaf himself bought 50 percent of the property. But since he also got 50 percent of the revenues, he got 50 percent of the land for free. After subtraction of taxes, legal charges, and intermediary costs, what small amount remained was paid out to the bondholders. Rocquette, Beeldemaker, and Elzevier wisely decided not to inform the bondholders (via the account) who actually bought the land, although they likely knew, and could not have been happy that they had been duped yet a second time by James Greenleaf.

In sum, Greenleaf, Morris, and Nicholson's initial difficulties stemmed from their failure to raise sufficient capital to allow them to be patient investors in the development and sale of properties. Like the Holland Land Company, they could not monetize the properties rapidly enough to meet cash obligations. These difficulties may have been compounded by the shady dealings and reputation of one or more of the three partners.

8.4   Path-Dependent Financial Innovation

Empirical studies of financial innovation are necessarily limited to unusual events. Frame and White (2004) argue that most analyses of financial innovation are forced to generalize from a few cases. Lerner and Tufano (2011) articulate this problem and use a set of historical examples—from the emergence of the venture capital industry to the appearance of mutual funds, to address the costs and benefits of financial innovation. Their approach considers the counterfactual; that is, what the economy would look like without a specific innovation.

In the first part of this chapter we detailed the many precedents for the Dutch property negotiaties, particularly the debt-like securities and funds issued in the Amsterdam market in the mid to late eighteenth century. We showed how the features of the Holland Land Company negotiaties and the Washington, DC, negotiaties could be traced to particular precedents in the Dutch market. Our hypothesis is that the innovations relied upon the marketplace's prior acceptance of bond-like instruments. This initially precluded offerings of common stock. The debt securities in the Dutch market at the time were characterized by features designed to secure expected future payments, although certain of them also contained "right-skewed" payoffs created by lottery features and rights in residual value to portfolios of securities. This framework of innovation is an exemplar of an institutionalist perspective in which frictions and information transactions costs of various types are minimized by reliance on precedent. One corollary is that path-dependent outcomes need not be first-best solutions or optimal in any measurable sense; only that they are improvements on existing technology.

The Holland Land Company found the debt service burdensome and restructured their negotiatie in 1805 into an instrument with an equity-like component, reducing the face value to be repaid and replacing it with a residual claim. They further supplemented this with a closed-end fund issue that partitioned proceeds into debt- and equity-like claims.

Shortly after issuing their two negotiaties, Greenleaf, Morris, and Nicholson also tried to engineer an equity-for-debt swap of their vast but highly levered American property holdings by creating the North American Land Company. This had some institutional precedent in the eighteenth-century American land, bridge, and canal companies trading on the Philadelphia Exchange—several of which Nicholson himself had been involved in launching. These institutional forms might have encouraged the hope that such a rescue was possible. While the Holland Land Company was less immediately constrained because its first two public offerings had been fully subscribed, it may have been restricted because of the lack of a market for equities in the Dutch market. This may explain the complexities of the 1805 residual claim certificates.

On the one hand, the land company negotiaties in the eighteenth-century Netherlands are extraordinary innovations: early and complex structured mortgage notes that demonstrate the remarkable sophistication of the capital markets of the time. On the other hand, the financial engineering required to make a debt instrument fit the needs of an enterprise whose value proposition is based upon patiently developing a market on the western frontier, or the growth of an entirely new city, is perhaps extremely inefficient. Had these firms been able to issue equity initial public offering (IPO)'s to a market that accepted them comfortably, the outcome—at least for Greenleaf, Morris, and Nicholson, might have been very different.

8.5   Conclusion

In this chapter we examine the development of an interesting class of mortgage-backed securities issued in the eighteenth century. Debt instruments evolved to support an innovative merchant tradition that used collateralized securities for financing. We conjecture that the American land negotiaties pushed the existing debt-based financial infrastructure of the Netherlands to its limits. Not designed to finance projects with long verification periods, fixed income issuances were used anyway with negative results, and led to recontracting to create what amounted to equity. This restructuring was successful in one instance, and completely failed in another.

References

Arbuckle, Robert D. 1975. *Pennsylvania Speculator and Patriot: the Entrepreneurial John Nicholson 1757–1800*. State College: The Pennsylvania University Press.

Barbour, Violet. 1950. *Capitalism in Amsterdam in the Seventeenth Century*. Baltimore: Johns Hopkins Press.

Evans, Paul D. 1924. *The Holland Land Company*. Fairfield, NJ: Augustus M. Kelley Publishers. Reprint, 1979.

Frame, W. Scott, and Lawrence J. White. 2004. "Empirical Studies of Financial Innovation: Lots of Talk, Little Action?" *Journal of Economic Literature* 42:116–44.

Fishback, Price V., William C. Horrace, and Shawn Kantor. 2001. "The Origins of Modern Housing Finance: The Impact of Federal Housing Programs During the Great Depression." Working Paper, University of Arizona.

Goetzmann, William, N., and Frank Newman. 2010. "Securitization in the 1920's." NBER Working Paper no. 15650, Cambridge, MA.

Hoonhout, Bram. 2012. "Subprime Plantation Mortgages in Suriname, Essequibo and Demerara, 1750–1800. On Manias, Ponzi processes and Illegal Trade in the Dutch Negotiatie System." Master's Thesis, Leiden University.

Lerner, Josh, and Peter Tufano. 2011. "The Consequences of Financial Innovation: A Counterfactual Research Agenda." NBER Working Paper no. 16780, Cambridge, MA.

Livermore, Shaw. 1939. *Early American Land Companies: Their Influence on Corporate Development*. New York: The Commonwealth Fund.

Riley, James. 2009. *International Government Finance and the Amsterdam Capital Market, 1740–1815*. Cambridge: Cambridge University Press.

Rouwenhorst, K. Geert. 2005. "The Origins of Mutual Funds." In *Origins of Value: The Financial Innovations That Created Modern Capital Markets*, edited by William N. Goetzmann and K. Geert Rouwenhorst, 249–71. Oxford: Oxford University Press.

Snowden, Kenneth A. 1995. "Mortgage Securitization in the United States: Twentieth Century Developments in Historical Perspective." In *Anglo-American Financial Systems*, edited by Michael D. Bordo and Richard Sylla, 261–98. New York: Irwin.

———. 2010. "The Anatomy of a Residential Mortgage Crisis: A Look Back to the 1930s." NBER Working Paper no. 16244, Cambridge, MA.

Van der Voort, Johannes P. 1973. *De Westindische Plantages van 1720 tot 1795, Financiën en Handel*. Eindhoven, Netherlands: De Witte.

White, Eugene N. 1995. "The French Revolution and the Politics of Government Finance, 1770–1815." *Journal of Economic History* 55 (2): 227–55.

Lending to Lemons
Landschaft Credit in Eighteenth-Century Prussia

Kirsten Wandschneider

9.1 Introduction

Landschaften[1] were cooperative mortgage credit associations, created in Prussia in the late eighteenth century. They facilitated the refinancing of loans to Prussian noble estates by issuing covered bonds—Pfandbriefe[2]—that were jointly backed by the member estates. Landschaften were public institutions that did not have a profit motive and, except for reserve funds, did not hold their own capital. Their emergence is an interesting example of successful financial innovation in historical mortgage markets, illustrating an important alternative to the financial products at the center of the recent mortgage market disaster.

The collapse of the housing bubble and ensuing 2008 financial crisis has induced American financial institutions and policymakers to search for alternate ways to finance mortgages and reduce their dependence on the asset-backed securities market. The superior experience of covered mortgage bonds has drawn considerable attention. Covered bonds are secured directly by a pool of collateral, typically consisting of mortgages or public

Kirsten Wandschneider is associate professor of economics at Occidental College.

I thank Timothy Guinnane and Larry Neal for comments and discussions throughout this project. I also thank participants at the 2010 Utrecht workshop for Intermediation and Financial Markets, the 2010 EHA meetings, the Berlin Colloquium in Economic History, the UCLA Economic History Proseminar, and the NBER-URC Conference on Housing and Mortgage Markets in Historical Perspective. Parts of this chapter were completed while in residence at the Humboldt University in Berlin. Support from the Prussian State Archive is gratefully acknowledged. For acknowledgments, sources of research support, and disclosure of the author's material financial relationships, if any, please see http://www.nber.org/chapters/c12796.ack.

1. *Landschaft* (sing.) is the German name for the Prussian cooperative mortgage credit associations discussed in this chapter.

2. *Pfandbrief* (sing.) is German for covered mortgage bond.

sector debt. They remain on the balance sheets of the issuing institutions, as opposed to the off-balance sheet transactions for unsecured mortgage-backed securities. Covered bonds carry a dual recourse feature, since they are backed by the collateral pool, as well as the issuers' creditworthiness (Packer, Stever, and Upper 2007). They therefore often receive the highest credit ratings, and are considered an alternative investment to government securities. For the US mortgage market, they have also been discussed as an alternative to replace the federal guarantees in the housing market. A bill to introduce covered bond legislation was proposed in the United States in 2010 (H.R. 4884 and H.R. 5823), but it narrowly failed to be included in the 2010 Dodd-Frank financial overhaul law. A similar bill was reintroduced in 2011 (H.R. 940) and was recommended by the House Financial Services Committee, but it failed to advance to a House vote.[3] In spite of the absence of a comprehensive covered bond framework for the United States, individual banks have introduced covered bonds, and foreign banks have expanded their US denominated covered bond offerings.[4]

In this ongoing debate, it is valuable to examine covered bonds—called Pfandbriefe in German. Covered bonds could only be found until recently in Germany and Denmark, and to a lesser extent in Austria and Switzerland (Packer, Stever, and Upper 2007). In the 1990s, covered bonds gained popularity with the introduction of covered bond bills in most of Europe. By 2011, the size of the European covered bond market had grown to 2.7 trillion euro, with the German market taking up about one third.[5] Covered bonds have remained stable investment options throughout the recent crisis. Yet few economists know about their origins and why they proved to be such successful and safe financial instruments. This chapter sheds light on the origins of the German Pfandbrief, which served as a template for modern covered bonds.

The current study is primarily focused on the five "old" Landschaften as Pfandbrief issuers: the Silesian Landschaft founded in 1770, the Kur- und Neumärkische Ritterschaftliche Kreditinstitut (1777), the Landschaft of Pomerania (1781), the Landschaft of West Prussia in Marienwerder (1787), and the Landschaft of East Prussia in Königsberg (1788) (Hecht 1908, 10). However, throughout the nineteenth century the concept of the Landschaften spread to other German regions.[6] While the old Landschaften were

---

3. For news coverage on the legislation compare, for example, "An Effort to Adapt a European-Style Tool to US Mortgages" *New York Times*, November 3, 2010, and "Geithner Backs New Financing Approach for Mortgages" *New York Times*, March 16, 2011.

4. See the US Covered Bond Investor Forum: http://www.euromoneyconferences.com/uscoveredbonds.html.

5. European Covered Bond Council, www.ecbc.hypo.org. The German Pfandbrief-market is the largest individual bond market in Europe (Mastroeni 2001).

6. Other examples of Landschaften established outside of Prussia were the Ritterschaftliches Kreditinstitut des Fürstentums Lüneburg in Celle (1766/1790), the Hamburgische Landschaft (1782), the Landschaft of Schleswig-Holstein (1811), Mecklenburg (1818 and 1840), Posen (1822), Würtemberg (1825), Calenberg, Grubenhagen and Hildesheim (1825), Bremen und Verden (1826), and the Hannoversche Landes Kreditanstalt (1840) (Frederiksen 1894).

closed down at the end of World War II, others were folded into modern Pfandbrief-issuing banks and some smaller institutions exist to this day.

From today's perspective, the study of Landschaften is relevant for several reasons:

First, as mentioned earlier, Landschaften provide the first institutional example of how safe bonds could be based on land (Frederiksen 1894). They are the only mortgage-lending institutions prior to the emergence of private mortgage banks in the mid-nineteenth century. While mortgage credit had been an important element in European finance since the Middle Ages, previous attempts at issuing mortgage-backed debt, including John Law's "système," failed.[7] The Pfandbriefe of the Landschaften therefore present an example for successful innovation in financial markets.

Second, Landschaften constitute a nonbank financial institution taking on the role of a delegated monitor.[8] In this function, they enrich the understanding of German financial history, which has predominantly been focused on the success of the large universal-style credit banks.[9] Landschaften, as nonbank financial intermediaries, were successful in recapitalizing the impoverished Prussian estates, for whom they provided credit and liquidity.

Third, by connecting the landholding Junker class to the financial market in Berlin, Landschaften enabled Junkers to increase their leverage using their estates, helping to solidify their economic dominance. However, as Landschaften were extended to include farmers and nonnoble landholders in the mid-nineteenth century, they expanded credit access beyond the nobility and eased the transition from serfdom to peasant proprietorship (Frederiksen 1894). Given the size of the market, Pfandbriefe constituted an attractive investment choice for investors.[10] Landschaften thus played an important role in the economic, political, and social development of Prussia and later the German Reich.[11]

This chapter focuses on the first of these aspects—how the Landschaften created a market for covered mortgage bonds. It describes the common operational features of the Landschaften and demonstrates how they served as financial intermediaries. Concentrating on the institutional details, the stability and relative success of the Landschaften can be traced back to their specific design, which helped overcome adverse selection, moral hazard, and auditing and enforcement problems related to lending. The chapter also briefly outlines the role and function of the Landschaften for the Prussian economy. To begin, this chapter describes the economic conditions in

7. Compare Hoffman, Postel-Vinay, and Rosenthal (2011).
8. Compare Stiglitz (1990).
9. For a review of recent developments in research focusing on German financial history compare, for example, Burhop (2006), Guinnane (2002), and Fohlin (2007).
10. For a more recent discussion, refer to Schiller (2003) and Hess (1990).
11. Compare Gerschenkron (1946) for a discussion of the role of the Prussian Junker class for German economics and political development.

Prussia at the time of the creation of the Landschaften. The next section discusses the features of the Landschaften, with special attention to how Landschaften overcame the informational problems related to lending. The fourth section examines their spread and performance by looking at the number of estates that borrowed, the number of Pfandbriefe issued, and their yields. The last section concludes with a discussion for possible future research.

9.2   Economic Conditions in Prussia and the Creation of the Landschaften

Prior to 1848 Prussia was a monarchy, ruled by the king and supported by the bureaucracy and the landed aristocracy—the Junkers. Prussian society was organized by a feudal class system, with the Junkers controlling local affairs through manorial courts and police powers. The Junkers dominated economic activity and have often been portrayed as being preoccupied with the status of agriculture and their estates and showing little interest in furthering industry (Schiller 2003; Hess 1990).

At the end of the Seven Years' War in 1763, Prussia emerged as a political and economic power in central Europe. However, economic conditions were bleak. The war had disrupted trade and economic activity. Areas east of the Elbe River had suffered from military operations and enemy occupation. Farms were neglected and landowners, farmers, and peasants were short on horses, cattle, sheep, fodder, and seed (Henderson 1962). To restore agricultural production, both landowners and farmers were in need of long-term credits at affordable rates.

Before the war, landowners had relied on private credit intermediaries who had offered loans at about 6 percent interest plus 1/2 to 1 percent commission. Traditional sources for loans included family, local merchants, and the Church (Enders 2008, 611). Loans were usually granted up to half of the last sale price of the estate and would often be secured by an entry into the district court's land registry (Mauer 1907, 19). The foundation for the formal use of land as collateral for loans had already been laid with the 1722 Prussian bankruptcy law, which stipulated the publication of liens in the land registry (Jessen 1962, 36). Revisions of the Prussian mortgage laws in 1748 and 1750 established a ranking for the seniority of debt, where secured debt was given the first lien (Weyermann 1910, 64). These legal changes improved creditor rights and facilitated the verification of collateral, setting the stage for lending on security of an estate's land.

During the Seven Years' War, the credit limit had been raised above the traditional threshold of 50 percent of the estate's last sale price, contributing to the high indebtedness of the manors by the end of the war (Mauer 1907, 20). Given this higher leverage, the postwar economic recession triggered a wave of defaults on estate loans.

The agricultural credit crisis coincided with a financial depression and general credit crunch in 1763. At the end of the war, speculative trading activities that had been profitable in wartime collapsed, leading to bank failures, notably of the bank house De Neufville in Amsterdam. The financial crisis was transmitted through bills of exchange from Amsterdam via Hamburg to Berlin, putting pressure on creditors. Distressed creditors started calling in previous estate loans to raise funds. Interest rates rose and available credit was restricted. This put additional pressure on borrowers, especially on those already experiencing financial strain. The credit market began to resemble a lemons market, as described by Akerlof (1970). At rising rates, only the high-risk borrowers that had an immediate need for credit remained in the market. This in turn discouraged liquid creditors from loaning out funds. Shrinking loan supply led to a complete credit collapse. That the drying up of credit was worsened by a lemon's problem and cannot solely be explained by the overall tightness of credit can be seen in the quick recovery of the market after the creation of the Landschaften, which helped match lenders and borrowers and verified collateral.[12] Similarly, some lenders relied on the Landschaft to carry out the estate's assessment but would then negotiate a private credit contract in place of the Landschaft loan (Ucke 1888).

To aid the landholders, King Frederick II had tried to halt the crisis's transmission to Berlin through the refusal of Wechselstrenge (holder in due course) and bailouts. However, both measures only heightened creditors' perception of risk, as the king colluded with the landed nobility, increasing pressure on lenders and worsening the credit crunch (Schnabel and Shin 2004). In 1765, Frederick II passed a three-year general moratorium on principal and interest payments for all outstanding debts, which only alienated creditors further. At the end of the moratorium in 1768 many estates went into foreclosure, and liquidations of estates in which less than half of the outstanding debt could be recovered were common (Weyermann 1910, 66). Land as collateral no longer sufficed to attract individual loans, and creditors shied away from all rural investments.

To illustrate the situation, a 1771 study of estates in the Kur- and Neumark reveals that the average level of indebtedness of the estates was 53 percent of their value, but about 15 percent of estates held debts over 100 percent, and some as high as 200 percent of the estate's value (Pr. Br. Rep 23B, Neumärkische Stände, Nr. 635). In addition, mortgage rates for the safest mortgage loans had climbed to 10 percent and the commission increased to 2 to 3 percent, substantially increasing the cost of credit (Frederiksen 1894).

Landschaften were created in this credit vacuum. The design of the Landschaften was based on a proposal made by a Berlin merchant, Diederich Ernst Bühring, in 1767. Bühring had spent the early years of his career in Amsterdam, trading bills of exchange that were used to finance eco-

---

12. Borchardt (1961) also shows that the lack of credit in Germany was in fact not a problem of supply, but rather of insufficient matching between creditors and debtors.

nomic activities of the Dutch colonies. Growing up in Bremen, he was also acquainted with Bremer "Handfeste-Urkunden," private bearer bonds that were backed with a claim on real estate belonging to the debtor (Jessen 1962, 40–41). Knowledge of these various financial instruments clearly influenced his thinking about mortgage credit, just as other innovations of mortgage securitization had been influenced by existing securities.[13] Bühring's plan combined these types of financial instruments and the creation of a general mortgage institute for Prussia, the "General Landschaftskasse," that would collectively hypothecate all of Prussia's noble estates. This Landschaftskasse would issue bearer bonds at 4 percent and would guarantee the convertibility and punctual payment of interest rates. Estate holders could join this mortgage bank and would pay 4.5 or 5 percent interest on their loans. The interest rate differential would be used for administrative funds and to assemble a reserve fund for emergencies.[14]

Bühring's proposal was presented to King Frederick II in February of 1767, who forwarded it to his minister of finance, Etat-Minister von Hagen. Von Hagen rejected the plan in March of 1767. But in 1768, Johann Heinrich Casimir von Carmer—the new finance minister and minister of justice—proposed a Landschaft for all of Prussia, similar to Bühring's original idea. Von Carmer stipulated that all noble estates would be mandatory members of this new organization. The Landschaft would issue covered bonds up to half the value of all estates and guarantee the interest payments as well as the principal, backing the Pfandbriefe with the joint liability of all member estates. Furthermore, Pfandbriefe should circulate as quasi-money to alleviate the general shortage of credit.

It is uncertain whether Bühring's plan served as the template for von Carmer's proposal. However, since Bühring's ideas laid out the key details, he is often referred to as the conceptual father of the Landschaften (Jessen 1962, 38). In 1777, after the first two Landschaften had already been established, Bühring was officially credited with the original concept of the Landschaften (Jessen 1962, 44).

Based on von Carmer's ideas but organized into regional Landschaften rather than one single institution for all of Prussia, King Frederick II signed a cabinet order to found the first of the Landschaften, the Silesian Landschaft, in August of 1769. In the summer of 1770 the statutes of the Silesian Landschaft were ratified by the general assembly of the Silesian feudal class, and in December of 1770 the first Pfandbriefe were issued (Jessen 1962, 47).

The creation of the Silesian Landschaft took up important elements of Bühring's as well as von Carmer's original plans. As von Carmer had suggested, the noble estates of Silesia were combined in a mandatory credit

13. See Frehen, Rouwenhorst, and Goetzmann on the development of Dutch bonds (chapter 8, this volume).
14. Compare Bühring's original plan, as cited in Maurer (1907, 190–95).

association and would jointly back all Pfandbriefe issued by the Landschaft. The key concept of the Pfandbrief went back to Bühring's original plan, with the Landschaft guaranteeing the interest payments as well as limited convertibility. Lenders could therefore rely on the Landschaft rather than on individual borrowers for their payments. They would purchase standardized Pfandbriefe rather than negotiating private loans with individual borrowers. Lenders also benefitted from reduced transaction costs and an emerging secondary market. The benefit of Landschaft credit for landholders was that it was long term and relatively low cost. Loans could not be called in by the lender, providing additional stability and security for the debtors.

9.3   The Design of the Landschaften and Their Lending Mechanisms

The key features of the Pfandbriefe can be seen in the example of a Pfandbrief issued by the Silesian Landschaft on June 24, 1774, shown in figure 9.1. The picture displays a Pfandbrief over thirty Reichstaler Courant, at fourteen Reichstaler per mark fine silver. It is made out for the estate named "Jaschkowitz" in the district of Tost in Upper Silesia, and it is backed by all combined estates in Upper Silesia. Interest was payable in cash in Cosel or Breslau and the coupons for the biannual interest payments were stamped on the Pfandbrief. Interest payments were payable through 1923 (noted on the back, not shown). In 1929, this Pfandbrief was stamped worthless and exchanged for a new gold Pfandbrief.

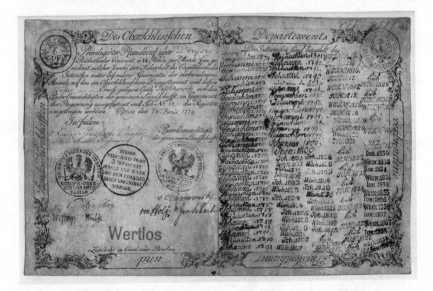

Fig. 9.1   An example of a Pfandbrief
Source: Courtesy of Auktionshaus Tschöpe.

9.3.1   The Design of the Landschaften

To obtain a loan, a landholder and member of the Landschaft would place a request with the Landschaft. The local assessor, who was also a member of the Landschaft, would estimate the value of the estate and determine a credit limit that was either based on the net profit of the estate (Grundsteuerreinertrag) or its last sale price. After the credit was granted, the Pfandbriefe were handed to the estate holder the following Christmas or Johanni (St. John the Baptist's Day, June 24). Estate holders could present these bonds to the Landschaft and ask to be paid in cash after a period of six months. Alternatively, estate holders could sell the bonds directly in the open market. Bonds were initially issued at 4 percent and borrowers had to commit to paying biannual interest payments in cash to the Landschaft, plus an added 1/2 to 1 percent for administrative purposes.[15]

To raise funds, the Landschaft sold Pfandbriefe to creditors, especially urban merchant bankers that were seeking investment opportunities. Pfandbriefe paid 3.5 to 4 percent interest to the lenders and were initially sold at their nominal value. With rising popularity their prices increased so there was an equivalent reduction of 1/4 to 1/2 percent, and it became easier for landholders to sell them directly to investors rather than cashing them in with the Landschaft. Figure 9.2 describes the transaction, assuming that the Landschaft was presented with the Pfandbrief, and figure 9.3 describes how borrowers could sell their Pfandbriefe directly. In both cases the Landschaft remained responsible for coupon payments to the lender and the borrower made regular biannual interest payments to the Landschaft, so that the creditor would always interact with the Landschaft and not have to seek out individual borrowers for payment.

Landschaften reduced transaction costs as they pooled loans and created a uniform debt instrument. They could realize economies of scale and scope by including up to 2,500 borrowers and reaching deeper into the pool of creditors.[16] As the Pfandbriefe were standardized, this offered creditors an emerging secondary market that increased liquidity. Pfandbriefe of the Prussian Landschaften were quoted on the Berlin Bourse and were available to a wide audience of investors.

9.3.2 Adverse Selection

Adverse selection is an ex ante informational problem where under certain conditions only borrowers that are a poor credit risk will be attracted into a market. In response, lenders will not be willing to supply capital to this

---

15. Here, the 4 percent interest rate was adjusted later to 3.5 percent, then raised again. Over their lifespan, most Landschaften created different issues of bonds, all priced between 3.5 percent and 5 percent.

16. By the early twentieth century, the East Prussian Landschaft had included over 15,000 Pfandbrief-issuing estates.

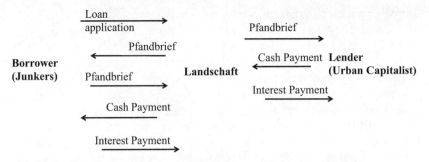

Fig. 9.2   Borrowing intermediated by the Landschaft–version 1

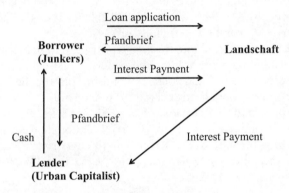

Fig. 9.3   Borrowing intermediated by the Landschaft–version 2

pool of "lemons." As described in section 9.2, this corresponds to the period following the Seven Years' War and the credit crisis of 1763. To overcome adverse selection, the old Landschaften, except for the Landschaft of the Kur- und Neumarkt, automatically included all noble estates situated within the Landschaft's geographic region.[17] This gave all estates, even Junkers in dire circumstances, equal access to credit at fixed interest rates. Since all estates that were part of the Landschaft had joint liability, landowners had an incentive to actively participate in the management of the Landschaft, improving its quality and thereby increasing the supply of credit.

In exchange for the compulsory membership, all members of the Land-schaften held a "right to credit" so the Landschaft could not discriminate against individual estates. Therefore, a key to prevent adverse selection was

17. Landschaften were built on the history of earlier financial functions of Prussian feudal organizations, which had provided banking services to its members. Most of these old credit banks had been shut down by a decree of the king in 1717. Only the "Kreditwerk der Chur-märkischen Landschaft" survived as the last of these old credit banks. It functioned as the credit institute for the Prussian upper class and remained in operation until 1820, issuing bonds that were traded on the exchanges of Berlin and Vienna (Jessen, 1962, 48).

the determination of the credit limit and the correct assessment of the estate to guarantee collateral. The assessment of the member estates prior to granting a loan followed two different procedures. Starting from the last sale price of the estate, the landholder could obtain a loan up to one quarter, one third, or one half of this price, depending on when the sale had taken place. Alternatively, the net profit of the estate (Grundsteuerreinertrag) was assessed by a tax commissioner, and the estate holder could then obtain a loan of fifteen to twenty times the assessed amount (Altrock 1914, 25).[18] Though in practice, the majority of the loans were based on previous sale prices, extending loans based on the net profit guaranteed that the cash flow of the estate would be sufficient to cover the interest payments on the loan, regardless of the value of the estate. To ensure a conservative assessment, the assessor could even be held personally liable for losses in the case of a too generous assessment (Weyermann 1910, 86).

Pfandbriefe were entered into the land registry and took precedence over all other outstanding debt, holding the preferred first debtor position. In cases where existing debt could not be extinguished prior to the Landschaft's loan, the amount of capitalized debt was subtracted from the maximum loan value. But often landholders could exchange Pfandbriefe for existing debt up to the credit limit (Altrock 1914, 60–61). Pfandbriefe were also used to service standing obligations such as rent payments or payments resulting from inheritance or estate settlements (Ritterschaftliche Haupt Direktion, Rep 23A Kurmärkische Stände).

9.3.3   Moral Hazard

Moral hazard constitutes an interim problem in the lending process in which borrowers that have received funds engage in risky behavior; for example, choosing a more risky investment project. Moral hazard can be avoided through improved incentives and monitoring. Moral hazard is also reduced when borrowers have to put up significant collateral. Without microdata on individual loans, it is hard to verify to what extent moral hazard presented a problem for the Landschaften. Generally, funds are described as being put to productive use, such as for the purchase of new agricultural machinery or construction or renovation of houses and barns on the estates. A case study of the East Prussian Landschaften finds limited evidence for moral hazard on the part of large landholders (Wandschneider 2013).

Moral hazard may not have been fully eliminated as some landholders used the proceeds of the Landschaften loans to buy additional land, which could then be mortgaged. Contemporaries worried that the Landschaften set off a speculative boom in real estate. Changes in ownership of estates were frequent between 1780 and 1806 and the noble estates were consolidated in the 1780s and 1790s (Mauer 1907, 21). In 1789 the king passed a law for

---

18. The same net profit measure was also used to determine tax liability of individual estates.

Silesia that limited the extent at which new estates could be purchased with Pfandbriefe. However, this law was difficult to enforce and was abolished in 1791. While the Landschaften failed to set up an effective mechanism to eliminate the speculative use of their funds, the practice appears to have been limited. Wandschneider (2013) finds little systematic estate enlargement for East Prussia between the years 1806 to 1834.

The key mechanism for Landschaften to address moral hazard was collateral and the principle of joint unlimited liability. Issuing the Pfandbrief, two legal obligations were incurred, which mirror the dual recourse feature of today's Pfandbriefe (Mauer 1907, 3–4). First, the owner of the Pfandbrief held a claim against the estate to which the Pfandbrief was tied. This claim was against the land on which the estate was situated, not against any private property or assets of the owner. Second, the Pfandbrief constituted a claim against the Landschaft, meaning that the Pfandbrief was backed by all liquid assets of the Landschaft as well as all land of the member estates of the Landschaft, whether they had borrowed money or not. This dual recourse can also clearly be seen on the Pfandbrief example, shown in figure 9.1.

The joint liability feature of the Pfandbrief resembles group-lending contracts used in modern microfinance groups, as well as the design of the credit cooperatives founded in mid-nineteenth-century Germany by Friedrich Raiffeisen and Hermann Schulze-Delitzsch.[19] While joint liability appears to have never been called on in practice, suggesting that there were adequate reserves, it served as an important signal of the safety of investing in a Pfandbrief, at least in the early years of the Landschaften's existence. It also increased the incentive for neighbors to monitor each other (Hagedorn 1978, 58). Since Landschaften were relatively large institutions, local monitoring was not always easy. But all members of the Landschaft belonged to the same social class, making the group fairly homogeneous and conscious of social stigma. Moreover, Landschaften built on the existing political and social order, continuing and often replacing the organization of the "Stände," which had historically ensured representation of the nobles. This reinforced the relationship between the Landschaft and the preexisting social structure. One more important feature was the fact that the Landschaften were subdivided in smaller regional groups for administrative purposes. For example, the Landschaft for East Prussia was split into three administrative regions (Angerburg, Königsberg, and Mohrungen), each of which again was divided into three to five districts.[20] These smaller administrative units reinforced monitoring, as the joint liability first covered the district, then the

19. A detailed discussion of the Raiffeisen credit cooperatives can be found in Guinnane (2001, 2002).

20. The Prussian administrative units of "Department" and "Kreis" are frequently translated as administrative district and county, respectively. Eddie (2008) argues that the terms administrative region for Department and district for Kreis are more accurate representations. Also, the Landschafts Departments and Kreise do not exactly follow the administrative units.

administrative region, and finally the Landschaft as a whole. This structured monitoring gave the Landschaften an advantage over private lenders.

9.3.4   Auditing and Enforcement

To help with auditing and enforcement, Landschaften relied heavily on local expertise and used local officers to inspect the estates and set the maximum loan amount.[21] Landschaften were self-governed, with elected officials coming from the membership of estate holders. Landschaften were managed by the "General-Landschaftsdirektion" (board of directors), headed by the Generallandschaftsdirektor (general director), elected for six years. Next to the director worked a corporate counsel, who had judicial powers to carry out foreclosure of delinquent estates. In addition, three "Generallandschaftsräte" with full voting rights were part of the board of directors. These had to be estate holders in the Landschaft and be fully employed in agriculture. In contrast to the director and the counsel, which were employed by the Landschaft, all other positions had no compensation. By relying on voluntary labor, Landschaften kept administrative costs to a minimum and reinforced the role of Landschaften members as stakeholders of the institution.

The board of directors carried out the important decision making and the day-to-day operations of the Landschaft. Members of the directorship were elected by a supervisory board called "Landschaftsausschuss," that represented the membership of the Landschaft. It included twenty to twenty-five members, and met at least once a year to supervise the activities of the board of directors (Jessen 1962, 119). Over time Landschaften supplemented the Landschaftsdirektion with additional tax and accounting committees that assisted with assessing the estates and supervising financial matters.

To strengthen their enforcement mechanism and provide a tool to address defaulting estate holders, Landschaften had the right to directly foreclose on estates whose payments were in arrears. The foreclosure process provided a credible threat, even if it was infrequently used. Due to the relatively conservative valuations for estates, Landschaften were usually able to recover the amount of the outstanding loan by selling the property (Wandschneider 2013).

9.3.5   Additional Measures

Additional mechanisms, which boosted the safety of the bonds issued by the Landschaften, were the accumulation of reserve funds, and over time, the introduction of amortization schedules. In addition to the land provided as collateral for the Pfandbriefe, Landschaften built reserve funds that were used

---

21. Landschaften refrained from valuing livestock early on, as it was found that livestock was difficult to value and estate owners sometimes "borrowed" livestock when an assessment was forthcoming (Frederiksen 1894).

to cover unexpected operating costs or losses. Over time, all Landschaften built sizable reserve funds; however, these assets were only used for emergencies and not to issue credit. The capital accumulated by the Landschaften resulted from the interest differential paid by the borrowers, as well as capital injected by the crown. For the Silesian Landschaft, for example, King Frederick II provided initial capital in the form of a loan of 200,000 Talers at 2 percent interest (Frederiksen 1894). However, not all Landschaften received this form of direct assistance. Moreover, the Landschaften did not depend on these loans for their day-to-day operations, but only counted on official support in times of crisis. The close relationship between the king and the Landschaften thus added an extra layer of security. It also served as a form of "bail-in" by the king who had an interest in supporting the Junkers. This support for the Landschaft also benefitted the creditors.

Landschaften varied to the extent to which the borrowers had to amortize their existing debt. While the Landschaften originally paid out the principal of the loans to the borrowers on demand, the individual borrowers were only obliged to make regular interest payments to the Landschaft and the "old" Landschaften did not carry provisions for how the existing debt should be retired. Only over time did Landschaften introduce obligatory amortization schedules (Frederiksen 1894). Between 1770 and 1777 borrowers could opt to retire their debt through Pfandbrief repurchases as well as cash payments to the Landschaft. In 1777 the bylaws of the Silesian Landschaft stipulated that debts could only be extinguished with Pfandbriefe having similar interest schedules. After 1785, cash payments were permitted again. The lack of amortization was seen as a structural weakness of the Landschaften since extinguishing outstanding debt was cumbersome. In the design of the subsequent Landschaften, in Posen in 1818, for example, provisions to pay off the debt were included from the start (Mauer 1907, 168). For the "old" Landschaften, however, estate holders resisted amortization, especially during the agrarian crisis of the 1820s. But as economic conditions improved, the West and the East Prussian Landschaften began creating amortization funds to extinguish some of the existing Pfandbriefe. In 1832, the East Prussian Landschaft even raised the interest payments for the estate holders by 1/6 percent (Mauer 1907, 169). But in practice, these funds were nothing but expanded reserve funds for the Landschaft as they were never used to pay off the principal. Mandatory amortization by the estate holders was only introduced in the 1920s (Jessen 1962, 78).

9.4   Empirical Evidence

The following section presents empirical evidence on Landschaften membership, the number of loans and Pfandbrief yields that is consistent with the previous description of the credit market, and highlights the importance of the institutional features of the Landschaften.

Data are scarce and often inconsistent, but they show that the Landschaften were successful in providing credit to the Prussian nobility. Contemporaries describe the Landschaften as averting liquidations of Junker estates and stabilizing economic conditions. For example, Frederiksen (1894) mentions that King Frederick II claimed in his memoirs that the Silesian Landschaft saved 400 of the best families in the province from ruin. The Landschaften lowered the cost of credit for agricultural estates from about 8 percent before the Seven Years' War to below 5 percent, and Pfandbriefe circulated widely soon after their issue. In Silesia interest rates in 1770 had been 6, 8, and 10 percent, while rates averaged 4.66 percent in 1777 and 4 percent in 1787 (Jessen 1962, 67). Homer and Sylla (1996, 258) show that interest rates in Prussia throughout the nineteenth century were consistently lower than in neighboring regions.

Pfandbriefe were deemed extremely safe investment choices, often at par with government securities. They also increased the value of the estates that could be used as collateral and brought a stabilization of and eventual rise in the price of land. In 1770 the value of all noble estates in Silesia was estimated to be sixty million Reichstaler, which were indebted for twenty-two million Reichstaler. By 1790, the value of the estates had doubled and Pfandbriefe valued at fifteen million Reichstaler were in circulation (Jessen 1962, 68).

The number of estates that borrowed through the system of the Landschaften (figure 9.4) rose steeply, especially from the mid-nineteenth century onward, and the totals for the Pfandbriefe increased (figure 9.5), emphasizing their popularity in financial markets. Pfandbriefe were also purchased by foreign investors, and the government worried about interest payments paid to foreigners and tried to curb foreign sales (Franz 1902, 26).

The steep rise in the number of estates for the Silesian and East Prussian Landschaften and the rising amount of Pfandbriefe issued corresponded to the changes in regulations of the Landschaften. Over time, they expanded to include smaller estates and farms. For example, in 1808 the East Prussian Landschaft decided to include nonnoble estates that belonged to the Köllmer, a group of free farmers. Beginning in 1849, the East Prussian Landschaft included all estates of a minimum tax value of 1,500 marks (Altrock 1914, 108). But the effect of the Landschaften for these smaller farms remained limited, as more large estates took advantage of the Landschaft credit than smaller ones. In the second half of the nineteenth century the system of Landschaften expanded not just in terms of members but also in terms of financial services offered. Many Landschaften added Darlehnskassen (savings and loan associations) and insurance companies (mostly fire and life insurance). In 1860, for example, the East Prussian Landschaft added the Landschaftliche Darlehnskasse to encourage savings by its members.

The central organization also expanded over time. Similar to the central organizations of the Raiffeisen credit cooperatives, a Central-Landschaft

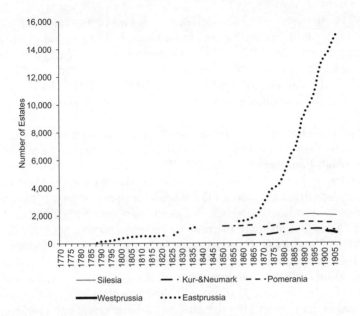

Fig. 9.4　Number of estates that issued Pfandbriefe

Sources: Hecht (1908), Kur- und Neumärkisches Landschaftliches Kreditinstitut: Tableau der mit Pfandbriefen belegten Domänen (1817), and Brämer (1867).

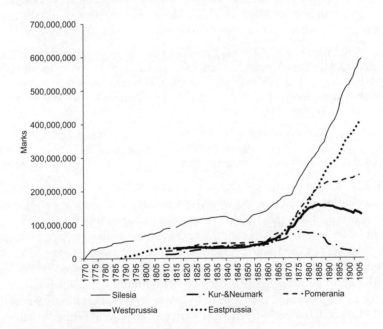

Fig. 9.5　Pfandbriefe outstanding (in marks)

Sources: Hecht (1908) and 125 Jahre Ostpreussische Landschaft (1913).

for all Prussian states was founded in 1873.[22] This central organization was a cooperation of twelve regional Landschaften. The Central-Landschaft issued unified Central-Pfandbriefe, which were thought to be more appealing to a wider group of buyers. However, since the individual Landschaften still issued their own Pfandbriefe alongside the Central-Pfandbriefe, the Central-Landschaft's success remained below expectations (Jessen 1962, 92).

In practice, Landschaften issued two different kinds of Pfandbriefe. First, "Capitalsbriefe" (capital bonds), which constituted 90 percent of the total share of all Pfandbiefe and second, "Realisationsbriefe" (realized bonds, 10 percent of the total). Realisationsbriefe could be exchanged on demand at the Landschaft into Prussian Taler. They were issued in smaller denominations of 20–100 Talers, while Capitalsbriefe were denominated up to 10,000 Talers. For Capitalsbriefe there was a six-month exchange period, after which the Pfandbriefe could be cashed in by the estate owner (Jessen 1962, 72). The Landschaft thus needed to hold reserves in the amount of all issued Realisationsbriefe. At an exchange rate of fourteen Talers to a mark of fine silver, Pfandbriefe were directly tied to the monetary base, but backed by land rather than specie. They helped expand the money supply similar to the early eighteenth-century US land banks, which had issued bank notes tied to mortgages (Thayer 1953). Often borrowers could pay obligations directly with the acquired Pfandbriefe, without cashing them in at the Landschaft.

Zöllner writes in his "Letters about Silesia" in 1793, describing the function of the Pfandbriefe as quasi-money:

> Und im Grunde war es für die Provinz so gut, as wenn 14 Millionen Taler bares Geld in dieselbe gekommen wäre, weil diese Summe in Pfandbriefen vorhanden war, deren man sich zu allen Zahlungen eben so sicher und mit noch grösserer Bequemlichkeit als der Klingenden Münze bedienen konnte. (Zöllner 1793, 399)

> In effect, it was as if fourteen million Taler in cash had entered the province, as this sum was available in Pfandbriefe, which could be used for all payments with the same security and even greater convenience as coins.

Figure 9.6 shows the development of Pfandbrief yields for the five old Landschaften in comparison with the 4 percent Prussian sovereign bond. The movements of these yields reflect the major economic and political events of Prussia at the time, but their peacetime overall stability also speaks to the success of the Landschaften. As can be seen from the graph, Pfandbriefe frequently traded at par with or above the Prussian state bonds.

All Landschaften initially issued 4 percent Pfandbriefe, which were converted to 3.5 percent in the 1830s to follow general market trends. From the 1830s forward, Landschaften issued a broader selection of Pfandbriefe with

---

22. Compare Guinnane (1997) on the Raiffeisen centrals.

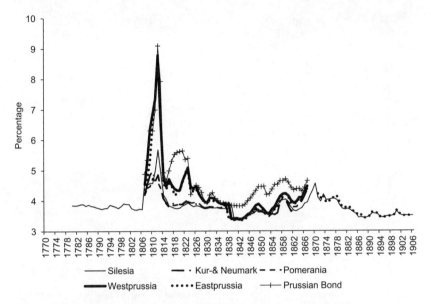

Fig. 9.6   Maximum yields of Pfandbriefe for the five old Landschaften and the Prussian 4 percent government bond

Sources: Hecht (1908) and Meitzen (1868).

varying interest rates (3.5 percent to 5 percent) to compete with changing conditions in the credit markets.

The yields of the Silesian Landschaft remained below 4 percent from the outset and were stable until the beginning of the Napoleonic Wars, when the yields of all Landschaften spiked. The wars halted agricultural productivity in Prussia. They also burdened East Prussia with approximately 260 million marks in wartime costs (Altrock 1914, 110). In response, Landschaften members were granted extensions on their interest payments between 1807 and 1818 (Ristau 1992). Also, after 1807, both the Silesian Landschaft and the East Prussian Landschaft incorporated territories of the Prussian state (Domänen) as member estates. This allowed the Prussian state to request Pfandbriefe backed by these territories and raise funds to pay off war debts. Both the Silesian and East Prussian Landschaften were used to increase the state's capacity to borrow, and the debt with the Landschaft was not amortized until 1900. However, other Landschaften refused to accept state territories as members, thus assuring their independence from the Prussian state (Jessen 1962, 74).

The years 1807 to 1815 were years of agricultural reform for Prussia. Following the proposals by Karl August von Hardenberg and Heinrich Friedrich Karl Freiherr von Stein, the old feudal system was abolished and farmers were liberated (Jessen 1962, 84). As part of the reforms, noble estate

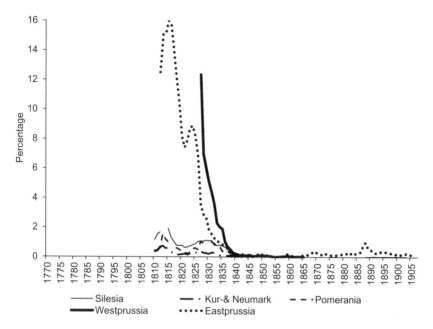

Fig. 9.7 **Interest payments in arrears as share of the total Pfandbrief volume**
Source: Hecht (1908).

holders were compensated for the loss of agricultural labor with part of the land that had belonged to farmers. The effect of these reforms on the value of the estates and on the value of the Pfandbriefe was unclear at first. The loss of workers reduced the productivity of the estates, but the additional land could be used as collateral for the issue of new Pfandbriefe (Mauer 1907, 52).

The Pfandbrief yields for all five Landschaften recovered with the end of the Napoleonic Wars, with the exception of spikes for East and West Prussia in the early 1820s, which were related to the agricultural crisis and the loss of British grain exports. They remained stable until the 1848 revolution. Beginning the in 1840s, the Landschaften struggled to attract capital due to competition from the demands from industry, especially railroads and mining, for credit (Altrock 1914, 113). Frequent Pfandbrief conversions also lowered their popularity in the 1860s. However, prices steadily recovered again after the German unification of 1871, trading close to par in the 1880s and 1890s.

Another measure for the stability of the Landschaften are data on interest arrears that the Landschaften accumulated as distressed borrowers failed to make regular payments (figure 9.7). The outstanding interest arrears mirror the changes in the yields. Arrears are generally low for the period after the 1830s, speaking to the Landschaften's stability and their overall successful monitoring of loans. Arrears spiked, especially for the Landschaft of East

Prussia, in the years before 1815 because the Crown ordered a suspension of payments during the war. They rose again, predominantly for East and West Prussia, during the early 1820s, mirroring other yields and reflecting the agricultural crisis that affected the estates (Ucke 1888).

With rising interest arrears, Landschaften made use of their right to take estates with nonperforming loans into receivership and ultimately foreclose on them to recover the outstanding loan amounts. Systematic data on estates in receivership and foreclosures are lacking, but for the time period 1806 to 1829 the Acta of the Königliche Oberpräsident of Prussia (XX.HA Hist. StA, Königsberg, Titel 22, Nr 46) list a total of 257 foreclosure sales in East Prussia (Wandschneider 2013). Data on West Prussia for the period after 1870 shows that Landschaften used this enforcement mechanism and foreclosed on two to twenty-three estates every year after 1870 (Hecht 1908). The seizure of estates was no empty threat and speaks to the effective design of the Landschaften to address moral hazard.

9.5   Conclusion

Landschaften were public nonprofit institutions that issued covered bonds, establishing the mortgage market in Prussia, beginning in the second half of the eighteenth century. They were effective in providing credit to Prussian noble estates. By demonstrating how bonds could be safely backed with land, they served as an early predecessor for credit cooperatives as well as private mortgage banks. They proved extremely durable, establishing an asset class of mortgage-backed securities—Pfandbriefe—that has remained popular to this day.

Landschaften assumed an important financial intermediary function by connecting the landholding but cash-poor Junker class with credit sources in Berlin. Landschaften reduced transaction costs for lenders and borrowers and relied on dual recourse, joint liability, local monitoring, and forced membership to avoid problems of moral hazard and adverse selection. They cooperated with the Crown, with some Landschaften mortgaging Crown lands, directly supporting government finances. Through the Landschaften, Junkers could easily take on large amounts of debt that were available long-term at comparatively cheap rates. The creation of a standardized debt instrument created a growing secondary market that increased the liquidity of mortgage loans. Issued in various denominations, Pfandbriefe circulated as cash equivalents.

Then as now, the value of the Pfandbriefe was anchored by their one-to-one correspondence to an underlying asset, which was guaranteed by the institution of the Landschaften. The dual recourse feature, which gave bondholders the double security of the underlying asset and the guarantee of the Landschaft, remains the key feature of Pfandbriefe today. The historical example highlights successful financial innovation, but also shows which institutional features made covered bonds successful. Future research to investigate the details of the loan portfolios of individual Landschaften will provide additional evidence and quantify the effects of the Landschaften on the economic and political development of Prussia.

References

Akerlof, George. 1970. "The Market for 'Lemons': Quality Uncertainty and the Market Mechanism." *Quarterly Journal of Economics* 84 (3): 488–500.
Altrock, Walther v. 1914. *Der Landwirtschaftliche Kredit in Preussen, I. Die Ostpreussische Landschaft.* Berlin: Verlagsbuchhandlung Paul Parey.
Borchardt, Knut. 1961. "Zur Frage des Kapitalmangels in der ersten Hälfte des 19. Jahrhunderts in Deutschland." *Jahrbücher für Nationalökonomie und Statistik* 173:401–21.
Brämer, H. 1867. "Grundkreditinstitute in Preussen." *Zeitschrift des Statistischen Bureaus* VII:216.
Burhop, Carsten. 2006. "Did Banks Cause the German Industrialization?" *Explorations in Economic History* 43:39–63.
Eddie, Scott M. 2008. *Landownership in Eastern Germany before the Great War, a Quantitative Analysis.* New York: Oxford University Press.
Enders, Lieselott. 2008. *Die Uckermark: Geschichte einer kurmaerkischen Landschaft vom 12. bis zum 18. Jahrhundert.* Veroeffentlichungen des Brandenburgischen Landeshauptarchivs. Berlin: Berliner Wissenschafts-Verlag.
Fohlin, Caroline. 2007. *Finance Capitalism and Germany's Rise to Industrial Power.* Cambridge: Cambridge University Press.
Franz, Robert. 1902. *Die landschaftlichen Kreditinstitute in Preussen, ihre rechtlichen und finanziellen Verhältnisse und ihre geschichtliche Entwicklung.* Berlin: Verlag F Schneider & Co.
Frederiksen, D. M. 1894. "Mortgage Banking in Germany," *Quarterly Journal of Economics* 9 (1): 47–76.
Gerschenkron, Alexander. 1946. *Bread and Democracy in Germany.* Ithaca: Cornell University Press. (1989).
Guinnane, Timothy. 1997. "Regional Organizations in the German Cooperative Banking System in the late 19th Century." *Research in Economics* 51:251–74.
———. 2001. "Cooperatives as Information Machines: German Rural Credit Cooperatives, 1883–1914." *Journal of Economic History* 61 (2): 366–89.
———. 2002. "Delegated Monitors, Large and Small: Germany's Banking System, 1800–1914." *Journal of Economic Literature* 40 (1): 73–124.
Hagedorn, Fred. 1978. *Die Landschaften, eine rechtsgeschichtliche Darstellung der preussischen Agrarkreditinstitute.* Inaugural Dissertation, Freiburg, Germany.
Hecht, F. 1908. *Die Organisation des Bodenkredits in Deutschland.* Dritte Abteilung, Erster Band. Leipzig: von Duncker & Humboldt.
Henderson, W. O. 1962. "The Berlin Commercial Crisis of 1763." *Economic History Review*, New Series 15 (1): 89–102.
Hess, Klaus. 1990. *Junker und Bürgerliche Grossgrundbesitzer im Kaiserreich: Landwirtschaftlicher Grossbetrieb, Grossgrundbesitz und Familienfideikomiss in Preussen.* Historische Forschungen. Stuttgart: Steiner.
Hoffman, Philip, Gilles Postel-Vinay, and Jean-Laurent Rosenthal. 2011. "History,

Geography, and the Markets for Mortgage Loans in Nineteenth-Century France." In *Understanding Long-Run Economic Growth: Geography, Institutions and the Knowledge Economy,* edited by Dora Costa and Naomi Lamoreaux. Chicago: University of Chicago Press.

Homer S., and R. Sylla. 1996. *A History of Interest Rates.* New Brunswick: Rutgers University Press.

Jessen, Hartwig. 1962. *Das Landschaftliche Kreditwesen.* Wiesbaden: Gabler.

Mastroeni, O. 2001. "Pfandbrief-style Products in Europe." BIS papers (5). Basel: Bank of International Settlements.

Mauer, Hermann. 1907. *Das Landschaftliche Kreditwesen Preussens, Agrargeschichtlich und Volkswirtschaftlich Betrachtet.* Strassburg: Verlag Karl J. Trübner.

Meitzen, August. 1868. *Der Boden und die Landwirthschaftlichen Verhältnisse des Preussischen Staates.* Prussia, Finanzministerium, Ministerium für Landwirtschaft, Domänen und Forsten. Berlin: Wiegandt und Hempel.

Ostpreussische Landschaft. 1913. *125 Jahre Ostpreussische Landschaft.* Königsberg.

Packer, Frank, Ryan Stever, and Christian Upper. 2007. "The Covered Bond Market." *BIS Quarterly Review,* September.

Ristau, Bernd. 1992. "Adelige Interessenpolitik in Konjunktur und Krise. Ein Beitrag zur Geschichte der landschaftlichen Kreditkasse Ostpreussens 1788–1835." In *Denkhorizonte und Handlungsspielräume: Historische Studien für Rudolf Vierhaus zum 70. Geburtstag,* edited by Rudolf Vierhaus. Göttingen: Wallstein Verlag.

Schiller, Rene. 2003. *Vom Rittergut zum Grossgrundbesitz: Ökonomische und Soziale Transformationsprozesse der ländlichen Eliten in Brandenburg im 19. Jahrhundert.* Berlin: Akademie Verlag.

Schnabel, Isabel, and Hyun Song Shin. 2004. "Liquidity and Contagion: The Crisis of 1763." *Journal of the European Economic Association* 2 (6): 929–68.

Stiglitz, Joseph E. 1990. "Peer Monitoring in Credit Markets." *World Bank Economic Review* IV:351–66.

Thayer, Theodore. 1953. "The Land-Bank System in the American Colonies." *Journal of Economic History* 13 (2): 145–59.

Ucke, Arnold. 1888. *Die Agrarkrisis in Preussen während der zwanziger Jahre dieses Jahrhunderts.* Halle: Max Niemeyer.

Wandschneider, Kirsten. 2013. "Landschaften as Credit Purveyors—The Example of East Prussia." Working Paper, Occidental College.

Weyermann, Moritz. 1910. *Zur Geschichte des Immobiliarkreditwesens in Preussen mit besonderer Nutzanwendung auf die Theorie der Bodenverschuldung.* Karlsruhe: Braunsche Hofbuchdruckerei und Verlag.

Zöllner, Johann Friedrich. 1793. *Briefe über Schlesien.* Berlin: Maurer.

Archival Sources

Brandeburgisches Landes Hauptarchiv, Potsdam

Pr. Br. Rep 23B, Neumärkische Stände, Nr. 635.
Ritterschaftliche Haupt Direktion, Rep 23A Kurmärkische Stände
Tableau der mit Pfandbriefen belegten Domänen (1817). Staatsarchiv Potsdam, Pr. Br. Rep 23A Kurmärkische Stände C 2919.

Geheimes Staatsarchiv Preussischer Kulturbesitz, Berlin Dahlem

XX.HA, Hist. StA Königsberg, Rep 2 Oberpräsident der Provinz Ostpreussen I, Titel 22, Nr 46.

IV

Postwar Housing Policies

The Twentieth-Century Increase in US Home Ownership
Facts and Hypotheses

Daniel K. Fetter

10.1 Introduction

The boom and bust in home ownership in the United States since the mid-1990s has recently revived interest in understanding the much larger increase in home ownership that occurred in the mid-twentieth century. Between 1940 and 1960, the share of households owning their own homes rose from 44 to 62 percent, and home ownership has remained high ever since. A growing literature has explored the causes behind the midcentury increase, but much remains to be explored.

In this chapter I use a variety of data sources to document several facts that potential explanations for the midcentury rise in home ownership should aim to match. The major period of increase was between 1940 and 1960, although the aggregate time series suggests that the Depression interrupted a steady increase in nonfarm home ownership that had begun decades earlier. Home ownership increased in every region of the country and in both rural and urban areas, but urban areas accounted for a larger share of the increase. In part, home ownership displaced renting, but equally important was a shift in household formation, as the young left home earlier in life. Finally, a key characteristic of the 1940 to 1960 period was a transformation in the

Daniel K. Fetter is assistant professor of economics at Wellesley College and a faculty research fellow of the National Bureau of Economic Research.

For helpful comments I am especially grateful to Claudia Goldin, Heidi Williams, and to each of the three editors. I gratefully acknowledge financial support from the Taubman Center for State and Local Government at the Harvard Kennedy School, the Real Estate Academic Initiative at Harvard University, and the Harvard Graduate School of Arts and Sciences. All errors are my own. For acknowledgments, sources of research support, and disclosure of the author's material financial relationships, if any, please see http://www.nber.org/chapters/c12801.ack.

age structure of home ownership: the young became owners at dramatically higher rates, as entry into home ownership shifted earlier in life.

After a discussion of these facts, I discuss the evidence on some of the leading hypotheses for the causes of the 1940 to 1960 rise in home ownership. Among these hypotheses are rising real incomes, the importance of the favorable tax treatment of owner-occupied housing as marginal tax rates increased in the 1940s, and the development of the modern mortgage finance system. Based on the evidence we have, no single factor seems to have had a direct effect sufficiently large to explain the aggregate increase by itself.

10.2   Some Basic Facts

I divide the discussion into two parts, according to how home ownership is measured. The conventional measure of home ownership is at the level of the household, or dwelling unit.[1] This measure represents the share of occupied dwelling units that are owner occupied (or the share of households that are owner-occupiers). This is the measure of home ownership for which the most extensive data exist, and is convenient for discussing the timing and geography of the increase in home ownership. It is also likely to be the more relevant measure for certain types of questions. For example, to the extent that the effort undertaken by the resident to maintain a dwelling depends on whether the resident owns or rents it (Glaeser and Shapiro 2003), one may wish to observe the tenure status of a dwelling rather than of an individual in order to answer questions about the rate of depreciation of an area's housing stock.

It is often more natural, however, to think of home ownership at the level of an individual rather than at the level of the household or dwelling. For example, a society in which most children lived with their parents until middle age, and then purchased a house of their own, would have a high share of owner-occupied dwellings. But one might reasonably wish to account for the fact that few young adults live in a home that they own themselves.[2] As will be evident, focusing solely on the dwelling-level measure of home ownership is particularly problematic for studying the 1940 to 1960 period given the dramatic transformation in household formation over the period. Unfortunately, data to measure home ownership at an individual level are scarce

1. Prior to the 1940 census, tenure was measured at the level of the census "family"; in 1940 and afterward it was measured at the level of the census "household." "Dwelling units" corresponded to households; in the 1940 census, for example, a dwelling unit was defined as the living quarters intended for occupancy by one household (US Bureau of the Census 1943).

2. Haurin and Rosenthal (2007) stressed the importance of considering household formation in interpreting home ownership rates in modern data. In his study of home ownership over the 1940–1960 period, Chevan (1989) used a definition of home ownership similar to the individual-level measure I use.

Rate of owner-occupancy for farm and nonfarm, 1890–2011

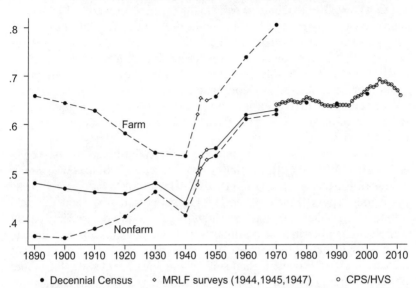

Fig. 10.1   Rate of owner occupancy, 1890–2011
Sources: Decennial census, Housing Vacancy Survey, and US Bureau of the Census (1945, 1946, 1947b).
Note: Figure shows share of occupied dwelling units that are owner occupied.

relative to data available to measure home ownership at the household level. In the second part of this section, I illustrate several facts about the 1940 to 1960 increase based on an individual-level measure of home ownership.

10.2.1   Home Ownership at the Household/Dwelling Unit Level

National Time Series

The pattern of the standard measure of home ownership—the share of occupied dwelling units that are owner occupied—is shown in figure 10.1. Decennial numbers are from the published volumes of the decennial census; annual figures for the overall rate from 1970 to 2011 are from the Housing Vacancy Survey.[3] Less well known are the figures for 1944, 1945, and 1947. These are estimates from supplements to the October 1944, November 1945, and April 1947 sample surveys for the monthly report on the labor force (US Bureau of the Census 1945, 1946, 1947b).

From 1890 to 1920, the overall home ownership rate declined slowly as

3. http://www.census.gov/hhes/www/housing/hvs/hvs.html.

both farm home ownership rates declined and the relative share of nonfarm housing grew. Overall, home ownership saw an increase over the 1920s and a sharp downturn over the 1930s before the dramatic shift from 44 to 62 percent between 1940 and 1960. Over the 1940 to 1960 period the steady prewar decline in farm home ownership was reversed; nonfarm home ownership had been increasing steadily when it was interrupted by the downturn of the 1930s. For understanding the long-run change in home ownership, based on the aggregate numbers it is likely that there was some commonality in the drivers of the increases in nonfarm home ownership in the pre-1930 and post-1940 periods.

Given the emphasis in the modern literature on the drivers of home ownership after World War II, the timing of the increase in home ownership is noteworthy in that the years from 1940 to 1945 saw the home ownership rate reach and surpass its earlier level. This fact complicates the frequently held notion of the increase in home ownership over this period as being a postwar phenomenon, associated primarily with new construction in suburban areas. With new construction severely curtailed during the war, much of the increase must have come from a shift of previously rented dwellings into owner occupancy. Indeed, a special tabulation of the 1950 census suggested that approximately three million units that were owner occupied in 1950 had been renter occupied in 1940 (US Bureau of the Census 1953).

In large part this rapid rise in home ownership in the early 1940s was likely related to the decrease in home ownership over the 1930s to a particularly low level in 1940. As Rose emphasizes in this volume (chapter 7), at the end of the 1930s many foreclosed properties were held by institutional lenders that wished to sell them. Fishback and Kollmann, also in this volume (chapter 6), provide evidence that house prices in 1940 were low relative to their 1930 levels. Yet the low level of home ownership in 1940 is unlikely to be the sole explanation for the rapid rise over the early 1940s. Ratcliff (1944), for example, suggested that many foreclosed homes had already been resold for owner occupancy by the time of the 1940 census. He estimated that on net, only about 600,000 to 700,000 dwelling units shifted from owner to renter occupancy between 1930 and 1940 as a result of foreclosure.[4] Many of these properties may have been held by institutions or individuals with little desire to be landlords, who would have supplied them elastically for

---

4. In particular, Ratcliff calculates the increase in the number of tenant units between 1930 and 1940, after adjustment for reclassification and demolitions, as 4,202,737. Of these, he estimates that 546,000 were units in new multifamily structures; 967,400 were new single-family units built for or shifted to tenant occupancy; 725,000 were added through conversion of existing structures to create additional units; 345,000 additional units were provided without structural alterations; and 722,300 units were vacant in 1930 but occupied by tenant households in 1940. This leaves a residual of 897,037 to be accounted for by a shift to tenant occupancy through voluntary abandonment, family dissolution, or foreclosure. He estimates that 200,000 to 300,000 were due to the first two factors, leaving about 600,000 due to foreclosure.

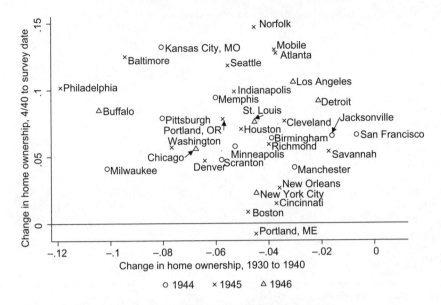

Fig. 10.2   Change in home ownership, 1930–1940 and early 1940s

Notes: Figure shows percentage point change in home ownership between the 1940 census and first housing survey against change from 1930 to 1940. Cities grouped by year of first survey. Sample correlation: −0.18.

owner occupancy in the early 1940s. A shift of these units into the owner-occupied stock would have raised the aggregate home ownership rate by about 2 percentage points in the early 1940s—a substantial share, but still leaving much to explain.

City-level housing surveys carried out toward the end of World War II provide further evidence suggesting that factors other than 1930s foreclosures were important in explaining the increase.[5] Figure 10.2 plots the 1930 to 1940 change in home ownership against the change in the early 1940s. The sample correlation between the two is relatively weak, at about −0.18 (corresponding to an R^2 of 0.033 in a regression of one on the other). This comparison weighs against a simple explanation of the increase in ownership in the early 1940s as a "rebound" effect after the Depression; other factors were surely at work as well. A list of possible explanations would include

5. The Census Bureau and the Bureau of Labor Statistics (BLS) carried out these surveys between 1944 and early 1947 in a selected sample of cities. Data were published in Humes and Schiro (1946), US Bureau of the Census (1947a), and US Bureau of the Census (1948). In order to have a roughly representative sample I use the thirty-four cities that the Bureau of Labor Statistics had begun tracking prior to World War II for its cost-of-living index.

Table 10.1   Geography of the increase in home ownership

Census division	Rate of home ownership (%)			Share of all occupied dwellings (%)			Share of overall change (%)	
	1940	1950	1960	1940	1950	1960	1940–1950	1940–1960
New England	42	51	59	6	6	6	4	5
Middle Atlantic	37	48	55	21	20	20	16	17
East North Central	49	60	67	21	21	20	19	18
West North Central	49	62	68	11	10	9	7	4
South Atlantic	41	52	61	12	13	14	15	19
East South Central	40	54	62	8	7	6	6	5
West South Central	41	56	64	10	10	9	12	11
Mountain	52	59	65	3	3	4	3	4
Pacific	47	57	61	9	11	12	17	18

Note: Alaska and Hawaii omitted in all years.

rising incomes and accumulating savings, the growing importance of non neutralities in the tax treatment of owner- and renter-occupied housing as marginal income tax rates rose, and the extraordinary conditions of housing markets during and after World War II. The relative roles of these different factors are not well understood.

Geography of the 1940–1960 Increase

The fact that city-level changes in home ownership were nearly all positive in figure 10.2 suggests that an increase in home ownership was widespread geographically. Indeed, over the longer period from 1940 to 1960 home ownership rose dramatically in all regions of the United States, and in both urban and rural areas. Table 10.1 shows the rate of home ownership in each census division in 1940, 1950, and 1960. From 1940 to 1960, the greatest increases were in the South, from about 40 to about 62 percentage points. The smallest increases were in the West, starting from a higher level—between 47 and 52 percentage points—and ending between 61 and 65 percentage points. The aggregate home ownership rate is a weighted average of the divisions' home ownership rates, with weights given by each division's share of all occupied units (its number of occupied dwellings divided by the nation's number of occupied dwellings). I show these weights and each region's share of the overall change, calculated for 1940 to 1960 as $(own_{d60}y_{d60} - own_{d40}y_{d40})/(own_{60} - own_{40})$, where own_t is the national home ownership rate in year t, own_{dt} the home ownership rate in division d in year t, and y_{dt} is the share of all occupied dwellings that were in division d in year t. By this measure, given the relative numbers of occupied units in each region and the changes in home ownership over the period, the Middle Atlantic, East North Central, South Atlantic, and Pacific regions were the most important in explaining the overall change in home ownership.

Increases in home ownership were large in both urban and rural areas over this period, but a greater share of the aggregate change was driven by increases in urban areas. This fact can be seen by expressing the aggregate change in home ownership between 1940 and 1960 as

$$(1) \qquad own_{60} - own_{40} = \sum_c own_{c60} y_{c60} - own_{c40} y_{c40}$$

where own_{ct} is the home ownership rate (owner-occupied dwellings as a share of occupied dwellings) in county c in year t, and y_{ct} is the share of all occupied dwellings that were in county c in year t. The right-hand side can be decomposed into two components: one associated with increased home ownership in a county, holding its share of dwellings constant, and another component associated with a county's relative growth as a share of all occupied dwellings, holding its home ownership rate constant. Thus, we can rewrite equation (1) as

$$(2) \qquad own_{60} - own_{40} = \sum_c \underbrace{(own_{c60} - own_{c40})\overline{y}_c}_{ownership\ term} + \sum_c \underbrace{(y_{c60} - y_{c40})\overline{own}_c}_{\#\ of\ dwellings\ term}$$

where $\overline{own}_c$ is the average of the 1940 and 1960 home ownership rates in county c and $\overline{y}_c$ is defined similarly. To assess the relative roles of rural and urban counties in the aggregate increase, I order all counties by their 1940 urban population share, and calculate the cumulative sum of the right-hand side of equation (1) as a share of the left-hand side; I plot the result as a solid line in figure 10.3. At a 1940 urban share of 18 percent, for example— roughly the median county—the value of about .03 implies that 3 percent of the aggregate 1940 to 1960 increase in home ownership can be explained by changes in counties that had a 1940 urban population share of 18 percent or below. I also illustrate the decomposition of the increase into ownership changes (the "ownership" term in equation [2]) and changes of counties' relative sizes (the "dwellings" term in equation [2]) by plotting the cumulative sums of each of these two terms.

The convexity of the cumulative share explained by 1940 urban population suggests that growth in home ownership in initially urban areas was the primary driver of the aggregate increase in home ownership. For example, in my sample of 3,095 counties, 1,253 had entirely rural populations in 1940, but by my measure these counties had roughly a zero, or slightly negative, contribution to the aggregate change in home ownership over the following

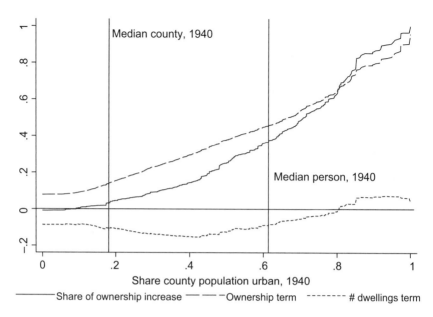

Fig. 10.3   Cumulative share of 1940–1960 increase explained, by 1940 urban population

Notes: Figure shows decompositions given in equations (1) and (2). The relatively large uptick just above an urban population share of 0.8 is Los Angeles County.

twenty years.[6] On average, home ownership increased substantially in these rural counties, but they also shrank relative to more urban counties; these two opposing effects netted out to about zero. As more urbanized counties are added the share of the aggregate change explained increases, but more urbanized counties continue to explain an even larger share. The median individual in 1940 lived in a county that was about 61 percent urban, but altogether the counties that were less than 61 percent urban explain only about 37 percent of the overall increase.

10.2.2 Home Ownership at the Individual Level

National Time Series

Integrated Public Use Microdata Series (IPUMS) census microdata (Ruggles et al. 2008) can be used to measure home ownership at the individual level. The microdata list a single head and tenure status for each household. Conceptually, one wishes to add one major classification to the possibilities of owning and renting, which is that the individual lives with

---

6. I aggregate some counties into groups as a rough correction for county boundary changes over this period; details are available on request.

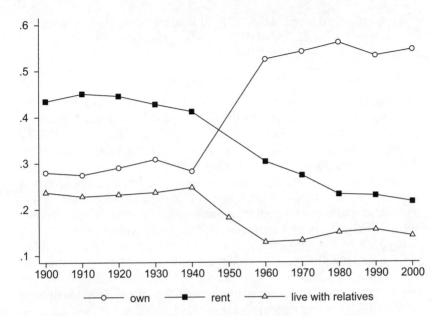

Fig. 10.4   Home ownership at the individual level, 1900–2000

Source: IPUMS (Ruggles et al. 2008).

Notes: Figure shows share of men eighteen and older owning, renting, and living with relatives. Residual category is omitted.

relatives—most often, with parents or with children. The approach I take is to limit the sample to men, and to classify an individual as a home owner if he was the household head or spouse of the head in an owner-occupied dwelling. I classify an individual as a renter if he is the head or the spouse of the head in a renter-occupied unit, or is identified as a boarder in a dwelling owned by someone else, and as "living with relatives" if he is otherwise related to the head. The remainder, always under 8 percent, encompasses group quarters, such as military barracks or rooming houses; domestic employees; and other arrangements that could not be classified. The schedules from the 1950 census of housing were destroyed after tabulation (US Bureau of the Census 1984), so this measure of home ownership cannot be calculated in 1950 (although the share living with relatives can be). Hence, I do not show the shares renting and owning in 1950.

Figure 10.4 shows that home ownership at the individual level also saw a remarkable increase between 1940 and 1960. But what is especially notable is that as much of the increase in home ownership at the individual level came out of living with relatives as did out of renting. The share of men eighteen and older renting, in fact, exhibits a fairly steady decline from 1920 to 1980; the unusual shift from 1940 to 1960 was in the share of men who lived with relatives.[7] In this respect the 1940 to 1960 increase in home ownership differed from the increase from 1920 to 1930: in the earlier period, increased ownership appears primarily to have displaced renting.

Patterns of Home Ownership by Age

It would be natural to expect that much of the change in living with relatives came from the youngest or the oldest individuals. Indeed, there are clear age patterns to the changes in home ownership. The early years of the Survey of Consumer Finances ([SCF]; Economic Behavior Program 1973), carried out annually beginning in 1947, provide a rare source of data to look at living arrangements at a high temporal frequency. The unit of observation in the SCF is a spending unit, defined as a group of related people living in the same dwelling who pool their incomes for major items of expense.[8] Unfortunately, the precise characteristics of the individuals in a spending unit cannot be fully disaggregated in a way that allows full comparability with the individual-level variables defined earlier.[9] For ownership, the 1960 numbers appear to match the individual-level measure from the census well; for living with relatives or renting, the SCF numbers do not match the individual-level census measure quite as closely.

Figure 10.5 illustrates the contrasting patterns of different age groups in their living arrangements from 1947 to 1960. The largest changes in home ownership over this postwar period were for ages twenty-five to forty-four. Yet for the older half of this age group—thirty-five to forty-four—increased home ownership primarily displaced renting, while for the younger half (twenty-five to thirty-four), renting remained roughly constant, and home ownership displaced living with relatives. Meanwhile, the youngest ages— eighteen to twenty-four—saw relatively little net change in home ownership but did see a shift from living with relatives to renting. If one were to attempt to infer life cycle patterns from the cross-age variation in a single year, it would appear that the 1947 to 1960 period was one in which a typical pattern of living with relatives (presumably parents), then renting, then owning, saw a sharp abbreviation of the early phases and extension of the period of ownership. Little change is evident in the oldest age group (sixty-five and older), although by the individual-level measure from the census, there

7. A similar pattern is evident for farm and nonfarm housing examined separately. Morgan et al. (1962) discuss attitudes toward living with relatives over this period.

8. For example, an adult son living with his parents would be classified as a separate spending unit if he does not pool his income with that of his parents, but otherwise would be part of the same spending unit. Spending units are further grouped into "family units" of related individuals, with a single "primary" spending unit and other "secondary" spending units. Housing tenure is not reported consistently for spending units living on farms, so these are excluded from the analysis that follows. Between 1947 and 1960, there were about 3,000 spending units interviewed in each year.

9. Because individuals living with relatives may often pool resources, it is likely that the spending unit-level measures understate the share living with relatives, and overstate the share owning or renting, for the youngest and oldest age groups.

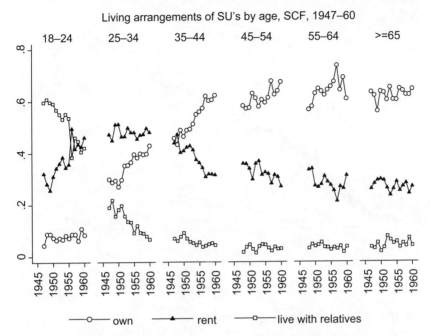

Fig. 10.5   **Living arrangements by age, nonfarm, 1947–1960**
Source: Survey of Consumer Finances (Economic Behavior Program, Survey Research Center, University of Michigan, 1973).

was an increase in home ownership, and a decrease in renting and living with relatives between 1940 and 1960. It may be that much of this change occurred before 1947, or that measurement of living arrangements at the spending unit level obscures these patterns in the SCF.

These patterns suggest that increases in home ownership between 1940 and 1960 were particularly large for young individuals. Indeed, home ownership rates by age in census data, measured at the individual level, suggest that a transformation in the age pattern of ownership was a crucial part of the midcentury increase in home ownership. Age-home ownership profiles are illustrated for 1900 through 1980 in figure 10.6, from Fetter (2013).[10] The age profile of home ownership was stable in every year up to 1940, and nearly linear up to age sixty, but from 1960 onward became strikingly more concave. Home ownership rates for men in their early thirties more than doubled, while home ownership among older age groups increased substantially less.[11]

10. For visual clarity in interpreting the 1940 to 1960 change, 1990 and 2000 are not shown. In these years, the age profile was somewhat less steep but its basic concavity persisted.

11. Here it is especially important not to condition on household head status, since doing so induces systematic differences in the characteristics of household heads of different ages. Conditioning on household head status gives, as one might expect, higher home ownership rates

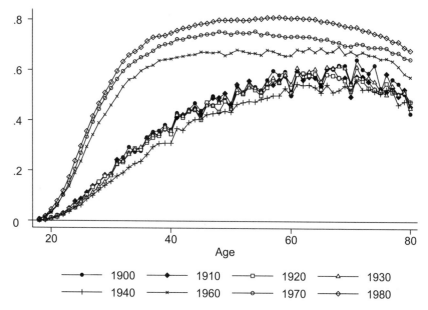

Fig. 10.6   Home ownership by age, 1900–1980
Source: IPUMS (Ruggles et al. 2008).

A natural interpretation is that the increase in ownership in the 1940s and 1950s largely represented earlier purchases among individuals who likely would have purchased later in life.

An alternative way of illustrating the changing age structure of home ownership is to plot home ownership by year of birth in each census. Doing so has the benefit of allowing one to trace the housing experience of a birth cohort more easily. Figure 10.7 and figure 10.8 illustrate cohort-ownership profiles for nonfarm and farm housing, respectively. Plotting the two separately has the added value of showing that the two had distinct age patterns of increased home ownership between 1940 and 1960. These two figures reveal several facts. The increased concavity of the age-ownership profile over these two decades was primarily a nonfarm phenomenon. For farm housing, increased home ownership between 1940 and 1960 was far more equally distributed across ages than for nonfarm housing. The pre-1940 profiles also illustrate contrasting experiences in the first part of the century. In farm housing there was a steady downward shift of the profile from 1900 to 1940, before the upward shift from 1940 to 1960. In fact, the age profiles of ownership in 1900 and 1960 for farm housing are quite close except at the oldest ages. Pre-1940 nonfarm age profiles exhibited more stability from year

---

for both the youngest and the oldest age groups. It gives a nearly linear age profile of home ownership well beyond age 60 in 1940 and earlier.

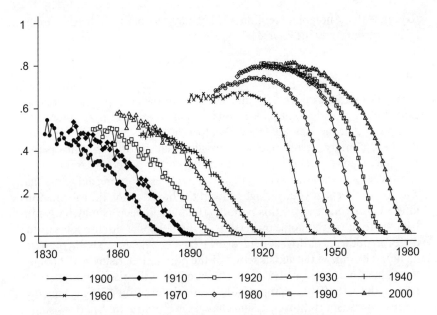

Fig. 10.7 Nonfarm home ownership by year of birth, 1900–2000
Source: IPUMS (Ruggles et al. 2008).

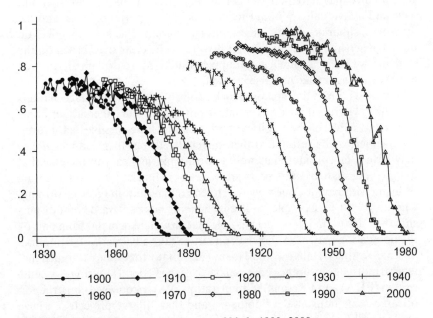

Fig. 10.8 Farm home ownership by year of birth, 1900–2000
Source: IPUMS (Ruggles et al. 2008).

to year, with the notable exception of what may have been a stalled beginning of an age shift over the course of the 1920s.

10.3 Hypotheses

What caused the midcentury increase in home ownership? The aforementioned facts provide some suggestions for places to look: from figure 10.1 it appears that the increase from 1940 to 1960 represented a return to the pre-1930 nonfarm trend; thus, it is possible that the drivers in this period may have some continuity with those of the earlier period of increase. The age-ownership shift observed in figure 10.6 suggests looking at factors that had larger effects at younger ages. Given the broad set of transformations in the United States over this period, a number of factors may have contributed to the rise in home ownership. In this section, I discuss some of the major hypotheses and what evidence we have for them. These hypotheses include a change in the age structure of the population, rising real incomes, the reduction in the relative cost of owning with the rise in marginal tax rates in the early 1940s, changes in the available terms on mortgage finance, decreased transportation costs and changes in city structure, and assistance to the elderly.

I discuss each factor in isolation, but of course these explanations are not mutually exclusive. For example, rising real incomes and changes in mortgage finance may have had a larger impact together than each one would have had individually. Without reductions in transportation costs and the growth of suburbs, other changes may not have had as large an effect on home ownership. In my discussion it will also be clear that, based on the evidence we have, no single factor appears sufficient to explain all (or even most) of the aggregate increase by itself.

A related point is that spillovers in housing markets or mortgage markets were likely a crucial part of the mid-twentieth-century increase in home ownership. Much of the empirical work on each of the possible factors driving the increase has estimated their direct effects, but their indirect effects may have been substantial as well. For example, it is easy to imagine that if a growing share of one's peers are purchasing houses rather than renting or living with parents, one's own preferences may shift in favor of owning; Chevan (1989), for example, discusses changing norms toward home ownership over this period. It is also possible that growth in demand from part of the population may have allowed builders to take advantage of economies of scale. Saulnier, Halcrow, and Jacoby (1958, 348), for example, argued that federal mortgage insurance programs such as the Federal Housing Administration (FHA) and Veterans Administration (VA) encouraged construction of large-scale housing developments, and that "[l]arge projects . . . have made possible the application of methods of production organization that have doubtless lowered costs in the building industry." In mortgage markets, government programs such as the VA and FHA surely influenced the terms on which conventional loans were available. To the best of my knowledge, there has been little work focusing on estimating the size of any spillovers, although in Fetter (2013) I attempt to shed light on the net direction of spillovers from mortgage benefits provided to veterans; I find suggestive evidence that they increased home ownership among nonveterans in the same housing market.

Much of the discussion that follows focuses on the factors likely to be important for explaining the twenty-year shift in home ownership, but it is important to keep in mind that the factors driving the overall shift may not overlap completely with those driving the timing of the shift. For example, factors that would have been temporary and hence might be thought primarily to drive the timing of the shift would include wartime policies such as "forced savings" due to price controls and rationing during the war, or disincentives to invest in rental housing due to wartime and postwar rent controls. Naturally, it is also possible that if spillovers were significant, such "temporary" factors may have had long-lasting effects by shifting the country toward a high home ownership equilibrium.

10.3.1   Demographics

We know from figure 10.6 that age-specific home ownership rates increased substantially over the 1940s and 1950s, but of course changes in the age structure of the population are also likely to influence aggregate home ownership rates; Chevan (1989) stresses the importance of demographic change in the midcentury rise in home ownership. Since home ownership increases more or less monotonically up to middle age, a decrease in the population share of the young will, all else equal, tend to increase home ownership rates.

A simple decomposition of the change in the aggregate home ownership rate from 1940 to 1960 provides a measure of the share of the aggregate increase that can be explained by changes in the age structure of the population. I decompose the 1940 to 1960 difference of .26 for US-born men eighteen and older as follows:[12]

$$own_{60} - own_{40} = \sum_{g=18}^{G} (w_{g60} - w_{g40})\overline{own}_g + \sum_{g=18}^{G} (own_{g60} - own_{g40})\overline{w}_g$$

where g indexes age and w_{gy} is the share of individuals of age g in the population in year y (bars indicate means over the 1940 and 1960 values). The first term gives the difference attributable to the change in the age structure of the population, the latter measures the difference due to increases in within-age rates of ownership. This calculation yields a value of .044 for the first term and .213 for the second, suggesting that changing age structure can account for an important share—about 17 percent—of the aggregate increase.

---

12. In 1940 I apply sampling weights to calculate averages; the 1960 sample is a flat sample of the population.

10.3.2   Income

Many observers at the time attributed the 1940 to 1960 increase in home ownership to rising real incomes. Humes and Schiro (1946) and Muller (1947) both suggested that rising incomes played an important role in the early years of the 1940s. Reid (1962), in her study of the income elasticity of demand for housing, noted the positive relationship between home ownership and income. Katona (1964) offers an overview of housing over the 1950s and early 1960s based on the Survey of Consumer Finances, discussing both attitudes toward home ownership and economic characteristics of owners and renters. He argues that both the availability of mortgage credit and rising incomes help to explain postwar patterns of home ownership, although he suggests a greater emphasis on the latter. One study that has provided quantitative estimates of the contribution of rising incomes to the increase in home ownership is Chevan (1989), which argues that changes in income can account for roughly half of the 1940 to 1960 increase.[13]

It would not be surprising for rising income to play an important role in the midcentury increase in home ownership, especially in combination with other factors. Yet I am not aware of work that attempts to isolate quasi-experimental variation in income for the purpose of estimating its causal relationship with home ownership at either the beginning or end of the period. Identifying promising sources of variation, perhaps to be used in combination with data from the Survey of Consumer Finances, could be a fruitful avenue for future research.

10.3.3   The Income Tax

An extensive literature has discussed the nonneutralities in the US tax code in its treatment of owner- and renter-occupied housing (Smith, Rosen, and Fallis [1988] provide a review). If a home owner were taxed as if she were her own landlord, she would have to pay taxes on her net rental income: the rent she would have obtained renting the house to a tenant, less deductions for maintenance, depreciation, mortgage interest, and property taxes. Instead, net rental income is not taxable for a home owner, and she can further deduct mortgage interest and property taxes from her gross income.[14] These features had been part of the federal personal income tax since 1913, but these nonneutralities became quantitatively significant only with the rise in marginal tax rates at the beginning of World War II (e.g., Aaron 1972).

---

13. Margo (1992) presents estimates of the role of income in the closely related phenomenon of suburbanization, concluding that about 43 percent of postwar suburbanization can be attributed to rising household incomes.

14. Hence, two identical individuals living in identical homes would have lower tax liabilities if each owned the home she lived in than they would if they rented to each other. There are many sources discussing the tax advantages of owning in more detail; two lucid expositions that discuss these nonneutralities in the context of the midcentury rise in home ownership are those of Goode (1960) and Aaron (1972).

Another explanation for the midcentury rise in home ownership, therefore, is that the rise in personal income tax rates reduced the relative cost of owner-occupied housing. Adding to these benefits was a provision, introduced in 1951, that capital gains from the sale of a principal residence were excluded from taxable income, provided that another residence costing at least as much was purchased within a year and a half (Congressional Budget Office 1981; Rosen 1985).

A number of studies have considered the role of the nonneutralities in the tax code specifically in the context of the midcentury rise in home ownership. Goode (1960) suggests that the income tax may have played an important role. Aaron (1972) argues that the personal income tax was the most important factor, but does not attempt to calculate a counterfactual home ownership rate in the absence of nonneutralities in the tax system. Rosen and Rosen (1980) provide a quantitative estimate, estimating a time-series regression over the period from 1949 to 1974 to assess the impact of eliminating the special tax treatment of owner-occupied housing.[15] They estimate that the national home ownership rate would have been 4 percentage points lower in 1974—60 percent rather than 64 percent—if the tax benefits to owners were eliminated. This is about a fifth of the increase from 1940 to 1974.[16] Most recently, Chambers, Garriga, and Schlagenhauf (chapter 11, this volume) calibrate a general equilibrium overlapping generations model to estimate home ownership rates under a variety of counterfactual scenarios, among them the taxation of home owners as if they were landlords or the elimination of the home mortgage interest deduction. Their results suggest that the incentives for home ownership induced by rising marginal income tax rates were important in the midcentury rise in home ownership.

I am not aware of any work that exploits disaggregated data and quasi-experimental methods for causal inference to quantify the role of federal taxes in the midcentury rise in home ownership—or, indeed, to quantify the relative roles of different aspects of the favorable tax treatment of home owners. Identifying variation across areas, across people, and over time in the impact of federal tax changes could provide illuminating counterpoint to the studies mentioned earlier.

10.3.4   Mortgage Finance

The middle of the twentieth century saw the development of the modern system of mortgage finance. The growing prevalence of fully amortized, low

---

15. They estimate their time-series regression at the annual level; their national home ownership rates are from the census for 1950, 1960, and 1970, and are imputed for intercensal years.

16. Hendershott and Shilling (1982) examine the period from 1955 to 1979 and conclude that in the absence of the tax provisions in favor of ownership, the home ownership rate in 1978 would have been 60 percent rather than 65 percent. Rosen, Rosen, and Holtz-Eakin (1984) suggest that both of these estimates may be overstated, due to the assumption that households know the user cost of owner-occupied housing with certainty.

down payment mortgage loans is an explanation for the increase in home ownership heard both now and at the time (Shelton 1968; Jackson 1985; Green and Wachter 2005). To the extent that the young are more likely to be liquidity constrained, the increased concavity of the age-ownership profile in figure 10.6 suggests that the finance channel may have been important. It is also in keeping with modern cross-country evidence that countries that have lower down payments tend to have higher home ownership rates among the young (Chiuri and Jappelli 2003).

The transition in mortgage finance during the 1930s and 1940s can be characterized very broadly as a shift away from high down payment, short-term mortgages (often supplemented with junior mortgage financing at high interest rates) to long-term, fully amortized, low down payment mortgages. Recent work, such as Snowden (2003, 2010), has done much to complicate and enrich this story; mortgage finance in the pre-Depression era defies any simple characterization. Nevertheless, it is fair to say that the mid-twentieth century saw broad changes in the terms on which mortgage finance was available for home purchase.

An important element of changes in mortgage markets over the 1940 to 1960 period was direct government involvement. The federal government played a central role in mortgage markets over this period, in part by guaranteeing and insuring mortgages through the Veterans Administration (VA) and Federal Housing Administration (FHA) programs. Each program provided protection to lenders against losses on loans that had been approved by the insuring agency. Relative to conventional loans—those without government guarantees—VA and FHA loans tended to be longer-term and to have lower down payments and interest rates. The VA loans in particular tended to have the lowest down payments, and over the fifteen years following World War II were often (although not always) available with no down payment.

Given the likelihood that government intervention in mortgage markets, or changes in mortgage terms more broadly, played a meaningful role in the midcentury increase in home ownership, there has been interest in quantifying the impact of credit availability. Yet much of the existing evidence is essentially a time-series comparison. Rosen and Rosen (1980), for example, attempt to estimate the impact of credit availability by estimating a time-series regression of the national home ownership rate on a measure of deposits in thrift institutions (as well as other factors). They find a positive relationship, but one not statistically significant at conventional levels; they draw no strong inferences from this result, admitting that it is an imperfect test. In this volume, Chambers, Garriga, and Schlagenhauf (chapter 11) provide stronger evidence on this question, using their calibrated model to predict what the 1960 home ownership rate would have been in the absence of mortgage market innovations. They find that the growing length of mortgage contracts over the 1940s and 1950s, encouraged by government interventions such as the FHA, can account for 12 percent of the overall 1940 to 1960 increase in home ownership.

In Fetter (2013), I attempt to bring quasi-experimental empirical methods to bear on the question of the role of credit availability. I shed light on this broad question by estimating the impact of the VA program, which allowed borrowing on easier terms than any other broad-based program over the period. I do so in a way that attempts to provide a rigorous empirical link between the aggregate increase in home ownership and the shift in the age structure of home ownership. In particular, I exploit two steep declines in the probability of military service by date of birth, induced by age requirements for military service interacted with the end of World War II and the Korean War. A "between-cohort" comparison allows estimation of the impact of military service on later-life outcomes such as home ownership, alleviating concerns with direct comparisons of veterans to nonveterans. The presence of two "breaks"—one associated with the end of World War II and one with the end of the Korean War—gives estimates of the effect of veteran status at two ages in each census year. Testing for differences at each break in 1960, I estimate the impact of veteran status at multiple ages; following the same cohorts to the 1970 and 1980 censuses allows estimation of the effects of veteran status at older ages. I find large effects of veteran status on the probability of home ownership in 1960. Consistent with the idea that easier credit terms should, roughly speaking, have larger effects at younger ages, the effects are larger for the younger individuals at the Korean War break, and there is no evidence of a positive effect of veteran status in 1970 or 1980, by which time the cohorts had reached their midthirties.

Given the large number of factors that also influenced the probability of home ownership, it is important to rule out alternative explanations of a "veteran effect" on home ownership. But in a number of complementary analyses, I show that the results cannot be explained by other veterans' benefits (such as education or job training) or by direct effects of military service (such as the possibility that service induces preferences for earlier family formation). I then use the estimates of the effect of veteran status in 1960 to estimate a counterfactual 1960 age-ownership profile (and counterfactual 1960 home ownership rate) in the absence of the VA. The results suggest that the VA itself can account for about 1.9 percentage points of the roughly 26 percentage point rise in individual-level home ownership between 1940 and 1960, about 7.4 percent of the overall increase (and 25 percent for the cohorts affected by the program). Because the VA was just one element in a changing mortgage market over the middle of the century, offering the easiest terms in a market moving more generally toward lower down payments and longer maturities, these estimates provide a lower bound on the broader increase in the availability of credit in the midcentury rise in home ownership. I provide a rough estimate that broader changes in finance may explain about 40 percent of the overall increase in home ownership from 1940 to 1960.

These results suggest that easing credit terms played an important role in the midcentury rise in home ownership, and also that government credit aids in particular contributed to this change. An interesting and unresolved question is the extent to which government credit aids influenced terms on conventional lending; this was an area of active interest at the time (discussed, for example, by Break [1961]), but it would be helpful to revisit the question using modern empirical methods.

10.3.5   Other Factors

A number of other factors were surely important in explaining the overall increase. There is a natural link between suburbanization and home ownership to the extent that a lower price of land more distant from city centers facilitates construction of larger, single-family detached dwellings, and for agency reasons these tend to be owner occupied more often than multifamily structures (Glaeser and Shapiro 2003). Baum-Snow (2007) shows that the construction of highways encouraged suburbanization in the postwar era; decreased transportation costs could have increased home ownership by lowering the cost of suburban residence. Boustan and Margo (2011) show that white suburbanization in the postwar period, in turn, increased home ownership rates for blacks who remained in central cities.

Much of the previous discussion has focused on influences on young individuals, but it is clear from figure 10.6 that home ownership increased substantially among older individuals as well. Costa (1999) shows that Old Age Assistance increased demand for separate living quarters for older, unmarried women; it is likely that greater financial security in old age tended to keep older individuals from leaving their homes to live with children, and instead to remain home owners later in life.

10.4   Conclusion

Among the most remarkable changes in the twentieth-century United States was the transformation in housing markets over the 1940s and 1950s. This chapter presents some important facts that hypotheses for the rise in home ownership would do well to address, and suggests that no single factor by itself appears to explain the entirety of the shift.

It is worth noting that the focus of this chapter has in many ways been quite narrow; it has not, for example, discussed the extensive literature on race and housing (see, for example, Collins and Margo [2001]). Yet it seems clear that much remains to be done to understand the drivers of the broad changes in tenure choice in the mid-twentieth century.

References

Aaron, Henry J. 1972. *Shelter and Subsidies: Who Benefits from Federal Housing Policies?* Washington, DC: The Brookings Institution.

Baum-Snow, Nathaniel. 2007. "Did Highways Cause Suburbanization?" *Quarterly Journal of Economics* 122 (2): 775–805.

Boustan, Leah Platt, and Robert A. Margo. 2011. "White Suburbanization and African-American Home Ownership, 1940–1980." NBER Working Paper no. 16702, Cambridge, MA.

Break, George F. 1961. *The Economic Impact of Federal Loan Insurance.* Washington, DC: National Planning Association.

Chevan, Albert. 1989. "The Growth of Home Ownership: 1940–1980." *Demography* 26 (2): 249–66.

Chiuri, Maria C., and Tullio Jappelli. 2003. "Financial Market Imperfections and Home Ownership: A Comparative Study." *European Economic Review* 47:857–75.

Collins, William J., and Robert A. Margo. 2001. "Race and Home Ownership: A Century-Long View." *Explorations in Economic History* 38:68–92.

Congressional Budget Office. 1981. *The Tax Treatment of Homeownership: Issues and Options.* Congress of the United States.

Costa, Dora. 1999. "A House of Her Own: Old Age Assistance and the Living Arrangements of Older Nonmarried Women." *Journal of Public Economics* 72 (1): 39–59.

Economic Behavior Program, Survey Research Center, University of Michigan. "Survey of Consumer Finances, various years." Institute for Social Research, Social Science Archive 1973. Distributed by Inter-university Consortium for Political and Social Research, 1999.

Fetter, Daniel K. 2013. "How Do Mortgage Subsidies Affect Home Ownership? Evidence from the Mid-Century GI Bills." *American Economic Journal: Economic Policy* 5 (2): 111–47.

Glaeser, Edward, and Jesse Shapiro. 2003. "The Benefits of the Home Mortgage Interest Deduction." *Tax Policy and the Economy* 17:37–82.

Goode, Richard. 1960. "Imputed Rent of Owner-Occupied Dwellings Under the Income Tax." *Journal of Finance* 15 (4): 504–30.

Green, Richard K., and Susan M. Wachter. 2005. "The American Mortgage in Historical and International Context." *Journal of Economic Perspectives* 19 (4): 93–114.

Haurin, Donald R., and Stuart S. Rosenthal. 2007. "The Influence of Household Formation on Homeownership Rates Across Time and Race." *Real Estate Economics* 35 (4): 411–50.

Hendershott, Patric H., and James D. Shilling. 1982. "The Economics of Tenure Choice, 1955–79." In *Research in Real Estate*, volume I, edited by C. Sirmans. Stamford, CT: JAI Press, Inc.

Humes, Helen, and Bruno Schiro. 1946. "Effect of Wartime Housing Shortages on Home Ownership." *Monthly Labor Review* 62:560–6. Reprinted with additional data as Serial No. R. 1840, U.S. G.P.O., 1946.

Jackson, Kenneth T. 1985. *Crabgrass Frontier.* Oxford: Oxford University Press.

Katona, George. 1964. *The Mass Consumption Society.* New York: McGraw-Hill Book Company.

Margo, Robert A. 1992. "Explaining the Postwar Suburbanization of Population in the United States: The Role of Income." *Journal of Urban Economics* 31:301–10.

Morgan, James N., Martin H. David, Wilbur J. Cohen, and Harvey E. Brazer. 1962. *Income and Welfare in the United States.* New York: McGraw-Hill Book Company.

Muller, Henry McCulley. 1947. "Urban Home Ownership: A Socioeconomic Analysis with Emphasis on Philadelphia." PhD diss., University of Pennsylvania.

Ratcliff, Richard U. 1944. "Notes on the Recent Decline in Home Ownership." *Journal of Land and Public Utility Economics* 20 (4): 373–7.

Reid, Margaret G. 1962. *Housing and Income*. Chicago: The University of Chicago Press.

Rosen, Harvey S. 1985. "Housing Subsidies: Effects on Housing Decisions, Efficiency, and Equity." In *Handbook of Public Economics*, volume 1, edited by Alan J. Auerbach and Martin Feldstein. Amsterdam: Elsevier.

Rosen, Harvey, and Kenneth T. Rosen. 1980. "Federal Taxes and Homeownership: Evidence from Time Series." *Journal of Political Economy* 88 (1): 59–75.

Rosen, Harvey, Kenneth T. Rosen, and Douglas Holtz-Eakin. 1984. "Housing Tenure, Uncertainty, and Taxation." *Review of Economics and Statistics* 66 (3): 405–16.

Ruggles, Steven, Matthew Sobek, Trent Alexander, Catherine A. Fitch, Ronald Goeken, Patricia Kelly Hall, Miriam King, and Chad Ronnander. 2008. "Integrated Public Use Microdata Series: Version 4.0." Minneapolis: Minnesota Population Center.

Saulnier, Raymond J., Harold G. Halcrow, and Neil H. Jacoby. 1958. *Federal Lending and Loan Insurance*. Princeton, NJ: Princeton University Press.

Shelton, John P. 1968. "The Cost of Renting Versus Owning a Home." *Land Economics* 44 (1): 59–72.

Smith, Lawrence B., Kenneth T. Rosen, and George Fallis. 1988. "Recent Developments in Economic Models of Housing Markets." *Journal of Economic Literature* 26 (1): 29–64.

Snowden, Kenneth A. 2003. "The Transition from Building and Loan to Savings and Loan, 1890–1940." In *Finance, Intermediaries, and Economic Development*, edited by Stanley L. Engerman, Philip T. Hoffman, Jean-Laurent Rosenthal, and Kenneth L. Sokoloff. Cambridge: Cambridge University Press.

———. 2010. "The Anatomy of a Residential Mortgage Crisis: A Look back to the 1930's." NBER Working Paper no. 16244, Cambridge, MA.

US Bureau of the Census. 1943. *Census of Housing: 1940, Vol. II: General Characteristics*. Washington, DC: United States Government Printing Office.

———. 1945. "Characteristics of Occupied Dwelling Units, for the United States: October, 1944." Housing–Special Reports, Series H-45, No. 2. July.

———. 1946. "Characteristics of Occupied Dwelling Units, for the United States: November, 1945." Housing–Special Reports, Series H-46, No. 1. May.

———. 1947a. "Housing Characteristics in 108 Selected Areas: 1946 Veterans' Housing Surveys and the 1940 Census of Housing." Current Population Reports: Housing Statistics. Census Series HVet- 115, Housing and Home Finance Agency Statistics Bulletin No. 1.

———. 1947b. "Housing Characteristics of the United States: April, 1947." Current Population Reports—Housing, Series P-70, No. 1. October.

———. 1948. "Vacancy, Occupancy, and Tenure in Selected Areas: 1945 to 1947." Current Population Reports: Housing, Series P-72, No. 1–2. June.

———. 1953. *Census of Housing: 1950, Vol. I: General Characteristics*. Washington, DC: United States Government Printing Office.

———. 1984. "Census of Population, 1950: Public Use Microdata Sample." Washington, DC: US Department of Commerce, Bureau of the Census and Madison, WI: University of Wisconsin, Center for Demography and Ecology. Distributed by Inter-university Consortium for Political and Social Research, 1999. doi:10.3886/ICPSR08251.

Did Housing Policies Cause the Postwar Boom in Home Ownership?

Matthew Chambers, Carlos Garriga,
and Don E. Schlagenhauf

11.1 Introduction

From a historical perspective, the recent expansion in home ownership is small compared with the one that started in 1940. Before the Great Depression there was little federal involvement in US housing except for land grants and the regulation of commercial banks. As a result of the foreclosure problem that coincided with the Depression, the role of government in residential housing expanded.[1] The government played a large role in shaping the future of US housing finance and housing policy.

Before the Great Depression many mortgages were short-term (five to seven years), balloon-type (nonamortizing) mortgages with large down payment requirements (50 to 60 percent). Partially as a result of New Deal

Matthew Chambers is associate professor of economics at Towson University. Carlos Garriga is a research officer and senior research economist at the Federal Reserve Bank of St. Louis. Don E. Schlagenhauf is an economist in the Center for Household Financial Stability at the Federal Reserve Bank of St. Louis and a professor of economics at Florida State University.

We acknowledge the useful comments of Daniel Fetter, Price Fishback, David Genesove, Shawn Kantor, Olmo Silva, Kenneth Snowden, Dave Wheelock, and Eugene White. Some of the ideas in the text have been presented at the 6th Meeting of the Urban Economics Association, the 2011 Society for Economic Dynamics Meetings, the 2011 Society for the Advancement of Economic Theory Meetings, the 1st European Meeting of the Urban Economics Association, the 2011 NBER-URC's Housing and Mortgage Markets in Historical Perspective Conference, and the Fifth Annual NBER Conference on Macroeconomics across Time and Space. The editorial comments from Judith Ahlers have been useful. Don Schlagenhauf acknowledges travel support from the De Voe Moore Center. The views expressed herein do not necessarily reflect those of the Federal Reserve Bank of St. Louis or those of the Federal Reserve System. For acknowledgments, sources of research support, and disclosure of the authors' material financial relationships, if any, please see http://www.nber.org/chapters/c12802.ack.

1. For example, the Home Owners' Loan Act of 1933 and the National Housing Act of 1934 were designed to stabilize the financial system. The National Housing Act established the Federal Housing Administration with the objective of regulating the terms of mortgages.

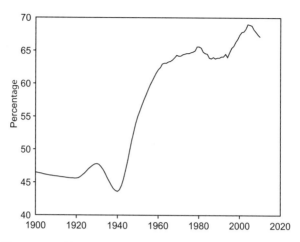

Fig. 11.1   Homeownership rate: United States (1900–2010)
Source: Census data.

policies, government agencies began to offer standard fixed-rate mortgage (FRM) contracts with longer maturities (twenty to thirty years) and a higher loan-to-value ratio (80 percent and above). A government agency was established to create a secondary market to provide liquidity and expand credit by buying primarily loans insured by the Federal Housing Administration.

During this period the government also changed the treatment of owner-occupied housing in the federal income tax code. This policy changed the effective price of owner-occupied housing services because of the deductibility of local property taxes, mortgage interest payments, and the omission of imputed rents from adjusted gross income. All of these interventions coincided with a significant expansion in home ownership (figure 11.1). Between 1940 and 1960, the percentage of owner-occupied households increased from 44 to 62 percent.

It is important to determine the contribution of government intervention in the expansion in the home ownership rate. An extensive empirical literature shows the important contribution of various government programs. Yearns (1976) argues that the increase in home ownership can be explained by the increased availability of mortgage funds from the Federal Housing Administration (FHA) and the Veterans Administration (VA), and the easy monetary policy of the Federal Reserve System. Housing provisions in the tax code have also contributed to increased ownership. Rosen and Rosen (1980) estimate that between 1949 and 1974 about one-fourth of the increase in home ownership was a result of implicit subsidies toward housing embedded in the personal income tax code. Hendershott and Shilling (1982) support this claim by finding that the decline in the cost of owning a home relative to the cost of renting during the period 1955 to 1979 was due to income tax provisions.

Some historians have credited the passage of the Serviceman's Readjustment Act of 1944 (the GI Bill) with playing a vital role in opening the doors of higher education to millions and helping set the stage for the decades of widely shared prosperity that followed World War II. Almost 70 percent of men who turned twenty-one between 1940 and 1955 were guaranteed an essentially free college education under one of the two GI Bills.[2] Fetter (2010) has estimated that the VA policy of making zero down payment mortgage loans available to World War II and Korean War veterans after 1946 accounts for a 10 percent increase in home ownership. The aforementioned research has attempted to measure the importance of a particular factor using a regression-based framework that attempts to hold other potential factors constant. As is known, the results from this empirical approach depend on the availability of data and the degree of interaction between the various factors.

This study employs a different empirical approach; we use a dynamic general equilibrium model and focus on the contributions of government interventions in housing markets to the expansion of US home ownership. The interventions include the role in housing financing as well as subsidies toward housing embedded in the federal income tax code. The framework is a modification of the life cycle mortgage choice framework developed by Chambers, Garriga, and Schlagenhauf (2009a). This approach allows the different factors to dynamically interact and thus provides a laboratory to study the effects of changes in government regulation on individual incentives and relative prices. It also allows us to perform counterfactual experiments.[3]

The model includes ex ante households that differ in education status and income risk. These households purchase consumption goods and housing services and invest in capital and/or housing. The purchase of housing services is intertwined with tenure and duration decisions. Housing is a lumpy investment that requires a down payment and long-term mortgage financing, and receives preferential tax treatment. The model allows economic agents to make optimal decisions in an environment that reflects the economic and institutional environment of the relevant time period. Home buyers have access to multiple types of mortgage loans. These loans are provided by a centralized financial sector that receives deposits from households and lends capital to private firms. The model has a home owner–based rental market that allows the ratio of house price to rental price to be endogenous. The production sector uses a neoclassical technology with capital and labor that produces consumption/investment goods and residential investment. In the model, a government implements a housing policy through various pro-

2. The 70 percent estimate is based on self-reported military service during World War II or the Korean War among males in the 1970 census.
3. This chapter follows the tradition of Amaral and MacGee (2002), Cole and Ohanian (2002, 2004), Hayashi and Prescott (2002), Ohanian (1997), and Perri and Quadrini (2002), who used quantitative techniques in the study of historical events.

grams and collects revenue via a progressive income tax system. The baseline model is (a) parameterized to match the key features of the US economy during the late 1930s, and then (b) used to determine the contribution of various government policies for the expansion of home ownership.

In the early 1940s, government-sponsored mortgages tended to be twenty-year duration contracts. By 1960, the duration of government-sponsored contracts increased to thirty years. The model suggests that the change in the length of the mortgage contract sponsored by the FHA can account for roughly 12 percent of the total increase in home ownership. When combined with a narrowing mortgage interest rate wedge, the total impact of mortgage innovation is approximately 21 percent. Given our assessment of the role of housing finance for home ownership, the implications of even longer maturity mortgage contracts are examined through a set of counterfactual experiments. The model indicates that increasing the maturity beyond thirty years has only a marginal (negative) effect on ownership. These results raise the question: "Why was the FRM not more effective in increasing home ownership in the 1940s?" The model suggests that slow income growth made this contract less attractive.[4]

Housing policies in the tax code have significant impact on the incentives to own a house, but the magnitude depends on the size of the general equilibrium effects. In particular, the elimination of the mortgage deduction only reduces ownership when prices are fixed and the tax surplus is not rebated back to the household sector. The taxation of housing services always reduces ownership.

This chapter is organized into five sections. Section 11.2 presents a brief economic history from 1930 to 1960 as well as some data for this period. Section 11.3 develops our model economy. In order to conduct a historical decomposition analysis the model must be calibrated and estimated to the late 1930s. This is discussed in section 11.4, which also discusses data used to calibrate the model to 1960 in order to conduct our decomposition analysis and discusses the results of the decomposition analysis. Section 11.5 concludes.

11.2   Government Programs and Housing Markets

In the late 1930s and early 1940s, the economy was recovering from the Great Depression. Not surprisingly, the economic environment substantially changed in the following years. This section describes some of the policy changes that occurred between 1930 and 1960.

---

4. The role of housing prices may be a factor. Conventional wisdom is that housing prices started to increase in the early 1930s and continued an upward trend through the 1950s. In this volume, Fishback and Kollmann (chapter 6) argue that housing prices were not increasing in the 1930s and were actually lower in 1940 compared to 1930.

11.2.1   The FHA and the Regulation of Housing Finance

In 1900, mortgage lenders consisted of mutual savings banks, life insurance companies, savings and loan associations (S&Ls), and commercial banks. Mutual savings banks were the dominant lenders, whereas commercial banks played a small role. After 1900 the importance of mutual saving banks declined while life insurance companies and S&Ls substantially increased their market shares. Commercial banks did not become dominant mortgage lenders until after World War II. The reason commercial banks were a relatively unimportant source of mortgage funds is the National Banking Act, which severely limited real estate loans. Hence, any commercial bank mortgage loans were restricted to state-chartered banks. In 1913, the Federal Reserve Act liberalized restrictions that limited participation in the mortgage market for national banks. As a result, the importance of commercial banks in this market steadily increased.

Perhaps a more important change occurred in the structure of the mortgage contract. Loan-to-value (LTV) ratios, length of contract, and contract structure as related to amortization were changing. For the period 1920 to 1940, mortgage loans were typically nonamortizing and characterized by a short-term balloon payment with a high LTV ratio. Grebler, Blank, and Winnick (1956) examine data from life insurance companies, commercial banks, and S&Ls and find that partially amortizing loans did exist during this period. Between 1920 and 1940, approximately 50 percent of mortgage loans issued by commercial banks were nonamortized contracts. For life insurance companies, approximately 20 percent of mortgage contracts in the period 1920 to 1934 were nonamortizing. For the same period, the share of this type of loan issued by savings and loan associations did not exceed 7 percent. However, by the early 1940s, Saulnier (1950) reports that 95 percent of mortgage loans issued by savings and loan associations were fully amortizing. Over approximately the same period, Behrens (1952) claims 73 percent of loans issued by commercial banks were fully amortized, and Edwards (1950) finds 99.7 percent of savings and loan association contracts were fully amortized.

This evidence supports the belief that mortgage contracts before 1950 were of shorter duration and with lower LTV ratios compared with the postwar period. Table 11.1 presents mortgage durations for loans originated at life insurance companies, commercial banks, and S&Ls. For the period 1920 to 1930, the average duration was between six and eleven years. After 1934, mortgage lengths (terms) increased and started to approach twenty-year mortgages; this was especially true for mortgages offered by life insurance companies. The LTV ratios also changed over this period and were around 50 percent. After 1934, LTV ratios began to increase, and by 1947 approached 80 percent.

An obvious question is why did mortgage contracts start to change after

Table 11.1   Properties of mortgage contracts between 1920 and 1950

	Mortgage duration (yr)			Loan-to-value ratio (%)		
	Life insurance companies	Commercial banks	S&L associations	Life insurance companies	Commercial banks	S&L associations
1920–1924	6.4	2.8	11.1	47	50	58
1925–1929	6.4	3.2	11.2	51	52	59
1930–1934	7.4	2.9	11.1	51	52	60
1935–1939	16.4	11.4	11.4	63	63	62
1940–1944	21.1	13.1	13.1	78	69	69
1945–1947	19.5	12.3	14.8	73	75	75

Sources: Data for life insurance companies are from Saulnier (1950); for commercial banks, from Behrens (1952); and for S&Ls, from Morton (1956).

1934? Before 1930, there was little federal involvement in housing except grants as exemplified by the 1862 Homestead Act. The Great Depression changed the government's role in residential housing. As a result of the wave of foreclosures, Congress responded initially with the Home Loan Bank Act of 1932. This act brought thrift institutions under the federal regulation umbrella. The Home Owners Bank Act and the National Housing Act of 1934 followed. These acts were designed to stabilize the financial system. The National Housing Act established the FHA, which introduced a government guarantee in hopes of spurring construction.[5] The FHA home mortgage was initially a twenty-year, fully amortizing loan with a maximum LTV ratio of 80 percent. Carliner (1998) argues that the introduction of this loan contract influenced the behavior of existing lenders, thus partially explaining the data trends in table 11.1. The changes in contract structuring took time to be implemented as state laws limiting LTV ratios had to be modified. The FHA also added restricted design, construction, and underwriting standards. These government programs, part of the New Deal legislation, are thought to have increased home owner participation.[6]

A second government policy with the potential to affect home ownership, especially after 1950, was the federal guarantee for individual mortgage loans. Because of the public view that World War I veterans received few benefits except the promise of a delayed bonus payment,[7] Congress

5. Eccles (1951), who was a central figure in the development of the FHA, made it clear the main intent of the program was "pump-priming" and not reform of the mortgage market.
6. The role that government policies played in influencing loan duration has been recently called into question. Rose and Snowden (2012) argue that the adoption of longer-term amortization was underway in the building and loan associations by the 1930s.
7. The 1920 Fordney Bill, a broader benefits program that would have allowed World War I veterans to choose among a cash bonus, education grants, or payments toward buying a home or farm, was defeated by the Senate. In 1924 Congress passed the Adjusted Compensation Act (the Bonus Bill), which promised World War I veterans a bonus. The plan was intended to

passed the Servicemen's Readjustment Act of 1944, or the GI Bill.[8] The new program included a housing benefit to veterans. Initially no down payments were required, based on the theory that soldiers were not paid enough to accumulate savings and did not have an opportunity to establish a credit rating. Under the original VA loan guarantee program, the maximum amount of guarantee was limited to 50 percent of the loan and was not to exceed $2,000. Loan durations were limited to twenty years, with a maximum interest rate of 4 percent. These ceilings were eliminated when market interest rates greatly exceeded this ceiling. The VA also set a limit on the price of the home. Because of rising house prices in 1945, the maximum amount of the guarantee to lenders was increased to $4,000 for home loans. The maximum maturity for real estate loans was extended to twenty-five years for residential homes. In 1950, the maximum amount of guarantee was increased to 60 percent of the amount of the loan with a cap of $7,500. The maximum length of a loan was lengthened again to thirty years.

Were these programs quantitatively significant? In table 11.2, the values of FHA and VA mortgages are reported as well as the relative importance of these mortgages in the total home mortgage market. While the impact of government mortgage programs was not immediate, by 1940 FHA and VA mortgages accounted for 13.5 percent of mortgages, and by 1945 these mortgages accounted for nearly 25 percent of mortgages. In 1950 the home mortgage share of FHA and VA mortgages was 41.9 percent. The increased role of these government programs is due to the growth of VA mortgage contracts. Between 1949 and 1953, VA mortgage loans averaged 24.0 percent of the market. Clearly, these statistics suggest that the VA mortgage program may have had a significant effect on home ownership and seem to support Fetter's (2010) claim that the VA program led to a 10 percent increase in the home ownership rate.

The important changes in the mortgage market could have implications for mortgage interest rates. Unfortunately, mortgage interest rates are more difficult to find for this period. Grebler, Blank, and Winnick (1956, table O-1, 496) report a mortgage rate series for Manhattan between 1900 and 1953 as well as a bond yield. Figure 11.2 shows the mortgage interest rate was 5.11 percent in 1900, while the bond yield was 3.25.

---

compensate veterans for wages lost while serving in the military during the war, but the bonus (paid as a bond) was to be deferred until 1945. In 1932, thousands of veterans (the "Bonus Army") marched on Washington, DC, and set up an encampment to urge the government to pay the bonus earlier. The Bonus Army was forced by the military to leave Washington, and the early payments (averaging about $800 per veteran) were not authorized by Congress for another four years.

8. A "veteran" was an individual who served at least ninety days on active duty and was discharged or released under conditions other than dishonorable. The qualifying service time was much higher for an individual who was in the military but not on active duty. For World War II active duty was between September 1940 and July 1947. For the Korean conflict the active duty period was June 1950 to January 1955.

Table 11.2   The role of government mortgage debt for home mortgages, 1936–1953

	FHA ($)	VA ($)	Combined ($)	Total home mortgages	FHA and VA home mortgages (% total)
1936	203		203	15,615	1.3
1937	594		594	15,673	3.8
1938	967		967	15,852	6.1
1939	1,755		1,755	16,402	10.7
1940	2,349		2,349	17,400	13.5
1941	3,030		3,030	18,364	16.5
1942	3,742		3,742	18,254	20.5
1943	4,060		4,060	17,807	22.8
1944	4,190		4,190	17,983	23.3
1945	4,078	500	4,578	18,534	24.7
1946	3,692	2,600	6,292	23,048	27.3
1947	3,781	5,800	9,581	28,179	34.0
1948	5,269	7,200	12,469	33,251	37.5
1949	6,906	8,100	15,006	37,515	40.0
1950	8,563	10,300	18,863	45,019	41.9
1951	9,677	13,200	22,877	51,875	44.1
1952	10,770	14,600	25,370	58,188	43.6
1953	11,990	16,100	28,090		

Source: Grebler, Blank, and Winnick (1956, 243).
Note: Values expressed in millions of dollars.

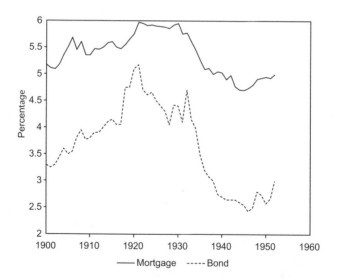

Fig. 11.2   Bond and mortgage rates (1900–1953)
Source: Grebler, Blank, and Winnick (1956).

Between 1900 and 1920, both interest rates had increasing trends. In the 1920s mortgage rates fell a little, while bond rates declined by a bit more. After 1930 mortgage interest rates declined from 5.95 percent to around 4.9 percent. This partially reflected an easy money policy clearly seen in the large decline in bond yields over this period. Some economic historians have used this information to argue that an easy money policy played a large role in the increase in home ownership, but it could also be due to the elimination of regional lending and a more homogeneous credit market.

11.2.2   Tax Treatment of Owner-Occupied Housing

During this period the US government used the tax code to promote owner-occupied housing. The most prominent provisions were the deductibility from taxable income of mortgage interest payments and property taxes as well as the exclusion of the imputed rental value of owner-occupied housing from taxable income. A large body of empirical and quantitative research evaluates the tax treatment of housing. This literature indicates that the elimination of these provisions would have significant effects for tenure and housing consumption. These provisions introduce a wedge into the decision to invest in housing relative to real capital, as well as the tenure (owner vs. renter) decision. Laidler (1969), Aaron (1972), and Rosen and Rosen (1980) estimate that the elimination of these tax provisions has sizable effects on the home ownership rate. There is also a growing literature that uses equilibrium models to assess the impact of changing such provisions and estimate significant effects. For example, Berkovec and Fullerton (1992) use a static disaggregated general equilibrium model and find that eliminating these provisions generates a decline of owner-occupied housing consumption ranging between 3 and 6 percent. Chambers, Garriga, and Schlagenhauf (2009c) find that the elimination of these provisions could increase the ownership rate if the resulting increase in government revenue is rebated to households. However, most of the empirical research on the implications of the tax treatment of owner-occupied housing are either estimated or calibrated to the postwar period. In addition, these studies in general ignore the implications of mortgage choice.

The progressivity of the income tax code changed significantly between 1940 and 1960. The Tax Foundation has constructed marginal tax rates by income level for 1940 and 1960. As Figure 11.3 shows, the marginal tax rates were substantially lower in 1940 than in the immediate postwar period. The highest marginal tax rate in 1940 was 63 percent for tax households earning $2 million or more. In contrast, the top marginal rate was 91 percent for households earning over $200,000 in 1960. During this period, income also changed significantly. Chambers, Garriga, and Schlagenhauf (2013) document the importance of education and income in ownership. The basic idea is that conditional on a certain level of income, a higher marginal tax rate increases the benefit of home ownership due to the tax break from the

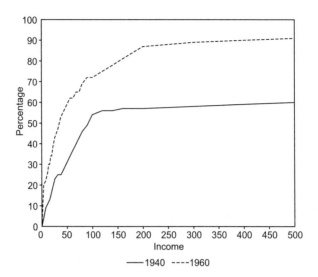

Fig. 11.3   Marginal tax rates in 1940 and 1960
Source: Tax Foundation (http://www.taxfoundation.org).

deductibility of mortgage interest payments and property taxes. This distortion not only provides an additional benefit of owning, but also an incentive to own larger homes.

11.3   Model

The model is based on the overlapping-generations economy with housing and long-term mortgages developed in Chambers, Garriga, and Schlagenhauf (2009a). A more detailed version for the pre–World War II period can be found in Chambers, Garriga, and Schlagenhauf (2013). The economy consists of households, a final goods-producing sector, a rental property sector, a mortgage-lending sector, and the government.

11.3.1   Households

Age Structure

The economy is populated by life cycle households that are ex ante heterogeneous. The heterogeneity is due to different education levels. Let i denote the education level of an individual and j represent the age of an individual. The term J represents the maximum number of periods a household can live. In every period, a household faces mortality risk and uninsurable wage earning uncertainty. The survival probability, conditional on being alive at age j, is denoted by $\psi_{j+1} \in [0,1]$, with $\psi = 1$, and $\psi_{J+1} = 0$. For simplicity, all individuals living in the household are subject to the same mortality risk. Earnings uncertainty implies that the household is subject to income shocks that cannot be insured via private contracts. As is usual in this class of models, annuity markets for mortality risk are absent. The lack of these insurance markets creates a demand for precautionary savings.

Preferences

Household preferences rank goods according to a momentary utility function $u(c,d)$, where c represents the effective consumption of goods, and d represents effective housing services over the life cycle. This function satisfies the usual properties of differentiability and Inada conditions. A comment is required to define effective consumption and effective housing services. At a particular age j, a household is comprised of adults and children. A household consists of up to two adults and children. Because of economies of scale in consumption (housing services), effective consumption (housing services) is simply household consumption divided by a household consumption aggregator.[9]

Asset Structure

Households have access to a portfolio of two assets to mitigate income and mortality risk. A financial asset is denoted by a' with a net return r, and a housing durable good is denoted by h' with a market price p, where the prime is used to denote future variables. This assumption simplifies the problem because households do not need to anticipate changes in house prices. A housing investment of size h' can be thought of as the number of square feet in the house. A house of size h' yields s services.[10] If a household does not invest in housing, $h = 0$; the household is a renter and must purchase housing services from a rental market. The rental price of a unit of housing services is R.

Mortgage Contracts

Housing investment is financed through long-term mortgage contracts. These contracts have a general recursive representation. Consider the expenditure associated with the purchase of a house of size h (i.e., square feet) with a unit price p (per square foot). In general, a mortgage loan requires

---

9. The aggregator used is the old OECD household aggregator. That is, if f_j is the average family size of an age j household, then effective consumption is

$$c_j = \frac{C_j}{[1.7+0.3(f_j-2)]},$$

where the denominator adjusts for economies of scale in household size. The term 1.7 indicates that the second adult accounts for 0.7 of the consumption of the first adult. The term $0.3(f_j-2)$ indicates that each child consumes 30 percent of the first adult. This formulation is a simple way to introduce changes in family structure into the model.

10. For the sake of simplicity, we assume a linear relationship between the house and services generated. In other words, $s = h'$.

a down payment equal to χ percent of the value of the house. The amount χph represents the amount of equity in the house at the time of purchase, and $D_0 = (1 - \chi)ph$ represents the initial amount of the loan. In a particular period, n, the borrower faces a payment amount m_n (i.e., monthly or yearly payment) that depends on the size of the original loan D_0, the length of the mortgage, N, and the mortgage interest rate, r^m. This payment can be subdivided into an amortization, (or principal) component, A_n, which is determined by the amortization schedule, and an interest component I_n, which depends on the payment schedule. That is,

$$(1) \qquad\qquad m_n = A_n + I_n, \qquad \forall n \,,$$

where the interest payments are calculated by $I_n = r^m D_n$.[11] An expression that determines how the remaining debt, D_n, changes over time can be written as

$$(2) \qquad\qquad D_{n+1} = D_n - A_n, \qquad \forall n.$$

This formula shows that the level of outstanding debt at the start of period n is reduced by the amount of any principal payment. A principal payment increases the level of equity in the home. If the amount of equity in a home at the start of period n is defined as H_n, a payment of principal equal to A_n increases equity in the house available in the next period to H_{n+1}. Formally,

$$(3) \qquad\qquad H_{n+1} = H_n + A_n, \qquad \forall n,$$

where $H_0 = \chi ph$ denotes the home equity in the initial period.

Before the Great Depression the typical mortgage contract was characterized by no amortization and a balloon payment at termination. A balloon loan is a very simple contract in which the entire principal borrowed is paid in full in the last period, N. The amortization schedule for this contract can be written as

$$A_n = \begin{cases} 0 & \forall n < N \\ (1-\chi)ph & n = N \end{cases}.$$

This means that the mortgage payment in all periods except the last one, is equal to the interest rate payment, $I_n = r^m D_0$. Hence, the mortgage payment for this contract can be specified as

$$m_n = \begin{cases} I_n & \forall n < N \\ (1-r^m)D_0 & n = N \end{cases},$$

where $D_0 = (1 - \chi)ph$. The evolution of the outstanding level of debt can be written as

---

11. The calculation of the mortgage payment depends on the characteristics of the contract, but for all contracts the present value of the payments must be equal to the total amount borrowed, $D_0 \equiv \chi ph = \sum_{n=1}^{N} m_n/(1 + r)^n$.

$$D_{n+1} = \begin{cases} D_n, & \forall n < N \\ 0 & n = N \end{cases}.$$

With an interest-only loan and no changes in house prices, the home owner never accrues additional equity beyond the initial down payment until the final mortgage payment is made. Hence, $A_n = 0$ and $m_n = I_n = r^m D_0$ for all n. In essence, the home owner effectively rents the property from the lender and the mortgage (interest) payments are the effective rental cost. As a result, the monthly mortgage payment is minimized because no periodic payments toward equity are made. A home owner is fully leveraged with the bank with this type of contract. If the home owner itemizes tax deductions, a large interest deduction is an attractive by-product of this contract.

After the Great Depression, the FHA sponsored a new mortgage contract characterized by a longer duration, lower down payment requirements (i.e., higher LTV ratios), and self-amortization with a mortgage payment comprised of both interest and principal. This loan product is characterized by a constant mortgage payment over the term of the mortgage, $m \equiv m_1 = \ldots = m_N$. This value, m, must be consistent with the condition that the present value of mortgage payments repays the initial loan. That is,

$$D_0 \equiv \chi p h = \sum_n^N \frac{m}{(1+r)^n}.$$

If this equation is solved for m, we can write $m = \lambda D_0$, where $\lambda = r^m [1 - (1 + r^m)^{-N}]^{-1}$. Because the mortgage payment is constant each period and $m = A_t + I_t$, the outstanding debt decreases over time, $D_0 > \ldots > D_n$. This means the fixed payment contract frontloads interest rate payments,

$$D_{n+1} = (1+r^m)D_n - m, \qquad \forall n,$$

and thus backloads principal payments, $A_n = m - r^m D_n$. The equity in the house increases each period by the mortgage payment net of the interest payment component: $H_{n+1} = H_n + [m - r^m D_n]$ every period.

Household Income

Household income varies over the life cycle and depends on (a) whether the household member is a worker or a retiree, (b) the return from savings and transfer programs, and (c) the income generated from the decision to rent property when a homeowner. Households supply their time endowment inelastically to the labor market and earn wage income, w, per effective unit of labor. The effective units of labor depend on the education level and the age of the household. The deterministic component of income is denoted by v_{ij} and a transitory type-dependent idiosyncratic component, ε_{ij}, drawn from a probability distribution, $\Pi_{ij}(\varepsilon_{ij})$. The expectations about income uncertainty are drawn from this distribution. For an individual younger than j^*, labor earnings are then $w\varepsilon_{ij}v_{ij}$. Households of age j^* or older receive a social security transfer that is proportional to average labor income and is defined as θ. Pretax labor earnings are defined as y_w, where

$$y_w(\varepsilon,i,j) = \begin{cases} \omega \varepsilon_{ij} \upsilon_{ij}, & \text{if } j < j^* \\ \theta, & \text{if } j \geq j^* \end{cases}.$$

A second source of income is available to households that invest in housing and decide to rent part of their investment. A household that does not consume all housing services, $h' > d$, can pay a fixed cost, $\varpi > 0$, and receive rental income $y_R(h',d)$; this is denoted as

$$y_R(h',d) = \begin{cases} R(h',d) - \varpi, & \text{if } h' < d \\ 0, & \text{if } h' = d \end{cases}.$$

Savings and transfers provide additional sources of income. Households with positive savings receive $(1 + r)a$. The transfers are derived from the households that die with positive wealth. The value of all these assets is uniformly distributed to the households that remain alive in an equal lump sum amount of tr. The (pretax) income of a household, y, is simply

$$y(h',a,\varepsilon,d,i,j) = y_w(\varepsilon,i,j) + y_R(h',d) + (1+r)a + tr.$$

The various income sources generate a tax obligation of T, which depends on labor income, y_w, net interest earnings from savings, ra, and rental income, y_R, less deductions available in the tax code, Ω. Examples of deductions could be the interest payment deduction on mortgage loans or maintenance expenses associated with tenant-occupied housing. Total tax obligations are denoted as

$$T = T(y_w(\varepsilon,i,j) + ra + y_R(h',d) - \Omega).$$

The Household Decision Problem

A single household's budget constraint cannot be easily written for this problem because such households make discrete tenure decisions. In each period, a renter could purchase a home or a home owner could change the size of the house or even become a renter. Hence, the household's budget constraint depends on the value of the current state variables. The relevant information at the start of the period is the education level (i.e., no education, high school, and college), i, household's age, j, the level of asset holding, a, the housing investment, h, the mortgage choice, z, the mortgage balance with the bank, n, and the income shock $\varepsilon(i,j)$, which is contingent on age and education, written as ε. To simplify notation, let $x = (i,a,h,z,n,j,\varepsilon)$ summarize the household's state vector. A household could face a number of budget constraints depending on the tenure decision. Individuals make decisions over consumption goods, c, housing services, d, and investment in assets, a', and housing, h'. Table 11.3 summarizes the five distinct decision problems that a household must solve with respect to shelter.

Table 11.3   **Choice diagram for the household**

Current renter: $h = 0$	$\left(\begin{array}{l}\text{Continues renting: } h' = 0 \\ \text{Purchases a house: } h' > 0\end{array}\right.$
Current owner: $h > 0$	$\left\{\begin{array}{l}\text{Stays in house: } h' = h \\ \text{Change house size (upsize or downsize): } h' \neq h \\ \text{Sell house and rent: } h' = 0\end{array}\right.$

The starting point is the problem of a household that starts as a renter, and then the decision problem of a household that starts as a home owner is considered.

Renters. A household that is currently renting, ($h = 0$), has two options: continue renting ($h' = 0$) or purchase a house ($h' > 0$). This is a discrete choice in ownership that can easily be captured by the value function v (present and future utility) associated with these two options. Given the relevant information $x = (i,j,a,0,0,0,\varepsilon)$, the individual chooses the option with the higher value, which can be expressed as

$$v(x) = \max\{v^r, v^o\}.$$

The value associated with continued renting is determined by solving

(4) $v^r(x) = \max[u(c,d) + \beta_{j+1}E_{ij}v(x')],$

$$\text{s.t.}\quad c + a' + Rd = y(x) - T.$$

The household is subject to nonnegativity constraints on c, d, and a'. These constraints are present in all possible cases and are not explicitly stated in the other cases.[12] The current decisions determine the state vector tomorrow x' $= (i, j + 1, a, 0,0,0, \varepsilon')$. A household that purchases a house solves a different problem as choices must now be made over $h' > 0$. This decision problem can be written as

(5) $v^o(x) = \max[u(c,d) + \beta_{j+1}E_{ij}v(x')],$

$$\text{s.t.}\quad c + a' + (\phi_b(z,x) + \chi(z,x))ph' + m(h',n;p) = y(x) - T.$$

The purchase of a home requires use of a long-term FRM loan. The mortgage contract is a function that specifies the length of the contract, N, the down payment fraction, $\chi(z,x) \in [0,1]$, and the payment schedule, m. The decision to buy a house of value ph' implies total borrowing must equal D_N $= (1 - \chi(z,x))ph'$. The payment structure depends on the mortgage available in any given period. The purchase of a house requires only an expenditure of the down payment and associated transaction costs, $\phi_b(z,x)$. The model

---

12. The change in the size of rental property (flow) is not subject to transaction costs; only the change in housing investment (stock) is subject to frictions.

formulation is fairly general and allows for down payment and transaction costs to depend on the mortgage choice, and potentially education status. The relevant continuation state is $x' = (i, j + 1, a', h, z, N - 1, \varepsilon')$.

Owners.   The decision problem for a household that currently owns a house $(h > 0)$, has a similar structure. However, a home owner faces a different set of options: stay in the same house $(h' = h)$, purchase a different house $(h' \neq h)$, or sell the house and acquire housing services through the rental market $(h' = 0)$. Given the relevant information state x, the individual solves

$$v(x) = \max\{v^s, v^c, v^r\}.$$

Each of these three different values is calculated by solving three different decision problems.

1. If the home owner decides to stay in the current house the optimization problem can be written as:

(6) $$v^s(x) = \max[u(c, h') + \beta_{j+1} E_{ij} v(x')],$$

$$s.t. \quad c + a' + m(h, n; p) = y(x) - T.$$

This problem is very simple because the home owner must make decisions only on consumption and saving after making the mortgage payment. If the mortgage has been paid off (i.e., $n = 0$), then $m(h,n;p) = 0$. Otherwise, the mortgage payment is positive. The next period state is given by $x = (i, j + 1, a', h, x, n', \varepsilon')$, where $n' = \max\{n - 1, 0\}$.

2. The home owner could continue to be a home owner but with a different housing position. This means the household must sell its housing position, h. The sale of the house generates revenue, $\pi = (1 - \phi_s)ph - D(h,n;p)$, from which transaction costs, $\phi_s ph$, and any remaining principal on the mortgage loan, $D(h,n;p)$, must be paid. The new house that is purchased, h', requires paying transaction costs and down payment costs, $(\phi_b(x) + \chi(x))ph'$, as well as making a mortgage payment on the new house, which depends on the type of mortgage selected to finance the new housing position, $m(h,n;p)$. For this case, the consumer problem is

$$v^c(x) = \max[u(c, h') + \beta_{j+1} E_{ij} v(x')],$$

$$s.t. \quad c + a' + (\phi_b(x) + \chi(x))ph' + m(h, n; p) = y(x) + \pi - T.$$

This household must sell the existing property to purchase a new one. The choices depend on the income received from selling the property, ph, net of transactions costs from selling, ϕ_s, and the remaining principal, $D(n)$, owed to the lender. The relevant future information is given by $x' = (i, j + 1, a', h, z', N - 1, \varepsilon')$.

3. The final option is for the homeowner to sell the current house, $h > 0$,

and become a renter, $h' = 0$, which means the household must make a rental expenditure of Rd.[13]

The consumer's optimization problem for this situation is

(7)
$$v'(x) = \max[u(c,d) + \beta_{j+1}E_{ij}v(x')],$$
$$s.t. \quad c + a' + Rd = y(x) + \pi - T,$$

and the future state vector is $x' = (i, j+1, a', 0, 0, 0, \epsilon')$.

Given the initial information summarized in x, the choice of whether to stay in the house, change the housing size, or sell the house and become a renter depends on the values of v^s, v^c, and v^r.

11.3.2   Mortgage Lending Sector

The financial intermediary is a zero-profit firm. This firm receives deposits from households, a', and uses these funds to make loans to firms and households. Firms acquire loans of capital to produce goods, and households use long-term mortgages to finance housing investment. This formulation does not derive the optimal mortgage contract from the model primitives. It takes the contract structure available during a period as given and imposes the mortgage structure as a constraint. Conditional on the legal lending arrangements, lenders provide credit and receive flows of payments to maximize profits. In addition, financial intermediaries receive principal payments from those individuals who sell their homes with an outstanding mortgage position, as well as the outstanding principal of individuals who unexpectedly die.[14]

11.3.3   Construction Sector

The stock of new homes is produced by a competitive real estate construction sector. Producers manufacture housing units using a linear technology, $I_H = C_H/\theta$, where I_H represents the output of new homes, C_H is the input of the consumption good, and θ is a technology constant used to transform consumption goods into new housing units. Technology is reversible; hence, homes can be transformed into consumption goods. The optimization problem of the representative real estate firm is given by

$$\max_{H,C_H} pI_H - C_H,$$
$$s.t. \quad I_H = C_H / \theta.$$

The first-order condition of the housing sector determines that the equi-

---

13. In the last period, all households must sell h, rent housing services, and consume all their assets, a, as a bequest motive is not in the model. In the last period, $h' = a' = 0$.

14. The formulation of the market clearing condition derived from zero profit on the lender side is in an appendix available from the authors upon request.

librium house price must satisfy $p = \theta$. The homes produced are added to the existing housing stock as either new units or as repairs of the existing stock. The aggregate law of motion for housing investment is

$$I_H = (1 + \rho_n)H' - H + \kappa(H, \delta_o, \delta_r),$$

where $\rho_n \geq 0$ represents the population growth rate. The depreciation of the housing stock $\kappa(H, \delta_o, \delta_r)$ depends on utilization (i.e., owner- versus tenant-occupied housing). The larger the size of the rental market, the larger the investment in housing repairs. If the depreciation rate is the same for owner-occupied and rental housing, $\delta_o = \delta_r$, then residential investment is linear in the stock, or $\kappa(H, \delta_o, \delta_r) = \delta H$. All the aspects of the supply side of the market can be controlled by changing the technological parameter θ. For example, shortages of materials can be captured by a decline in θ, whereas innovations in the process of producing homes (i.e., Levittown on the East Coast) would be an increase in θ.

11.3.4   Production of Final Goods

A representative firm produces a good in a competitive environment that can be used for consumption, government, capital, or housing purposes. The production function has the property of constant returns to scale, $F(K,L) = K^\alpha L^{1-\alpha}$, where K and L denote the amount of capital and labor, respectively, and the term α represents the labor share. The aggregate resource constraint is given by

(8) $$C + C_H + I_K + I_H + G + Y = K^\alpha L^{1-\alpha},$$

where C, I_K, I_H, G, and Y represent aggregate consumption, capital investment, housing investment, government spending, and various transactions costs, respectively.[15]

11.3.5 Government Activities

In this economy, the government regulates markets by imposing particular lending arrangements on the mortgage loan market. It also provides tax provisions toward housing. In addition to these passive regulatory roles, the government plays a more active role through other programs. First, retirement benefits are provided through a pay-as-you-go social security program. Social security contributions are used to finance a uniform transfer upon retirement that represents a fraction of average income. Second, exogenous government expenditure is financed by using a nonlinear income tax scheme. The financing of government expenditure and social security is conducted under different budgets. Finally, the government redistributes

---

15. The definitions for aggregate housing investment and total transaction costs appear in the appendix.

the wealth (housing and financial assets) of individuals who die unexpectedly. Both housing and financial assets are sold and any outstanding debt on housing is paid off. The remaining value of these assets is distributed to the surviving households as a lump-sum payment, tr.

11.3.6 Stationary Equilibrium

In the model, a stationary equilibrium includes optimal decisions that are a function of the individual state variables, $x = (i,j,a,h,z,n,\varepsilon)$ prices $\{r,w,R\}$,market clearing conditions, and a distribution over the state space $\Phi(x)$ that are constant over time.[16]

11.4 Quantitative Analysis

11.4.1 Parameterization

The objective of the chapter is to quantify the role of government policy in housing markets during 1940 to 1960. During this period many other important changes occurred that could account for the large increase in the home ownership rate. In order to measure the role of government policy toward housing, other important factors must be incorporated into the model. Otherwise, the model could mismeasure the role of government policy. The methodology used in this chapter incorporates the key factors that have been mentioned in the literature but focuses on counterfactual experiments pertaining to government housing policy. The change in ownership rates that occurs in these experiments allows us to quantify the importance of government housing policies over this period.[17]

The parameterization technique is based on moment estimation to replicate key properties of the US economy between 1935 and 1940. This period is chosen to minimize the potential structural effects on the housing market due to the National Housing Act. While this act was passed in 1934, the substantive effects of this legislation did not begin to impact housing markets until late in the1930s. Some of the parameters are taken directly from data or other empirical work.

Population Structure

A period in the model corresponds to five years. An individual enters the labor force at age twenty (model period 1) and lives a maximum of eighty-three years (model period 14). Mandatory retirement occurs at age sixty-five (model period 11). The survival probabilities $\{\psi\}$ are from the National Center for Health Statistics, *United States Life Tables* (1935, 1940). The

---

16. A formal definition of the recursive equilibrium is available from the authors.

17. The details of the full decomposition over all of the factors that influence the ownership rate are provided in a companion paper (see Chambers, Garriga, and Schlagenhauf 2013).

initial size of a cohort, μ_{ij}, is endogenously determined by the share of these individuals at age twenty-five or younger and the population growth rate.

Functional Forms

The utility function is CES specified as

$$u(c,d) = \frac{\left[\gamma c^{-\rho} + (1-\gamma)d^{-\rho}\right]^{\frac{1-\sigma}{\rho}}}{1-\sigma},$$

where the parameters γ, σ, and ρ need to be determined. The parameter σ is set to 2, and the intertemporal elasticity of substitution is taken from the range of estimates in the literature and set to 1. The parameters γ, which measures the relative importance of consumption to housing services, and the discount rate β are estimated. The first parameter, γ, is estimated to be consistent with a housing-to-consumption ratio of 0.180. The individual discount rate is determined to match a capital-output ratio for 1935, which was 2.54. The capital stock is defined as private fixed assets plus the stock of consumer durables less the stock of residential structures (to be consistent with the capital stock in the model). Output is gross domestic product (GDP) plus an estimate of the service flow from consumer durables less the service flow from housing.

Goods outputs are produced with a Cobb-Douglas function. The capital share parameter, α, is set to 0.24 based on National Income and Product Accounts (NIPA) data for 1935. Total factor productivity is normalized to unity. The depreciation rate of the firm's capital capital stock, δ, is estimated to be consistent with the observed ratio of fixed capital investment to GDP (as previously defined) for 1935.

Income Endowments

A household's income depends on its education level, i. Four exogenous education levels are available: (a) fewer than eight years of education, (b) between eight and eleven years of education, (c) twelve years of education, and (d) more than twelve years of education. For each education level, a household's income has two components; one is deterministic and the other is stochastic. The values of these components are constructed from Public Use Microdata Samples (PUMS) for the 1940 and 1960 censuses. The deterministic, or life cycle component, v_{ij}, is generated using the average salary and wage income by age and education. A polynomial is fit to age-specific averages per education to smooth this component. The determination of the uncertain component hinges on the available data. The reliance on census data (which restricts data availability to once every ten years) does not allow the estimation of a serially correlated income process.[18]

---

18. Storesletten, Telmer, and Yaron (2004) find that income shocks have a persistent component even when you condition on all the observables. Their finding is based on a sample of

Our strategy is to assume the stochastic component, ε_{ij}, is independent and identically distributed over education and age. This component of income, along with the associated probabilities, is estimated using a kernel density estimation for every age cohort, $\Pi_{ij}(\varepsilon_{ij})$, for the cross-section of individuals. Since the unit in the model is the household, the estimation considers only households that work full-time. Therefore, the model captures the dispersion of labor income for a given education. This approach has the attractive property that it reproduces, by construction, the coefficient of labor income dispersion observed in the data for both periods.

Family Size

The size of the average household family is constructed using census data for the relevant years. Since the baby boom takes place during this period, the goal is to allow for the effects of changing household family size in the demand for owner-occupied housing. In a more detailed theory, changes in institutional arrangements could affect fertility decisions. In the model, the demographic structure is taken as exogenously determined and does not depend on education types.

Government and the Income Tax Function

In 1940, the US Social Security program was in its infancy. The payroll tax rate for a worker was 1 percent of wage income. In addition, wage income for payroll tax purposes was capped at $3,000. The model uses a 30 percent replacement rate.

The income tax code in 1940 differentiated wage income from total net taxable income, which is equal to wage and interest income less interest payments such as mortgage interest payments. Each household receives an earned income credit. This credit is equal to 10 percent of wage income as long as net income is less than $3,000. If net income exceeds $3,000, the credit is calculated as 10 percent of the minimum of wage income or total taxable income. The tax credit is capped at $1,400. In addition to the earned income credit, each household received a personal exemption of $800. If these two credits are subtracted from total net taxable income, adjusted taxable income is determined. The actual tax schedules for 1940 and 1960 are programmed to determine a household's tax obligation. The tax functions for 1940 and 1960 are summarized in figure 11.3. For the 1940 tax code, the marginal tax rate is 0.79, which is applicable to income levels exceeding $500,000. In 1940, an income tax surcharge equal to an additional 10 percent of income which must be included in the income tax obligation. The documentation for the 1940 tax code is the Internal Revenue Service and

---

household data over many periods from the Panel Survey on Income Dynamics. Other recent works (e.g., Castaneda, Diaz-Giminez, and Rios-Rull [2003]) find that a smaller persistent component is needed once ex ante heterogeneity is considered. Their model is constructed to generate the observed income and wealth differences.

the Tax Foundation. To ensure that the income tax function generates the proper amount of revenue for 1940, an adjustment factor must be added to the tax code. This parameter can be considered as adding an intercept to the tax function. If too much revenue is generated, this parameter, τ_0, can be reduced. This factor is estimated by targeting the personal income tax revenue-to-GDP ratio. In 1935, this ratio was 0.01.

Housing

In the baseline model, home owners have two mortgage choices: a short-duration balloon loan restricted to ten years with a 50 percent down payment and a twenty-year FRM with a 20 percent down payment. Formally, $\chi(1) = 0.5$ and $\chi(2) = 0.2$. The transaction costs from buying and selling property are $\phi_s = 0$ and $\phi_b = 0.06$. The minimum house size, $\underline{h}$, is estimated to be consistent with the set of specified targets. The values δ_o and δ_r are from Chambers, Garriga, and Schlagenhauf (2009a), where the annual depreciation rates for owner- and tenant-occupied housing are $\delta_o = 0.0106$ and $\delta_r = 0.0135$, respectively.

Wealth Endowments

Bequests appear to have been an important source of home ownership for young households in 1940. Table 11.4 presents IRS data on real estate bequests in both 1940 and 1960.[19]

Although the number of returns tripled between 1940 and 1960, the total gross value of real estate bequests grew by less that 10 percent. However, the amount of outstanding debt on bequeathed real estate more than tripled in the same twenty-year period. As a result, the net value of real estate bequests actually dropped by 23 percent between 1940 and 1960. The apparent importance of real estate bequests in 1940 requires the introduction of an additional parameter W_0 to the model. This parameter represents the percentage of age 1 households that receive a bequest of a minimum-size home. The percentage is adjusted so that the model generates a home owner-ship rate for young households similar to that found in the data. The value of transfers from accidental death is adjusted to equal the amount of housing bequests to individuals.

The estimation of the set structural parameters $(\delta,\gamma,\beta,\underline{h},\tau_0,W_0)$ for 1940 is based on an exactly identified method of moments approach plus the computation of market clearing (capital market and rental market) under the restriction that the government budget constraint is balanced. Table 11.5

---

19. The data in table 5 are from the US Treasury Department, Bureau of Internal Revenue, *Statistics on Income for 1940, Part 1*. These data are compiled from individual income tax returns, taxable fiduciary income and defense tax returns, and estate tax returns prepared under the direction of the commissioner of revenue by the statistics section, income tax unit. A similar document is used for 1960.

Table 11.4   Real estate bequests in the United States, 1940–1960

Year	Returns	Gross bequest value ($)	Mortgages and debts ($)	Net bequest value ($)
1940	16,156	2,649,492,000	229,866,000	2,419,626,000
1960	52,070	2,857,330,000	690,038,000	1,867,292,000

Source: Internal Revenue Service, Historical Data.

Table 11.5   Parameterization of model

Statistic	Target	Model
Ratio of wealth to gross domestic product (K/Y)	2.540	2.5470
Ratio of housing services to consumption of goods (Rs_c/c)	0.180	0.1800
Ratio of fixed capital investment to GDP ($\delta K/Y$)	0.112	0.1120
Home ownership rate	0.436	0.4350
Ratio of personal income tax revenue to output ($T(ay)/Y$)	0.010	0.0099
Balanced bequests	0.000	0.0003

Variable	Parameter	Value
Individual discount rate	β	0.928
Share of consumption goods in the utility function	γ	0.947
Depreciation rate on capital	δ	0.197
Minimum housing size	$\underline{h}$	0.637
Lump-sum tax transfer	τ_0	0.081
Initial-period bequested homes	W_0	0.565

reports the parameter values that generate aggregate statistics consistent with the US economy. Parameters are estimated within 1 percent error for all the observed targets.

11.4.2   Baseline Economy: 1940

The model can be evaluated from various perspectives. The objective is to measure the performance by considering home ownership rate statistics for various years and age groups. As table 11.6 shows, the home ownership rate in 1930 was 48.1 percent, whereas after the Great Depression it ranged between 42.7 and 45.5 percent. Since the baseline model attempts to focus on the home ownership rate prior to the impact of the National Housing Act, the targeted home ownership rate is 45.5 percent.

Since the aggregate home ownership rate is an estimation target, it not surprising that the baseline model generates a number close to the selected moment. The age-specific home ownership rates also can be used to evaluate the model. The model captures the hump-shaped behavior observed in the data. The lowest home ownership rate is for the youngest age cohort;

Table 11.6   Home ownership (%) by age

Age	Data		Model 1940
	1930	1940–1943	
Under 35 years	20.0	19.1	22.7
36–45 years	48.5	42.1	49.5
46–55 years	57.7	51.0	61.8
56–65 years	65.1	57.5	69.5
65 years and over	69.7	60.3	69.4
Total	48.1	42.7–45.5	45.7

Source: US Census Bureau.

Table 11.7   Housing finance

Statistics	Model 1940
Home ownership rate	45.7
No mortgage (%)	83.5
Mortgage loan (%)	16.5
Share balloon (5-year)	100.0
Share FRM (20-year)	0.0

this pattern is apparent in 1930 and 1940 with the difference that home ownership rates are higher in 1930. The model does generate a pattern by age cohort consistent with the census estimates. The model also makes predictions about mortgage holdings. Table 11.7 summarizes some aggregate statistics about housing finance.

It is difficult to find micro data on the holding of specific mortgage contracts, but given the short duration and the predominance of balloon-type mortgages, this contract would be expected to be dominant in the model. In the model the majority of home owners (83.5 percent) do not have a mortgage. In the model all the home owners purchase housing using the balloon loan. The share of FRMs predicted by the model for 1940 is zero.

11.4.3   Baseline Economy: 1960

Many factors could have been important in the determination of the ownership boom. The objective of this section is to isolate the contribution of government programs from other relevant factors that could influence the increase in ownership. Government programs potentially affect home ownership through policies that have an impact on financing of housing, changes in the federal income tax structure, the role of the mortgage interest rate deduction, and the reduction of transaction costs in mortgage rates. To measure the contribution of these government policies, the model must account for other factors that have been argued as critical.[20] The relevant factors that changed between 1940 and 1960 are summarized as follows:

1. Demographic factors: These include changes in the survival probabilities, education composition, and family structure.
2. Endowments: These include a change in the distribution of the i.i.d. idiosyncratic income component, the efficiency units by age and education, and the fact that real wage income increased by a factor of 2.25.
3. House prices: According to Case-Shiller price data, real house prices increased by 41.5 percent. Since house prices in the model are determined by the productivity parameter in the construction sector, this parameter must be adjusted to generate the increased cost of housing per unit.
4. Housing finance: Changes include the extension of the FRM maturity from twenty to thirty years and a decline in the spread between the mortgage interest rate and the risk-free rate from 2.53 to 1.63 percent annualized.
5. Taxation: This includes the relevant changes in the tax code.

Table 11.8 summarizes the implications of allowing all factors to change in the model.[21] The model accounts for a significant amount of the total change in ownership (level) as well as the compositional differences across age groups. It is important to note that these are endogenous variables, not a result of estimating the parameters for 1960.

For example, the actual aggregate housing participation rate in 1960 was 62.5 percent and the model predicts a similar magnitude. The model-generated age-cohort ownership rates have a more pronounced hump compared with actual 1960 data, but this is likely due to the fact that home owners do not face mobility or health shocks that could require them to sell their house and rent. Despite the small differences in levels, the change between both periods in the model and data is quite similar, suggesting

20. The federal income tax code changed significantly by 1960. Using data from the Tax Foundation and the US Treasury Department Internal Revenue Service publication no. 17, it is possible to construct a representative tax function. This tax function had to account for the fact that renters were not likely to itemize their deductions. A model assumption is that in 1960 all renters did not itemize deductions. As a result, these individuals used tax tables different from the households that did itemize. In fact, nonitemizing households with income levels under $5,000 were able to use a tax table that differed from nonitemizers with income over $5,000. Individuals were allowed an individual deduction worth $600 that could be used to minimize the tax obligation. If a household itemized expenses because of the mortgage interest rate deduction, another tax table was to be used to calculate the income tax obligation where taxable income excluded the mortgage deduction and the individual exemption. The tax adjustment coefficient, τ_0, is set to be consistent with a federal income tax-to-GDP ratio of 7.73 percent. Income tax obligations were much higher in 1960 and marginal tax rates were higher (see figure 11.3). The top marginal tax rate in 1960 was 91 percent for income over $2 million. The payroll tax increased to 1.5 percent of wage income up to a cap of $4,800.

21. In 1960, households have mortgage choice (thirty-year FRM mortgage and a balloon contract). In equilibrium, households do not hold a balloon-type contract. In other words, the twenty-year (or thirty-year) fixed-rate contract is a dominant contract.

Table 11.8   Model prediction for home ownership rate, 1940–1960

Age cohort	Data (%)			Model (%)		
	1940	1960	Difference	1940	1960	Difference
Under 35 years	19.1	56.2	37.1	22.7	53.5	30.8
36–45 years	42.1	68.1	26.0	49.5	80.0	30.5
46–55 years	51.0	69.5	18.5	61.8	86.5	24.7
56–65 years	57.5	69.3	11.8	69.5	85.4	15.9
65–72 years	60.3	69.8	9.5	69.4	73.3	3.9
Total	45.5	62.5	18.9	45.7	63.5	17.8

that this dynamic model of tenure and mortgage choice provides a useful laboratory to assess the importance of government interventions in housing finance and housing policy.

11.4.4   Policy Intervention in Housing Finance

In this section, the model is used to measure the contribution of federal housing policies to the increased home ownership rate.[22] The focus is on the importance of amortizing contracts, mortgage duration, and mortgage interest rate costs. Chambers, Garriga, Schlagenhauf (2009a, 2009b) found that mortgage market innovation was the key factor in explaining the increase in the home ownership rate between 1996 and 2005. More precisely, the introduction of highly leveraged loans with graduated mortgage payments was found important as this type of contract attracted first-time buyers to the housing market, while more established households still had the availability of the standard thirty-year FRM contract. Significant mortgage contract innovation also occurred in the mortgage market between 1930 and 1960. As discussed previously, stimulating the flow of mortgage funds to residential construction was a goal of federal housing policies since the early 1930s. Grebler, Blank, and Winnick, (1956, 238) state:

> Stimulating the flow of mortgage funds to residential construction has been the principal aim of federal housing policies since the early and middle thirties . . . [T]hese policies in fact have operated almost exclusively through the use of various devices influencing the flow of private institutional mortgages funds, that is, mortgage insurance or guarantee and improved marketability of loans through the Federal National Mortgage Association. . . . Another major objective of federal housing policies has been to reduce the periodic payments of mortgage borrowers, by lowering interest rates and lengthening contract terms. Policy makers looked

22. It is interesting to note that Grebler, Blank, and Winnick (1956, 238) stated that the "precise effects of the Federal Housing Administration and Veterans Administration programs on the volume of residential mortgage lending are as indeterminable as their impact on residential building activity."

to easier borrowing as a way to increase demand for new residential construction.

As noted in the previous section, the starting point is the benchmark model where the 1940 estimated parameters are used with all factors at their 1960 values. Households have access to a thirty-year FRM mortgage with a 20 percent down payment requirement as well as a ten-year balloon contract with a 50 percent down payment. As documented earlier, the home ownership rate would be at 63.5 percent. Since the baseline model captures the magnitude of the increase in ownership, one way to measure the contribution of the thirty-year FRM is to replace this contract with a twenty-year FRM contract. This latter contract corresponds to the initial offering of FRMs in the 1940s.

As table 11.9 shows, the model predicts that the aggregate home ownership rate should fall from 63.5 percent to 61.6 percent. The model suggests that the extension of the FRM contract from twenty to thirty years can explain around 12 percent of the increase in ownership. The effect is more dramatic by age cohorts, particularly in young and middle-aged buyers. For these groups, a more leveraged contract reduces the magnitude of the mortgage payments and makes housing more attractive. In both economies, the fraction of individuals who use the balloon loan with 50 percent down payment is zero.

All households use the FRM but the change in duration, combined with the general equilibrium effects, makes this contract more attractive to a larger percentage of the population. The higher aggregate LTV ratio implies that the percentage of home owners with no mortgage is substantially reduced from the 1940s figure. In the economy with a twenty-year FRM, only 6.3 percent of home owners do not have a mortgage and when the maturity is extended the number does not change. The lesson learned is that mortgage innovation did make a significant contribution to the increase in home ownership between 1940 and 1960.

The ten-year increase in loan maturity had a positive effect on the aggre-

Table 11.9	Contribution of thirty-year FRM in 1960				
	Data			Model predictions (1960)	
Age cohort	1940	1960	1940	FRM = 20-year	FRM = 30-year (%)
Under 35 years	19.1	56.2	22.7	50.7	53.5
36–45 years	42.1	68.1	49.5	78.7	80.0
46–55 years	51.0	69.5	61.8	86.2	86.5
56–65 years	57.5	69.3	69.5	84.0	85.4
65–72 years	60.3	69.8	69.4	64.7	73.3
Total	45.5	62.5	45.7	61.6	63.5

Table 11.10   Loan maturity of FRM and ownership

Age (yr) Cohort	1940 (%)	Model predictions (1960)		
		30-year (%)	35-year (%)	40-year (%)
25–35	22.7	53.5	54.1	54.3
36–45	49.5	80.0	77.4	77.2
46–55	61.8	86.5	84.7	84.4
56–65	69.5	85.4	84.7	84.0
66–82	69.4	73.3	52.7	52.6
Total	45.7	63.5	63.0	62.5

gate home ownership rate. One could ask whether additional extensions in the maturity would have resulted in even larger increases in home ownership. The model can be used to examine implications of increasing the maturity beyond thirty years. Table 11.10 summarizes the findings of extending the maturity of FRM to thirty-five and forty years.

The model suggests that extending the loan maturity beyond thirty years has only a very marginal (negative) effect in the aggregate ownership rate. The aggregate effects mask some interesting distributional implications. As the maturity increases, the mortgage payments for an equivalent home are reduced and housing becomes more attractive for the young working cohorts. The decline in the older cohorts is mainly due to the terminal condition that forces individuals to sell the home before they die. Given the extended loan maturity, the fraction of retired home owners carrying a mortgage increases and properties are sold earlier.

Overall, the introduction of the thirty-year FRM can account for roughly 12 percent of the total change in ownership. The model suggests that the length of the mortgage contract sponsored by FHA had a significant effect on ownership; however, increasing the maturity beyond thirty years seems to have a small negative effect in ownership. Since FRM contracts already existed in the 1940s and 1950s, an obvious question is why the FRM contracts were not more popular in the 1940s when this type contract first became available. As documented in Chambers, Garriga, and Schlagenhauf (2013), given that average household income was lower in 1940 than 1960 by a significant factor, the 1940 household might not have been financially able to take advantage of the leverage features available in a FRM contract.

In addition to federal policies that impacted home ownership through mortgage contract structure, Grebler, Blank, and Winnick (1956) argue that a policy of lower mortgage interest rates and increased mortgage market efficiencies were important in the increase in home ownership. Data for 1940 and 1960 suggest the spread between the mortgage interest rate and risk-free rate declined 85 basis points. The model can be used to quantify the impor-

Table 11.11   **The importance of the interest rate**

Experimental factors	Ownership (%)
1. Baseline: 1960 factors, 1940 parameters, 30-year FRM, 1960 spread	63.5
2. Model: 1960 factors, 1940 parameters, 30-year FRM, 1940 spread	62.1

tance of the decline in the spread that resulted from an improved mortgage market. The test maintains the baseline model for 1960 but assumes the 1940 spread. If the interest spread is increased to the 1940 value, while maintaining the other factors at their 1960 values, the model-predicted ownership rate would be 62.1 percent as summarized in table 11.11. The decrease in the spread accounts for an 8.5 percent change in homeownership.

11.4.5   Housing Policy: The Tax Treatment of Housing

This section explores the direct role of housing policy, taking as given the innovations in housing finance. The purpose is to use the model to understand how housing tenure and investment decisions can be affected by housing policy embedded in the tax code. Part of the analysis is based on Chambers, Garriga, and Schlagenhauf (2009c). The key difference is that the previous model does not consider mortgage choice, but in the current framework mortgage choice is an important consideration.

Understanding how this type of housing policy affects a household's tenure and duration decisions requires examination of the household's budget constraint. Some additional notation is required. Let κ_o and κ_r represent the taxable fraction of housing services consumed by owner- and tenant-occupied housing, respectively. The terms ι_o and ι_r represent the fraction of maintenance expenses from owner- and tenant-occupied housing that is deductible. Given these definitions, taxable income can be defined in the model as

$$(9) \qquad y = \omega + ra + \kappa_r R(h' - d) + \kappa_o Rd - \iota_r \delta_r p(h' - d) - \iota_o \delta_0 pd - \Omega,$$

where Ω represents other types of deductions. The mortgage interest rate deduction would enter through this variable as it obviously reduces taxable income.[23] For home owners who do not pay the fixed entry cost ($\varpi > 0$), the definition of taxable income is reduced to

$$(10) \qquad\qquad y = \omega + ra + \kappa_o Rd - \iota_o \delta_0 pd - \Omega,$$

as $h' = d$.

The first-order condition of a household that supplies rental housing services to the market can be expressed as

---

23. These terms are relevant only for home owners since renters are not affected because they cannot be property owners in the model.

(11) $$\frac{u_d}{u_c} = R - p\Delta\delta + T'(y)[p(\iota_r\delta_r - \iota_o\delta_o) - R(\kappa_r - \kappa_o)],$$

where u_c measures the marginal utility with respect to consumption c, and u_d represents the marginal utility with respect to housing services consumption, d. The first term on the right-hand side is the rental price of a unit of housing, R, and measures the benefit to a household of foregoing a unit of housing services. This benefit is reduced the greater the spread in the depreciation rate for renter- and owner-occupied housing, $\Delta\delta = (\delta_r - \delta_o)$. Ignoring tax considerations, the effective cost of owner-occupied housing services is $R_e = R - p(\delta_r - \delta_o)$. The implicit moral hazard problem makes renting more expensive than owning as in Henderson and Ioannides (1983). The last two terms on the right-hand side of the equation reflect the asymmetric treatment of owner- and tenant-occupied housing. The benefit from supplying services to the rental market is reduced when the spread in the fraction of rental income relative to owner-occupied imputed income is larger. In addition, the benefit increases when the spread between maintenance expenses on renter- and owner-occupied housing increases. Removing the asymmetries, $\iota_r = \iota_o\delta_o/\delta_r$ and $\kappa_r = \kappa_o$, and eliminating the progressivity of income taxation, $T'(y)$, reduces the benefits from housing policy. As a result, the first-order condition without distortions is:

(12) $$\frac{u_d}{u_c} = R - p\Delta\delta.$$

The US tax code has explicit provisions toward housing that imply $\kappa_o = \iota_o = 0$ and $\kappa_r = \iota_r = 1$. That is, the income from the consumption of tenant-occupied housing services is taxable, whereas owner-consumed housing services are not taxable. Maintenance expenses are treated asymmetrically in the tax code. Owner-occupied maintenance expenses cannot be deducted whereas maintenance expenses incurred with respect to tenant-occupied housing are deductible. Under the US code, the first-order condition becomes

(13) $$\frac{u_d}{u_c} = R[1 - T'(y)] + p[T'(\bar{y})\delta_r - \Delta\delta].$$

In addition to the asymmetric distortions just discussed and housing deductions, Ω, that affect adjusted gross income, y, the degree of progressivity of the marginal tax rates, $T'(y)$, affects housing decisions. For example, under a more progressive tax code, the taxation effects are large, which changes the incentives to own and supply rental property. At the aggregate level some of these incentives can disappear due to general equilibrium effects. Since the model has mortgage choice, changes in the tax code can change the incentives on when to buy and the size of the house.

The Home Mortgage Interest Deduction

One of the hallmarks of US housing policy is the deductibility of mortgage interest payments for households that itemize. This deduction creates an incentive to both own and consume more homes, generating an asymmetry between housing and financial investment. The view among many economists is that the removal of the interest deduction would reduce owner-occupied housing consumption and thus result in smaller home sizes. Home ownership would be lower because the incentives to own have been reduced. Under revenue neutrality, the elimination of the deduction for mortgage interest costs results in additional revenue, thus leading to a tax reduction.[24]

The baseline model assumes complete deductibility of mortgage interest payments. Formally, the deduction on taxable income can be expressed as $\Omega = \chi I_n = \chi r^m D(h',n;p)$, where the term χ captures the percentage of mortgage interest costs that is deductible. If $\chi = 1$, then mortgage interest expenses are fully deductible. It is also important to point out that the benefits from the mortgage interest deduction are enhanced when the tax rates are more progressive.

The importance of the mortgage interest rate deduction can be determined if the model is resolved under the assumption that this deduction is eliminated, $\chi = 0$. Table 11.12 summarizes the quantitative implications of this change in policy.

By comparing the baseline version of the model, (i.e., the model with estimated 1940 parameters with the various factors that existed in 1960), in which a mortgage interest rate deduction is allowed with the same model except the mortgage interest deduction is removed, the home ownership rate would increase from 63.5 percent to 67.6 percent, or a 22 percent increase.[25] The importance of general equilibrium effects can be tested by solving the model with fixed prices. In this case, ownership declines to 50.2 percent, a value more in line with Rosen and Rosen (1980) who estimate a negative effect in ownership. Their framework ignores the importance of income effects and the analysis indicates the importance of using a general equilibrium approach over a partial equilibrium approach when relative prices change significantly.

Taxation of Owner-Occupied Housing Service Flows

Many economists argue that the primary distortion in the current tax code is the treatment of housing services. Previous studies of the postwar period

---

24. This point is important to keep in mind in policy analysis as the lowering of tax revenue to maintain revenue neutrality can reverse the intuition implied from a partial equilibrium analysis.
25. In this model all home owners can choose to either use the standard deduction or itemize, picking the choice that generates the lower tax liability.

Table 11.12   The importance of the mortgage deduction

Experimental factors	Ownership (%)
1. Baseline: 1960 factors,1940 parameters, $\chi = 1$	63.5
2. Removal of the mortgage deduction, $\chi = 0$	67.6
3. Prices fixed, revenue neutrality not imposed, $\chi = 0$	50.2

Table 11.13   The importance of taxation housing

Experimental factors	Ownership (%)
1. Baseline: 1960 factors,1940 parameters, $\kappa_o = 0$ and $\kappa_r = 1$	63.5
2. Taxation of services, $\kappa_0 = \kappa_r = 1$	60.4
3. Prices fixed, revenue neutrality not imposed, $\kappa_0 = \kappa_r = 1$	55.9

suggest that the elimination of this asymmetry should lead to the consumption of smaller homes and lower home ownership. For example, Berkovec and Fullerton (1992) find that the taxation of housing services should reduce average housing consumption between 3 and 6 percent, whereas Gervais (2002) finds that taxing imputed rents of owner-occupied housing would increase the capital stock by more than 6 percent but decrease the housing stock by 8 percent.

Under the current tax code, income generated from rental property is subject to taxation, but the implicit income from owner-occupied housing is not taxed. As shown in equation (13), this policy introduces an asymmetry in the tax treatment of owners and landlords that favors the consumption of owner-occupied housing services and reduces the incentive to supply rental property. The landlord supply decision when housing services are taxed at different rates is determined by

$$(14) \qquad \frac{u_d}{u_c} = [R - p\Delta\delta] + T'(\tilde{y})p\delta_r - T'(\tilde{y})R(\kappa_r - \kappa_o).$$

The US tax code for the period 1940 to 1960 would set $\kappa_o = 0$ and $\kappa_r = 1$. In equation (14), the term $T'(\tilde{y})R(\kappa_r - \kappa_o)$ measures the impact of the failure to tax housing services. As can be seen, this term reduces the effective cost of owner-occupied housing and thus introduces a bias toward owner-occupied housing consumption. This asymmetry is eliminated when the fraction of imputed rental income from owner- and tenant-occupied housing is taxed at the same rate, $\kappa_r = \kappa_o$, but not necessarily zero. The analysis considers the case where the imputed rental income (measured as Rd) is fully faxed, $\kappa_o = \kappa_r = 1$. Table 11.13 presents these results.

The model suggests that the lack of taxation of housing services has an important impact in accounting for the increase in home ownership. The model suggests that if housing services were taxed, the home ownership rate would be 21 percent lower. Again, a partial equilibrium analysis would overstate the importance of the policy of not taxing owner-occupied housing services. With fixed prices, the taxation of housing services reduces the home ownership rate to 55.9.

11.5   Conclusion

After the collapse of housing markets during the Great Depression, the government, as part of the New Deal, played a large role in shaping the future of housing finance. By 1960, the housing market had more than recovered as the home ownership rate soared to over 60 percent. This chapter quantifies the role of government intervention in housing markets in explaining the expansion in US homeownership between 1940 and 1960; this role is quantified with an equilibrium model of tenure choice. In the model, home buyers have access to a menu of mortgage choices to finance the acquisition of the house. The government also provides special programs, consistent with the provisions in the tax code. The parameterized model is consistent with key aggregate and distributional features in the United States in 1940. The model can account for the boom in home ownership when adjusted to a 1960 economy.

Government intervention via the mortgage market was a key part of the housing boom. The model suggests that moving from a twenty-year to a thirty-year FRM accounts for roughly 12 percent of the increase in home ownership. When combined with a narrowing mortgage interest rate wedge, the total impact of mortgage innovation is approximately 21 percent. Government intervention via tax policy was also a significant factor in the housing boom. The model suggests that housing policy can have important effects in ownership. For example, the elimination of the mortgage deduction only reduces ownership when prices are fixed and the tax surplus is not rebated back to the household sector. The taxation of housing services always reduces ownership.

These estimates have ignored the implications of the GI Bill for US housing markets. This legislation could affect housing markets in two ways. First, the GI Bill made housing markets more accessible to veterans through down payment and mortgage payment subsidies. Fetter (2010) presented some empirical findings on this question. Second, this bill provided benefits for human capital investment. The number of college graduates increased substantially under this program. This means an individual with this level of human capital will operate on a higher income path in expected terms than an individual with less education, which has implications for housing investment. The quantitative implications of these policies are analyzed in more detail in Chambers, Garriga, and Schlagenhauf (2011).

References

Aaron, H. 1972. *Shelter and Subsides*. Washington, DC: Brookings Institution.
Amaral, P. S., and J. C. MacGee. 2002. "The Great Depression in Canada and the United States: A Neoclassical Perspective." *Review of Economic Dynamics* 5 (1): 45–72.
Behrens, C. F. 1952. *Commercial Bank Activities in Urban Mortgage Financing*. New York: National Bureau of Economic Research.
Berkovec, J., and D. Fullerton. 1992. "A General Equilibrium Model of Housing, Taxes and Portfolio Choice." *Journal of Political Economy* 100 (2): 390–429.
Carliner, M. S. 1998. "Development of Federal Home Ownership Policy." *Housing Policy Debate* 9 (2): 299–321.
Castaneda, A., J. Diaz-Gimenez, and J. V. Rios-Rull. 2003. "Accounting for the U.S. Earnings and Wealth Inequality." *Journal of Political Economy* 111 (4): 818–57.
Cole, H. L., and L. E. Ohanian. 2002. "The Great U.K. Depression: A Puzzle and Possible Resolution." *Review of Economic Dynamics* 5 (1): 19–45.
———. 2004. "New Deal Policies and the Persistence of the Great Depression: A General Equilibrium Analysis." *Journal of Political Economy* 112 (4): 779–816.
Chambers, M., C. Garriga, and D. Schlagenhauf. 2009a. "Accounting for Changes in the Home Ownership Rate." *International Economic Review* 50 (3): 677–726.
———. 2009b. "The Loan Structure and Housing Tenure Decisions in an Equilibrium Model of Mortgage Choice." *Review of Economic Dynamics* 12 (5): 444–68.
———. 2009c. "Housing Policy and the Progressivity of Income Taxation." *Journal of Monetary Economics* 56 (8): 1116–34.
———. 2011. "The New Deal, the GI Bill, and the Post-War Housing." Florida State University. Working Paper.
———. 2013. "Constructing the Post-War Housing Boom." Florida State University Working Paper.
Eccles, M. 1951. *Beckoning Frontiers*. New York: Knopf.
Edwards, E. 1950. "Urban Real Estate Financing by Savings and Loan Associations" NBER Working Paper, Cambridge, MA.
Fetter, D. K. 2010. "Housing Finance and the Mid-Century Transformation in US Home Ownership: The VA Home Loan Program." Unpublished Manuscript, Harvard University.
Gervais, M. 2002. "Housing Taxation and Capital Accumulation." *Journal of Monetary Economics* 49 (7): 1461–89.
Grebler, L., D. M. Blank, and L. Winnick. 1956. *Capital Formation in Residential Real Estate*. Princeton, NJ: Princeton University Press.
Hayashi F., and E. Prescott. 2002. "The 1990s in Japan: A Lost Decade." *Review of Economic Dynamics* 5 (1): 206–36.
Hendershott, P. H., and J. D. Shilling. 1982. "The Economics of Tenure Choice, 1955–1979." In *Research in Real Estate*, edited by C. Sirmans. Greenwich, CT: JAI Press.
Henderson, J. V., and Y. M. Ioannides. 1983. "A Model of Housing Tenure Choice." *American Economic Review* 73 (1): 98–113.
Laidler, D. 1969. "Income Taxation Incentives for Owner-Occupied Housing." In *The Taxation of Income from Capital*, edited by A. Harberger and M. Bailey, 50–76. Washington, DC: Brookings Institution.
Morton, J. E. 1956. *Urban Mortgage Lending: Competitive Markets and Experience*. Princeton, NJ: Princeton University Press.
Ohanian, L. 1997. "The Macroeconomic Effects of War Finance in the United States." *American Economic Review* 87 (1): 23–40.

Perri, F., and V. Quadrini. 2002. "The Great Depression in Italy: Trade Restrictions and Real Wage Rigidities." *Review of Economic Dynamics* 5 (1): 128–51.

Rose, J., and K. Snowden. 2012. "The New Deal and the Origins of the Modern American Real Estate Loan Contract in the Building and Loan Industry." Working Paper, University of North Carolina, Greensboro.

Rosen, H., and K. T. Rosen. 1980. "Federal Taxes and Home Ownership: Evidence from Time Series." *Journal of Political Economy* 88 (1): 59–75.

Saulnier, R. J. 1950. *Urban Mortgage Lending by Life Insurance Companies.* New York: National Bureau of Economic Research.

Storesletten, K., C. Telmer, and A. Yaron. 2004. "Consumption and Risk Sharing Over the Life Cycle." *Journal of Monetary Economics* 51 (3): 609–33.

Yearns, M. H. 1976. "Governmental Housing Programs: A Brief Review." In *Housing Perspectives: Individuals and Families,* edited by C. S. Wedin and L. G. Nygren. Minneapolis, MN: Burgess Publishing.

Contributors

Michael Brocker

Matthew Chambers
Department of Economics
101B Stephens Hall
Towson University
Towson, MD 21252

Daniel K. Fetter
Department of Economics
Wellesley College
106 Central Street
Wellesley, MA 02481

Alexander J. Field
Department of Economics
Santa Clara University
Santa Clara, CA 95053

Price Fishback
Department of Economics
University of Arizona
Tucson, AZ 85721

Rik Frehen
Department of Finance
Faculty of Economics and Business
Tilburg University
P.O. Box 90153
5000 LE Tilburg, The Netherlands

Carlos Garriga
Research Division
Federal Reserve Bank of St. Louis
P.O. Box 442
St. Louis, MO 63166-0442

Steven Gjerstad
Economic Science Institute
Chapman University
One University Drive
Orange, CA 92866

William N. Goetzmann
School of Management
Yale University
Box 208200
New Haven, CT 06520-8200

Christopher Hanes
Department of Economics
State University of New York at
   Binghamton
P.O. Box 6000
Binghamton, NY 13902

Trevor Kollmann
School of Economics, Finance and
  Marketing
Royal Melbourne Institute of
  Technology University
Building 80, Level 10, Room 57
445 Swanston Street, Melbourne
  Victoria

Jonathan D. Rose
Board of Governors of the Federal
  Reserve System
20th Street and Constitution Avenue,
  NW
Washington, DC 20551

K. Geert Rouwenhorst
Yale School of Management
Box 208200
New Haven, CT 06520-8200

Don E. Schlagenhauf
Federal Reserve Bank of St. Louis
Center for Household Financial
  Stability
St. Louis, MO 63166-0442
and
Department of Economics
246 Bellamy Building
Florida State University
Tallahassee, FL 32306-2180

Vernon L. Smith
Economic Science Institute
Chapman University
One University Drive
Orange, CA 92866

Kenneth Snowden
Bryan School of Business and
  Economics
University of North Carolina at
  Greensboro
P.O. Box 26165
Greensboro, NC 27402

Kirsten Wandschneider
Economics Department
Occidental College
1600 Campus Road
Los Angeles, CA 90041

Eugene N. White
Department of Economics
Rutgers University
New Brunswick, NJ 08901

Author Index

Subject Index

Page numbers followed by the letter *f* or *t* refer to figures or tables, respectively.